DEMOCRACY OFF BALANCE

Freedom of Expression and Hate Propaganda Law in Canada

Freedom of public expression is becoming ever more contested in Canada. The idea that official messages, meanings, and histories can take the place of publicly constructed ones – for fear of what an uncensored public might themselves construct – is gaining widespread acceptance. Public invocation of hate propaganda law, its language, and its moral authority in otherwise ordinary discursive contexts, has contributed to, and is symbolic of, this trend.

Democracy Off Balance offers an analysis of hate censorship as a paradox of modern democratic discourse. In this controversial work, Stefan Braun argues against the supposed public interest served by hate speech laws and dissects the complex forces – the politically self-contradictory thinking and the socially self-defeating assumptions – that drive censorship in Canada today.

Braun draws on censors' own terms of social and political reference to show how they undermine their own causes with hate censorship. He demonstrates how hate speech law reaches beyond its strictly legal confines and essentially conditions and corrodes public discourse. Timely and absorbing, *Democracy Off Balance* offers a multidimensional approach to the debate and challenges traditional views on the legal boundaries of freedom of expression.

STEFAN BRAUN is a barrister and solicitor in Thornhill, Ontario.

STEFAN BRAUN

Democracy Off Balance

Freedom of Expression and
Hate Propaganda Law in Canada

UNIVERSITY OF TORONTO PRESS
Toronto Buffalo London

© University of Toronto Press Incorporated 2004
Toronto Buffalo London
Printed in Canada

ISBN 0-8020-8959-3 (cloth)
ISBN 0-8020-8636-5 (paper)

Printed on acid-free paper

National Library of Canada Cataloguing in Publication Data

Braun, Stefan, 1954–
    Democracy off balance : freedom of expression and hate propaganda law in
    Canada /Stefan Braun.

    Includes bibliographical references and index.
    ISBN 0-8020-8959-3 (bound).   ISBN 0-8020-8636-5 (pbk.)

    1. Freedom of speech – Canada.   2. Hate speech – Canada.   I. Title.

    KE4418.B73 2004   323.44'3'0971   C2003-906108-6
    KF4483.C524B73 2004

This book has been published with the help of a grant from the Canadian
Federation for the Humanities and Social Sciences, through the Aid to
Scholarly Publications Programme, using funds provided by the Social Sciences
and Humanities Research Council of Canada.

University of Toronto Press acknowledges the financial assistance to its
publishing program of the Canada Council for the Arts and the Ontario Arts
Council.

University of Toronto Press acknowledges the financial support for its publishing activities of the Government of Canada through the Book Publishing
Industry Development Program (BPIDP).

Contents

Acknowledgments

This book brings together three fields – political theory, public law, and communications – to explore the dilemma of balancing hate speech law and freedom of speech in Canada. Developing the ideas that would become this book was the product of numerous influences. I am indebted to too many people to acknowledge them all adequately. I owe a special thanks to Professors Ian Greene, Bernard Frolic, and Fred Fletcher at York University. Professor Fletcher's work in political communications gave me early appreciation for the value of a threefold approach. Professor Frolic's insights into the trials and tribulations of twentieth-century Communism convinced me that the discursive lessons of those failed regimes are as relevant as ever to the challenges posed to freedom of speech in our own liberal democratic polities. I am particularly grateful to Professor Ian Greene. Professor Greene was most generous not only with his time and critical suggestions in the formative stages of my ideas but also with his moral support for turning them into this book. The point of view expressed by this book is strictly my own, as are any defects, omissions, or errors in conveying it.

I gratefully acknowledge the research assistance of Kris Dickinson and the technical assistance of Mr Arthur Di Leo. Mr Di Leo's insights into the mysterious crashes and temperament of the modern computer were exceeded only by his patience for the deficiencies of my own acumen.

Finally, I wish to thank my dear wife, Helen, for her understanding and for putting up with me during my long hours barricaded behind closed doors.

DEMOCRACY OFF BALANCE

Introduction

I

In the last fifteen years, a legally unfettered right of public discussion on all matters of society, history, and governance has become 'ever more contested' in Canada.[1] The idea that official messages, official meanings, and even official histories may properly take the place of publicly constructed ones, for fear of what an uncensored public might themselves construct, is no longer confined to the margins of elite thinking or the edges of public policy. It finds its premier expression in a triad of 'at-large' speech offences (hate, pornography, discriminatory utterances),[2] in university speech codes,[3] in civil actions against 'discriminatory speech,'[4] and in criminal actions against hate propaganda.[5] The perennial challenges to freedom of public expression from the political right of course antedate Canada's 1982 constitutional entrenchment of freedom of expression.[6] What has changed is that the most profound challenges are now coming from the political left, in particular, the progressive left. As Borovoy recounts, the progressive left has evolved from being the sole or chief target of oppressive politics and repressive laws against socially disconcerting and politically disturbing speech to being one of the leading agitators of such politics and laws.[7]

Public discourse that is vital to a more adaptable society and robust self-government in Canada is caught in the grip of a five-sided vice squeezing speech from diverse directions: public apathy and participatory malaise; concentration and cross-ownership of important media of public communication; left-wing intolerance of socially disconcerting political expression; a judicial mindset increasingly sympathetic to the silencing thinking of the censoring left; and a growing risk of right-wing backlash facilitated by public indifference to the abuse of rights of public expression.

Hate speech law is seminal to and symbolic of this discursive devolution. Today, popular opinion, influential commentators, respected scholars, leading jurists, and the majority of the judges of the Supreme Court of Canada agree that hate speech is beyond the pale of permissible public communication in a democratic society. Hate propaganda against identifiable groups is a crime, and those who speak it are criminals.[8] The problem is that what is called hate propaganda is not just about hate and the evil it can do. It is also about political communication and self-government. It is about our society, our polity, and ourselves and about communicating our deepest grievances and truest feelings about these things to each other. It is about disturbing, disrupting, and transforming society. It is about the pace of social change and the character of political transition. And it is about public self-enlightenment, social transparency, and political accountability. Hate propaganda law is more than an exception to freedom of expression. It is all about freedom of expression.

Where the legitimacy of public authority springs from the 'rule of law' rather than the 'whims of men,' authority clothed in the language of the law occupies a place of special significance in the body politic.[9] This is especially true in modern constitutional democracies. Constitutional sanction engraves a shining stamp of moral authority and imprimatur of public legitimacy on those who act, or can make public claim of right to act, under it. Constitutionally sanctioned criminalization of hate speech in Canada demarcates the official boundaries of legitimate public discourse and morally permissible discursive public conflict on weighty matters of state and society – boundaries to which the public must pay special heed.

Criminal law derives its essential moral authority not from the number of prosecutions but from its status. The moral authority that hate propaganda law symbolizes neither begins nor ends at its legal doorstep. The language of hate silencing criss-crosses social, political, and even commercial boundaries, cross-fertilizing public meanings with its moral authority, demarcating the perimeters of permissible public discourse, and conditioning public discursive activity in subtle and seductive ways.[10] Its authority, as we shall see, can be called upon by almost anyone in almost any discursive context, not just out of public duty, personal conviction, or legitimate fear of public injury but also to occupy the moral high ground, for legal cover or political advantage, or even for retribution or financial return.[11] Criminalization of public discourse is ordinarily thought of as a last resort in a democracy, when it is felt that all else has failed or would fail. Public invocation of hate law, its language, or its moral authority in otherwise ordinary public discourse is, therefore, a telling gauge of the depth of public discursive intolerance and a bellwether of future social directions and political trends.

Today there is a diverse and loose collection of defenders of freedom of public expression in Canada. This includes public pretenders to freedom of speech – those who support the right to speak when it is their own right to socially disturb and politically disrupt that is threatened but not when it is the right of their social and political rivals to do so. Repressed reactionaries, aided by 'maverick' counsel, are particularly good pretenders. With friends like that, however, freedom of speech needs no enemies. There are, of course, true public contenders for the vacancy. The Canadian Civil Liberties Association (CCLA) combines a rich history of social activism with politically organized defence of freedom of expression. But the free speech splintering of the social activist camp and the ongoing departure of many, if perhaps not quite all, of the progressive wing from the liberal fold has meant that the historic role of the CCLA, too, has evolved. The CCLA has had to take some troubling stands on behalf of freedom of expression.[12] Feminists, minorities, and left-wing academics alike have assailed the CCLA for undermining social progress and equality in taking these stands.[13] Without active progressive support, the association's defence of freedom of speech can no longer claim the moral high ground it once did, when the left spoke far more with one voice against silencing public expressions of social discontent.

Many of the same forces can be observed at work in the United States.[14] But there are some very important differences, particularly in how these forces work. The squeeze on speech may be formidable, but the vice is not nearly as impervious to outside penetration and organized resistance as it is in Canada. First, there is nothing in the United States comparable to Canada's hate propaganda law, and guiding pronouncements by U.S. courts would seem to argue vigorously against the constitutionality of hate laws.[15] There is political correctness, to be sure, but there is no constitutionally sanctioned right of official message making and legally 'correct' public meaning construction (or resort to hate law's moral authority) on matters of state, history, and society.

Second, the more discordant structures and processes of American government – fragmented law making, separation of powers, checks and balances – erect formidable obstacles in the way of legislative construction of a comprehensive law to suppress hate.[16]

Third, Lockean legacies of minimalist government, a revolutionary past, and a history of social progress through civil disobedience have helped to fashion in America a discursive landscape that is less deferential to established authority or resigned to the idea of exclusive rights of public meaning construction by officialdom on behalf of the public good.[17] Fourth, the America media establishment is much larger and more diverse than it is in Canada. It has shown itself more conscious of its independence and more willing to challenge attempts by established authority to trespass on it.[18] Moreover, it has been buttressed in its independence by the more press-friendly libel pronouncements of the U.S. courts.[19] Fifth, the Cold War witch-hunts of the 1950s (the term 'McCarthyism' is now part of popular vernacular signifying the dangers of censorship) have left an indelible mark on the American discursive landscape. They provided first-hand experience of the risks of political censorship, lessons on which influential and well-organized opponents of progressive silencing routinely draw to counterbalance current censorship trends.[20]

Finally, the U.S. Supreme Court has had much longer legal and political experience in theorizing free speech values in the noble traditions of eminent jurists such as Brandeis, Holmes, and Douglas and a long history of judicial activism to imbue its abstractions with meaningful social and political content.[21] The devolving discursive landscape in Canada is, therefore, of a qualitatively different and potentially more ominous order. It is officially embracing, sanctioned by law, and politically more seamless.

II

How should a consolidated postindustrial representative democracy such as Canada deal with public communication that is most testing of its tolerance, its diversity, its social harmony, and its beliefs about all these things? Should it work to silence such communication by law? Or should it work to challenge it by other means? Can hate censors effectively silence such messages and their meanings? Can they do so both effectively *and* successfully – in a way that would not subvert the very democratic values and social goals underlying the cause of repression* of this kind of public expression? Is there any role for hate censorship?

Today a kind of intellectual stalemate has developed beyond which thinking on these questions seems unable to move. This impasse serves no one well, least of all the cause of social progress and political democracy. Free speech advocates are not without blame here. Too often, they simply dismiss hate censorship theorists as enemies of freedom. In turn, hate censorship advocates often dismiss free speech theorists as enemies of social progress. Both tend to see each other as bad for the cause of democracy. Battle lines are drawn. Thinking becomes paralysed – in familiar forms. Neither side is able to move the debate forward. Unless a way can be found to better join issues in dispute and bridge discordant minds, the stalemate will continue as before.

III

The key to moving thinking forward may never be found. This, however, is not the same as saying it does not exist. It will not be found if we continue to search in the wrong places. Those who begin with the assumption that the standoff is rooted in fundamentally different values and goals are searching, I would suggest, in the wrong place. As Sniderman and his colleagues have observed, 'the values of freedom of expression and racial or religious tolerance remain in tension in Canadian society even though they both draw on the same underlying liberal principle.'[22] The key to moving thinking forward is to unravel the reasons why these values remain in tension despite this common ground. Approaches to date have not done this very well, mainly for three reasons.

First, the values and goals underlying the rights in dispute are not singular or monistic but plural and overlapping. Tolerance, equality, social harmony, diversity, and strong democracy are politically multidimensional causes housing socially multifaceted goals. But the debate over hate censorship has tended to be one-dimensional. Too often, the common social and political threads that bind these causes together, as well as the tensions and conflicts that separate them, are missed or under-appreciated. This book addresses the problem through a multi-

---

* Throughout this book, the phrase 'cause of repression' is used in this sense of a set of social and political principles, beliefs, or purposes that are explicitly advocated or implicitly held.

faceted approach utilizing overlapping themes – an approach that lets one turn recurring issues in dispute around in one's mind to make important connections and disconnections from different but overlapping perspectives. To see key points in contention from different but related angles is not just to see some of the same issues in different ways and some different issues in the same way. It is to see them better. I am reminded of Marvin Minsky's words:

> [I]f you understand something in only one way, then you do not really understand it at all ... The secret of what anything means to us depends on how we have connected it to all the other things we know ... Of course, making too many indiscriminate connections will turn a mind into mush. But well-connected representations let you turn ideas around in your mind, to envision things from many perspectives ... And that is what we mean by thinking![23]

Second, and derivative of the first, is this idea of 'hate.' In principle, it is unambiguous. But in censorship practice, it is a socially malleable and politically pliable concept of public injury. Framing the cause against intolerance, ignorance, and prejudice in the language of hate as progressive censors do can become a strait-jacket on more nuanced and balanced thinking. Once the problematic is successfully packaged in the socially singular and politically absolute language of hate, the case for censorship becomes almost self-evident. One can see the contours of this kind of thinking in the writings of leading social advocates and influential progressive scholars such as MacKinnon, Mahoney, Bakan, Anand, Mckenna, and many others.[24] This packaging is a primary intellectual definer that unduly restricts thinking on the censorship problematic. It does not simply conceal the tensions and conflicts among censorship goals and the dilemmas they pose for the progressive cause. It masks the politically self-contradictory thinking and socially self-defeating assumptions that underlie the progressive case for censorship. This book unwraps the package.

Finally, an economistic approach seems to have taken hold of the debate, one that lends itself well to societally reductionist answers to the problem of intolerance.[25] Communicative resources in Canada are unequal, and the marketplace of ideas is often far from free or fair. But what follows from this in a system of occasional governing majorities and changing social agendas? Official histories, fixed public meanings, and final political triumphs guaranteed by hate law? 'Social character' understandings of freedom of speech in the context of intolerance are flawed not for what they notice but for what they miss. They artificially depoliticize the silencing dilemma, reducing the question of hate censorship to apolitical, time static choices – choices that miss the overarching importance of the movement of society, history, and the political dynamics that drive the interactive processes of censorship itself. These variables need to be restored to the debate and better understood.

IV

My approach is unconventional. Chapter divisions and subheadings are analytical divisions (there is no 'one right' way to organize them) along a continuum of overlapping themes – rather than intrinsic, required, or independent demarcations. I unwrap packaged censorship thinking from different but overlapping perspectives, disentangle points of contention, and spotlight self-contradictory assumptions. My arguments, like the issues they address, are overlapping. Each chapter draws from and expounds on common themes explored in earlier chapters with a view to deepening understanding and enriching insight into those themes. I systematically construct a multifaceted case for rethinking hate censorship, consisting of overlapping arguments stressing an overarching theme: as a feature of ordinary democratic discourse, the right to silence hate is theoretically deficient and functionally flawed. On balance, hate censorship does not and cannot do what progressive hate censors want and expect it to do – promote tolerance, equality, and harmony, combat ignorance and prejudice, and protect and promote democracy. It is politically self-contradictory and slippery, socially self-defeating, pragmatically unworkable, and jurisprudentially flawed. I conclude that hate censors undermine their own cause in the very process by which they promote it.

Chapter 1 sets out the foundations for this thesis from a historical perspective. I briefly revisit the historical enactment of hate propaganda law and trace the subsequent devolution in the thinking on its meaning. Chapters 2 to 7 then highlight different aspects of my core thesis. Chapters 2 and 3 spotlight the deficiencies of hate speech law from an intersubjective theoretical perspective on the functions and assumptions of freedom of speech and hate censorship. Chapters 4 and 5 focus on the political dilemmas and slippery political dynamics, respectively, of the repression of this kind of public expression. Chapter 6 follows with a 'pragmatic' perspective on the functional deficiency of censorship – why silencing intolerance not only does not do what censors want it to do but why it cannot. Chapter 7 rounds out the discussion with an exploration of why the legal 'exceptions defence' of hate speech law is a democratically flawed jurisprudential justification. Chapter 8 draws on the insights of the previous chapters to explore the comparative strengths and weaknesses of alternative juridical 'balancing by legal silencing' options. Chapter 9 concludes the discussion with an exploration of alternatives to legal silencing as the more appropriate answer in 'ordinary' conditions of democratic discourse and governance.

My unorthodox approach is not without its difficulties, nor, I am sure, its critics. Analysis invariably involves separation, and there is an element of artificiality in my chapter divisions and choices of themes, the perspectives I adopt, and my allocation of ideas, issues, and arguments. Questions may arise that have no easy answers, at least none satisfactory to all, particularly as to where the lines of perspective are drawn and what should be included or excluded under particular headings and subheadings. As well, a multifaceted, multidimensional approach utilizing conceptually overlapping themes invariably involves repetition, for the same or similar issues need often be considered under the headings and subheadings of different perspectives. However, I do not believe that disagreements over lines of analytical demarcation warrant not drawing them in the first place or discredit the insights gained from exploring the issues within them or the linkages between them. As for thematic overlap and issue repetition, I believe that exploring the finer points and nuances of the debate from different but connected 'angles' is justified by the deeper insight into the silencing dilemma it will provide.

V

The ideas of 'balance' and 'balancing' pervade this book. By these terms I mean both the practice of weighing competing rights and the weight of the claims to those rights. Hate censorship is not simply a noble idea in the minds of theoreticians. It has a functional purpose. The measure of strength of a balancing choice backed by censorship law is relative to the strengths and weaknesses of alternative possible choices, sanctioned by law, in achieving that purpose. Imbalance describes, at a minimum, a result that is self-contradictory and self-defeating on its own terms of reference. In balancing competing rights it may not be possible to serve them all equally well. But a comparatively better balance cannot be one that undermines its own social and political cause in the very process of promoting it. Whatever more a successful hate censorship may mean it cannot mean less than this. My thesis should not be taken to mean that the freedom of speech position is a panacea without social problems or political risks. Rather, it is that balancing by legal silencing is, by those same measures and on censors' own terms of reference, likely worse over time than the alternatives, notwithstanding such problems and risks. This comparative and relative frame of reference centrally informs all my 'balancing' arguments, though it sometimes will remain implicit. Ultimately, this is a thesis that argues against choices that may seem theoretically ideal but that are not in practice viable.

Balancing rights of expression against rights of hate suppression is not about discovering 'objective truth.'[26] Debates concerning social and political causes such as tolerance, equality, harmony, and democracy are ultimately normative questions. I therefore make no pretence to 'objectivity' in a 'scientific' sense. My 'balancing conclusions' are drawn from an intersubjective understanding of juridical alternatives measured (tested) against shared values, goals, and terms of reference articulated by – or implicit in the assumptions of – the opposing sides themselves. In particular, finding the 'right' balance in Canada from the perspective of hate censorship theorists' own deeper social aspirations and democratic terms of political reference is an occupying theme of this book.

1

Foundations of the Imbalance

I The Malady and the Prevention: A Brief Historical Perspective

Canada has not been untouched by the racial, ethnic, religious, and related animosities that have scarred democracy, poisoned social harmony, and subverted political stability elsewhere. Still, compared to most multiracial nations of the world, Canada has come to enjoy a relatively high degree of tolerance, social peace, and political stability. Were it not for the horrors visited on Europe from 1940 to 1945, one might almost forget that in the 1920s and 1930s Fascists in this country were busy attacking democracy and scapegoating Communists and minorities, especially Jews, for the social and economic ills of the nation.[1] More than any other single event, the Holocaust focused the attention of Western democracies on the dangers of racial and ethnic hatred, suggesting that no country was immune to its ravages. With signs of the revival of Nazi and neo-Nazi activity in the late 1950s and early 1960s in Canada, there was growing concern that, unless 'something was done,' the fascist scourge might gain a political foothold through the subconscious prejudices of a vulnerable public.

At the forefront of this concern was the Canadian Jewish Congress. It had been unsuccessfully pressing Parliament for some time to enact criminal legislation prohibiting public expressions of hate against historically vulnerable groups.[2] By 1963, it was beginning to make real headway, and in 1966 the 'Special Committee on Hate Propaganda' reported to Parliament, giving its assessment of the problem.[3] Concluding that existing laws were insufficient to deal with the threat, it wrote that,

[H]owever small the actors may be in number, the individuals and groups promoting hate in Canada constitute 'a clear and present' danger to the functioning of a democratic society. For, in time of social stress, such 'hate' *could mushroom into a real and monstrous threat to our way of life* ... In the Committee's view, the 'hate' situation in Canada, although not alarming, clearly is serious enough to require action. It is far better for Canadians to come to grips with the problem now, before it attains unmanageable proportions, rather than deal with it at some future date in an atmosphere of urgency, of fear and perhaps even of crisis. (emphasis mine)[4]

In the voting on the bill that would become the Hate Propaganda section of the Criminal Code,[5] no hearings were held in the Senate. In the House, the bill passed 89 to 45 with 127 MPs not voting or absent from the chamber.[6] Given the importance of the issue to democracy, earlier parliamentary resistance to criminalization of speech, and, one would have thought, the controversial nature of the corrective remedy, the dearth of parliamentary and public debate is rather disturbing, although, for some of the same reasons, perhaps not surprising. Whether this paucity of debate reflected a fear of being perceived to be on the wrong side of hate, a yielding to growing political pressure, public indifference, political weariness, or some combination of all four is hard to say. But the criminalization of 'hate propaganda,' would set the political and moral stage for an intellectual and juridical slide of momentous proportions in this nation's understanding of how to deal with ignorance and prejudice.

II The Political and Intellectual Slide: From Open Bigotry to Subconscious Prejudice to Structural Discrimination – from National Survival to Social Transformation

With the constitutional entrenchment in 1982 of the *Canadian Charter of Rights and Freedoms,*[7] the work of the Cohen Committee would come under increasing scrutiny from academic scholars and jurists alike. The committee's conclusions both about the nature of the problem and the appropriate purpose and scope of the legislation enacted to deal with it would come to be questioned. But what has come to be more questioned than the wisdom of the Cohen Committee in criminally restricting public speech was its 'failure' to see public expressions of subconscious prejudice and problems of systemic discrimination as within the

ambit of the law's purpose. The perspective driving this thinking originated not from better understandings of the nature and functions of
freedom of expression but from abhorrence of unacknowledged or
subconscious thoughts of prejudice and the structures of systemic discrimination that help sustain them.

In the last decade, this perspective has come to fundamentally shift
thinking on the underlying public purpose and social role of hate censorship. It finds its premier expression in the 'structuralist' approach to
hate and prejudice of progressive scholars. Anand, for example, criticizes the Cohen Committee for their 'erroneous conclusion' that 'racial
hatred in Canada was confined to marginal extremists.'

> They came to this conclusion because their focus was on an extreme symptom
> of racism: the creation and dissemination of hate propaganda ... Racist
> publications are not the only evidence of racism in Canada. Further evidence
> of racism may be found by considering the position of some of Canada's
> visible minority groups, historically and currently, and by considering other
> manifestations of race-based discrimination, government laws and actions
> and societal attitudes and practices.[8]

He concludes that,

> [h]ate propaganda perpetuates barriers to the dismantling of systemic racial
> discrimination ... employers, teachers, landlords and police are likely to be
> active consumers of hate propaganda. It is the existence of hate propaganda
> in general society that makes this effect possible ... [T]he vulnerability of
> every member of society to the subtle effects of hate propaganda is made
> more clear. Perhaps a landlord, at even an unconscious level, will prefer
> renting to a white couple as opposed to an East Indian couple after being
> subject to a 'dot busters' campaign [derogatory remarks about the cosmetic
> red dot traditionally worn by married Indian women].[9]

Progressive structuralists such as McKenna actively recommend a larger
role for hate speech law:

> [r]acial hatred has long been promoted officially in Canada and ... when
> managed at the appropriate level, serves the corporate interests that domi-
> nate the contemporary political agenda. One of the current effects of a
> managed level of racial hate propaganda is to consolidate a social climate that
> is hostile to the dismantling of systemic discrimination ... [T]his paper

recommends that the law focus not only on the extremist purveyor of hate propaganda but on those private corporations and public authorities who condone it by failing to exercise their power to stop it.[10]

Structuralists say that their expansive understanding is well justified by numerous studies on prejudice and intolerance: '[t]he demons of racial and cultural prejudice have never been either officially or unofficially exorcised from Canadian society. We may, on occasion, have been marginally more enlightened than our southern neighbors, but instances of racism and intolerance are deeply etched in the historical record and, for that matter, not hard to find in the daily newspapers.'[11] The structuralist perspective on sexism, racism, and homophobia argues that it would be wrong to see in the progress made by historically oppressed groups meaningful movement in public attitudes. 'The tolerance we know,' writes Anand, 'is historically only a thin and recently applied veneer on Canadian society.'[12]

It is not necessary here to revisit the well-worn debate on how far Canadians have come in the battle against intolerance and ignorance. There is no paucity of evidence of the persistence of prejudice long after the Cohen Committee completed its work.[13] I take issue not with structuralist assertions that prejudice extends beyond the marginal extremist or that correction is desirable but with the slide or leap in thinking from such evidence to a far more politically pliable and problematic social understanding of the appropriate corrective role of hate censorship.

This slide may not be apparent in preliminary structuralist definitions of 'hate.' Anand, for example, echoes the Cohen Committee's characterization of hate propaganda.[14] He writes, 'In this paper, the phrase "expressions of racial hatred" is used synonymously with the term "hate propaganda" as both refer to the dissemination of a malevolent doctrine of vilification and detestation of a group of individuals based on racial, religious or ethnic identification.'[15] The leap becomes apparent, however, in the ease with which the 'malicious injury' definition slips into a purely social conception of the law for enlistment in the service of partisan politics. The requirement of malicious intention is subtly abandoned, and a proactive thinking pushing for social transformation takes its place. The delimited Cohenian understanding of hate propaganda law – that Canadians, indeed, all peoples everywhere, have the right to be free of malicious utterances aiming to injure them not for anything they have done but for who they are – no longer adequately describes progressive thinking on the legitimate public policy making function of hate speech law.

Progressive hate censorship thinking raises more questions than it answers. Anand, for example, cites an Angus Reid finding that 43 per cent of Canadians polled in August 1989 'felt that there were too many immigrants coming to Canada' at a time when '71% [of immigrants] were from predominantly non-white source countries.'[16] While the suggestion of prejudice or bigotry here may well be justified, the case for a more expansive *social* understanding of the role of hate propaganda law is less obvious. What, one might ask, is the numerically 'correct' (unbigoted) balance of immigrants, at any given time, that hate propaganda law is supposed to serve? And how is it to serve it? Is the answer self-evident? For now? For all time? For all but the bigoted? Is there room for disagreement on the numbers? How much room? Structuralists link criminal sanctions against speech to singularly correct (unprejudiced) answers to such problems. But are the answers to more contentious social issues – issues that go beyond simple questions of marginal extremism and malicious intentions – as obvious as such thinking and linking suggest?

Consider McKenna's even less self-conscious slide. McKenna makes an open case for expanding criminal sanctions against speech. True, for now at least he would limit enforcement to violations involving employment and the performance of governmental functions such as policing and the provision of social services. But his thinking on the appropriate public policy making function of censorship is anything but politically confined. First, he complains that the 'recommendations of the Cohen Committee serve well the corporate agenda of maintaining public order' by targeting only marginal extremists. Then he lays the causes of a slew of domestic social and foreign policy ills squarely at the doorstep of a corporate culture of 'racist and sexist' hatred. In the list of social ills that follows, notice how he links hate propaganda law to politically correct policy prescriptions:

[l]ogging and mining interests that benefit from the low self-esteem in which aboriginal people and their interest are held – expression of racial hatred helps to perpetuate such low self-esteem ... [The] destruction of rain forests and other natural habitats [because] racial hatred supports corporate interests [that are] rendered politically more palatable by the low regard that white societies have for the non-white populations that bear the brunt of environmental devastations ... [Corporate demands for military intervention

in Central America or the Middle East] justified by an appeal to racism and xenophobia ... [The scapegoating of immigrants] which is greatly enhanced by a strategic stirring of the pot of racial hatred ... [The striking down of the rape shield law] which illustrates the task facing human rights advocates who seek effective legal control of public expressions of hatred.[17]

Social inequalities tend to be derivative of economic inequalities and their power differentials. Premier expression of this, historically, has been along lines of gender and race. In much progressive thinking, therefore, the need to correct disproportionate white male representation in higher income and occupations is often spotlighted to buttress the case against structures and institutions of economic oppression that promote hate and prejudice in other areas of public intercourse. In this view, systemic remedies against discriminatory practices and hate propaganda law against discriminatory speech can be linked as complementary weapons in a common cause. But what, one might ask, is the naturally correct (non-hate) view on the number of women in engineering for the purposes of hate speech repression? What is the necessarily right (unbigoted) view on the number of Blacks, or for that matter Jews or Chinese (who are 'grossly over represented') in law, medicine, or the sciences?[18] What is the socially correct (unprejudiced) vision on the right distribution of income among Jews, Chinese, Blacks, Portuguese, Gypsies, and 'WASPS'? What is the non-hate view on abortion rights, women in combat, and immigration numbers? Would Jews favouring more Jewish and less Arab immigration be 'incorrect' (prejudiced) for the purposes of corrective hate propaganda law?[19]

It is less than clear what the unprejudiced view on any, much less all, of these things should be. Might people who don't 'hate' other people – or see them as inferior or suffer from a false social consciousness manufactured by a racist hegemony – honestly and legitimately (openly) disagree on these things?[20] The points of agreement and disagreement on policy issues can themselves change over time with evolving technology, demographic trends, economic needs, social mores, and political climates.[21]

In posing the issue this way, my purpose is not to suggest that progressive goals are socially undesirable. On the contrary, as Borovoy himself attests, many such goals, if not necessarily all, are shared by thoughtful free speech advocates. My purpose is to suggest that social problems worth arguing about are inescapably value laden and to highlight the political implications of an approach to freedom of public discourse that would make claims to social infallibility in answering them. There are no 'objectively correct' answers to many, if any, of these issues even for the foreseeable future, much less for the unforeseeable one. We can't know the answers with the kind of certainty that could justify legally, much less criminally, immunizing them from effective and open political challenge. The structuralist view belies a problematic conceptual slide from Cohen of significant and unsettling political proportions. The slide challenges not only free speech thinking but also original censorship thinking.

In the structuralist view, prejudice is largely a symptomatic manifestation of socio-economic structures of domination and exploitation. In this view, intolerance is essentially structurally caused and culturally sustained primarily by two complementary systems of cognitive domination: capitalism and patriarchy.[22] Hate censorship focused solely on individuals, malicious intentions, and marginal extremists misses the mark by neglecting the subtle invidiousness of more subconscious expressions of public prejudice and the socio-economic structures of domination that sustain them.[23] These structures are as much cognitive and cultural as they are material. What follows is a societally reductionist approach to freedom of public expression rooted in an economistic understanding of intolerance and prejudice. Proactively correcting subconscious expressions of public prejudice with hate speech law for the purposes of social transformation is no less legitimate than negatively containing deliberate expressions of overt hate to preserve social peace and ensure regime survival.

The political lineage for this 'apolitical' censorship thinking may be traced to structural Marxism and Marx's thoughts on 'false consciousness' or to more sophisticated Gramscian notions of hegemony, where the self-fuelling institutions of dominant ideology combine with the exploitative structures of production to the detriment of 'free' or independent thinking. In this latter view, the public at large take on the interests, values, and prejudices of the dominant (and dominating) as their own and come to view the existing social order as natural, necessary, and inevitable.[24] A socially transforming hate censorship is a logical and legitimate answer to intolerance and ignorance, given the depth and breadth of existing cognitive and productive (structural) illegitimacies.

All-embracing socio-economic conceptions of censorship, however, raise all-embracing democratic problems of political legitimacy. The model of public discourse touted by progressive censors is one that would legally mandate correct public cognition on ever more complex, fluid, and politically contentious social issues. Progressive public silencing does not neutrally correct structures of cognitive oppression, replacing them with structures of cognitive freedom. It substitutes structures of cognitive oppression of its own – a legal regime of state-enforced official right. Legally engineering one correct public consciousness for another, incorrect one leaves progressive claims of emancipatory public silencing vulnerable to objections that it is discursive social engineering by another name.[25]

The political character of this slide and its implications should not be minimized. It is not against the law to overcome dominant meanings sustained by structures of hegemony. But it is against the law to defy the strictures of censorship. The only dissident answer to legal repression of non-conforming public expression is either illegal acts of clandestine resistance or open force. Dissident inroads challenging and piercing hegemonic assumptions and structures of domination have been forged in Canada through freedom of expression.[26] The more democratic answer to a relatively porous hegemonic wall of social message making and public meaning construction can hardly be to erect a legal brick wall of official message making and state meaning fiat in its place.

The assumption that rightful legal censorship is the corrective to wrongful social hegemony forgets that the essence of hegemony is denial of independent cognitive choice. Legal silencing deprives public discourse of the very public choice essential to a non-hegemonic cognition. To pervert constitutional protection of freedom of public expression into a tool for officially ensuring a certain correct social agenda, by legally excluding public expressions of the incorrect thoughts of another, is to attempt to guarantee indirectly (through the legal system) what cannot be guaranteed directly (through the ballot box). The right to legally prejudge the legitimacy of public discourse works to predetermine social outcomes – a coercive 'end run' around the political process.[27] Effectively, progressive censors would substitute found social truths, fixed public meanings, and final political triumphs for the political process. Ought not social policy disagreement to be a matter for the ballot box, even a highly imperfect box, rather than for hate law? Moreover, if the progressive left can silence for social 'right,' what is to prevent the reactionary right or, for that matter, any political group from asserting the same legal right?

Appreciating how justification for this slide in censorship thinking is intellectually engineered is helpful to understanding its deficiencies further. While the social agenda in whose cause the slide is enlisted exudes the very essence of politics and politicking, a partisan political justification for public silencing would hardly qualify to sustain its authors' aspirations to apolitical social legitimacy. Justification requires intellectually engineering politics out of hate censorship. But social reality requires engaging in those very politics. The dichotomy is 'resolved' by a historically *unqualified* transportation of the evidence of past prejudice into a static, fixed view of society and polity of the future.

The best structuralist evidence justifying hate censorship 'today' in the interest of desired social transformation for tomorrow is drawn not from today but from 'yesterday.' It begins far back – too far back to sustain a conceptually expansive understanding of the appropriate role for censorship. The more distant the past, the more emotively probative the evidence may be. But it is not empirically more probative. The evidence includes abuse of Chinese labourers working on the Canadian Pacific Railway in the eighteen hundreds, the arrival of the first Black slaves in Canada in 1608, and the enslavement of Aboriginals in the seventeenth century in New France.[28] Although this historical record is abhorrent, the blanket and unqualified use to which such 'deep history' of prejudice is put is highly problematic. But it serves its purpose. By evoking the sins of the father to taint the sentiments of the child, this approach can dismiss significant public progress – social, political, legal, and even economic – to justify a far more socially embracing and politically consequential censorship thinking.[29] It is an approach that enlists what was intended to be a carefully confined and narrowly purposed abridgment of public discourse in the questionable service of a broad-based, politically partisan intellectual slide.

The progressive left are quite right in saying that the Cohen Committee failed to see hate censorship in the way that the progressive left do today. But I believe it is terribly misleading to read the committee's understanding of the problem as the progressive left do.[30] The committee's conclusion was not that the *problem* of prejudice was confined to marginal extremists. It was that *criminal censorship* should be confined to marginal extremists. The two are not the same. It is quite possible to see the problem as socially wide and structurally deep, but the remedy as necessarily narrow. As Anand himself writes, 'The [Cohen] Committee also doubted that man's rationality would always allow him to distinguish truth from falsity. The Committee cited the successes of modern advertising, the persuasiveness and invasiveness of modern media, and the success of Nazi propaganda in pre-World War Two Germany as the empirical basis of its scepticism.'[31] It can hardly be that the

Canadian Jewish Congress in the 1950s and 1960s believed that Jewish vulnerability to anti-Semitism in Canada was confined to a few fringe fanatics. The gravamen of the Cohen Committee's justification for the law – its 'mushroom' thesis of possible social disintegration and political conflagration absent criminal repression of hate propaganda – belies such assumptions.[32] For the left today to suggest that, aided by modern empirical tools, they understand the depth and breadth of prejudice better than a committee advised by a people that had six million of its members exterminated in a nation at the forefront of modernity is patronizing and implausible in the extreme.

It is not hard to see why the Cohen Committee would not want the law of criminal censorship to become entangled in partisan social politics. Consider politically contentious social issues such as the wearing of religious headgear in the RCMP; the size of women's financial support on marriage breakdown; gay marriage rights; ethnic representation on corporate boards; equitable rental practices; hiring, firing, and promotion policies; or immigration policy. Social, political, and economic questions raised by these issues may also raise important questions of sexism, racism, homophobia, or xenophobia that a democratic legislature might wish to address directly with corrective legislation. But it was not the intention of the Cohen Committee that 'inappropriate' public discourse about such questions should one day be viewed as thought crimes.[33] It was the Cohen Committee's wisdom, not its folly, to leave such questions to the political arena of legislated public *acts* – rather than to try to pre-fix the correct answers, now and for later, by legislating public thoughts.

In declining to see hate censorship as the progressive left do, the Cohen Committee did so by foresight and design rather than as an oversight or out of ignorance. It sought to eschew entrapment in a slippery political slope, the kind that reducing economic, domestic, and foreign policy ills of liberal capitalism to a matter for hate censorship entails. In choosing to anchor its justification for criminal censorship in the 'mushroom' thesis of potential social conflagration, the Cohen Committee was sending a clear message on both the purpose and the limits of the law. Its purpose was to better protect the existing 'Canadian way of life' from those who would knowingly and maliciously destroy it, not to shield progressive agendas from effective public challenge. The Cohen Committee's concern with 'symptoms' of prejudice stemmed from fear of the danger to freedom of expression and Canadian political democracy if censorship got too deeply involved in politically partisan battles over socio-economic 'causes.' I would suggest that the Cohen Committee understood prejudice not any less than the committee's detractors do today. They understood freedom of expression better.

I have been careful to use the term 'political' or 'intellectual slide' because even committed social activists have resisted criminally pursuing a prejudiced public 'at large' for their socially and politically incorrect views. None the less, as subsequent chapters will show, a deliberate policy to broaden the legal reach of hate speech law is not needed to expand its proscriptive social and political net, or threat. There is an unrelenting pressure for censorship expansion inherent in the very processes and politics of hate silencing itself – subtly moving thinking beyond its focus on the marginal extremist to more socially opaque and politically problematic matters of public expressions of intolerance.

It took much behind-the-scenes work to get hate propaganda enacted into criminal law. Back in 1964, NDP Member of Parliament David Orlikow asked in the House of Commons why there was no progress on such legislation to stem the tide of hate literature 'now being distributed in various cities.' Justice Minister Favreau responded that '[i]t was reported [by the joint committee on criminal law studying the problem] that while the objective sought to be attained was eminently desirable, no recommendation was made because no formula devised would deal adequately with the problem without affecting the general freedom of expression of opinion in an adverse way.'[34] Depending on the degree to which progressive scholars of the structuralist school of censorship thinking succeed in enlisting Canadian courts in their expansive and expandable understanding of the social function of hate propaganda law, the concerns voiced by the minister may well turn out to be prescient. Recent evidence of judicial slippage suggests that the courts enjoy no innate political immunity to the intellectual slide. That is the subject of discussion of the following section.

III The Juridical Slide: From a Right of Expression to a Question of Content – the Evolution of Asymmetry in Judicial Balancing[35]

Canadian courts have resisted a criminal speech jurisprudence that would enlist suppression of speech directly in the service of politically partisan battles over social policies. Publicly saying such things as 'there is too much non-White immigration; affirmative action is reverse discrimination against Whites; same-sex marriages undermine the family;

or women in combat weaken the military' may well invite social disapprobation, even blacklisting or professional ostracism for racism, sexism, xenophobia, or homophobia.[36] But no one has yet been prosecuted for saying them. And unless, someone intends to make a career out of saying such ill-considered things, it is unlikely, in the immediate future at least, that the courts would interpret hate propaganda law so as to catch such speech. Instead, courts have focused on correcting intolerant or inequitable social practices. They have generally upheld 'discriminatory practice' proscriptions in provincial and federal human rights codes, labour and housing acts, and assorted other legislation covering the provision of services and use of public facilities.[37] While they have upheld certain civil and administrative speech proscriptions within spatially confined and already regulated contexts, such as employment,[38] they have been resistant to applying a structuralist understanding of public discourse to procure policy goals.

None the less, a structuralist understanding of certain types of public discourse as 'social offences' that injure Canadian society at large by promoting public cognitions that help sustain structures of domination and discrimination is gaining legal favour. A growing number of 'discriminatory speech' actions reflecting this kind of thinking are being successfully brought under non-criminal penal provisions. For example, in Canada (Human Rights Commission) v. Taylor,[39] the Supreme Court of Canada upheld, on this basis, a human rights complaint, under section 13 of the Canadian Human Rights Act,[40] against hateful telephone recordings made available to the general public by a White supremacist. In Ross v. New Brunswick School District No. 15,[41] it upheld an at-large 'discrimination complaint' under the New Brunswick Human Rights Act against the Moncton school board arising from a public school teacher's off-duty anti-Semitic comments and activity.[42]

Proponents of hate propaganda law point to provisions in the Charter such as the derogation clause,[43] equality rights,[44] multiculturalism,[45] language rights,[46] Aboriginal rights,[47] equalization, and the regional disparities clause.[48] These, they contend, constitutionally ground their case for reading the Charter's guarantee of freedom of expression to include a right to proscribe hate propaganda. The argument, however, does not stop there. These 'positive' Canadian constitutional provisions are often contrasted with their absence from the U.S. Constitution and with the latter's 'negative' provisions, such as the Fifth and Fourteenth Amendments protecting property and economic rights.[49] The point of these 'textual' comparisons, and their accompanying political labelling, is to better legally ground a socially progressive case arguing for an expansive understanding of hate censorship. However, they expose their advocates' social agenda more than they disclose true constitutional meaning. It is important to unpack tenuous assumptions and to separate labelling from law.

The community- and culture-promoting provisions of the Canadian constitution do indeed contrast with the more singular and individual focused legal language of the U.S. Constitution. Not only plain legal language but also the social and political history of the Canadian constitution(s) would suggest a more multicultural and socio-economically level vision of society.[50] In areas other than public discourse, 'plain readings' of substantive provisions consistent with policy prescriptions promotive of this vision are constitutionally sound. Indeed, one can even find, textually, a constitutional mandate in Canada towards this end – directive provisions stipulating legislative obligation to actively promote it. Whether viewed textually, historically, or, as it should be, in both textual and historical terms, constitutional development in Canada reflects a far more communitarian vision of society than does American constitutional development. Far less obvious is that, textually and historically, the Canadian constitution envisages a legal right to silence public communication that may not be promotive of this vision (or that may be promotive of it in different ways or respects from those envisaged by multicultural structuralists) as a legitimate means for achieving it.[51]

A constitutional right, or even mandate, to legislate social or commercial practices towards a progressive end is one thing. A constitutional right or mandate to legislate public discourse for that end is not the same thing. Failure to distinguish the two is to confuse public policy with public process. It is to mistake particular normative ends of democracy with the generic means of democracy. Patrick Monahan, who developed the idea of a distinctive *communitarian* approach to Charter review, has himself written that,

[s]ignificantly, the elements of the American experience which were rejected or modified by the Canadian drafters were those constitutional provisions which required judges to vindicate particular substantive values. Those features of the American constitution which required judges to police the integrity of the political process were imported, largely unchanged, into the Canadian *Charter* ... The Canadian drafters went on to add a series of provisions which either recognise the positive contribution of the state in

securing individual freedom or protect communitarian values ... [J]udicial review should be conducted in the name of democracy, rather than as a means of guaranteeing or requiring 'right answers' from the political process.[52]

Canadian courts have actively enlisted principles of multiculturalism and concepts of equality both in aid of constitutional interpretation and as key goals of Canadian democracy. But they have never *required* speech promotive of that vision. There is no positive duty on Canadians at large, no legal requirement, to speak to promote these goals. They can choose to remain silent.[53] But neither have the public at large been the subject of legal stricture merely for expressing themselves in ways that might be contrary to the official vision. While I would not disagree with Anand that the Charter 'constitutionalizes' the policy of multiculturalism,[54] it is hardly obvious that it does so, much less that it should do so, by constitutionalizing legal suppression of public discourse suggesting alternatives to the official vision. In *R. v. Morgentaler*,[55] Madam Justice Bertha Wilson, a leading progressive jurist, said, 'the basic theory underlying the Charter [is] that the state will respect choices made by individuals and, to the greatest extent possible, will avoid subordinating those choices to any one conception of the good life.'[56] Surely this 'respect' applies to respecting the essential means by which those social choices are made – political communication.

In judicial practice, structuralist linkage of specific social *policies* (on immigration, abortion, gay rights, and many others) to constitutional prescriptions of equality and multiculturalism have been well received. But at the same, such linkages have proven too politically contentious for the courts to directly and openly take one side of the *speech* debate by upholding censorship against the other. Judicial pronouncements on state strictures against speech based on such linkages have, therefore, been relatively circumspect. Judicial balancing methodology, however, has been slipping. And this can have important *substantive* implications for the future.

Since its initial sweeping support for social choices and expression of respect for freedom of public communication in making them, the Supreme Court has slowly clawed and crawled its way back to a far more diffident approach to the subject. It has adopted a 'balancing asymmetry' in its approach to socially divisive public communication. Hate propaganda law is at the very bedrock of this clawback – creating a disquieting foundational imbalance. This judicial devolution is one that serves well the cause of a politically partisan and, for now, structuralist slide against public discourse. It is also one that risks provoking an equally partisan reactionary slide, detrimental to public discourse in the future. It is important to understand how the court's approach creates a foundational asymmetry in juridical balancing, how it came to adopt it, and the implications of this approach for the balancing problematic.

There is a legal prerequisite to the progressive slide – a political movement that, at bottom, targets society at large for cognitive correction. It requires that the court first accept as constitutionally legitimate *some* state censorship of the general public for 'illegitimate social, historical or political' expressions. For only when the court discards *all* notions of contentual illegitimacy in public discourse on matters of society, history, and governance is there no possibility for a politically driven legal slide. Judicial acceptance of the Cohen Committee presumptions for enacting hate propaganda law is therefore foundational to later developments. *R. v. Keegstra*,[57] a much-publicized case, has been pivotal in giving this foundational acceptance the official stamp of judicial sanction and the moral imprimatur of the criminal law.[58]

The facts of *Keegstra*, however, are particularly problematic for the purpose it has come to serve.[59] James Keegstra, a schoolteacher in Eckville, Alberta, was convicted of promoting hate propaganda for teaching Holocaust denial and the usual canards about world Jewish conspiracy and media control in his social studies class. In contrast, Ernst Zundel was charged, but acquitted, for saying much the same thing to the *adult* public at large under the 'false news' section of the Criminal Code.[60] Of course, preaching to the adult Canadian public at large, who are free to listen to or reject the speaker, is not the same as preaching to a captive audience of impressionable school children by a person in a position of authority over them. But that, as it turned out, was not the ground for the different results. The court could have reached the result it wanted in *Keegstra* without integrally violating, as it did, the public's right to freedom of social and political expression.

The court could have applied the doctrine of *in loco parentis* to limit hate propaganda law to the very specific facts of *Keegstra*. It could have weighed the values served by hate propaganda legislation in the *instant* case against the values served by a constitutionally protected right of public expression and still served the former without violating the fundamental assumptions and functions of the latter. The court could have upheld conviction on the basis of absence of listener choice, position of authority of the speaker, and presumptive inability of the listeners to judge the message.

First, a corollary of the right to speak is the right not to have to listen – a choice effectively denied to a captive audience of schoolchildren who could either listen and 'learn' or suffer the consequences. These consequences included the stigma of in-class rejection, teacher disapproval, or involuntary student withdrawal. Second, a right of the speaker to speak presupposes that the speaker has no special controlling or coercive power over the listener – a presumption clearly violated where the listeners are schoolchildren and the speaker is an adult teacher in a position of authority over them. Finally, a meaningful right of public expression on matters of state, society, and history presumes an ordinary ability to judge the social messenger and the credibility of his message. Such is the general presumption for enfranchised adults in systems of self-government. It need not and may not be the general presumption for the mentally ill, the legally incompetent, or impressionable schoolchildren below the age of majority.

Alternatively, and even better, the court did not have to uphold hate propaganda law at all – a law reaching all Canadians and extending far beyond the classroom – to protect the children and stop the teaching. It could have accomplished the same thing simply by upholding the right of the school to fire Keegstra for academic incompetence. The court's failure to qualify its decision with due regard to these distinctions effectively reduces all Canadians to the status of a captive audience of impressionable schoolchildren and hate propaganda law to the role of *in loco parentis* over them. That the court chose to uphold the law as it did, even given the free speech escapes provided by the facts of *Keegstra*, is therefore very significant for the future of freedom of expression in Canada.

It is not difficult to distinguish *Zundel* from *Keegstra*.[61] Different facts and circumstances, and the different provisions (language) of the Criminal Code under which each was charged, raise the possibility that *Keegstra* might not serve as precedent for *Zundel*, if Zundel is ever recharged under the hate propaganda section of the Criminal Code. However, the court did not decide either *Keegstra* or *Zundel* on grounds that would suggest judicial recognition of the significance of these fundamental distinctions. In striking down the offending false news section of the Criminal Code in *Zundel* (mainly for vagueness/overbreadth), the court was dutifully careful not to tread on the constitutionality of the hate propaganda provisions of the Criminal Code – provisions that clearly cover 'Zundelite' speech and are, equally clearly, aimed at muzzling expression directed to the general public. And, in upholding the hate propaganda provision in *Keegstra*, the court was equally careful not to restrict or to delimit the application of the law to the narrow confines of the school classroom. While one cannot completely rule out the possibility that a challenge to hate propaganda law based on facts of listener choice or voluntariness, at-large dissemination, and adult audience reception would be decided differently, it seems extremely unlikely. In *Keegstra*, the court made some sweeping assumptions and reached some broad conclusions echoing the Cohen Committee's foundational view that criminalization of certain speech directed to the general public can be sustained for the protection of society at large and political democracy in particular.[62] This thinking and the reasons articulated for it would make it very difficult for the court to reach a contrary conclusion on a different, but equally propagandistic, set of 'hate' facts.

The problem for freedom of expression, in the context of hate propaganda law, has been in making out an effective juridical case for a balance in its favour. The case for freedom of expression is far more difficult to make than the case against it. But this is not because the case for it is intrinsically less cogent. On the contrary, as subsequent chapters will show, the case for freedom of expression is far more compelling than the case against it. For now, it is sufficient to observe that part of the difficulty resides in the subtler reasoning required to justify the free speech side – the kind of thinking that the court has decided to avoid. The social and political values served by freedom of social expression are much less tangible than the social and political values served by hate propaganda law. The linkages between abstract thinking and concrete application of such thinking are much more complex in arguing for freedom of expression than in denying it. This is particularly true in the context of social expression – such as Holocaust denial – whose content is patently devoid of intrinsic social value.[63]

Messages of hate such as Holocaust denial are, literally and figuratively, loud and clear. The values served in allowing their expression are not as clear. While the political wisdom or social benefits of public censorship are open to debate, hate itself is an eminently tangible hurt, measurable by at least three of the human senses – touch if physically manifested, sight if written, sound if heard (and both sight and sound if televised). In short, the public hurt of hate is visible, dramatic, and newsworthy. The public hurt of denial of freedom to express hate is not. That something of existing value to democratic society may be lost or some prospective social or political good foregone as a result of such suppression are much less tangible, but no less important, possible hurts.

The intuitive response, in case of doubt – and doubt there will invariably be in any debate about balancing political rights and social values – is to balance in favour of the tangible harm and against the unquantifiable right. Courts are not immune to such response. Indeed, they are contextualizing institutions of a particular kind. They are charged with resolving concrete, fact-based disputes. They are not particularly well equipped either in terms of institutional structure or historical mandate to articulate general or abstract rights, much less to 'speculate' about foregone social and political benefits from denial of such rights. This is especially true of the Supreme Court of Canada, coming as it has from a historic tradition of judicial deference to the legislature anchored in the doctrine of parliamentary supremacy.[64]

The problem with a juridical approach that a priori discounts the values served by the more abstract is that it is disposed to prejudge the balancing outcome against those values. It is in imbalance from the start, laying the foundations for future imbalances. Yet that is the approach to freedom of speech taken by the Supreme Court of Canada in the context of hate speech law. A brief case history tracing the evolution of judicial thinking on freedom of speech is helpful to understand how the court came to this point.

Juridical balancing of freedom of expression and hate propaganda does not take place in isolation, divorced from other social and political concerns. Development of jurisprudential thinking here has been part of a broader general development of thinking about freedom of speech. The court has had to decide the constitutional ambit of freedom of expression not just in the context of hate propaganda but in a host of diverse contexts ranging from the commercial speech of dentists[65] to the solicitation of sex between prostitutes and their customers.[66] Most, if not all, of these cases focused on situational resolution of relatively tangible problems, an exercise that stresses the concrete and the immediate over the more abstract and theoretical. This is not to say that balancing competing rights in these cases did not require judicial regard for the larger social issues and the political linkages connecting them. But, comparatively speaking, they stressed more an *adjudicative* function of courts than the abstract one demanded of them by hate speech.

In the landmark case *R. v. Oakes*,[67] the Supreme Court of Canada laid down the test for limiting Charter guarantees under section 1, the derogation clause. It was a most demanding test reflecting early fears that, in a straight balancing between rights wrapped in individualistic terms and those packaged in larger social or collective concerns, the case against the 'individual' right would be a foregone conclusion.[68] Early thinking on enumerated rights tended to stress the importance of the Charter as a contra-majoritarian, contra-parliamentary-supremacy device. The purpose of enumeration was to protect civil and political rights from abridgment by the onerous police powers of the state. This thinking was well exemplified by Madam Justice Bertha Wilson herself in an immigration context where she suggested that there was an implicit constitutional bias, a 'commitment' to not allow constitutional derogation under section 1 to 'emasculate' enumerated rights.[69] Yet it would be a mistake to see in such pronouncements a particularly insightful appreciation of the social and political values served by enumerated 'individual' rights such as freedom of expression. In early Charter cases, the courts could afford to be more generous to 'individual' rights because such generosity tended not to collide directly with fundamental concerns for multiculturalism and equality. It was only later, with regard to cases more testing of judicial appreciation for abstract values, that the court created what Jamie Cameron has called an 'asymmetric and hierarchical analysis' that a priori 'privileged section 15 (equality) and section 27 (multiculturalism) at the expense of freedom of expression.'[70]

In *Quebec* v. *Irwin Toy*,[71] the court suggested that all expressive activity (activity intended to 'convey meaning') is 'inherently valuable,' while finding that competing values served by statutory protection of children from exploitation by commercial advertising was a reasonable limit in a free and democratic society.[72] Early cases stressed what became known as the 'content neutral' or 'content blind' approach – the idea that, in balancing freedom of expression against competing values, the intrinsic worth or content of the impugned expression was irrelevant to the question of the right to its expression. It was the values served by the right of expression, not the value of the content of such expression, against which competing values were to be balanced and weighed.

The developing problem, as Cameron writes, was that *Irwin Toy* and *Oakes* created 'abstract standards that provided little or no guidance for resolving concrete questions about the scope of expressive freedom.'[73] Hence, the move to what became known as the 'contextual' approach – a 'balancing' formula where, effectively, the value of public thought would increasingly come to be judged on the circumstantial merits of its content, not on the value of the right to its expression. Commercial speech cases helped fuel this shift. It was apparent in *Rocket*. Madam Justice Beverley McLachlin advised a 'sensitive, case-oriented approach,' one with careful regard to 'the special features of the expression in question.'[74] This approach sat well with the traditional adjudicative role of the courts – one that stressed the situational and the concrete. The instant case may have been well served by it. But it was ill-suited to better appreciation of the more abstract social values and political rights that are served by constitutional protection of freedom of expression – rights and values that extend far beyond the concrete, situational, or evidentiary gauge.

It would remain to *Keegstra* to put such judicial appreciation directly to the test. And it would be *Keegstra* that would show just how short the court had fallen. In *Keegstra*, Chief Justice Dickson was content to pay lip-service to *Irwin Toy* when noting that 'the content of expression is irrelevant in determining the scope of [the guarantee of freedom of expression].'[75] He acknowledges commenting 'at length upon the way in which the suppression of hate propaganda furthers values basic to a free and democratic society' but hardly ponders whether or how 'these same values' may be 'furthered by permitting hate propaganda.'[76] Rather, he warns against a balancing formula that depended on placing a 'high value' on 'freedom of expression in the abstract.'[77] That the 'high value' of freedom of expression that the Chief Justice had earlier so eloquently espoused cannot be appreciated apart from the 'abstract' no longer seemed to matter in the learned justice's balancing equation. Adopting a 'balancing' formula that depended on placing a low value on freedom of expression in the concrete, he effectively made the right of expression conditional on the merits of the content of the expression in the instant case. The intrinsic worth of the message would become equated with the value of the constitutional right to its expression, consuming the latter in the valueless vacuum of the former. The juridical slide from a right of expression to an issue of content was now complete.

Social and political values ostensibly served by hate law would be balanced not against the competing social and political values served by a right of public expression on matters of society and polity but against the intrinsic value of the content of the malevolent message. Effectively, bad content would be 'balanced' against itself – in an exasperating example of tautological judicial reasoning. Using disagreeable content as the defining test for deciding the right to its expression leaves hollow the very idea of 'balancing' competing values. The outcome against speech is a foregone conclusion – the 'worse' the speech, the more foregone the conclusion. Effectively, the value of the right to speak is prejudged and predetermined – before the relative strengths or weaknesses of competing rights and values are even weighed in the balance.

Agreeable or popular public thought would not be put at risk. But then, there is hardly a need to accord constitutional protection to a right to its expression in a system of majority rule. Offensive thought would be put at risk – the more offensive the content, the more at risk it would be. But it is precisely here that protection from suppression is most needed. Meaningful constitutional protection is turned on its head. So too, therefore, is meaningful balancing. Content- or merit-dependent protection emasculates the right of expression of the very indicia for its constitutional protection. The foreboding words of Madam Justice Bertha Wilson in *Singh* are discarded here. In privileging the concrete over the abstract and content over the right to expression, the Supreme Court of Canada has laid the foundations for an asymmetrical juridical balancing of values, one pre-slanted against the very indicia for constitutional protection of expression.

It is very unlikely that the court's approach is a 'momentary' slip. More likely, it is a momentous one. It highlights the kind of weakness in judicial thinking that Greschner and Colvin foresaw early as a problem for the Canadian court.

> The resolution of 'legal' questions often demands some inquiry into 'political' matters. Consider, for example, the interpretations and applications of the abstract concepts which are included in Charters of rights and freedoms. Moreover, the boundaries of the world of 'law' are debatable and reasonable people can disagree on whether an issue is legal or political ... Indeed, if judges are to engage in legal work at all, they must take preliminary positions on recognitory criteria and, therefore, on matters of political theory. It is only conditions of substantial political stability and consensus, under which recognitory criteria operate as implicit assumptions, which enable this facet of judicial reasoning to be disguised ... The Canadian experience cautions against optimistic expectations of the courts' present capacity to appreciate and handle questions of political theory.[78]

For freedom of speech, at perhaps its most foundational test of meaningfulness, Greschner and Colvin's observations are turning out to be prescient. Recognitory criteria of political theory assume criteria of political theory that are recognized. The court has chosen not to seriously 'ponder,' much less recognize, them here. It has openly expressed its hostility to the abstract where regard for the abstract is most crucial, in the matter of silencing the socially most disconcerting and politically most disagreeable. In the result, a meaningful understanding of freedom of expression and the democratic values served by that right where it counts most has been stripped from judicial thinking on intolerance. Until it is put back into the balancing exercise, the 'balance' in the claimed balancing will be largely hollow. A foundational imbalance from which all later thinking can grow is the new reality.

Conclusion

This brief historical examination of the events and fears leading up to the enactment of hate propaganda legislation and later developments in thinking on the problem identifies two distinctive but intersecting paths – one political, the other juridical – laying the foundations for an imbalanced approach to social progress and democracy. The last fifteen years has seen an economistically rooted, societally reductionist, 'political' slide in influential thinking on the function of hate speech law. What began as a relatively bipartisan view of hate speech law as legal protection of vulnerable minorities and democratic society against deliberate and malicious attempts to injure them has turned into a far more problematic ideological understanding of the law as a legitimate instrument for securing desired (necessary) social change. In this thinking, legal silencing may legitimately be enlisted into political service, officially prejudging and authoritatively predetermining public policy outcomes.

While the courts have not openly embraced this view, they have laid the juridical foundations allowing for progression in that direction. Judicial adoption of an asymmetrical balancing approach privileging the concrete and the tangible over the abstract and the general is seminal to the slide. It a priori allows the court to prejudge and predetermine political outcomes against speech if the speech is particularly socially offensive – before the competing values of a meaningful understanding of freedom of expression in the instant case can be weighed in the balance. Rights of expression have slipped to questions of content. Common ground now exists for the political slide to cross-fertilize with the juridical slippage.

2

Functions and Assumptions of Freedom of Expression

The challenge to freedom of expression presented by hate censorship is formidable. Open-ended free speech theories or rights-based morally grounded 'Dworkinian' rationales[1] that may be persuasive in some other public silencing contexts have not served *this* one well (a human or moral right to openly propagate hate?). If the free speech side is to meet the 'theoretical' challenge of hate speech law head on, it must do so on censors' own functionally reductionist terms of social and political reference. This chapter adopts a functionally anchored intersubjective theoretical approach.[2] I consider the functions and assumptions of freedom of expression not in all their aspects but from the perspective of hate censors' own underlying social goals and democratic political premise and suggest that the censors' case for silencing is seriously wanting on their own terms of reference. I divide my discussion into three analytically distinctive but conceptually overlapping theoretical perspectives and four subperspectives.

I Participation, Self-determination, and Self-government

'Freedom of expression,' observed Judge Belzie, 'is the first to be suppressed by totalitarian regimes.'[3] With good reason. As Borovoy writes, freedom of public expression on public matters is the 'freedom on which other freedoms depend.'[4] Freedom of public expression includes corollary rights such as freedom of the press, freedom of public assembly,[5] and freedom of political association.[6] Freedom of public expression not only can unite in a common cause but also can divide in a common cause. It can be destructive as well as constructive. But without freedom of the one (to divide in a common cause), there cannot be freedom of the other (to unite in a common cause).[7]

Constitutional protection of freedom of expression in a democracy is not intended for the numerous but to be a limit on them. As U.S. Supreme Court Justice Brandeis said, '[r]ecognizing the occasional tyrannies of governing majorities, [the Founding Fathers] amended the Constitution so that free speech and assembly should be guaranteed.'[8] In capitalist polities premised on majoritarian governance, the numerous have the numbers and the economically powerful the political clout to command attention. The unpopular, the socially outcast, and the politically excluded possess none of these advantages.[9] To abridge their right to speak is to abridge freedom of expression where it counts most.

Hate censors are not enemies of democracy. In outlawing public expression of intolerance, it is not their purpose to injure freedom of expression and diminish democracy but to better protect it. Successful self-government is the best shield against the scourge of intolerance. Hate propaganda law is not concerned with private expression on public matters[10] or public expression on private matters[11] but with public expression on public matters. Hate, censors contend, is about ignorance and intolerance. But it is also about social discontent and the right to publicly communicate such discomfort. It is about self-expression and self-revealing expression of the socially disaffected's most deeply held feelings and beliefs about the state of society and polity. The main purpose in publicly communicating such feelings is to convert as many people as possible (the proselytizing function) to their cause and, ultimately, to change existing society and polity to one that is more to their liking. It is, in short, intrinsically political communication that is at issue here. The more the message can be said to be publicly disconcerting and socially challenging, the more profoundly 'political' or 'politically important' the communication is.

Politically important communication should be distinguished from 'politically correct' communication. Communication is politically correct if it is officially agreeable. Communication is politically important if it stirs public thought, provokes public controversy, or converts publics' minds.[12] Politically important speech, like politically correct speech, can be socially meritorious or socially unmeritorious. Hitler's *Mein Kampf* ('my struggle') today is both politically incorrect and patently socially unmeritorious, but its message is hardly politically unimportant. Hate propagandists are, quintessentially, politically important communicators.[13] Hate propaganda law itself is shining testimony to this.

Suppressing politically important public communication abridges more than just individual or personal self-determination. It abridges public self-determination. Self-expression, wrote Sartre, is an expression 'of choosing ourselves,'[14] a human voicing of our distinctive self-identity. Political self-expression is an 'act' of choosing our public selves, an expression of our distinctive public self-identity. Suppressing political communication, however, is more than a denial of the public self of the wrongheaded speaker. That would be to confuse the messenger with the purpose of the prohibition. Preventing the speaker from speaking hate is only the means. Preventing the audience from hearing hate is the end. Protecting the public from itself, its feared worst self, is the essential reason for hate propaganda law. The hatemonger is only as dangerous as his audience. Hate propaganda law denies the political self of the wrongheaded listener, the public at large. It abridges public self-determination.

Repression of hate propaganda and rights of self-government are inextricably linked, as proponents of hate censorship themselves illustrate. As Prutschi complains,

> [m]embers of hate groups, or those I have labelled 'bigotry's fellow travellers' are not merely content with carrying out their activities on the periphery. They very consciously involve themselves in our political process. Zundel ran for the leadership of the federal Liberal party in 1968 (Pierre Trudeau won that contest); Andrews [Western Guard; Nationalist Party] has repeatedly vied for municipal office, and Keegstra ran for Social Credit in the 1984 federal election. Fromm [Edmund Burke Society], in this last federal election, ran in Mississauga East for the Confederation of Regions Party; and Christie [Keegstra's and Zundel's lawyer], a vigorous advocate of western separatism, founded the Western Canada Concept party, and has run twice in federal election contests as an independent.[15]

Yet, for hate censors, hate *censorship* is not political. But hate *speech* observably and lamentably is. Thinking that both acknowledges and dismisses the political link (as illegitimate) serves a useful but self-deceptive and self-serving purpose. Censors connect the link to emphasize the harm. But they disconnect the link to justify the repression. What ought not to be substitutes for what is – for the convenience of censorship. The rights to self-determination of one side, the politically less important side, are focused – the *individual* rights of the malevolent speaker to speak publicly. The rights to self-determination of the more important side – the *collective* rights of every interested member of the public to hear – are obscured. Yet, if it is true that the collective welfare of the public is the ultimate object of hate propaganda law, it must equally be true that the collective right of the public to hear and choose is the subject of true contention. An abrogation of the public's collective right to self-determination cannot be turned into a mere abrogation of extremists' individual right to speak.

Canadian representative democracy gives each enfranchised member of the public a legal right[16] to participate in publicly choosing between alternative courses of action on competing and divisive political, social, and economic matters affecting family, community, and country.[17] This right does not depend on the members' political views, good intentions, intellectual acumen, or moral integrity.[18] 'The people's claim to rule,' writes Walzer, 'does not rest upon their knowledge of truth ... but in terms of who they are. They are the subjects of the law, and if the law is to bind them ... they must also be its makers.'[19] Freedom to openly convey and openly receive messages on public matters is an expression of who we, the public, are, social warts and all. This is a public right to self-determination, not the right to self-determination of only some of the public. It is not a right only of the socially right or the morally good to be exercised on behalf of the socially wrong or morally bad. An abridgment of the 'individual' right of anyone to political communication is an abridgment of the collective right of everyone to political self-determination.[20] Dearth of robust participation by the public in their own destiny, decried by progressive censors, has many causes besides abridgment of public discourse by legal censorship.[21] But it is precisely because there is so little public discourse on important matters of state and society in contemporary representative democracies that further abridgments of that discourse by force of law become so significant.[22]

A legally protected right of political communication is not, nor is it intended to be, a political guarantee of either more, or more open, participation. It is not a promise of effective self-government. Its function is facilitative not assurative. Nor is it a substitute for other possible remedies, social, political, or legal, for the participatory malaise that afflicts postindustrial contemporary political democracies. As facilitator, it is inclusionary not exclusionary. To speak against laws that abridge political communication is not to speak against other laws or measures that could or would extend and broaden political communication.[23]

More participatory self-government itself is not a guarantee of good government. Public self-determination can no more guarantee constructive public growth than individual self-determination can guarantee constructive personal growth. Even the freest and most equitable marketplace of ideas cannot guarantee only socially responsible public communicators and politically wise self-government. Indeed, legally unfettered public participation may produce not socially responsible self-government but irresponsible licence. As Monahan writes, 'Democratic politics is not guaranteed to produce right answers. No matter how much debate and discussion is encouraged, there is still the possibility that the community will make a choice that is mean-spirited or unenlightened ... A choice for democracy means that the community has the right to be wrong.'[24]

Hate propaganda law is a rejection of the view that the community has a right to be wrong. Censors fear the public more than the propagandist. They do not fear the public with respect to all or even most political communication. They fear the public where trust is a foundational test of self-governance – the public's ability to get along as it should. Hate law distrusts public expression where trust counts most. This is hardly a more meaningful understanding of freedom of expression and self-government.

Hate censors' democratic dilemma may explain the growing attractiveness of the progressive structuralist position. It is one that seeks to reconcile the right to silence with a meaningful understanding of freedom of expression and effective self-government. Democratic structuralists argue that what they fear is not a flawed public but a flawed polity – a flawed system of social justice and public choice.[25] The difficulty is that their legal remedy does not agree either with their own understanding of the problem or with the more meaningful freedom of expression and self-government they extol. Hate propaganda law targets precisely the public it ostensibly does not fear. And it does not target the flawed system of choice it ostensibly does fear. The real but unacknowledged object of hate propaganda law is not a flawed system but a flawed public. If a flawed system of choice was what hate censors really feared, they could not and would not dismiss from the cognitive balance the many public choices and voices for tolerance, equality, and harmony. But they do. All proponents of censorship do – even those proponents of censorship who are of the view that most Canadians are 'solidly tolerant' and 'the largest circle' of voices.[26]

The problem for hate censors cannot be that voices, visions, and policies for social progress, equality, and tolerance in Canada have been altogether absent or not heard.[27] If that were the case, it might be credible to cite a flawed system as justification for hate propaganda law.[28] But that is not the case. It cannot even be that such voices occupy an insignificant place in the hierarchy of public meaning and message

making in Canada today.[29] Nor can the problem be that it is just enlightened elites who hate propagandists who spread hate. So, too, do
the general public. Public revulsion against hate propagandists in Canada
runs wide and deep – as popular support for hate propaganda law itself
strongly suggests. Progressive censors may fear that transparent messages of hate will resonate with the public. But the concern of the
public itself is more one of public dissonance than resonance – having
to suffer offensive messages of transparent hate.

At bottom, hate censors have a problem not with the absence of
choice but with its existence. To them, it matters not if the choice for
hate is marginally expressed or marginally received.[30] As long as there is
any independent public choice, they feel that there is justification for
official censorship. Even one Zundel is one too many to tolerate. Even
many right choices and correct voices are vulnerable to contamination
by marginal racist voices and their publicly expressed choices. But if
this is true, the problem cannot simply be with a deficient system of
choice. It must be with the people who choose. In fact, hate censorship
law is not directed to the system of public choosing but to the public
who choose. Hate law abridges not bridges. It does nothing to 'free up'
or replace structures of cognitive closure that block independent public choice. Rather, it imposes its own system of closure. The goal is to
ensure that all of the public thinks right by denying every member of
the public the right to think wrong. The public is *in* danger because the
public *is* the danger.

To see hate censorship as a counterbalance for more choice in a
flawed system of choice is therefore highly problematic. The counterbalance to blindness in one eye cannot be to blind the other eye.
Without the right to hear and speak wrong where it counts most, there
can be no public *choice* to speak right *instead* of wrong where it counts
most – whether the system is flawed or not. The structures and institutions of hate censorship are intended to be a brick wall – not a porous
wall. They are erected precisely to guarantee what choice can only risk
– right results. Guaranteeing right results, rather than the right to choose,
makes sense if what is feared more than a flawed system of choice is a
flawed public choosing. Effectively, what structuralists really distrust are
flawed publics in the name of flawed polities.

While progressive censors may speak of a flawed system of choice,
liberal censors openly fear flawed publics that choose. But for the purposes of hate law, this is a distinction without a difference. Neither
group is willing to risk the wrong choice, flawed-system justification or

not. Liberal censors are just more apt to recognize and acknowledge this fact. In neither case does the legal remedy agree with the more meaningful freedom of expression and self-government extolled by censors. Progressive censors, in particular, call for measures to open up political democracy to excluded and marginal voices. They speak of building more effective bridges of public participation and more transparent faces of political expression in order to open doors closed by official structures and vested interests. And they often do, or at least try to do, as they say – except when those bridges and faces are uncensored ones crossing fundamentally troubled waters for their cause. Then they believe that no one should have the right to cross independently, for there is no assurance that some won't lose their balance, fall in, and even drag others with them.

For hate censors, there can be no freedom of choice or need for discursive transparency where there is most to lose. But it is precisely where there is most to lose that choice and transparency become most important. Where choice and transparency should count most, for hate censors it is correct results that count more than choice and transparency. Hate censors may call for more meaningful freedom of expression. They may extol bridges to politically more effective rather than politically correct self-government. But hate propaganda law is not one of these bridges.

II Enlightened Publics, Honest Politics, Accountable Politicians, and Self-government

Successful self-government, many would argue, is about much more than just open and effective public participation. It is also about more enlightened public participation, meaningful public discourse, social harmony, honest politics, and accountable politicians.

1 Enlightened Participation and Social Division

Unenlightened public participation risks social division and public discord. This can diminish democracy, and even destroy the polity.[31] More enlightened publics are more self-knowing publics. Self-knowing publics cannot fear to know the truth about themselves. The more prejudices they have, the more they need to know about themselves. They need to understand their worst falsehoods and vilest secrets no less than their best truths and finest virtues. Those kept in the dark because they cannot be trusted to see the light for themselves are likely to become less, not more, able to see the light for the dark that they are kept in. The longer their time in the dark, the less likely they are to see the light.

Enlightened public choice is not more likely when publics 'choose' right because they fear prosecution if they choose wrong. Nor does it result from unreflective minds required to reflexively parrot what is legally required and officially expected. It cannot be dictated by right thinkers from above on behalf of a public of wrong thinkers below, but must come from the people themselves. There is no more reason to think that it can be legally crafted and officially mandated in a structurally flawed system of public choice than in a structurally unflawed one. A flawed structure of choice is more reason against such legal construction.

This is not to suggest that legally unfettered public expression on public matters can ensure against ignorance and prejudice. Public self-enlightenment, like personal self-development, takes learning as well as freedom. Public learning takes public practice. And even then, practice is no assurance of success. But without the right to practise – to hear, reflect, and decide – public learning and growth are handicapped. Enlightened self-government, like positive personal self-development, must be risked to be learned. It is not that all members of the public, or even the majority, will necessarily, or inevitably, or on each controversy, grow as desired. Barring a presumption of flawless publics, even in an ideally structurally unflawed system of public choice, no such assurances can be given.[32] However, the possibilities for public growth are lessened to the extent that leaders fear rather than respect the very means by which the public may *learn* to grow.[33]

Public choice is not a guarantee of uninterrupted public success, much less of a final one. Assurances are the task of censorship not the promise of freedom of expression. Tolerance for public choice, where it counts, risks the possibility of intolerant public choice, where it counts. But intolerance of public choice cannot produce right public *choices* when it allows no choice. 'Right' without choice is to preach to the converted, to think for those who need to think for themselves, and to procure compliance in place of consent from the recalcitrant. This may 'work' to silence what is feared to be heard for a while, perhaps even a long while. But neither passive obedience nor resentful compliance is the stuff of which a more enlightened social harmony, secure equality, and genuine public tolerance are made.

Progressive censors point to an unenlightened public in defence of their public silencing.[34] They spotlight latent prejudices hiding beneath the thin veneer of social civility – the self-denying, self-deceiving, and self-serving (subconscious) prejudices concealed behind a facade of politically correct public pronouncements.[35] But, then, is that not the very kind of 'tolerance' that public silencing promotes? Censorship's abridgment of disconcerting public discourse helps perpetuate the very conditions that serve as reason for abridging it. Silence, or its effects, becomes reason for silencing. The assumption that the people cannot be trusted to get along as they should without hate censorship takes on a disturbing circularity. Where the answer to a problem serves both as cause and effect, the problem becomes self-realizing and the answer self-justifying.

More self-knowing publics may not make for more tolerant publics. But less self-knowing ones are apt to make for even less tolerant ones. The reasons for the travails of post-Communist societies are many and complex. But in no other social experiment this century was so much effort expended to officially craft, socially mould, and legally compel the desired enlightened consciousness as an ordinary feature of public discourse – egalitarian and tolerant.[36] Nor is there a stronger example of unmitigated failure. Ethnic conflicts, self-regarding licence, and public prejudices of the most virulent kind have erupted in all multi-ethnic post-Communist regimes where once political peace and social harmony reigned supreme.[37] Discourse-deprived, choice-inexperienced publics became more not less vulnerable to demagoguery and uncivil pursuit of the self. Communism's failure to promote public growth in the absence of public choice was unequivocal and universal – transnational, transcultural, and transhistorical. Mandated harmony turned out to be artificial harmony, official truth empty truth, and enforced stability instability when force was gone. Egalitarian quiet, mistaken at first for genuine cognitive triumph, proved more pyrrhic than profound.

It may be objected that Communism did not do what it set out to do. Fixing desired public thinking by force of silencing became socially self-serving and politically total.[38] Democracies such as Canada hardly seek to prohibit all socially or politically incorrect public discourse, only intolerant discourse where it counts. The censorship, the circumstances, and the histories are hardly identical. The laboratory of comparative history is rarely contextually untainted or politically unequivocal. There are both quantitative and qualitative differences, even between Communist regimes, in terms of public growth. But the essential point of the comparison remains – shielding publics from self-knowledge with hate censorship gets in the way of public growth by diminishing the very means by which they may learn to get along as they should. The lesson of this century's premier experiments in crafting a more progressive, egalitarian, enlightened social consciousness cannot be that shielding publics from self-knowledge where it counts most gets in the way of public learning and public growth in Communist dictatorships but not in more self-governing polities. Rather, it suggests that the more encompassing the shield, the more it gets in the way.

2 Meaningful Public Discourse, Social Truth, and Social Division

More meaningful public discourse on public matters is central to more enlightened public participation. Meaningful public discourse requires better public understanding of public matters in dispute. Such discourse assumes special regard for truth. Hate censors would officially guarantee truth by legal silencing – where it counts most. Free speech advocates would not. Free speech theorists seem to value public choice over public truth. However, what they value is public truth *through* public choice. Freedom of speech protects the right of the public to search for truth, not 'correct' public results.

A public right to search for truth is not, of course, synonymous with truth itself. It is not meant to be. A right to search is not an assurance that the search will be successful.[39] Nor can it depend on the truthful intentions of the searcher. That would be to prejudge the right to search.[40] Freedom of expression is a facilitative right protecting a content-neutral process; it is not meant to dictate the direction of that process or guarantee right results or the good intentions of the searcher. A meaningful right to search for truth can no more assure that everyone will search rightly and that truth will be found than the discursive right to public self-determination can assure that everyone will speak responsibly and that responsible self-government will be found. It is not that free speech advocates believe that truths do not exist. It is that they believe that without meaningful public choice a different kind of truth from the one wanted and expected will be more likely to exist.

More meaningful public discourse is not synonymous with the intention of the speaker to seek truth, her success in finding it, or the truth or falsity of the content of the expression. For one thing, the speaker may intend truth but completely miss the mark.[41] Or, the speaker may not intend truth but may produce it none the less.[42] Or, a speaker may produce truth but fail to impress an indifferent society. Then again, she may not produce truth, but society may be aroused by her failed search to more meaningfully discover it. Or, the fearful but truthful might exercise self-censorship rather than risk legal stricture for misspeaking.[43] Alternatively, opportunists may say what society expects them to say rather than what they truly believe. Public understandings need not accord with officially made or legally required ones. More meaningful ones are publicly made not publicly mandated.

John Stuart Mill's thoughts on the matter are salient. Noting first that 'if the opinion is right they [society] are deprived [by censorship] of the opportunity of exchanging error for truth,' he continues, 'if wrong, they lose, what is almost as great a benefit, the clearer impression and livelier impression of truth, produced by its collision with error.'[44] Censoring theorists summarily dismiss Mill's famous 'collision' thesis as the 'doctrine of rationality,' routinely attributing its 'naive faith' in the inevitable 'triumph of human reason' to free speech advocates.[45] But this misunderstands the assumptions and functions of freedom of speech in a most fundamental way.

Freedom of expression, meaningfully understood, cannot assume the inevitable triumph of rational results, for it does not assume the guaranteeability of any results. A freedom intended to reflect 'who we are' can hardly be said to assume that only the right and the rational 'will be.' That is censors' purpose and expectation. There is nothing consequentially inevitable in free speech assumptions. The free speech position accepts that truth making cannot be made risk free. Freedom of speech is about relative risks and lesser evils precisely because its adherents reject faith in absolute guarantees.[46] Assurances of rational results belie censors' assumptions and expectations of silencing not speech advocates' assumptions about relative risks and social and political uncertainties.

Construction of meaning by the public does not turn simply on rational considerations – on the intrinsic merit of the message. Public meaning construction is a function of ongoing intersubjective and interactive, not linear, cognitive exchanges that defy both the cerebral meanings and finality of 'found truths' demanded by censors.[47] Emotion, symbolism, personal experiences, and countless other factors weigh as heavily in public 'reasoning' as the intrinsic merit of the message itself. This, of course, is as true for the social divider as it is for the social harmonizer. But messaging causes here successfully is asymmetrical. Bridging public divides and correcting latent prejudices requires right *understanding* – deeper public appreciation of the *reasons* why the right message is correct – not simply right results. Social harmonizers need *knowing* publics, not simply *nodding* publics, if their 'success' is not to be fleeting or fragile – especially in systems of occasional governing majorities and changing social agendas. Uncritical public acceptance may work very well for the cause of hate and ignorance but not for the cause against it. A law that fears public thinking where it counts most – officially and finally fixing a correct public understanding – is more likely to compress further than to 'expand the space for critical judgement' required for *deeper* public appreciation of its message.[48]

Public understandings evolve through time, place, and change – censors' attempts to legally 'fix' or 'correct for' the uncertainties of these things notwithstanding. Time and change, especially, are the enemies of memory and therefore of the lessons of historical wrongs. Time and change fade original meanings – the more distant the time, the less relevant and meaningful are the lessons of past wrongs to later generations untouched by them.[49] In this sense, what social injustice is not time and change dependent? As I have said elsewhere, '[s]ocial truth must be regularly challenged – its message kept alive – if it is to remain current and meaningful ... The process of vigorous clash and interplay of social truth with social falsehood rejuvenates the message of truth. Silence, not falsehood, allows the message to die.'[50]

The Holocaust is no exception to this observation but an illustration of it. Enforced protection of the truth of its occurrence risks becoming a paper preservation of its lessons. The meaning of the Holocaust is more than its genocide. It is about memory and relevance and currency. Censorship works at cross-purposes with these goals. A truth-revitalizing project such as filmmaker Steven Spielberg's video testimonials of 51,661 surviving eyewitnesses of the Holocaust for posterity is a case in point.[51] The need to construct discursive substitutes for real-time history, to preserve its deeper meanings, and guard against time-worn public indifference to its message, testifies to the problem of meaning atrophy. Ordinary people don't experience important social or historical meanings in the timeless and final terms that censors committed to the cause do and expect them to.

For increasingly distant Canadian generations untouched by it, the horrors of the Holocaust can hardly resonate with the same deeper meaning if their current incarnations are shielded behind the silence of censorship rather than exposed through freedom to speak. Is a good answer to 'Evil like that can't happen here' to say, 'Yes, it can, but won't. It is not heard here'? How can the silence of the unrepentant clandestine hatemonger improve on the words of an open free-speaking one like Zundel – who testifies in the flesh to the evil feared, and rejuvenates in 'real time' the deeper meanings that people like Spielberg seek to keep alive? How can minds be opened to see more vividly what is right about the truth if they are closed to seeing for themselves what is wrong about the falsehood?

Collision between wrong and right is hardly a guarantee that right will win. Assurances are censorship's task, not freedom of expression's promise. There can be no absolute guarantees that right will triumph either way, only relative risks. Advocates of free speech believe that promoting enlightened public meanings that are better understood is less risky to society and polity than legal assurances of correct meanings officially given. They would rather risk absolute triumph than risk comparative success. Open hatemongers in Canada have brought history to life for the public at large where before it languished behind closed doors or in academic books. Daily protests in front of Zundel' headquarters in downtown Toronto juxtaposed frail, elderly Holocaust survivors protesting against steel-helmeted, leather-booted, foul-mouthed storm troopers – painting a particularly poignant and persuasive message against hate and hatemongers. Once nonexistent, Holocaust education across Canada has revitalized the lessons of the Nazi campaign of genocide.[52] Seven of ten provinces in Canada today (the remaining provinces are expected to follow) have enacted legislation officially marking Holocaust Memorial Day.[53] The long-dormant conscience of Canadian churches has been reawakened in response to open expressions of Holocaust denial. Rev. G. Malcolm Sinclair has said '[o]ur remembrance is a profound form of resistance and a radical act of solidarity. We resist the forces of forgetfulness and denial.'[54]

In October 1999, the lessons of the Holocaust were brought to life in Canada through more than 100 programs hosted by dozens of community organizations, including thirty-six churches, in what has been described by its organizers as 'North America's premier Holocaust Education Program.'[55] Writes co-chair Howard Driman, '[t]he amount of interest in the event is a testament to the relevance and importance of the subject matter, as well as the mandate of the program.'[56] There has been a veritable proliferation of films, videos, and movies on the Holocaust.[57] Permanent courses on the Holocaust are being launched at universities all across Canada.[58] This has been the 'free speech' response to an exposed and venomously expressed public threat. It is hard to imagine such enthusiastic response to an effectively hidden or concealed one.

Today, ever more Holocaust 'rediscovery' in Canada is proceeding with ever less benefit of legally unencumbered clash and collision of minds in the flesh. The fear that Holocaust education is increasingly being carried on the back of a more meaningful education *in* the Holocaust because of hate censorship is not groundless. Censorship works to abridge more thoughtful public understandings of the meaning and message of important social and historical truths not only by *devaluing* the importance of falsehood to such understandings but also by *overvaluing* the importance of *only* truth to such understandings. The partner of truth atrophy in marriage is truth overload. There is growing reason to believe that even in the case of history's most incontrovertible truth there can be such a thing as too much of *only* a good 'think.'

Message overload can produce feelings of bombardment, frustrating more meaningful appreciation of the message loaded.[59] Bombardment can, of course, flow from too many conflicting or different kinds of messages hitting the senses at one time.[60] But it can also flow from too much of only one exclusively correct or official kind hitting the senses all the time. Over time, desensitization to the message, withdrawal, indifference, even resentment can occur. Hate censors wish to ensure that the message about tolerance 'freely' hitting the senses is of only one kind – the correct kind. The thinking that says even one free-speaking Holocaust denier is one too many to tolerate, expresses it well.

Truth overload is becoming a problem even for members of the Jewish community. As Morton Weinfeld writes,

[f]or some time, I have felt Holocaust overload from the world of the arts and entertainment ... the Jewish community continues to use the Holocaust as a central vehicle of identity and socialization ... Everywhere there are symposia, institutes, academic chairs, museums, memorials, centres, curricula, political sloganeering, pilgrimages of adults and teens ... On a personal level, I now feel sufficiently confused that I am no longer receptive to artistic interpretations of the Holocaust, of ever increasing subtlety.[61]

Hate censors may speak of legal silencing as a force only for unity and understanding, not for division and intolerance. Yet when even distinguished members of the Jewish community begin to complain about message overload, what effect might this be having on those outside the community – those less committed to the cause? Truth overload can breed not only desensitization to the message and indifference to its meaning but also resentment of the cause. A backlash in place of belief has already been observed against the expansion of antiracism education in Canada.[62] Backlash is served well by public indifference. Divisive demagogues thrive best in the soil of public indifference. Ultimately, received truths are more fragile than self-constructed ones. As Louis Brandeis put it, 'public discussion is a political duty' and the 'greatest menace to freedom is an inert people.'[63]

Truth without genuine choice is an idea of public meaning construction that fails to distinguish between truth prized for its intrinsic worth (where, we may all agree, patent falsehoods such as Holocaust denial have, of themselves, no value) and truth prized for its public worth (where falsehoods, when juxtaposed to truth, may be valuable). Public worth is simply subsumed or swallowed up by intrinsic worth. Messenger intention and message content then become the deciding criteria for freedom of expression, and bad intentions and bad messages cease to deserve constitutional protection.

Censoring theorists see falsehood and choice in their socially and politically constructed contexts. But they see truth and censorship in an apolitical and time static theoretical vacuum – a final event of 'found' meanings, fixed public growths, and final political triumphs.[64] Censors' minds and censors' meanings may be fixed, but public minds and public meaning making are ongoing processes. Meanings of even irrefutable historical truths are not self-contained, self-regenerating, and self-rejuvenating. They depend for their continuing social relevance and deeper public appreciation on renewal in the face of changing times – and this requires ongoing challenges.

3 Multiplicity of Public Truth and Social Division

All social, historical, or public truths are not equal. Some are more distinct, more consequential, or more visible than others. But such truths do not speak to the public of their own accord. People do. People give truths their meanings. Public meaning construction on such matters, however, is not simply a function of education. It is also a function of politics. In the push and pull of political competition for the public mind, even irrefutable public truths can acquire multiple meanings and take on the dimensions of elusive goals and fluid ideals. Diverse interests can give the same truth diverse meanings or diverse truths the same meaning. The Holocaust is no exception to this observation but a good illustration of it.

Abu-Zahra, a duly qualified member of an Ontario Race Relations Committee, was found distributing what Jewish groups argued was 'hate material' – M.H. Faruqui's review of Norman Finkelstein's book *The Holocaust Industry – Reflections on the Exploitation of Jewish Suffering* – at an antiracism teachers' conference. The committee's director of education refused to remove Abu-Zahra, arguing that the vote against removal was 'democratic' and that the Race Relations Advisory Committee 'represents the total community in terms of the nine jurisdictions and it seeks a balance racially.'[65] An outraged Canadian Jewish Congress threatened to bring Abu-Zahra before the Ontario Human Rights Commission for disseminating 'hate material at an equity-in-race conference.'[66]

In a letter defending his actions, Abu-Zahra argued that a special focus on teaching the Holocaust in Canada's school curriculum is 'exclusive and marginalizes the suffering of other people' (citing the killing of 1 million Armenians between 1915 and 1924, the slaughter of 14.5 million Ukrainians, the wounding of 3.5 million Chinese during the Second World War, and the cultural genocide directed against Canada's First Nations). He went on to say that 'The notion that the suffering of Jewish people should be featured in the school curriculum over that of others is without merit from either an educational or human rights perspective' and that promoting the Holocaust message outside a commemorative context encourages a 'self-serving industry.' Parroting Finkelstein, he maintained that the legacy of Jewish suffering 'has been shamelessly exploited for the financial advantage' of the elite and to quell political opposition to Israel's handling of the Palestinian uprising.[67] The dilemma of the political multiplicity of even patent public truths can, it seems, strike and scorch the houses of even hate censors themselves.

The suggestion that a commemorative context could escape what a duly constituted race relations context could not is groundless. The Jewish community has been pressing Ottawa to build a commemorative Holocaust museum in the capital. An alternative campaign, spearheaded by a Toronto-based Ukrainian organization (Ukrainian Canadian Civil Liberties Organization) has been pressing the federal government for a museum to commemorate genocide throughout the twentieth century. While the latter's members and observer groups are mostly 'European in background,' others include Asian participants, First Nations groups, and Palestine Heritage Canada (PHC). This has raised deep concern in the Jewish community, which fears 'that such an effort could derail efforts to establish a dedicated Holocaust museum' and could 'pit various ethnic communities against each other with each vying for inclusion as a victim group at the expense of the others.'[68] Manuel Prutschi, national director of community relations for the Canadian Jewish Congress, has said that 'our clear impression was that this was an effort to dilute the national Holocaust museum project.'[69] Others have warned that the 'situation has potential to turn very ugly, very quickly, unless a more creative alternative is developed that can allow everyone to save face.'[70]

Fears of dilution of meaning have been raised in many other contexts as well. Criticizing Holocaust 'mis-imaging' associated with the war in Kosovo and the NATO campaign against Yugoslavia, Professor Irwin Cotler writes,

> [i]f the Holocaust is a metaphor to understand or manipulate the understanding of what is happening in Kosovo today, many commentators and critics, including not a few Israelis and Jews, invoke Kosovo as a metaphor for the Holocaust ... [T]o suggest that Kosovo is another Holocaust, runs the risk of trivializing the Holocaust, while minimizing the evil of Kosovo. For if Kosovo is a Holocaust, then the Holocaust was like Kosovo, which means that in the Holocaust there were no gas chambers, no death camps, no 'final solution' to kill every Jew anywhere simply because they were Jews.[71]

Even former prime ministers of Israel are not spared. Hebrew University philosophy professor Avishai Margalit has argued that Israel itself acutely debased the meaning of the Holocaust under the governments of Golda Meir and Menachem Begin, citing Begin's comparison of a Syrian attack against Christians in Lebanon – which left few casualties – with the Holocaust.[72]

The political multiplicity of meaning construction is highlighted in crises, particularly those that strike closest to home. Following the destruction of the World Trade Center in New York, Professor Howard Adelman wrote a scathing piece on the dangers of misappropriation of language. Linking vitriolic Holocaust mis-imaging at the world antiracism conference in Durban, South Africa, to the Trade Center attack, he wrote, 'The most repugnant assault on language was the attempt to appropriate the term [Holocaust] to apply to any disaster [such as the displacement of Palestinians from their homeland].'[73] But even otherwise politically innocuous commercial or social contexts can illustrate the dilemma. Following a complaint by the Simon Wiesenthal Center, the British arm of U.S.-based sportswear maker Umbro apologized and promised to rename or withdraw a line of shoes that bore the name 'Zyklon,' the same name as the poison gas used to kill Jews during the Holocaust.[74] The U.S. chain store Target removed the numbers '88' from a line of baseball caps and shorts because the numbers have been used as symbols or 'code' for 'Heil Hitler' by White supremacists.[75] In Vancouver, a city councillor apologized for comparing a police proposal that drunk drivers should display a 'D' on their cars for a year to the Nazi practice of requiring Jews to wear a Star of David on their clothes.[76]

Attempts to appropriate exclusive social or political meanings are, of course, not confined to the symbols of the Holocaust; nor are they the prerogative of any single group. The Federal Court of Canada recently rejected the attempt of the Chosen People Ministries (CPM), a messianic 'Jews-for-Jesus type group,' to *legally* appropriate the menorah, the ancient seven-branched candelabrum symbolizing the Jewish faith, by registering it as the CPM's 'Official Mark.' Keith Landy, Canadian Jewish Congress national president, argued that such groups 'create the misleading perception of Jewish affiliation through their appropriation of Jewish religious symbols (such as the menorah), holidays, traditions and terminology, all to facilitate their proselytizing campaign.'[77]

As this illustrates, in the contentious politics of public meaning construction, the symbols and meanings of even patent public truths are plural – socially multifaceted and politically multidimensional. Disagreement, division, and discord are intrinsic to public pursuits of exclusively correct meanings in a multitude of diverse, social, political, religious, economic, and even educational contexts – from the commemorative (Holocaust memorial) and the spiritual (menorah) to public safety (drunk drivers), commercial activity (shoes and baseball caps), international relations (terrorism), and even the work of race-relations committees (the Abu-Zahra debacle). It is the mainstream intercommunity competition to privilege a singular correct meaning within multiple possible meanings, rather than the transparent falsehoods of marginal extremists such as Zundel, that presents the more formidable challenge to tolerance, social harmony, and public enlightenment in Canada today.[78] Of course, division and discord do not result only from censorship, as illustrated above. They are a function of the political multiplicity of public meaning construction on matters worth arguing about. But where censorship is enlisted or threatened, silencing works more to sharpen than to blunt those divisions. Exclusionary truth practices, by dint of law, risk generating not only greater intercommunity conflict but also hollow rather than the enlightened and meaningful public victories desired by censors.

Recognition, implicitly or explicitly, of these dilemmas can be found in creative forms of cooperative truth splitting – inclusionary discursive models modifying exclusionary truth-making practices. The Museum of Tolerance in Los Angeles, a multiracial, multihistorical educational arm of the Simon Wiesenthal Center, 'challenges visitors on two fronts,' writes Kirshner.[79] The museum 'highlights two interlocking themes – the history of racism in the United States and the story of the Holocaust.' It includes the 'Other America,' depicting the history of hate groups from the Ku Klux Klan to the Aryan Nations; 'Ain't You Gotta Right?' depicting the African-American civil rights movement; 'In Our Time,' a documentary on the genocides in Rwanda and Bosnia and a chronicle of contemporary neo-Nazi organizations and other human-rights violations worldwide.

Cooperative truth splitting can be implicit. A full-page ad in the *Canadian Jewish News* soliciting funds for a Holocaust project states, 'Your support will guarantee that future generations will know what befell the Jewish People *and so many others* ...'[80] Or consider the Alberta Jewish community's relatively muted response to the Alberta government's decision to change its commemorative 'Holocaust Memorial Day Yom ha-Shoah Act' to 'Holocaust Memorial Day and Genocide Remembrance Act.' The change, made in response to complaints by the Ukrainian and Islamic communities, intends to 'encourage Albertans to recognize the Holocaust and consider other instances of systemic violence, genocide, persecution, racism and hatred.'[81]

Even the controlled message making and meaning constructing that occur in the school classroom are not immune to the dilemma of the political multiplicity of truth. Segal cites the frustrations of one Toronto-area high school teacher after his course on the Holocaust attracted only between 10 and 15 per cent of the school's non-Jewish students. The teacher decided it was time for some cooperative truth splitting. To make Holocaust education 'relevant to everyone,' he required students to 'do an independent study project that is not on the Holocaust, but must be on another example of a genocide, such as Rwanda or Bosnia-Herzegovina [Yugoslavia].'[82] The only thing feared by this antiracist educator more than the dilution or corruption of the meaning of the Holocaust was that its message not be heard in the first place.

Modified truth-making practices such as these illustrate how competing political interests can give the same truth diverse meanings or diverse truths similar meanings but within the context of cooperation rather than conflict and confrontation. Spotlighting and understanding such dilemmas better is not to deny unique historic meanings or intrinsic truths. It is not to argue for moral relativism but to recognize that absolutism in social message making and the construction of public meaning may not come without a price, even in the case of 'irrefutable' truths. That price, paradoxically, may include the sacrifice of wider social harmony and better public appreciation of the meaning of the cause itself. However, whereas public meaning construction through public choice forces the truth makers to confront such dilemmas or face the social and political costs of ignoring them, truth making through censorship allows them to dismiss such dilemmas and deny their costs altogether. Found truths, fixed meanings, and final triumphs, guaranteed by law, tend to do that to 'unfound' ones.

The dilemma for the construction of public meaning, however, is more than the political multiplicity of truth. It is also that the link binding falsehood to truth is inextricable in such construction. It is harder to bridge divides – to meaningfully enlighten unknowing or ignorant minds – without benefit of independent choice or risk of division. Segal describes how the high school teacher in the previous example recalled that questions asked by a non-Jewish student might 'have offended many kids. She said "wasn't Hitler just being efficient or why didn't the Jews stand up for themselves?"'[83] Should she have been 'educatively' censured? Or unimposingly answered? Real-life dilemmas such as this suggest that while true meaning may be officially given and legally enforced, true understanding must be independently discovered, freely arrived at, and fearlessly searched for. And that requires true choice – and the risks of falsehood.[84] Censoring theorists may reject such 'messy' dilemmas, but truth making in practice illustrates them.

The right to quiet messages that deny, dilute, or corrupt the meaning of the Holocaust should be the easiest case for censors to defend and the hardest for free speech advocates to attack. The Holocaust is perhaps the best-documented 'hate fact' of the twentieth century. Yet even here, censors' case for truth without independent choice, as the better way to promote public tolerance, enlightenment, and harmony, falls far short of their own social intentions and political expectations. If censors' idea of truth officially guaranteed by law is a less than convincing answer even in the most common 'best case' contexts, where is it convincing? Abortion, immigration, affirmative action, social justice, poverty, cloning, euthanasia are far more complex and pressing public concerns where ignorance may better hide and prejudice more subtly play out than is Holocaust denial. But it is also within them where public truths are far less cerebrally obvious, fixing exclusively correct public meanings is more politically elusive, and hate silencing is even more socially problematic.

Free speech advocates do not think that public meaning construction, where it counts most, can be legally stripped of its socially multifaceted, politically multidimensional contexts, the movement of time or the risks of political challenge – to better assure public rationality and social harmony. In matters of public tolerance, message making and meaning construction, comprehension and education, truth and falsehood, talk and thinking are inextricably politically bound up. Hate censors' 'public truth without public choice' approach to the public good fails to fully appreciate the political character and cognitive complexity of these links and the dilemmas they pose for a cause that would legally guarantee against such dilemmas by denying them.

4 Honest Politicians, Accountable Politics, Public Division

Successful self-government is more than just participation, in still another way. As Greene and Shugarman argue, it is also about honest politicians and accountable politics.[85] Participation may be the fuel of self-government. But enlightened participation, honest politicians, and accountable politics are the measure of its social and political performance. We shouldn't expect more honest politicians and accountable politics without more honest and self-accountable publics. The latter, of course, is no guarantee of the former. But its absence is a virtual assurance against it.

Public self-accountability begins with self-knowledge. Legal repression of open expressions of intolerance 'works' not only to deprive the public of the unpleasant facts it needs to know itself better but also of the responsibility to do so. Such repression works to free the public from having to openly and honestly take stock of itself on matters it otherwise would and should confront. Silencing public discourse on public matters works to deprive public political exchange of the challenge of self-responsibility, the experience of self-accountability, and, in a polity premised on self-government, a sense of public duty for both.

The more effective the censorial protection, the more such protection works to so debilitate the public.

What the public does not know, or is chilled by censorship from knowing, can hurt it in more ways than one. Public silencing works its injuries not just on the publics silenced but also on the public silencers. Those who have 'found' the truth (or think they have) and try to legally fix its correct meanings and officially assure its public triumph need not only not search for it – they need not tolerate those who have not found it. Whether or not such infallibility is justified in the instant case is less important for public accountability than its official assumption in the first place.[86] Self-ignorant publics are not only less able to account for themselves. They are less able to hold their leaders accountable. Nor do leaders of such publics have much incentive, of their own accord, to hold themselves accountable to the public. On the contrary, they have more incentive not to. It is self-ignorant publics who must account to their more knowing leaders. Self-government is turned on its head.[87] Self-ignorant publics promote arrogant and self-ignorant censoring elites. Public discourse on public matters promotes publicly responsive elites. Public silencing risks producing self-serving ones. The more censorship there is, where it counts, the greater the risk.

The dilemmas of legal truth making – public accountability, meaningful public discourse, multiplicity of truth – have led to some imaginative attempts to salvage the case for hate censorship. Some theorists have suggested that social or racial harmony is paramount. All other goals and values, including truth, must bow to it. Let's assume, writes Barendt, that claims of racial superiority/inequality are true. '[B]ritish legislation outlaws the publication of insulting speech likely to cause racial hatred, a prohibition which might well cover such pseudo-scientific statements. A society is arguably entitled to take the view that for the foreseeable future racial harmony is such an important goal that an absolute tolerance of free speech is too great a luxury.'[88] Can the case for legal silencing be rescued this way, or does it make a weak case weaker still?

Effectively, Barendt would replace the official truth with the official lie – for the sake of social harmony and public peace. It is hard to see how legally enforced public lies can construct the more enlightened publics, much less the more accountable politics and honest politicians, wanted and expected by censors. By the terms of this argument for legal silencing, the civil rights movement in the United States could have been suppressed 'for the foreseeable future.' Demonstrators protesting discrimination, while expressing social truth, fuelled some of the worst public unrest, racial enmity, and political discord seen in America since the Civil War. If racial harmony trumps truth, South African apartheid and pre-civil rights America should be extolled. They were, while they lasted, far more racially harmonious and publicly peaceful regimes than their free speech successors. Temporary respite may be bought this way, but at what cost to a more meaningful social harmony and a less fragile and more accountable self-government?

How long will society be required to live the lie, and when will it be safe to think and speak the truth? By whom is public silencing for the sake of social peace and public order rather than truth to be enforced? Absent political dictatorship, how will censors ensure that official silencing in the cause of social harmony will be applied only as intended? In systems of occasional governing majorities, such censorship cannot be guaranteed to apply only when it is 'your' social truth that endangers public harmony and social order and not when it is 'my' social truth that does.

An overriding concern for social peace and public order has been the most favoured ground for political dictatorships to suppress speech. Their concern, too, has been that a public enlightened to the truth would be a sufficient danger to themselves to justify keeping them in the dark, 'for their own good' – a self-realizing, self-justifying prophecy, as I argued earlier.[89] The Barendt approach buys artificial quiet at the price of public accountability and more genuine social harmony – for the public good. Thinking like this came to its fullest fruition under Communist rule where, first, truth through choice, and then truth for its own sake, came not to matter, and a chilling political culture of deceit, cynicism, and dishonesty, in and out of public life, came to engulf ever more corrupt but quiet polities.[90]

Free speech theorists' idea of accountability, social harmony, and more honest politics through discursive public choice does not harbour a naïve and 'boundless faith in the people' to make the right choices.[91] Censoring theorists' idea of social harmony without discursive public choice posits a naïve and boundless faith that accountable censoring elites can honestly (or dishonestly?) and *legally assure* such choices. Free speech theorists hold a naïve and boundless faith in no one. A choice for public speech over public silencing is a recognition of both the public's and their leaders' shortcomings. It is a recognition of relative risks and comparative success in light of those shortcomings. It is a recognition that more honest politicians, more accountable politics, and more tolerant polities cannot be officially given or legally mandated but need to be publicly self-made.

III Adaptation, Change, and Enduring Self-government

Tolerance left to discursive public choice and self-government left to public chance are no guarantee against social or political failure. That is the task of censorship not the promise of free speech. But the public goods that freedom of public discourse on public matters offers are more than just fleeting goods based on faith. They rest on socially less fragile, politically more sturdy, foundations of public progress (read Churchillian 'less worse') than the alternatives. By facilitating change, freedom of public discourse on public matters helps balance social movement with social continuity to promote political stability.

'End-of-history' theories have still to come to fruition.[92] Until the march of time comes to an apolitical close, human societies will continue to be confronted with the uncertainties of social, economic, and technological change. A politics of public empowerment is one that can deal well with change.[93] Such politics is particularly important in the information age where, measured against past history, both the scope and pace of change have assumed near-revolutionary proportions. Change entails uncertainty and the risk of social disruption, public division, and political discord.[94] The more rapid the change the greater the risk. The question for the 'foreseeable' future is not *whether* there will be social division or political disruption but how best to manage them – in short, how best to manage change. Societies that do not manage change well today are apt to find that change will manage them badly 'tomorrow.' More successful polities will be those that grow, innovate, and adapt to 'better cope with the exigencies of their period.'[95] Those that cannot adapt well risk social stagnation, economic deprivation, and even political collapse.[96] The need to manage change well, to balance permanence and movement, is therefore foundational to all the goals of hate censors.

Managing the uncertainties and risks of change well requires not official assurances and legal guarantees but the ability to adapt. More successful adaptation requires political depth and the social resilience not to 'break' in the face of challenge and crisis. It requires learning from, growing with, even harnessing – rather than 'arresting' – the challenges of change. Polities more able to 'roll' with the punches of social division, political challenge, and economic displacement are more

apt to manage change well than ones that try to prevent them altogether. This requires a willingness to deflect or absorb the blows of
social division and public discord. Free speech advocates are willing to
trade a social quiet of the present and a public order of the moment
for a 'social compact where differences are exercised at large within the
framework of freedom and order on [a] broader and deeper ... basis of
social stability.'[97] Managing change and its uncertainties well requires
more not less knowledge of its challenges.

More successful political systems tend to 'know themselves' better
than less successful ones. They get timely feedback on the true state of
their society and polity.[98] Time and change are the enemies of feedback. The more rapid the changes of a period, the more timely this
feedback needs to be. History suggests that states, at least postindustrial
states, that suppress unpleasant information about themselves wholesale, impairing or delaying timely social and political feedback, threaten
their own survival.[99] But even polities with relatively more restrained
forms of such censorship work at cross-purposes with their feedback
needs. For when public expression tells leaders and publics only what
they want to hear, what they hear may not be what they need to know.

All public knowledge is not equally important, and not all deficiencies in feedback are equally risky. It is deficient feedback concerning
deep-seated hate and prejudice that is potentially most threatening to
social harmony and political stability. It is here that accurate and timely
feedback is particularly important.[100] A secure society, but especially a
secure self-governing society, needs to know its enemies as well as its
friends – how they think, who they are, where they are, what they
intend to do, and how and when they intend to do it. Unless it knows
these things, even some friends may turn out to be enemies – and their
reassurances, threats.[101] Abridged, inaccurate, or delayed feedback can,
over time, become more dangerous than the feared feedback itself.
More successful transition depends on honestly and correctly assessing
the true character, intensity, sources, and resources of the forces of
public divisions and political tensions. The more faulty the assessment,
the more problematic is successful transition.

This kind of knowledge requires tolerance. Tolerance should not be
confused with acceptance. The right to speak does not mean that what
is said is right. Discursive forbearance is the price to secure a less fragile
social progress. Effective silencing of *determined* hate (what other kind
worthy of repression is there?) might take divisive messages out of public sight. Out of public sight, however, does not mean out of public

mind – or the public out of danger. Repression of determined speech encourages movement from the open to the hidden and the transformation of feared words into feared acts. Extremists are more likely to be driven underground than to give up the fight. Repressed extremists are more likely to become concealed extremists than the public is likely to be freed of the danger. Concealed extremists are more dangerous than exposed extremists. They have more cover to substitute feared acts for the impermissible feared words. As U.S. Supreme Court Justice Louis Brandeis wrote,

[the Founding Fathers knew] that it is hazardous to discourage thought, hope and imagination; that fear breeds repression; that repression breeds hate; that hate menaces stable government ... [They] did not fear political change. They did not exalt order at the cost of liberty ... [N]o danger flowing from speech can be deemed clear and present, unless the evidence of the evil apprehended is so imminent that it may befall before there is opportunity for full discussion. If there be time to expose through discussion the falsehoods and fallacies, to avert the evil by the process of education, the remedy to be applied is more speech, not enforced silence.[102]

Further, effective repression of divisive speech does not just silence important speech. It also promotes speech. But the speech it promotes includes speech it would rather discourage. Some may fear to say what they really think. But many others may say what they do not really think but are expected to say. Repression facilitates dishonest publics and pandering politicians. This also impedes accurate feedback on the true state of society and polity. The extent of the problem, the identity of repressed believers and their sympathizers, becomes more difficult to gauge, the depth of the threat more difficult to assess or demonstrate, and the steps needed to guard against it more difficult to formulate.[103]

What the polity doesn't know, know well enough, or know in time can hurt it in more ways than one, especially here. First, there is the risk of overestimating the danger. Zealotry and overreaction in speech repression, even for a good cause, are not without their social and political costs. Zealotry provokes resentment or disdain for the cause from those unjustly harassed or accused. Overreaction can provoke the very divisions it fears. Alternatively, the problem may be underestimated. A society effectively blocked from expressing its worst prejudices is more vulnerable to the 'feedback failure' of complacency. The public may see acts of violence by determined extremists as socially unrepresentative or politically inconsequential. The true depth and breadth of racial intolerance and social prejudice may be temporarily masked by repressive laws against intolerant speech, only to be revealed in times of social crisis to a vulnerable, unsuspecting, 'protected' public lulled into a false sense of complacency.[104] Public discourse on disconcerting public matters can best expose extreme views, identify accurately the threat, provide a safety valve to let off 'steam,' avoid making martyrs of maniacs, and respond in a measured way to danger. In short, a law that would conceal or camouflage the problem by sweeping it under the rug of fear, favour, and force is likely to produce a polity that is less, not more, politically secure and socially adaptable.

Free speech theorists' assumptions regarding adaptation to change are not assumptions of absolute political stability or uninterrupted social harmony but of relative risks and comparative success over time. Freedom of expression is not a panacea for the social and political ills that may befall the nation. For one thing, as Justice Brennan once said, quoting Madison, 'some degree of abuse is inseparable from the proper use of everything.'[105] For another, unfettered freedom of expression on divisive matters of society and governance may not only expose but also fuel the fires of social discord and political turmoil.[106] What a regime cannot successfully absorb or deflect it cannot successfully manage. But then, neither can it successfully repress what it cannot successfully absorb or deflect – at least not for long, if it is to remain much of a democracy. A more secure social harmony is apt to be a more adaptive social harmony, a socially transiting, politically enabling harmony – one that absorbs, deflects, and manages, rather than represses, conceals, and denies its most testing divisions.

Conclusion

Public growth, successful adaptation to change, accountable politicians, responsible publics, and honest politics are not just the foundations for a more successful self-government. They are also the foundations for a more tolerant society. Freedom of expression is an idea of social progress and democratic government that sees these goals not as a one-time or final event, fixable 'for good' in time and place by silencing law, but as a discursive work in continuous progress. Official histories, found truths, fixed meanings, and final triumphs are ideas of social progress and political democracy of hate censors that, effectively, deny this.

An idea of democracy that would officially 'fix' public discourse on vital public matters where freedom to speak means the most does not promote a more effective and transparent self-governance. An idea of public growth that would shield the public from first-hand knowledge of its own worst prejudices and hide from public view its most transparent bigots does not promote a more self-knowing public or responsible self-governance. An idea of social harmony and political stability that would conceal society's most disgruntled extremists, allowing publics and their leaders to hear not what they may need to know but what they want to hear, does not promote a more risk-free adaptation to change. An idea of public politics that would legally fix important truths, according their meanings official status and their makers relative freedom from public challenge, does not promote a more honest politics or accountable and responsive self-governance. The purpose of hate censorship is to assure what freedom of expression can only risk. But how can it assure when it cannot even offer a better risk?

3

Functions and Assumptions of Hate Propaganda Law

Chapter 1 explored how the court in *Keegstra* adopted an asymmetrical balancing methodology that a priori rejected the abstract in favour of the concrete. Hate propaganda law was enacted to prevent 'tangible' not 'theoretical' injuries. Yet even on its own self-limited terms of reference, the court did not do a very good job of 'balancing.' The functions of hate propaganda law are socially multifaceted and politically multidimensional – to promote inclusion, equality, community, multiculturalism, harmony, and strong democracy. This is a complex and unwieldy 'package of social and political aspirations,' concealing often conflicting and self-conflicting choices. The case for hate silencing largely ignores these conflicts. It would be helpful to do what the court failed to do – critically and systematically unwrap the package and expose the dated, flawed, and self-contradictory assumptions it conceals.

This chapter unpacks four principal functions of hate censorship and the assumptions of hate censors underlying them that, explicitly or implicitly, framed the court's thinking: (1) to prevent disruption to public order and social peace stemming from retaliation by victims; (2) to prevent psychological harm to targeted groups that would effectively impair their ability to positively participate in their community and contribute to society; (3) to prevent both visible exclusion of minority groups that would deny them equal opportunities and benefits of Canadian society and invisible exclusion that would prevent their being accepted as equals; (4) to prevent social conflagration and political disintegration.

The gravamen underscoring all four functions is a key causal assumption – that serious public injury will result from the hatemonger's attempt to convert his audience to his point of view (proselytization).

The law explicitly speaks to the welfare of targeted victims. But injury to the targeted victims is not *per se* the larger public concern. Injury to society and polity resulting from injury to the targeted victims is. As Manuel Prutschi puts it, 'an assault on them [targeted victims] is an assault on all Canadians.'[1] Censorship is intended to prevent this.

I Peace and Order: Victim Retaliation and Disturbance to Public Order

That members of communities targeted for public opprobrium suffer emotional distress is indisputable.[2] But preventing emotional distress, even great emotional distress, is not *per se* the purpose of public protection under this branch of justification for the law. If allowing disconcerting public discourse on public matters worth arguing about were to hinge on not causing emotional distress to some segment of the public, no meaningful discursive exchange would be exempt from the censor's knife. Sanitizing Canadian society of robust debate for fear of offending community sensibilities would not serve the cause of public growth and strong democracy well.[3] Injury to public peace and order resulting from the hatemonger's *failure* to convince targeted victims that they are unworthy and inferior is the fear here.

The concern of this branch of fear is not that targeted victims will passively accept the hatemonger's demeaning depiction of them but that they will retaliate in anger against their tormentor, threatening public peace, order, and safety. Protection of public order and safety is everywhere recognized as a legitimate 'police function' of government, including, of course, a democratic one. Proselytization directed to victims is unlike proselytization directed to third parties. For the hatemonger it is a 'win-win' proposition, serving the cause of hate in both success and failure. For society it is 'lose-lose.' While compliant victim servitude and humble assumption of inferiority is preferred, victim retaliation and violence can often serve the hatemonger's cause equally well.

But there is a major problem here – with the assumed injury feared. There is no probative evidence, let alone compelling evidence, that members of targeted groups (or their supporters) in Canada are prepared to lash out *en masse* at their tormentors.[4] Even were some isolated or insulated instances of violence to occur, there is no reason to think that the myriad of ordinary civil and criminal laws deterring or punishing illegal conduct would be inadequate to deal with them. To reduce hate propaganda law to an ordinary police power – a mere regulatory instrument to quell containable disturbances to public peace and order – would not only be to duplicate powers of prevention and punishment that already exist. It would also be to dilute the meaning and trivialize the purpose of hate propaganda law.[5]

A far better case for the fear, historically, was addressed and rejected by a pre-Charter Supreme Court of Canada a half-century ago.[6] Comparatively speaking, Canada at the start of the 1950s was still a rather inexperienced and relatively fragile political democracy. Quebec was on the eve, if not quite yet in the throes, of momentous social change. Boucher, a devout Jehovah's Witness, was charged with seditious libel for promoting 'social disaffection and ill-will' in Quebec. His immediate offence was the public distribution of a socially and politically venomous tract denouncing the people of Quebec, the Catholic church, and the Government of Quebec for their intolerance. At the time, the Witnesses were conducting a very visible and aggressive proselytizing campaign in the province.[7] Given the depth and breadth of hostility this attracted, the fear for public order and safety in the Quebec of 1951 was a very real one.

Much, though hardly all, of Boucher's venomous tirade was true.[8] In contrast, those of hatemongers like Zundel and Keegstra (albeit not their authors' complaints of majority intolerance of their right to communicate it) is not. But the gravamen for suppression under this branch of fear turns not on the truth, falsity, or disagreeableness of the message *per se* but rather on its likelihood to cause the public disturbances feared. Notwithstanding the volatile social and political context, the court in *Boucher* did then what the court in *Keegstra* just recently declined to do – it carefully explored and balanced the values upheld by freedom of disconcerting public expression on matters of society and polity against the value of social peace and public order. Justice Rand explicitly focused on the different sources of strength and stability between a consolidated democracy and the monarchical polity from which Canada had emerged. He then distinguished the different kind of social peace and public order required to cultivate such consolidation.

> Freedom in thought and speech and disagreement in ideas and beliefs, on every conceivable subject, are of the essence of our life. The clash of critical discussion on political, social and religious subjects has too deeply become the stuff of daily experience to suggest that mere ill-will as a product of controversy can strike down the latter with illegality ... Controversial fury is

aroused constantly ... but our compact of free society accepts and absorbs these differences and they are exercised at large within the framework of freedom and order on broader and deeper ... basis of social stability. Similarly in discontent and hostility ... they and the ideas which arouse them are part of our living which ultimately serve us in stimulation, in clarification of thought and, as we believe, in the search for ... truth.[9]

In the context of the social peace and public order needs of a politically consolidated modern democracy, such as Canada today, suppression of socially disconcerting political communication is, at best, grossly disproportionate to the threat feared. At worst, it is simply not justified at all. The refusal of today's censoring court to articulate now what it was prepared to articulate in more socially volatile and politically fragile circumstances in the 1950s may, however, be less surprising than it seems. Social activist pressures for censorship, a heightened awareness of prejudice, elite intolerance of public disturbances, and the traditional Canadian reverence for public peace and order seem to have coalesced in the last decade, causing the court to effectively, if not explicitly, rethink the gravamen of the reasoning in *Boucher*.[10] Moreover, the advantage of couching at least some aspect of hate propaganda law in the politically neutral garb of protecting public order and safety is not hard to see. It masks the political essence of the law and dodges the troublesome questions that suppression of public communication for fear of disturbing social content or community distress alone might otherwise raise. More often than not, public peace and order justifications that resort to heavy hammers such as hate propaganda law conceal much deeper political fears of social change, challenge to accepted or expected societal norms, or threats to official wisdom and established authority.

Twenty-four years before *Boucher*, U.S. Supreme Court Justice Louis Brandeis directly addressed such concerns in *Whitney* v. *California*.[11] The defendant, a Marxist labour activist, had been charged with teaching criminal syndicalism. Today, it is easy to forget both the domestic and international context within which these events unfolded. This was a scant ten years after the Bolshevik revolution, in the midst of a brutal campaign to annihilate all vestiges of religious, class, and social distinctions in what became the Union of Soviet Socialist Republics. This was a period characterized by virulent expressions of hate for particular classes of people, violent challenges to established social norms, and disturbing questions about fixed political beliefs. Brandeis's words, admonishing not the intolerance of the speaker but the public's intolerance of his speech, are as remarkable for their prescience in not overstating the danger as they are insightful in understanding the deeper strengths of democracy in resisting it:

> [m]oreover, even imminent danger cannot justify resort to prohibition of those functions essential to effective democracy, unless the evil apprehended is relatively serious. Prohibition of free speech and assembly is a measure so stringent that it would be inappropriate as a means for averting a relatively trivial harm to society ... The fact that speech is likely to result in some violence or in destruction of property is not enough to justify its repression. There must be probability of serious injury to the State. Among free men, the deterrents ordinarily to be applied to prevent crime are education and punishment for violations of the law, not abridgement of the rights of free speech and assembly.[12]

II Community Participation and Multiculturalism: Hate-induced Self-exclusion, Self-withdrawal, Negative Participation, and Assimilation

This branch of hate law is also victim-impact or victim-reaction oriented, but it is the flip side of the first one. Censors here fear the success of hate propaganda – that it psychologically damages its targets of opprobrium. They assume that the targeted victims will consciously or unconsciously assimilate (be converted to) the hatemonger's pejorative and demeaning message. Like the first fear, this one has a socially and politically broader preventive public purpose. The concern here is that open expressions of opprobrium will produce involuntary self-denial in the victims, causing their alienation from their true selves, their community, and the larger society.[13] The psychologically injured victim either withdraws from his or her community or society in despair or participates negatively in frustration.[14] Societal self-exclusion by dint of public expressions of opprobrium assumes that the target cannot surmount the messages' presumed debilitating effect without censorship.

Broadly, self-denial by victims can be expressed in three ways: individually distinctive, group distinctive, or both. Where enough members of a targeted community come to deny their distinctive group identity, the community can no longer contribute to society as a distinctive community. Community delegitimization can express itself in two very different ways. As cultural breakdown or cultural genocide, it expresses itself in self-debilitating and societally alienating forms of withdrawal or negative participation. As cultural flight, it expresses itself, where possible, in assimilation or integration into the dominant culture. Given the multicultural objectives of public policy in Canada, either form would be a grave societal loss. Hate propaganda law is intended to help prevent this. In the words of Manuel Prutschi, 'prosecution of hatemongers ... helps keep our multicultural society intact.'[15]

The blanket assumption that *open* expressions of opprobrium, in particular, psychologically cripple their targeted victims in Canada today in the ways feared is highly problematic. First, the theory suffers from protective overinclusion. It includes far too many minority groups. It cannot be sustained as a universally valid justification for hate propaganda law in Canada today.[16] Second, even a more selective or particular protective application of the causal thesis is deficient. Where once the causal link may have been rooted in good empirical soil, it is now, for the most part, highly tenuous – and increasingly so. Third, a more particular protective approach would result in discriminatory applications contrary to the very terms of reference by which hate censors justify their censorship.

Positive participation in Canadian society may be considered in two ways: as individually distinguished contribution or as group distinctive contribution. Group distinctive contribution, as we saw in chapter 1, is central to a particular vision of Canadian democracy. Pierre Trudeau probably stated it best when he said, '[i]n essence, multiculturalism's aim is to make Canada a pluralistic mosaic. It eschews the process of assimilation and instead embraces the integration of all groups into the Canadian community, so as to ensure that those who wish to maintain their distinctive cultural identities may do so.'[17]

Are either or both of these goals in danger in Canada because of psychological hurt suffered by targets of open expressions of hate? The causal assumption that it is endangered is not limited. All historically vulnerable groups in Canada are covered. The court in *Keegstra* treated the thesis as universally valid. Yet the evidence for this is simply not there. Indeed, even a particularist application, which at one time may have been valid, is now dated and untenable.

First, universal application of the thesis systematically ignores the societal progress of the vast majority of historically vulnerable groups. It was the history of grievous prejudice directed particularly against Jews (but also other minorities, such as the Chinese, Japanese, Catholics, and most East Europeans) that led to the formation of the Cohen

Committee and the enactment of hate propaganda law. But it is precisely these groups who are oddly missing from empirical proof of the feared causal nexus. While accepting an unqualified causal thesis of minority harm – open prejudice equals psychological harm equals negative withdrawal from society – the court in *Keegstra* was concerned, specifically, with opprobrium directed against Jews. Jews have suffered thousands of years of persecution, prejudice, and even attempts to physically exterminate them. But historical evidence for the causal link is not only missing – it suggests the very opposite.

Despite millennia of both physical and verbal abuse, Jews, as a distinct community, have not simply survived their indignities but have thrived despite them – wherever they suffered and wherever they fled. Whether one looks to science, technology, business, literature, or the arts, the participation of Jews in Canadian society has demonstrated the very psychological capacities – pride, worth, confidence, accomplishment – that these indignities were supposed to irreparably injure.[18] As documented by one of Canada's foremost authorities on the subject, Canadian Jewry is flourishing and is among the most affluent, educated, and integrated of all ethnic communities in Canada.[19] Hate's failure to break the Jewish spirit is imprinted in the deep and pervasive impact of Jewish culture on the mainstream Canadian landscape itself.[20] Neither the legacies of genocidal homicide in Germany nor the indignities suffered by Jews with respect to housing, employment, education, or the use of public facilities in Canada could harvest, even marginally, the feared injury.

Much of the most dramatic social progress made by most minorities in Canada (the single most significant being legal recognition of their indignities and the outlawing of discriminatory practices through human rights codes) preceded hate propaganda law. Hate propaganda law itself followed, was belatedly tacked on to, and was made possible by social progress that was well underway.[21] If a cogent causal link is to be found between social progress and minority psychological well-being, a far stronger one can be found in the exercise of freedom of minority expression to disturb popular beliefs and disrupt conventional wisdom than in the suppression of open expressions of hate. In the United States, where the court has not accorded minorities the protection of hate propaganda law,[22] Black self-awareness and push for civil rights erupted with the eruption of minority freedom of expression, not with majority suppression of 'hateful' public expression. The more effective cognitive road to minority inclusion and psychological self-sufficiency has, historically, been one that respected more what minorities thought of themselves through freedom of expression than one that dictated what others must think of them by censorship.

The universal causal assumption is problematic in still other ways. Ethnic, religious, or cultural self-denial alone is not necessarily societally exclusionary. In some cases, it can equally produce positive participation in the larger society as negative withdrawal from it – where assimilation into the dominant culture is possible. A desire to assimilate may be defined as a rejection of one's sense of belonging to one's own community in favour of identification with the larger community. The desire may be self-willed or induced by prejudice. But the reason, though morally highly objectionable in the case of the latter, does not deny the inclusion.

An individual may, because of outside prejudice, reject only his group identity not his individual or personal identity. He may do so not to withdraw from the larger society but to more easily and ably participate in it – achieving self-promotion by integration or assimilation.[23] In that case, the individual's societal contribution may be diluted of its group distinctive value but not of its individual distinctive value.[24] In either case, whether the yardstick of inclusion is individually distinguished or group distinctive, the level of positive contribution by some of history's most grievously oppressed minorities may be noticed not for falling short of egalitarian expectations but for exceeding them.[25] On the whole, societal inclusion in Canada has not been insurmountably injured even by historically permitted discriminatory *acts*, much less by intolerant *words*. To suggest otherwise is to fly in the face of overwhelming evidence to the contrary and to diminish the psychological resilience of historically targeted minorities too numerous to ignore.

Of course, individually distinguished participation is not the same as group distinctive participation, especially for the purposes of a law and a nation with a multicultural vision of society. If enough members of Canadian ethnic communities were to deny their distinctive community self-identity to escape outside prejudice, this would indeed undermine the goal of Canadian multiculturalism – distinguished individual participation notwithstanding. Assimilationist tendencies are strong indicia of the waning strength of distinctive community self-identity. Self-dilution may be a growing problem for many ethnic communities in Canada.[26] However, to the extent that such dilution is a function of dominant attitudes, it is, paradoxically, due less to open expressions of outside prejudice than to their absence. Many in the Canadian Jewish community today fear the twin dangers of secularization and intra-community strife – promoted more by the fact of living in a culturally pluralistic society that is largely free from open expressions of prejudice or state-sponsored anti-Semitism than by external hostility.[27] As Professor Irving Abella has written, 'today's [Jewish] community worries more about rates of assimilation than rates of anti-Semitism. Its greatest concern is for its children and grandchildren; will they remain Jewish? ... Burgeoning assimilation rates in the United States are a growing concern to Canadian Jews. In North America, living as a Jew is only one option among many.'[28]

It is not only Canadian Jewish leaders today who recognize that the dangers to Jewish continuity of 'love you to death' can be greater than the dangers of 'hate you to death.' Golda Meir, a former prime minister of Israel, went so far as to warn that the danger to the Jewish community posed by spiritual destruction through cultural assimilation would be worse than the destruction of the Holocaust.[29] One would, however, be hard pressed to find a single historical community in Canada that has, as a community, forsaken its distinctive self-identity as a condition of entry into mainstream society, much less done so to escape open expressions of prejudice. Indeed, the richness and diversity of thriving ethnic, religious, cultural, and social communities in Canada in the face of the very prejudices that are supposed to threaten them belies the thesis.

Is censorship's dilemma here a problem of protective overinclusion – perhaps the causal thesis holds true for some communities but not others – or a problem of untenable assumptions? Some of the strongest empirical evidence linking open expressions of prejudice to self-alienation and community withdrawal comes from segregation studies done of Afro-American school children in the United States in the 1950s and 1960s.[30] However, the uniquely enslaving mix of social exclusion and political oppression that existed then is hardly comparable to the very different social and political conditions that exist today. The strongest evidence linking prejudice and self-esteem predated civil rights and voting rights, Afro-American mayors, Afro-American congressmen and women, Afro-American senators, an Afro-American secretary of state, Afro-American lawyers, Afro-American judges, Afro-American professors, Afro-American studies, and Afro-American presidential candidates.

If past causal validity is to have equal current probativity, one would expect to see today an equally strong correlation. But even to the casual observer it is obvious that Afro-American socio-economic progress has not nearly kept pace with the growth in Afro-American self-esteem. Afro-American psychological self-sufficiency has far outpaced Afro-American societal inclusion.[31] Here, as is often the case elsewhere, a time static historical view of the problem is a major weakness in the censorship case. Censors continue to advance as 'contemporary' their psychological harm thesis for those who are still disproportionately denied positive participation in society, while giving short shrift precisely to contemporary developments – developments that are coming to overwhelmingly refute that thesis.

Psychological resilience depends on better self-awareness of prejudice and more public self-consciousness about prejudice. Both have grown greatly. Racists openly espousing prejudice no longer enjoy the public discursive monopoly or political stranglehold they once had, or the social power to psychologically cripple targeted communities and prevent them from rejecting the lie and demanding their due. Once, the stigma of open expressions of prejudice had to be suffered in self-debilitating silence. Today, a myriad of uplifting official, unofficial, and often interconnected networks – political, social, cultural, legal, and everything in between – work tirelessly to raise self-awareness and expose the evil of such expressions.[32] Oppressed minorities today are astutely aware of and keenly prepared to expose even subtle expressions of public prejudices. The mainstream community and the mainstream media have had to become more sensitive and have become more self-conscious so as not to offend minority sensibilities precisely because minorities will no longer stand for it.[33] Rather than bringing hapless victims who are too traumatized to reject the racist's view of them to serve the cause of the racist, open vilification today is more apt to arouse immediate outrage and public demands for apology. Where once the public emphasis was on educating the victim about his inferiority, today it is on educating the racist on the finer points of his unconscious prejudice.[34] Both hate propaganda law itself and relentless calls for wider, deeper censorship to 'eradicate' intolerance testify to awakened minority pride, self-empowerment, and vigilance, rather than hapless acquiescence.

The more distant the history of racial oppression – the history from which censors most prefer to draw their proofs – the stronger the causal evidence of debilitating psychological harm. However, this is also to say (what censors ignore) that the more current the history the weaker the causal evidence. Even in the 'best' case, the evidence for the causal contention has become far too tenuous to sustain a case for public censorship. As time passes, the causal thesis is apt to become even more tenuous. It is one thing to observe as fact that certain communities are still excluded or are disproportionately forced to participate negatively in society. It is quite another to continue to attribute this to psychological injury caused by open expressions of prejudice.

Finally, even if a best or selective case could be made out today, it would not help the censorship argument. Legally speaking, minorities could be segregated and protection allotted on the basis of differential psychological need. Protection could be granted to only some historically vulnerable groups but not others, or more protection could be granted to some than others. Malevolent speakers would be punished accordingly. But imagine a hate censorship law that would exclude, or accord lesser protection against, hateful expressions aimed at Jews or Chinese (or any other historically vulnerable groups who participate disproportionately in the larger society) on the grounds that they are not in equal need of psychological protection from prejudice.[35] Imagine the stigmatization, the division, the rivalry, and, most of all, the inequality. A psychological harm thesis for repression of expression that is not protectively overinclusive would be vulnerability underinclusive and politically untenable on censors' own egalitarian terms of reference. Effectively, either the psychological thesis of harm must be universally valid as touted – which it patently is not – or it cannot sustain its case for hate censorship at all. In short, this branch of justification for censorship cannot satisfactorily validate itself in any case.[36]

At bottom, the problem for censorship is not simply that societal exclusion no longer turns on psychological injury but that vulnerability to prejudice need not turn on deficiencies in societal participation or open expressions of outside prejudice.[37] That a proud, 'well-to-do,' relatively integrated community such as European Jewry could suddenly be brought to virtual extinction is a case in point. Even in the 'melting pot' of the United States, as Michael Alexander documents, Jewish success and penetration into mainstream society had historically failed to alter that community's status as 'outsider.'[38] Vulnerability to hate and prejudice depends on minority status and group distinctive social, political, and historical circumstances.[39] In a self-governing polity, to borrow the words of M.E. Turpel, 'the minority is always defined by and in subordination to the majority.'[40] If there is a universally valid thesis of vulnerability to hate and prejudice, Turpel's is the more telling one.[41]

III Community Participation and Multiculturalism: Societal Exclusion
   – Visible and Invisible

The third branch of justification for hate censorship sees open expressions of hate working their social harm not through the targeted victims but through the larger society. It is concerned with conversion of
the dominant public to the cause of the malevolent speaker. The concern here is also with the social consequences of psychological injury.
But it is not psychological injury to the targeted community but to the
larger society that is feared. Minority exclusion here is not a problem of
minorities involuntarily 'choosing' to abstain from participating or partaking equally but of a prejudiced society that won't allow them to.

   This branch of fear seeks to explain why targets of open opprobrium
that are not self-debilitated by it can still be excluded as equal participants in society because of it. In this thinking, open expressions of
prejudice are seen to do their harm in two ways: first, by working on
society to visibly exclude targeted groups from equally sharing in social,
economic, cultural, political, and economic opportunities; second, by
working on society to invisibly exclude targeted groups by denying them
acceptance as equals.[42] The persistence of prejudice in Canada, or of its
socially detrimental effects, is not at issue here; nor that some groups
have had or may still have to suffer more prejudice than others.[43] The
question is, in what form is the prejudice persisting and by what means
can we better address it? Suppression of open expressions of hate is a
dated answer to a past problem (visible exclusion) and the wrong answer to the current one (invisible exclusion).

1 Visible Exclusion

Censors' causal assumption that open expression of hate sustains visible
exclusion in Canada is problematic in several ways. The theory is not
limited only to some historically vulnerable groups. The court in *Keegstra*
made no distinctions between minority groups and treated the theory
as universally valid. Historical evidence for this assumption is simply not
there. On the contrary, history suggests the opposite. In Canada, open
expression of prejudice has not succeeded in visibly excluding the majority of historically vulnerable minorities from actively partaking of
and participating in society. Where they were once visibly excluded,
most Canadian minorities – cultural, linguistic, ethnic, racial, or reli-

gious – are now visibly included. Indeed, if there is a complaint, it is more likely the one made by racists that some of the historically most visibly excluded, such as Jews and Chinese, now visibly participate and partake unequally and should therefore be selectively or systemically excluded.

When this inclusion began is critical to a better understanding of what did and did not make it happen. Some of the most dramatic breakthroughs occurred despite, during, and in the very face of what, compared to today, was a far more openly and expressively prejudiced society – that of the 1950s, the 1960s, and even the early 1970s. The connecting link between public prejudice and societal exclusion, for the vast majority of historically oppressed minorities, can more readily be found in public practices than in open public expressions of prejudice. For oppressed minorities, the history of their visible inclusion in Canada is not defined by the legal suppression of open expressions of public prejudice but by the successful tearing down of exclusionary *practices* of prejudice – despite open public expressions of prejudice.[44] The right to silence intolerance did not lead inclusion but followed inclusion and was made possible by a growing tolerance of rights to speak. Where expressions of prejudice have failed to visibly exclude, repression of such expressions of prejudice cannot visibly include.

Of course, not all groups are equally vulnerable to exclusion. Some groups are more excludable and have been visibly more barred than others.[45] The reality of public prejudice is that difference is exclusionary. And the greater the difference, the more vulnerable to exclusion the different are apt to be. The frame of reference against which the dominant culture measures difference is itself. That which departs from its practices, beliefs, or physiological characteristics is different. The more it departs, the more different it is. It matters not that the difference is more apparent than real. Difference, for the purposes of prejudice, is a function not of real inferiority but of real visibility. The greater the visibility, the greater the vulnerability to exclusionary practices of prejudice.[46] Visibility can be the product of unalterable physical characteristics such as gender or colour (the latter still salient in a mainly White but rapidly changing Canadian society) or of differences in cultural, social, religious, or other customs, or of some combination of all these things. Blacks are particularly vulnerable to exclusion because of visibility. Unlike Jews, even Blacks who would be willing to deny their heritage to garner inclusion cannot deny their colour. Where physical assimilation is not possible, societal exclusion is more probable.

But if visible minorities are more vulnerable to exclusion, it is no longer because of *open* expression of prejudice. Open expression of prejudice is the exception not the rule in Canada today. Continuing exclusion of visible minorities has gone hand in hand with dramatically lower levels of open expression of prejudice. It is hidden not open expression of prejudice that both visible minorities and censors themselves routinely cite today as the cause of minorities' exclusion. This suggests that the better answer to overcoming exclusion may be found not in public censorship but in a better understanding of exclusion.

Even among visible minorities, exclusion never lent itself well to a censorship answer, much less the one-size-fits-all censorship answer of hate censorship theorists today. Historically, unique minority circumstances and different public and official policy responses to prejudice have raised different issues, timelines, and paths to overcoming exclusion. The particularist features of participatory failures suggest that hate censorship is not simply a blunt instrument in a refined cause but the wrong instrument in the right cause. Indeed, for Native peoples, one of Canada's most visible and most oppressed communities, hate speech law is not even relevant. It was never relevant to their needs to begin with.

Until fairly recently, the Canadian government's official policy *vis-à-vis* the Native populations included confiscation of their lands, destruction of their livelihood, and a deliberate agenda of cultural genocide. Alan Borovoy writes that Wilson Head, a long-time leader of the Canadian Black community, 'has told audiences of his fellow blacks that the most victimised people in the country are Aboriginals.'[47] Nowhere is this victimization better highlighted than in the system of residential schools – a particularly vile policy of forced integration that saw Aboriginal children literally snatched from their homes and communities and isolated in special schools that force-fed them a steady 'educational' diet of Aboriginal inferiority.[48] In the case of no other minority has the Canadian government conducted such a patronizing campaign of 'visible' inclusion or so blatantly abrogated freedom of minority self-expression in order to do it.[49] And in no other case has the government failed so miserably.[50]

This policy was not a failure of freedom of speech. It was a failure of the denial of it. What the Canadian government failed to allow was what it failed to understand – social and cultural self-expression. For non-individualistic cultures there can be no 'positive' individual participation separate and apart from group distinctive participation. Group self-identity and individual self-identity are inseparable.[51] To destroy the group is to destroy the individual. The residential school system was alien to both Aboriginal culture and the democratic precepts of the non-Aboriginal society whose assimilationist goals it was to serve. It depended for its 'success' on a policy of systematic silencing of Aboriginal rights to political, social, economic, and cultural self-expression.

Where inclusion is not the solution, exclusion could not have been the problem. It was not the absence of hate law that failed Aboriginal people and robbed them of their dignity and initiative. It was forced integration and denial of Native self-expression that did. It is in the correction of these problems, not in public censorship, that both the dominant culture and Native peoples today are finding their solutions. The creation of Nunavut testifies not to the case for censorship but to the importance of respect for freedom of social, cultural, and political self-expression. Tolerance, multiculturalism, and social progress here – to be 'equal' – have meant being visibly separate.[52] This is a belated recognition that, for territorial-based communal cultures, positive participation may have to take place alongside, not within, the dominant society.

2 Invisible Exclusion

Locating minority vulnerability to prejudice in invisible exclusion – the failure of society, in some way, to fully *accept* all minorities as equal – does correct for a great many of the problems suffered by the other censorship theories. Inequality of acceptance succeeds as a universally valid test of minority vulnerability. It does not depend on evidence of visible exclusion for its validity or suffer that test's deficiencies of coverage. It is not protectively overinclusive or vulnerably underinclusive. This approach is one that can equally include participatory 'overachievers' and participatory 'underachievers.'[53] It is not time dependent. It does not suffer from dated evidence of the causal link. All minorities, from Jews to Blacks to Native people, can locate their vulnerability, actual or potential, in some part of the larger society's failure to fully accept them in some way as equals.

The persistence of prejudice without its open expression is today's and tomorrow's problem of 'hate,' just as open practices and unabashed expressions of it were yesterday's. As Borovoy writes, '[i]n the early 1940's racial and ethnic discrimination was practised overtly with public approval. By the 1990's, this discrimination is practised covertly over public objection.'[54] While one may object to Borovoy's assumptions of the extent of public objection, his observations about the dramatic shift of prejudice underground, out of sight but not out of mind, is what is most important here. Censorship thinking that does not mirror this shift is stuck in time, chasing shadows from the past in place of addressing problems of the present and the future. Censorship thinking that substitutes what was for what is quiets symptoms when it seeks and needs to treat causes instead. As progressive censoring theorists themselves are at pains to point out, a more inclusive society is not one that merely tolerates its minorities. It is one that accepts them as equals. Where there is only tolerance there is also prejudice. Where there is acceptance there is not. Acceptance embraces both visible and invisible exclusion.

The acceptance thesis of invisible exclusion harbours certain implicit assumptions. It assumes that a more real inclusion cannot come from a less genuine inclusion. A society that accepts, not just tolerates, equality is more likely to practise equality. This is especially important in times of social stress and political crisis, when the depth of people's acceptance becomes the test of their tolerance. This is also what distinguishes a meaningful understanding of hate (speech) censorship from other laws against hate and prejudice. The public may be forced to do right by human rights laws that outlaw discriminatory practices. But this is not the same as thinking right. Hate propaganda law abridges what people say. But its purpose is to correct what people think. It is intended to prevent socially undesirable thinking so that the public will do right not because it has to but because it wants to – this is what is meant by 'acceptance.' Acceptance is, singularly, what distinguishes a law correcting societal mal-expressions from a law suppressing societal malpractices.

The acceptance thesis of invisible exclusion is, in just about every way, the most meaningful understanding of vulnerability to prejudice. It is also the most compelling understanding of the problem of hate in Canada today that censors can make. But it is also here, where it should count most, that their case for repression of public expression stumbles the most. Silencing open expressions of hate contradicts censors' own assumptions about acceptance as the gravamen of societal inclusiveness. What society thinks is hardly synonymous with what society says, where what society says can only be what the law will allow them to say and not what they may really 'think' to say. A truly inclusive democratic society is one that does right and says right not because it has to but because it wants to. Visible inclusion can be required by law. Invisible inclusion cannot be. Visible exclusion is a state of public fact. Invisible exclusion is a state of private mind. Antidiscriminatory law may require a racist landlord to rent to a Black person. And, hate speech law may require the landlord not to speak ill of that person. But no law can require the landlord to accept that tenant as an equal. Required speech is no more an answer to psychological rejection than required conduct is an answer to invisible exclusion.

The dilemma here is not simply that hate censorship cannot do what it is supposed to do. The problem is that it is more apt to impair than promote the very thing that censors want and need to do. Censorship of open expressions of prejudice 'works' to conceal the very things it should reveal. The price of effective suppression of open prejudices is failure to expose concealed ones. If the problem of prejudice in Canada is the invisible exclusion that stems from failure to accept, the better answer must surely be to make that exclusion more, not less, visible.

Finally, more selective applications of the acceptance thesis of harm do not offer escape for censors here, either.[55] On the contrary, such applications would make the problem worse in two ways. First, as with minority discriminatory applications of the other branches of justification, a visibility-based censorship would be politically untenable and contradictory to egalitarian censors' own terms of justifying reference. Second, and more basic, in making such distinctions, it would be even more self-defeating in terms of its purpose. Those groups still disproportionately unaccepted by society may very well be the victims of a deeper, more hidden, public prejudice. However, if censorship works to conceal, more onerous censorship works to conceal still more. Prejudices that are more hidden require not more public silencing but less. Deeper prejudices in Canada today require more, not less, public exposure.

Where censors diagnose the pathology of the disease in Canada today most accurately (invisible exclusion), the medicine they prescribe (hate censorship) is, curatively, least appropriate. Suppression of open expression of hate is, at best, a dated answer to a past problem (visible exclusion) and the wrong answer to the current one (invisible exclusion).

IV Social Disintegration and Political Conflagration: The 'Mushroom' Thesis

A fourth function of hate propaganda law is what I have described as the Cohen Committee's mushroom thesis.[56] The mushroom thesis, as we saw in chapter 1, was the gravamen of the case for enacting hate propaganda law. It was not intended to secure or to immunize from future challenge structurally transforming ideologies and their partisan social politics. That a more enlightened society than now exists might be facilitated by hate censorship may very well have been a hope of its authors but was not the reason for their censorship. Censorship was not intended to be a legal end run, an official shortcut, around the democratic political process but was viewed as a necessary evil to save from destruction that very process. Echoing this idea, Prutschi writes, 'hatemongers, however, are not only a threat to the security of vulnerable groups but to society as a whole. [The danger] is no more and no less than the destruction of the open, democratic and pluralistic society we have built and hold so dear.'[57] Criminalizing hate propaganda was intended to underscore the gravity of the feared threat.

Under this branch of justification, one need not worry about what censorship conceals, for the far greater danger is with what freedom of expression may reveal. According to this thesis, public prejudices in Canada are not just irrational. They are potentially crippling. Below the surface of public calm and social propriety today there is not just offensive prejudice. There is a latent cauldron of potentially monstrous hate waiting to boil over at some time in the future. Open hate, unfettered by free speech, can turn even disbelievers into acting and active hatemongers. Left legally unchecked to chance, social intolerance cannot be prevented from growing, expanding, and, ultimately, consuming all of society.[58] All society must therefore be preventively protected from hate with censorship – adults as well as children, the sympathetic as well as the unsympathetic, targeted victims as well as untargeted 'bystanders' – because anyone, and therefore everyone, is vulnerable.[59] This is a preventive purpose on a grand scale.[60]

The mushroom thesis is a conserving, but not a 'conservative,' fear. It is not about different conceptions of Canadian democracy.[61] Liberalism, socialism, regionalism, or multiculturalism are not the issue. The issue is survival. The fear is that if society and polity, 'as we live them' in Canada[62] are lost to hate nothing else – equality, multiculturalism, social progress – can be saved, much less elevated. The concern of the mushroom thesis is to prevent a Hitler, a Milosevic, or a Stalin. Unlike the second and third branches of justification, which emphasize positive social transformation, the defining purpose driving this fear is societal preservation. It is censors' least politically partisan purpose and their most compelling case for abridging freedom of political commu-

nication. To abridge public discourse on public matters in order, arguably, to save democracy is a more compelling 'balancing' objective than
to do so in order, arguably, to improve it.

For all four branches of hate law justification, the function to protect
is *timeless*. Safeguarding the public cannot be time limited, for eradicating hate is not time dependent. Found truths and official guarantees
are about achieving final triumphs not temporary ones. However, this
branch of protection is often *explicitly* expressed as timeless for two
reasons – the first is of a cast common to all, the second distinctive to
this one. First, social disintegration and political conflagration feared
from hate are not transitory threats but timeless evils – the public is in
permanent danger because the public *is* the danger. Second, while the
danger feared is in the nature of a prospective emergency, the character and gravity of the threat turn it effectively, into a state of *present*
emergency. To wait for the catastrophe when it is upon us before acting
would be to act when it is too late to prevent it.[63] Certain extraordinary
social, political, or economic conditions may fan hate but are not the
reasons for public protection. Their presence is not necessary for the
law's continuation, nor is their absence grounds for its termination.
Preventive protection here is not temporary. It does not mean 'a cool-
ing off period,' after which wiser and saner heads are expected to
prevail so as to allow the law to be lifted. The law applies equally in
social calm and in social crisis, in ordinary conditions and in extraordinary times, in economic plenty and in economic hardship, in peace
and in war. In short, it is intended to apply indefinitely into the future
as it does in the present.[64]

The thesis has *no* boundaries, literally or figuratively. It is neither
particularist nor temporal but universal and transcendental – crossing
time and space. Differences in history, national character, state of economic development, political culture, or system of government – none
of these things *ultimately* matter. Mushroom censors make no distinction between nations (Canada or Austria); democratic and undemocratic governments (Canada or China); fledgling democracies and ma-
ture, established, or consolidated democracies (South Korea or Canada);
authoritarian and totalitarian governments (Singapore or Nazi Germany); economically developed and economically underdeveloped nations (Barbados or Bangladesh); unstable governments in transition
between dictatorships and consolidated democracies (the Weimar Republic, Kerensky's Russia, or the United Kingdom). The lessons of the
worst (Nazi Germany) are equally foreboding for the best (the Nether-

lands). In the end, no polity anywhere – not even consolidated Western democracies – is secure if speech is left to chance.

Boundless assumptions grounded in boundless fears resist demands for bounded justification. Grand fears call for grand remedies. However, as Jeremy Bentham cautioned, 'the object of the legislature' ought to be that 'the incidents which he tries to prevent are really evils and, secondly, that if evils, they are greater than those which he employs to prevent them.'[65] Does the mushroom thesis pass this critical balancing test?

One objection to the mushroom thesis is that its fears are socially subjective and politically speculative. The defining injury feared here exists *totally* prospectively.[66] Mayton has written on the problem of preventive criminal punishment for harm not yet and, arguably, never to be caused:

Physical acts such as battery of a public officer, destruction of governmental property ... or even destruction of a draft card ... can be detected and measured by the five senses ... But with laws against speech ... the offence consists of the speakers' instilling a certain state of mind in the listeners; the offence consists of speech 'directed' to 'inciting' lawless acts. But no such acts need occur, and the state therefore gains the power to make relatively subjective and unconfirmed assessments about mental events.[67]

No case against the mushroom thesis, however, can rest solely or even mainly on this objection. For one thing, subjective and speculative fears can and do sometimes turn out to be right, and in this case the consequences would be disastrous for society and polity. For another, the case against such fears is also socially subjective and politically speculative. The thesis cannot be disproved for the same reason that it cannot be proved – it is a timeless fear about the political future at its most profound. The test of this branch of fear must turn on the cogency of its assumptions and the quality of the evidence marshalled in support of it.

For evidence, mushroom theorists turn to history. But their use of history is both far too underinclusive and far too overinclusive to sustain their case. It includes those cases it should exclude and excludes those cases it should include. Genocide in Germany, pogroms in Tsarist Russia, ethnic repression in the former Soviet Union, persecution in Communist Eastern Europe, and assorted conflagrations and internecine conflicts in ancient history are routinely advanced in support of the thesis. Comparative history, mushroom theorists argue, demonstrates that hate and prejudice 'left to themselves' (read 'absent censorship') recognize no cognitive boundaries and know no physical borders – the disease is endemic to humanity. If it can happen in Germany, a country at the forefront of medicine, art, science, and technology – the land of Schiller, Goethe, and Beethoven – it can happen anywhere.[68] Is history being properly used or improperly misused here?

There is good reason why not one example advancing this censorship thesis is drawn from developments in long-standing, consolidated, political democracies. Even the United States, despite its sordid history of oppression, slavery, and violent racial divisions (and despite being the only major Western democracy without a comprehensive, constitutionally sustained hate propaganda law), does not buttress the fear of proponents of the mushroom thesis, of social disintegration and political conflagration absent legal repression of intolerant expression. 'Compelling' examples are all drawn from fledgling democracies (e.g., in Eastern Europe) struggling to recover from authoritarianism or from historically failed attempts at political democracy. The best examples from the latter are drawn from war-ravaged or economically debilitated authoritarian regimes in transition between political dictatorships (e.g. Germany's Weimar Republic, Kerensky's Russia) – regimes that did not and could not respect freedom of political expression for long. Indeed, the best examples, even as between authoritarian regimes, are taken from the politically worst of these regimes – those with long traditions of intolerance for public expression of political criticism – such as the totalitarian polities of Nazi Germany and Stalinist Russia.[69] Mushroom theorists highlight short-lived periods of liberalized expression in the failed life of these regimes, but ignore the much longer periods of its relative suppression. They mistake the legacies of denial of freedom of speech for freedom of speech itself. Freedom of speech is not synonymous with freeing up speech where what is freed up can only be what has been concealed by repression or ignored by denial. Politically and socially stunted mindsets were not suddenly and magically fabricated from short-lived liberalization of critical public discourse; they predated it.[70] They were gestated in the wombs of authoritarian political governances that nourished social division's greatest friend – unquestioning obedience, official deference, and public self-denial.[71]

The rise of Hitler is not a good illustration of the benefits of suppression of public expression. It is a better illustration of the dangers of a political culture that would officially craft reflexive minds and legally mandate correct responses for fear of socially more questioning and politically critical ones. A political culture that grows to respect public words in place of deeds as the better way to 'settle' disagreement may be no guarantee against a Hitler, a Stalin, or a Milosevic. But a public that is impoverished in such respect is an open invitation to them.[72] Demagogues thrive best among uncritical, especially 'unselfcritical,' minds – those best promoted by censorship. Unchallenged truths, as I have argued elsewhere, are more prone than challenged ones to 'lose their contemporary social significance' and atrophy, leaving a more perilous cognitive vacuum 'where social evil, unappreciated where un-heard, can in times of social crisis more easily take [the place of truth.] The deceitful and the dominant, rather than the honest and the mod-erate, can then take the place of truth.'[73]

Historical evidence used in the unqualified way of the mushroom theorists misunderstands freedom of speech as a social and political phenomenon. Fixed fears require fixed histories. But public growth is an ongoing process, not a one-time or final event. Snapshots in time, of discursive freedoms, miss this. Moving pictures capture it. In this ongo-ing process, the legacy of long denial of freedom of speech taints the subsequent attempts at freedom to speak. Unstable periods of political transition, where the repressive legacies of the past become the crises of the future, are particularly ill-suited to serve as the democratic lessons for the politically consolidated. For consolidated liberal democracies such as Canada, the historical lesson of intolerance is not simply that the 'cure' of legislated silence may well be worse than open expressions of the disease but that it is part of the disease. That is the more cogent mushroom thesis.

Thoughtful proponents of hate censorship have countered that free-dom of speech does not create but can facilitate or precipitate the worst of subsisting latent prejudices. The conventional censorial as-sumption is that Hitler might not have gained power were it not for Weimar's legal unfettering of racist communication. In fact, Hitler did not rise to power with legal unfettering of racist communication. Nazi Germany came about *with* hate propaganda law.[74] If freedom of expres-sion was part of the problem, it was not legal freedom to promote racial hate and social intolerance that was the problem. In the years before Hitler came to power there were more than two hundred prosecutions against anti-Semitic speech.[75] Consider not only what hate law in the Weimar Republic could not do for racial harmony, but also what an unselfcritical public mindset nestled in a long tradition of official deference and social obedience did to freedom of expression. There is a reason why hate law could not be limited to the suppression of racist propaganda as intended but came to be perverted in monstrous ways not intended. Freedom of expression failed for the same reason that silencing could not be limited. An uncritical public mindset of official deference and social obedience would not allow it.

Failure of freedom of expression in Weimar Germany is better understood not as the cause of social division and political disintegration but as its symptom. Given that democracy in Germany failed with the benefit and active application of hate law, what was the alternative to freedom of speech – continued political authoritarianism? Could freedom from hate and prejudice have been bought at the cost of democracy? Should freedom of disagreeable public expression be discouraged for fear of what democracy might bring? What is the mushroom thesis without the political democracy that it seeks to protect and preserve?

The magnitude of the historical difficulties in forging new social realities from mindless legacies left by old ones is more an indictment of denials of free speech than of its dangers. In mushroom theorists' reference to 'speech-failed' regimes, two things stand out. One is the extraordinary latent social enmity and political fragility that suddenly burdened freedom of expression during inter- or post-authoritarian transitions. The other is that the alternative to freedom of speech was to continue with repressive authoritarian governances that imposed social harmony and political stability at the end of a barrel of a gun.[76] Neither feature of the silencing dilemma buttresses the case for hate censorship in Canada. Nevertheless, references to 'speech-failed' or 'speech-failing' regimes are the best examples that mushroom theorists can offer. For consolidated Western liberal democracies that have long departed from debilitating authoritarian social and political legacies and their transitional dangers, these are hardly the 'compelling' historical lessons that proponents of hate censorship claim they are.

In terms of the gravity of the harm feared, the mushroom thesis of hate censorship stands as the quintessential preventive remedy. But prevention is precisely where this thesis stumbles the most. Where the need for hate propaganda law can best be called upon (in cases of virulent hatreds endemic to authoritarian governances in transition to more politically unfettered systems), attempts to squelch public enmity by public silencing are least likely to be effective.[77] The problem is already too far along – too many people already think to do wrong – to speak of 'cognitive' prevention.[78] Alternatively, where, prevention is most feasible (as in a consolidated political democracy such as Canada), forging public enlightenment from public silencing is most questionable. Effective public silencing of social discontent conceals determined dissentient expressions, and concealment is the single greatest enemy to timely, accurate, and balanced prevention.[79] In short, where the cognitive prevention may be meaningful because the feared harm has not yet set down endemic social and political roots, censorship is more likely to impede and impair than to facilitate and promote prevention. And, where the feared harm has already set down endemic cognitive roots, prevention by censorship can no longer be meaningful.[80]

Mushroom theorists mistake the symptoms for the causes of demagoguery. Over time, the cognitive repression they call for is more likely to heighten than to lessen the risks by worsening those causes. The mushroom thesis does not pass the test of balancing rights articulated by Jeremy Bentham – 'the object of the legislature' ought to be that 'the incidents which he tries to prevent are really evils and, secondly, that if evils, they are greater than those which he employs to prevent them.'[81]

Conclusion

If the function of hate propaganda law is to act as a sweeping preventive substitute for ordinary police powers (justification one), the case for it cannot be sustained. A veritably flawless social peace and politically seamless public order do not serve well the needs of a consolidated modern democracy dependent for its political resilience and social strength on robust debate and vital discussion. If the function of public silencing is to promote psychological self-sufficiency and thereby further community continuity, positive participation, and multiculturalism in Canada (justification two), evidence of the causal link between open expressions of prejudice and the feared harm, or that public silencing can correct it, is at best dated, at worst altogether wanting. Assumptions of universal causal validity fly in the face of overwhelming evidence to the contrary, while more discriminatory protective applications of the law would be neither politically feasible nor socially tenable on censors' own terms of reference. If the function is to ensure a more visible *and* more genuine inclusiveness (justification three), hate propaganda law is at best a dated answer to a past problem (visible exclusion) and the wrong answer to the current one (invisible exclusion). Finally, if the function is to prevent social conflagration and political disintegration (justification four), history suggests that building a politically less fragile polity on the strength of more open, probing, and self-knowing publics – rather than artificially guaranteeing political stability by quieting discursive public conflicts and papering over determined differences – is the better way to do it.

Unwrapped, all four justifications for hate propaganda law fall well short of what their authors claim for them. They fall short not just on free speech advocates' terms of reference. They fall short on censors' own egalitarian and democratic terms of justifying reference. Each justification suffers, in varying degrees, from problems of time dependency; factual, circumstantial, and contextual insensitivity; assumptive inconsistency; diagnostic symptomaticity; and remedial disproportionality or outright legal irrationality. Censors' case for repression of public expression is seriously flawed regardless of the investigating frame of reference – whether it be competing functions and assumptions, shared assumptions and functions, or censors' own terms of justifying reference.

4

The Political Dilemma, Part I

Legally Definable and *Politically Defensible* *Hate Censorship*

This chapter explores the balancing dilemma from the perspective of the politics of hate censorship in practice. My purpose is to bring a conceptually overlapping but analytically distinctive perspective to bear on the themes explored in the previous two chapters. I unwrap the dilemma of reconciling legally definable with politically defensible hate censorship from three overlapping perspectives on the politics of hate speech repression in Canada: the politics of content, the politics of victimhood, and the politics of fixing social right. I have two related goals: first, to contextualize and concretize the political dilemmas of the practice of hate censorship in Canada; second, to counterbalance societally reductionist approaches, fashioned from economistic under-standings, that present hate censorship as a limited and limitable apo-litical answer to a structurally flawed marketplace of ideas.[1]

The perspective of this chapter accepts the arguments of hate censor-ship theorists that economic freedom in Canada is not equally distrib-uted, that communicative resources are not equal, and that the market-place of ideas can often be far from free or fair.[2] But the question remains – what follows from this? Found truths, fixed meanings, and final triumphs? And are these ideals that can be guaranteed by law in a system of occasional governing majorities and changing social agendas?

For hate censorship theorists, politics ceases to exist meaningfully when the law protects censorship. Politics seems to count only when the law protects freedom of expression. Even then, it counts only, or essen-tially, as an instrument of exploitive structures of production or un-equal resources or relations of communication and social intercourse. Politics, however, cannot be written out of the practice of hate speech repression any more than it can be written out of the practice of freedom of speech. The politics of hate censorship is not a peripheral issue, as censorship theorists would have it, but is overarching. While economistic and societally reductionist arguments in justification of censorship may be theoretically attractive, they are also politically vacuous and functionally deceptive – the unfreedoms of the marketplace of ideas notwithstanding. Proponents of censorship take the political and pragmatic dilemmas of hate censorship out of the practice of hate censorship. This chapter puts them back into the balancing equation.

The purpose of hate censorship in Canada is not simply to silence. Canada is not a political dictatorship. Thoughtful censorship theorists would rather not find, hiding beneath a veneer of public tolerance, a deeper, more problematic prejudice. They want to promote a more enlightened public and a stronger Canadian democracy and believe they can do so better with hate censorship than they can without it.[3] Just and worthy goals alone are not enough, however – they must be translated into working reality. And that reality must reflect those just and worthy goals in its practice. That much is clear. Much less clear is how hate censors are going to do this by public silencing.

Politics is about power. Those exercising political power are not infallible, and unquestioned power can corrupt even those with the wisest and most honest of intentions. Political power can be self-serving as well as public serving. This is ordinarily true for all exercises of politics, but is especially true for the politics of hate propaganda repression. The politics of hate speech repression is particularly unwieldy. It lends itself well, especially over time, to error, abuse, and self-serving practices. While usually associated with the politics of the censoring few in political dictatorships, the politics of the censoring many, or influential few, in political democracies enjoys no natural immunity from these problems. The 'right' politics required by hate censorship can no more be successfully 'fixed' in political democracies than in political dictatorships. Indeed, the very idea is self-contradictory.

Ordinarily, the certainties of found truths, fixed meanings, and final triumphs on matters of state, society, and history that are worth fighting about are associated with the ruling guarantees of dictatorships, not the governing assumptions of systems of occasional governing majorities and changing social agendas. Ordinarily, too, progressive theorists would see officially constructed meanings on such matters as politically self-contradictory in a system premised on self-government, and socially self-defeating in a public-interest cause. They are among the first to reject, as specious and self-serving, claims of authoritarian rulers that only through their official decrees setting down correct public discourse can racial harmony, social progress, and political stability be assured. Even if this were true, the social and political price, over time, of *that kind* of harmony, progress, and stability is deemed too high to pay.

Ordinarily, progressive theorists would not accord presumptions of social infallibility, disinterested public service, and unswayable good judgment to any individual, group, or entity claiming exclusive knowledge of the public cognitive good or official right to legally fix it. Nor would they assume that, to better assure that good, any one social message or public meaning could be *successfully* fixed by law, to the exclusion of contrary ones. Yet these are the very things they assume with respect to hate censors and their censorship.[4] Points of view on matters that touch vitally on the well-being of society and polity cannot be put beyond political challenge or public debate. The assumption that they can is an idea about and for the public good that cannot allow for social fallibility, self-serving political interest, or simply bad judgment and still remain true to its public-interest cause.

Progressive censorship theorists place extraordinary trust in what they would ordinarily suspect and otherwise reject – for two main reasons: the importance of the cause to democratic society, and the presumed dependability of the means to advance it. In this view, hate censorship in a democracy is not anything like hate censorship in a political dictatorship. It is narrowly limited in terms of subject, scope, and injury to only that which is necessary for public growth and political democracy. The content of hate proscription is presumed to be legally definable, the targets of proscription politically manageable, the subjects of protection socially ascertainable, and the injury indisputable. It is political dictatorship that is self-serving. Hate propaganda law is public serving. As the Supreme Court of Canada suggested in *Keegstra*, hate censorship law is better seen as a positive requisite of social and political democracy than as a restriction on it.[5]

To merit its extraordinary status of trust, hate censorship should meet certain criteria reflecting its proponents' exceptional assumptions. First, it should proscribe only those threatened injuries that merit prevention. Selections of injuries for prevention should not lend themselves to applications that are arbitrary, capricious, or politically self-serving, depending on prevailing social times and changing political climates.[6] Nor, alternatively, should they lend themselves to applications that are potentially discourse suffocating by silencing most everything. Second, hate law should protect only those needing protection.

Selections of victims for protection and targets of proscription should not lend themselves to applications that are arbitrary, capricious, or politically self-serving, depending on prevailing social times and changing political climates. Nor, alternatively, should they lend themselves to applications that patronize victims and trivialize public injuries by making victims of most everyone.

Finally, those who would have power to put important public matters beyond public challenge or debate should be competent in and accountable for their work and their decisions free of political or personal conflicts of interest. Their decisions to silence, or the threat to do so, should reflect the exceptional trust placed in them by censorship theorists and express the strong sense of disinterested public service expected of them. Punishment for misspeaking should be based on the persuasiveness of the threat, the vulnerability of the threatened, the proximity of the feared injury, and the gravity of the threatened harm, not on inappropriate considerations extraneous to these criteria. However trustworthy or personally reliable particular censors may be, they are no substitute for a trustworthy and reliable system of censorship.

I Unwrapping the Politics of Content: What Is Hate Propaganda and How Do You Fix It?

Proponents of hate censorship, especially those of the 'social character' school of free speech thinking, would like to *reduce* open expressions of intolerance to just a criminal or 'legal' matter. Hate *silencing*, however, cannot be so reduced.[7] Hate propaganda may be intolerance packaged in the language of politics, but hate censorship may be politics packaged in the language of tolerance. In censorship practice, the two are not easily separable. What Sniderman and his colleagues observe about the politics of rights is also true of the politics of hate censorship – it 'is more complex, more fluid than has been customarily supposed.'[8] First, hate propaganda is hard to define. There are five reasons why: political indeterminacy; conflict between goals; conflict within goals; conflict both between and within goals; and time dependencies.

Neither the intrinsic deficiencies of the message of intolerance nor its feared public injuries ordinarily come conveniently wrapped in singular social meanings or apolitical truths for the convenience of censors. The content of 'proscribable' hate cannot be absolved of the contentious and subjective politics of its repression. The social malleability and political pliability of the idea of hate propaganda is well illustrated in disagreement over its boundaries.

Does hate propaganda include speech that 'perpetuates barriers to the dismantling of systemic discrimination'? Respected scholars like Anand think so.[9] If 'a landlord, at even an unconscious level, will prefer renting to a white couple as opposed to an East Indian couple after being subjected to a "dot busters" campaign' shouldn't speech disparaging tenants generally as unclean, irresponsible, destructive, and untrustworthy be considered hate propaganda? Do non-White immigrants not make up a disproportionate share of renters?[10] Does hate propaganda include speech promotive of a 'social climate that is hostile to the dismantling of systemic discrimination,' as McKenna suggests?[11] If 'instances of racism and intolerance are deeply etched in the historical record and, for that matter, not hard to find in the daily newspapers,'[12] as the Canadian Human Rights Commission itself has said, should the news not be far more carefully scrutinized for violating the hate propaganda provisions of the Criminal Code? As Dickey and Stratford say, '[t]here can be no doubt that media distortion contributes to a general climate of discrimination and abuse of women.'[13] Might hate propaganda include a personalized definition of group hurt feelings? The B.C. Human Rights Tribunal found that four impersonal articles written by columnist Doug Collins in the *North Shore News* 'collectively and through representation of anti-Semitic themes' promoted hatred of Jews; it ordered him to pay Harry Abrams, a Jewish complainant, $2,000 for 'injury to dignity and feelings of self-respect.'[14]

If the environment suffers because 'of the low regard that white societies have for the non-white populations that bear the brunt of environmental devastation,'[15] should not certain messages of logging companies, recreational developers, or travel agencies be considered beyond the bounds of legally acceptable speech? If the striking down of the rape shield law 'illustrates the task facing human rights advocates who seek effective legal control of public expressions of hatred,'[16] why exempt from hate silencing public expressions that effectively speak against such laws?

Does hate propaganda include the proselytic activities of messianic Christian organizations attempting to convert Jews? B'nai Brith Canada's League for Human Rights included them in its 2000 annual report on anti-Semitism and hate crimes in Canada.[17] Take, for example, the offensive messaging activities of the evangelical group 'Jews for Jesus,' which has launched a vigorous campaign of deception and half-truths counselling Jews to come back to their 'true Jewish roots' through the 'words of Jesus Christ.' Should these not be more effectively quieted?[18] If porn is hate propaganda because it 'mutilates women's fight for equality,' as suggested by prominent feminist writer Michele Landsberg, should the lascivious messages of licentious liberals (or the graphic depictions of aborted fetuses by pro-lifers) not be more carefully scrutinized for promoting hate propaganda?[19] If Canadian immigration policies are 'racist and exclusionary,' as Professor Irving Abella has suggested, is it not time to include speech advocating immigration quotas, which promote such policies, in the definition of intolerable hate propaganda?[20]

What can be said of a scholarly book about Canada's Natives that *inter alia*, recommends cultural assimilation so that they can 'acquire the skills and the attitudes to become self-supporting and get beyond the social pathologies that are ruining their communities'?[21] Is this 'nothing more than racism,' as Phil Fontaine, former Grand Chief of the Assembly of First Nations has called it?[22] Or is this book 'disagreements' notwithstanding, 'the most thoughtful and comprehensive of the critiques of aboriginal policy offered so far,' as Professor Alan Cairns seems to think?[23] Is a library display showcasing the contributions of Palestinians to the local community hate propaganda if it includes graphic depictions of 'injustices suffered by Palestinians' in Israel and highlights a 'UN resolution calling for Israeli withdrawal from occupied territories'? Many in the Jewish community in Windsor thought so.[24]

Does comparing public funding of faith-based schools in Ontario to South African apartheid promote an environment of religious intolerance? Is such comparison an 'outrageous, hateful and completely unjustified' statement that may contravene the antidiscrimination provisions of the Ontario Human Rights Code – as suggested by prominent lawyer Joseph Adler and Charles McVety, president of Canada Christian College? They have called for a public retraction, resignation, and investigation of none other than the chief commissioner of the Ontario Human Rights Commission for making just that comparison.[25] Or consider, again, the case of Abu-Zahra.[26] If a duly constituted race relations committee cannot itself agree to know what is hate propaganda when one of its own members promotes a book such as Norman Finkelstein's *The Holocaust Industry – Reflections on the Exploitation of Jewish Suffering,* how is the rest of society to know, without risking punishment for error?[27]

Perhaps these examples make more of the problem than it is – they are difficult cases that harbour sensitive issues. Consider, then, transparent messages or messengers of hate where there should be no problem drawing the line between what should be silenced and what should be exposed and challenged. Should Hitler's *Mein Kampf* be pulled from public libraries because it is hate propaganda? An 'upper echelon official' of the Ontario Human Rights Commission thought so.[28] Should the scurrilous anti-Semitic forgery *The Protocols of the Elders of Zion* be pulled from the World Wide Web for the same reason? Jewish outrage at 'reputable booksellers' such as Barnes and Noble, Amazon.com, and Borders for selling the detestable tract would suggest so. Would a set of children's Pokemon cards with an obscure illustration of a swastika on one card qualify for suppression? Many Jewish families think so.[29] Do the tapes of the interviews of talk-show host Phil Donahue with Bill Wilkinson, former Imperial Wizard of the Ku Klux Klan, qualify as hate propaganda? Canada Customs seems to think so.[30] If the meanings of even transparent messages of hate cannot tell us when we should repress and when we should express, challenge, and educate instead, how can society know in the case of more subtle messages of division and discord – the kind that more commonly confront ordinary Canadians daily?

The messages of even transparent hate do not ordinarily come already de-linked from socially and politically more problematic meanings for the convenience of censors.[31] Linkage is a common, not an exceptional, feature of intolerance. It is a dilemma for hate censorship for which proponents have no answers, only illustrations.

A United Church was smeared [by White supremacists] with graffiti because United Church headquarters had 'collaborated,' with communists. Bethune College, at York University, was defaced because it honoured Norman Bethune ... Theologians of hate [such as Keegstra and Malcolm Ross] view modern society as atheistic, secular, materialistic and immoral ... The world is engaged in total war between good and evil, Christianity and Judaism ... Aryan Nations ... are part of what has become known as the Identity Movement. It holds that the British, German, Scandinavian and American people, rather than the Jews, are the real Israel ... Ultra conservatives tending towards racism [such as Ron Gostick of the Canadian League of Rights] subscribe to an extreme chauvinism and xenophobia. [This] is a rather exclusive club made up of individuals who are British, or northern European, preferably monarchist, Christian (essentially Protestant Christian), and white ... Their racism is not advanced as overtly; racism is more-or-less masked, and promoted through their advocacy of issues which they put forward as of national concern. They are bigotry's fellow travellers.[32]

Where it counts most, intolerance is inescapably a political issue with multifaceted public features that do not respect the artificial legal boundaries set for it by censors. It is a problem that messengers of hate know all too well and exploit to great advantage. Laments Prutschi,

> One of the strategies of groups in this category [covert racists] is to plug themselves into issues which find a positive resonance in certain segments of the broader community. The opposition to bilingualism and the extension of French-language service is one example. In Ontario we find the Canadian League of Rights linking itself to such movements as the Alliance for the Preservation of English in Canada (or A.P.E.C.). [Edmund Burke Society co-founder] Paul Fromm heads two institutes: the Canadian Association for Free Expression (C.A.F.E.) and the Citizens for Foreign Aid Reform (C-Far).[33]

Even proponents of hate law cannot agree on proscribable content. Compare the position of a much-reserved supporter of hate censorship such as Professor Richard Moon with the far more expansive thinking on the subject articulated by scholars such as Anand or McKenna.[34] A socially correct hate standard, one justifying the exceptional status of apolitical trust accorded it, needs to be a defensible one. But how can a standard claiming found truths and fixed injuries be defensible if it is unknowable or, if knowable, indefensible beyond the thinking or thinkers of the times? Hate law proponents do not meet their own content requirement for exceptional trust. Important social policy decisions can be no more reduced to apolitical choices in the exercise of hate censorship than they can be in the exercise of freedom of expression.

Second, hate propaganda is hard to define because the 'cause' of hate censors is not monistic but plural. We may all agree with a singular notion of a shared purpose held in common when it is presented as a theoretical abstraction and packaged in broad terms. How many persons of conscience and tolerance do not want equality, racial harmony, cultural diversity, or a more democratic polity? Does hate not injure all these goals? When socially multifaceted and politically multidimensional goals are packaged in the singular language of hate, there are no conflicts. But in concrete applications, these goals may, and often do, come into direct conflict with one another. The observation of Sniderman and his colleagues that it is 'deeply deceptive to understand rights in the abstract'[35] describes well the dilemma of hate censorship. A 'political point of view,' they write, 'can be coherent, but not monistic.' It is 'not aimed at just one goal to the exclusion of all others' but is a 'pluralistic assemblage of related concerns that at some levels are mutually reinforcing and at others capable of coming into conflict.'[36] In censorship practice, choices and tradeoffs, often socially subjective or politically speculative, may have to be made that are inconsistent with the notion of a singularly purposed or apolitically definable social censorship.

Consider the possibilities for conflict between the goals of tolerance and diversity. If diversity is the social goal and intolerance is the injury of its breach, why not censor the Bible or the pronouncements of the Pope and his Canadian faithful?[37] Are antichoice, antigay, antisex statements less a threat to tolerance and diversity because they are couched in religious language, espouse an entire way of 'correct living,' or tout the Bible as their authority? Or, is proscription of the message of strict adherents to the Bible the greater harm to tolerance and diversity? Are tolerance and diversity complementary or conflicting here?

Third, hate propaganda is hard to define because particular goals of hate censors may harbour conflict within themselves. The language of hate repression may conceal a pluralistic assemblage of related concerns in the package of a singular goal, for the convenience of censors. But when unbundled, in particular contexts, the package often splits into socially multifaceted and politically multidimensional concerns that can come into conflict with each other. It can often be unclear which silencing choices (if any) further the goal espoused and which do not.

Consider the goal of equality in the context of patriarchal practices in Canada. Is open defence of these practices by, for example, some traditional Muslim groups less a threat to women's equality in Canada than less invasive mal-expressions about women that routinely raise the ire of censors? Or is proscription of such utterences inconsistent with ethnic, religious, and cultural diversity? Is ethnic, religious, and cultural diversity not also women's equality? What is the correct understanding of hate propaganda here? What is the ascertainable and defensible standard for repression, one that is not arbitrary, capricious, or politically self-serving? Calling equality a chameleon right, Sniderman and colleagues write that 'equality is a complex rather than a unitary idea.' It embraces, as Michael Walzer (1983) has argued, '[a] variety of domains of life and social goals capable of taking on different but coherent meanings in different cultures or even in the same culture at different times ... [E]quality encompasses a plurality of concerns and acquires its special political dynamic because its various conceptions can both complement and conflict with one another.'[38]

Fourth, the content of hate propaganda is hard to define because it may involve a particularly complex and troublesome mix – conflict both between and within particular goals of hate censorship at one and the same time. Consider hate censorship's goals of racial peace, public order, and equality in the context of the Los Angeles riots following the acquittal of four White police officers charged with the brutal beating of Rodney King. If racial peace and public order are the goal, should not the inflammatory speech of Blacks, directed at the Los Angeles Police Department and the local Korean community, have been proscribed? Or would this have conflicted with the goal of equality? Whose equality? Equality for disadvantaged Afro-Americans routinely stopped and harassed by a racist police force because of the colour of their skin? Or equality for the local Korean community threatened by such inflammatory speech with imminent and actual 'mob' violence? Are peace and public order for one community inequality for the other? Or is equality for one community division and disorder for the other? What is the 'right' understanding of hate propaganda in such cases for the purposes of repressing intolerant expression and preventing public injury?

Finally, the content of hate propaganda is hard to define because, while the definition of its injuries may be timeless in theory, they are time and circumstance dependent in political practice. Found truths, fixed meanings, and final triumphs assume unchanging injuries. But social, political, economic, demographic, and technological circumstances change. Social injuries change. New ones may arise. Old ones may fade. Some may become more grave, others less so. Ones thought solved may arise again. Ones thought unsolvable may eventually be gone for good. Others may change in intricate and complex ways we cannot imagine today. Social censors are not clairvoyant, and hate propaganda law does not come with a crystal ball. Censoring theorists may have 'found' truth. But history and politics do not stand still for fixed meanings and final triumphs – at least, not for a system premised on occasional governing majorities and changing social agendas.

What may have been an especially pressing public concern at one time and under one set of social and political circumstances (for example, women's glass ceiling at least to the end of the 1990s) may become less so in different social and political circumstances at a future time. School uniforms, religious instruction, and parental rights – socially comforting to society and polity at one time – have become politically divisive and socially disconcerting ideas for many minds in today's different era and different times. Then again, they may become comforting once again at some time in the future. Message, meaning, and injury choices on matters of society and polity worth fighting about are inescapably vulnerable to arbitrary, capricious, or politically self-serving standards of proscription, depending on prevailing social attitudes and changing political climates.

Contrary to what censorship theorists may think, these are not 'theoretical' dilemmas. Even in the relatively short life of hate law, there are already numerous illustrations of such dilemmas in censorship practice. Hate law tends to become whatever those with the power to threaten or enforce it think it is in the particular circumstances. In practice, it may be stretched, narrowed, even redefined, depending on prevailing social times and changing political climates, without a single word being changed. In 1975, several young people distributing literature with the words 'Yankee go home' at a Shriners' parade in Toronto were arrested for distributing hate propaganda and held for a couple of days in jail before charges were dropped.[39] In 1989, Salman Rushdie's fictional *The Satanic Verses* was ordered detained at the Canadian border in response to pressures from the Muslim community, many of whom found the book a contemptuous social slur and a veiled attack on their religious dignity and moral integrity.[40]

Even those who are clearly meant to be protected are not immune from becoming the unintended suspected – without a single word being changed in the law. In 1986, a film detailing Nelson Mandela's struggles for South African Blacks was detained for more than a month at the Canadian border because of allegations that it promoted hatred.[41] In 1989, prominent Jewish leader Edgar Bronfman found himself the target of a hate propaganda complaint for his intemperate language lambasting Austrians for their refusal to denounce Kurt Waldheim following reports of Waldheim's pro-Nazi past. In 1992, the Canadian Jewish Congress (CJC) tried to keep widely published British historian and Holocaust revisionist David Irving from speaking in Canada. The CJC's case was based on a section of the *Immigration Act* [42] that gives discretion to exclude anyone convicted in another country of an offence that, if committed in Canada, could be prosecuted 'by way of indictment.'[43] Under this section, Martin Luther King could have been (and future 'Kings' may still one day be) denied admission, since he had been convicted and jailed for disobeying a court injunction against a desegregation march.[44]

Hate censorship theorists face a content dilemma they would rather not confront. Repression of divisive expression can be narrow and exclusive or it can be unbounded and inclusive. What it cannot do is escape the political problems of both. It cannot be narrowly 'fixed' and exclusive without lending itself to applications that are arbitrary, capricious, or politically self-serving, depending on prevailing social attitudes and changing political climates. And it cannot be unbounded and inclusive without risking suffocation of vital public discourse. Neither is in the public interest.

Under Soviet Communism, there was not much difficulty knowing what was and what was not hate propaganda. The feared social injury was fixed and frozen in time. Communism realized that found truths, fixed meanings, and final content require truly final triumphs, and so politics, too, had to be frozen in time. The content of hate propaganda was politically broad and socially inclusive. All inegalitarian and socially divisive public discourse was officially outlawed, for now, for later, forever. The problem of dissent was not lack of knowledge but lack of acceptance. All citizens knew what was and what was not expected of them. The price of such social certainty was the political suffocation of virtually all meaningful public discourse. But even Communism could not freeze the politics of social division forever. The politics of content illustrates well hate censors' dilemma of self-contradiction and self-defeat.

II Unwrapping the Politics of Victimhood: Absolute Victims and Absolute Victimizers

To merit its extraordinary status of trust, hate law needs to silence only those whom it should silence. Found victims, no less than found truths, should not depend for their protection on the exigencies of prevailing social times and changing political climates. Selections of subjects of protection and targets of proscription should not lend themselves to applications that may be arbitrary, capricious, or politically self-serving. Nor, alternatively, should they lend themselves to applications that patronize victims or trivialize public injuries by threatening to make victims of most everyone of us. Confining the law to designated or 'ascertainable' victims is supposed to accomplish this. It is through their victimization that injury to society and polity is feared.

Just as not every derogatory utterance should be a legally proscribable public injury, so too not everyone against whom it is uttered should be a censorially protected victim. That would be to patronize victims and trivialize social injuries. Hate law proponents themselves are the first to point out that the law is not concerned with just any victim or any social or political injury. But if discovering and distinguishing the content of public injuries worthy of censorial protection is, in practice, socially malleable and politically pliable, can the criteria for selecting the deserving victims through whose victimization all of society is injured not be? If the first is politically boundless can the second be politically bounded?

Found truths and final triumphs guaranteed by law need found victims and final victimizers. Hate propaganda law in Canada attempts to find them by de-linking problems of the 'what' of repression from the 'who' of protection. The law defines the victim with a degree of precision that its authors have not been able to fashion with respect to the content of the proscribable injuries to society. The law protects only *identifiable* groups from intolerant public expressions.[45] The designation 'identifiable' substitutes for the word 'vulnerable' and is meant to limit victim inclusion to only those groups found to be in need of protection. The identifiable are defined as 'any section of the public distinguished by colour, race, religion or ethnic origin.'[46] There is, however, no reason in principle, either social or political, for this list to be exhaustive and, in fact, developing social wisdom and political pressure are working to expand it.[47] Victimhood can be both expanded and contracted – and that is the problem. Victimhood may be socially reduced and legally defined, but can it be politically assured? Assured how and by whom in a system of occasional governing majorities and changing social agendas? Politics is an ongoing process. Today's 'found' victims need not be the same as tomorrow's – as evolving calls on the moral authority of hate law attest. There are three related victim-victimizer identification dilemmas for hate censorship: changing (conflicting) times, conflicting victims, and conflicting self-identities.

First, it is hard to relate the idea of victimhood to a fixed notion of vulnerability of the kind required by progressive censors. History does not stand still for today's categories of 'protected maligned' any more than it does for the content of feared public injuries.[48] Consider what should be one of the least difficult grounds for protection – those minorities found vulnerable to intolerance because of their religious convictions. Should devout Catholics and their social agendas fall within the class of those requiring protection today? Was Martin Luther, in the sixteenth century, a dangerous heretic and a proselytizing hate propagandist as branded by the Catholic church? Or was the heretic the victim? Were Jehovah's Witnesses proselytizing hate propagandists as found by the church, the government, and the Catholic population of Quebec? Or were they the victims of intolerance? Are Jews for Judaism the victims of a self-hate campaign by evangelical Jews for Jesus or the other way around? Who is the victim when faith, race, and religion become increasingly indistinguishable from politics? After the destruction of the World Trade Center in New York, the Toronto police Hate Crimes Unit was asked to launch a criminal investigation of the website 'Muslims of America Islamic Center' for its 'vitriolic' and 'vilifying attacks' aimed mainly at Jews.[49] This was a time when Muslims were personally targeted and openly vilified by formerly veiled racists and the understandly anguished alike. Who are the victims here, for the purposes of progressive censorial protection?

To be a minority is to be vulnerable. That (see chapter 3) is the only timeless condition universally denoting vulnerability to intolerance and injury – at least in systems of majority rule. But is it any more of a workable criterion for fixing a socially definable and politically defensible hate censorship? Minority-based protection may include minorities disadvantaged in height, weight, or appearance. Short, fat, bald men have been vulnerable to timeless, derisive, stereotypical depictions as sexually, socially, physically, and even intellectually less adequate than tall men. Is abusive stereotyping of the short, the obese, or the physically unattractive ('midget,' 'porker,' 'a face to stop a truck') not hate? Disadvantage in such cases stems partly or wholly from unalterable personal or physical characteristics. These groups have suffered economic, occupational, social, psychological, physical, and other disadvantages throughout history. Arguably, some still suffer their indignities more than some currently included groups. Yet they do not have an at-large legal redress against the contemptuous stereotypical messages and derisive meanings of their tormentors.

Why is the hurt of these minorities necessarily less than the hurt of those currently enjoying protection? Does ridicule of them not contribute to a social climate hostile to the goals of equality, diversity, tolerance, and inclusion? Indeed, why should any of the marginalized or outcast – the destitute, debtors, renters, the aged, the mentally ill, the once incarcerated, the illiterate, smokers, hermits, swingers, fringe ideologues, and all the downtrodden and disadvantaged who pick up our garbage or unclog our toilets for a living – be excluded from cognitive protection? And if we include them, why not others? On what grounds of 'found' victimhood or 'found' social truth should any minority be excluded – or included? Can one construct the 'right,' broad, inclusive criteria for public silencing from the disadvantages of minority status without patronizing victims or trivializing public injury by making victims of most everyone? Alternatively, can one 'fix' narrow, exclusive criteria that are not arbitrary, capricious, or politically self-serving, depending on prevailing social attitudes and changing political climates – in short, that are not discursively discriminatory?

Second, it is hard to define victims worthy of official censorship protection because vulnerability to injury even of 'recognized' victims is not absolute but relative, as well as time dependent. The historically vulnerable do not just come into conflict with the 'invulnerable.' They can equally come into conflict with each other – and today increasingly do so. It is in the mainstream conflicts between recognized rival minority groups in an increasingly multicultural Canadian society – rather than in *open* expressions of prejudice by a dominant White society or fringe vilifications by marginal fanatics outside of any recognized group – that intolerance is becoming most consequential and the need for a meaningful law of hate silencing most pressing. Yet it is also in such conflicts that absolute victims and absolute truths can be most difficult to find and official triumphs most difficult to fix. Socially divisive messages are least amenable to politically undivisive standards of victimhood where such standards count most. Public choices based on relative degrees rather than absolute 'findings' of victimhood are a function of subjective and shifting social sympathies and fluid political vulnerabilities.

When two Arab-language newspapers in Quebec published a series of scathing articles attacking Jews, the Canadian Jewish Congress called on Montreal police to 'investigate,' suggesting that the pieces could violate Canada's anti-hate laws.[50] When Stockwell Day, then leader of the Official Opposition of Canada, gave a 'rousingly pro-Israel speech,' Atif Kubursi, president of the National Council of Arab-Canada Relations, threatened to bring a lawsuit against Day for 'inciting hatred' against Arabs.[51] When best-selling author Leon Uris published the pro-Zionist novel *The Haj*, there was relentless pressure on public libraries to withdraw the book because an Arab organization maintained that the book amounted to 'hate propaganda.'[52] At the University of Ottawa, the Student Council denied recognition to the Jewish Students' Union because 'they claim for themselves the right to propagate their racist ideology, which precisely goes against all principles of democracy.'[53] Meanwhile, at the University of Western Ontario, the Student Council denied recognition to a pro-Palestinian group, 'Canadians for Peace in the Middle East,' because of its anti-Jewish, anti-Israel 'bias.'[54] Those who were protected at the University of Western Ontario became the 'suspected' at the University of Ottawa and those who were protected at the University of Ottawa became the 'suspected' at the University of Western Ontario.

Finding and fixing the 'right' victim is a political dilemma for which there are many illustrations but no satisfactory legal answers. Consider one Jewish writer's thoughts: '[t]he Nation of Islam attempts to promote black pride by portraying blacks as the exclusive victims of racial intolerance ... In exalting their own race at the expense of others, the Nation of Islam claims to be working for the betterment of the black person's quality of life in America [but this masks a hateful message].'[55] In 1996, the Canadian Jewish Congress invoked a section of the *Immigration Act* that allows for the exclusion of aliens if there is reasonable grounds to believe that they 'would violate' a Canadian law, in order to keep Louis Farrakhan, the Afro-American head of the Nation of Islam, from entering the country. Though unsuccessful, at least for now, the CJC's argument was that Farrakhan was 'likely' to breach Canada's hate propaganda law.[56] When Al-Jazeera's plans for cable television carriage in Canada became known, the Canadian Jewish Congress and B'nai Brith said they would move before the Canadian Radio-television and Telecommunications Commission (CRTC) to block the application on the grounds that the twenty-four-hour 'Arab CNN' fanned anti-Semitism and would violate the hate propaganda provisions of the Criminal Code.[57]

Historically, animosities between free-speaking rival minorities have proven to be among the greatest threats to *all* the underlying goals of hate censorship. Can a censorship choice be made between such competitive claims to exclusive victimhood that is not socially subjective or politically self-serving on behalf of one victim at the expense of the other? Who decides? How do they decide? Are virulent tracts by published and respected academics such as York University's Professor Aijaz Ahmad (author of *The Nazification of Israel and Israel's Killing Fields*), singling out the Jewish state for special public opprobrium, less a threat to Jews, public truth, social harmony, and multiculturalism than the words of Ernst Zundel?[58] Is the socially 'just' and offically 'correct' understanding of victimhood, that hate censors' trust can be legally guaranteed, to be based on truth, the persuasiveness of the threatener, the vulnerability of the threatened, the proximity of the injury feared, and the gravity of the potential harm, or on rival groups' political clout in wielding or warding off the censor's knife?

Hate censorship theorists may assume absolute victims and absolute victimizers. Vulnerability, however, cannot be so reduced. It is a socially relative, historically time dependent, and politically pliable concept. The 'social character' of victimhood may be fixed and clear in the minds of censorship theorists. But in political practice its boundaries are opaque and fluid. Power relations and public perceptions of them change over time – sometimes over a short time. The adage 'we are all victims in some ways and some times and victimizers in other ways and other times' may be only partly true, but to dismiss it is to dismiss an important truth about the movement of time, politics, and social relations. Consider the evolving power relations between Jews and Arabs, Catholics and Muslims, men and women. The politics of victimhood may accord with objective movements in power relations, but it need not do so. Moreover, it need not accord with original censorial intentions. As we have seen, applications of hate law that reflect neither the original intentions of the Cohen Committee (or progressive censors) nor objective movements in social power relations since then have been made, or attempted, or proposed. All that is needed for 'victim shifting' are changing political climates and evolving social times. The availability of the threat to silence is always ripe for time-dependent political manipulation. Self-serving or self-righteous censoring politics can do the rest. Hate may stand still for theoretical censors, but history and politics do not stand still – even for the historically vulnerable.

The Jewish community's alarm at a growing disregard for their historic vulnerability – a disregard buttressed by a shift in media depictions of the Jewish state, from a nation of stateless victims to a nation of empowered victimizers, illustrates the dilemma for censors.[59] Professor Laurie Zoloth points to the complicity of the progressive left in an increasingly ugly misappropriation of Holocaust imagery that depicts the Jewish state as a brutal, racist, colonial pariah.[60] The executive committee and council of the Canadian Labour Congress, historically an ally of Israel, adopted a policy statement comparing the Jewish state to South Africa during apartheid.[61] Over time, such shifts in public and elite perceptions of victimhood make hate censorship a double-edged political sword. No victim, no group, is invulnerable to being publicly hoist one day on its own censorial petard. Yesterday's historically protected may well become tomorrow's newly suspected. In October 2002, Canada Customs seized, on suspicion of hate propaganda, a newsletter put out by the Ayn Rand Institute, *In Moral Defense of Israel*.[62] The newsletter consisted of thoughtful pro-Israeli articles, many of which had appeared in the mainstream U.S. press, including the *Chicago Sun Times*, the *Houston Chronicle*, and the *Orange County Register*. As an outraged editorial in the *Canadian Jewish News* declared, 'It stuns the mind that an official at CCRA [Canada Customs and Revenue Agency] would even remotely consider the need, let alone the propriety of examining this pamphlet. Given the undisguised hostility towards Israel and brazenly anti-Semitic attitudes that appear so commonly these days in public discourse, it is now appropriate to ask: Is it incompetence, madness, mischief, or something more malign, more sinister taking root at CCRA?'[63] This may not be the law of hate censorship, as censorship theorists see it. But it is the politics of victim protection, as they do not.

In a political culture that looks to hate law for solace, the politics of rival censorship can cross legal boundaries, spreading its moral authority and its language of silencing across diverse arenas and cross-fertilizing public discourse with its chilling meaning, in unintended ways. Even the 'historically' suspected may become tomorrow's legally protected. In 1998, a New Brunswick court ordered cartoonist Josh Beutel to pay Malcolm Ross $7,500 in damages for 'going too far' in depicting Ross as a Nazi.[64] Even Zundel got into the victim protection act, albeit in politically most unpropitious circumstances, trying unsuccessfully to convince a justice of the peace to criminally charge Sol Littman, the Canadian representative of the Simon Wiesenthal Center, with 'spreading false information.'[65] In the summer of 1998, he launched a defamation suit against the Canadian prime minister, leading parliamentarians, the Canadian Jewish Congress, and others, alleging injuries of 'humiliation, ridicule, hatred and contempt' as a result of a unanimous all-party resolution banning him from parliamentary precincts. The Canadian Jewish Congress instructed its legal counsel 'to study the suit with a view to issuing a counter-claim against Zundel.'[66]

Canadian Secretary of State Gerry Weiner felt more vulnerable, finding it necessary to publicly defend and 'explain' himself against a defamation suit filed against him by Holocaust revisionist David Irving, after he called Irving an anti-Semite who subscribes to 'pseudo-historic theories' and 'myths and distortions' about the Holocaust.[67] The 2000 annual audit on anti-Semitism and hate by B'nai Brith Canada's League for Human Rights reported 'a recent trend [in Canada] involving libel suits by extreme right wingers against human rights advocates.'[68]

Victimhood is an inherently subjective, shifting, and discriminatory 'identity' politics. Its political contexts are boundless. The threat to silence may come, as illustrated above, from rival victims, official institutions, or even historic victimizers – indeed, from almost anywhere. Asserting victim status, the National Ballet of Canada launched a $1-million defamation suit against *Now* magazine for publishing an advertisement by supporters of a Jewish artist who had been dismissed from the ballet; the advertisement compared the dance company to the Nazis in their treatment of their Jewish artists.[69] In a 'political' world, on public matters worth arguing about, there are no such things as absolute victims, absolute victimizers, and apolitical choices – there are only comparative vulnerabilities, subjective and shifting social choices, and often self-serving, even vindictive, censorship politics. In short, one cannot know the censorship politics, much less assure the socially desired (correct?) one, in changing public climates of the future.

Third, it is hard to define the victim because *social self-identity* itself is neither monistic nor fixed but multifaceted and fluid. Censorship theorists may package victimhood into singular and fixed notions of vulnerability. But vulnerability invariably involves not one but multiple, and ongoing self-identities. Unbundled, vulnerability can split into several, often self-conflicting, identities – a pluralistic assemblage of related vulnerabilities that are mutually reinforcing at some levels and some times and capable of coming into conflict at other levels and other times. As Professor Epstein observes,

> I think that basing politics primarily on identity creates several problems ... For instance, I am a woman and a Jew; but I am also a product of the left, in particular the Old Left, and an intellectual. These latter terms are also important parts of my identity – and of my experience of objectification, in a society not particularly fond of either Communists or intellectuals. A political language that ... tries to fold all experience into categories of race, sexuality, and gender ... makes it more difficult for people to understand their own experience in a complex way, to understand that different aspects of identity can take on different meanings at different times or can be more or less important at different points in people's lives. [P]olitical correctness [is the product of a] political atmosphere, that is dominated by identity politics ... [T]he dangers [are] ... assigning of moral status in terms of exclusion or subordination, and the use of moral judgements as clubs against ourselves and others.[70]

Consider the self-conflict of reconciling being Jewish with being left in the context of the shifted victim politics of today.[71] Or consider Professor Nora Gold's finding that Canadian Jewish women today feel more vulnerable to anti-Semitism than to sexism.[72] Today, a woman who is obese, pro-life, and an intellectual may find herself more vulnerable to prejudice because of stereotypes about 'fatsos,' 'religious fanatics,' and 'bookworms' than because she is a woman. Different aspects of one's self-identity bear different vulnerabilities that can take on different meanings at different times or be more or less important at different points in one's life. Monistic notions of victimhood, fixing human experiences and stripping human identities of the multifaceted and fluid aspects of their vulnerability for the purposes of censorship, are a blunt instrument ill-suited to the needs of a refined cause.

Dilemmas of victim selection cannot be de-linked from the dilemmas of content selection. Vulnerability can be made narrow and exclusive or unbounded and inclusive. What hate censors cannot do is to escape the political problems of both. Vulnerability cannot be narrowly 'fixed' and exclusive without lending itself to applications that are arbitrary, capricious, or politically self-serving, and dependent on prevailing social times and changing political climates; and it cannot be unbounded and inclusive without lending itself to applications that patronize victims and trivialize public injury. Neither serves the public interest.

Under Communism there was no difficulty in knowing who was a victim and who was not. Vulnerability was broad and inclusive – all who were socially and materially disadvantaged were victims and all who were socially and materially advantaged were victimizers. The price of such legal certainty was a politically suffocating patronizing of victims and trivializing of public injury – where almost any anti-egalitarian or intolerant public pronouncement became a generic public contempt. To openly challenge official social wisdom was an offence not against anyone in particular but against everyone in general – it was to 'slander' the 'people.' Fixed truths and found victims required final political triumphs, and so vulnerability became an idea frozen in time. But even Communism could not freeze the politics of vulnerability forever. The politics of victimhood also illustrates well hate censors' dilemma of self-contradiction and self-defeat.

III Unwrapping the Politics of Fixing Social Right: Trusted Censorship and Trustworthy Censors

Censorship theorists do not trust the public to make the right choices on a matter so fundamental to their well-being as the ability to get along as they should. Their mistrust may well be justified – at least sometimes. A flawed public may not always think or act as they should, and a flawed system may often not permit them to. But who, in a system premised on occasional governing majorities and changing social agendas (and for a cause committed to revitalizing not denying such governance), should assure that the public think on public matters as they should, if not the public themselves? Those empowered to do so in place of the public must merit the extraordinary trust placed in them that they will do it right. Five dilemmas stand in the way of theorists' faith in trustworthy hate censors and a trustable censorship: competence, chilling effects, accountability, conflict of interest, and fixability.

1 Competence

Trust in hate censorship assumes censors competent for their task – skilled in their work, judicious in their decisions, and experienced in their subject matter. Trust in the decision to silence depends on trust in the decision maker. Even in ordinary civil disputes, incompetence, poor training, or inexperience of the decision makers would be considered unacceptable. In matters of criminal justice concerning the public welfare at its most basic, they should be considered fatal. Ordinarily, progressive censorship theorists would be among the first to distrust adjudication so deficient – but not when it comes to the silencing of hate. Writes MacKinnon, 'because the Canadian law of equality ... knows the difference between disadvantaged groups and advantaged ones, it is less worried about the misfiring of restrictions against the powerless and more concerned about having nothing to fire against abuse of power by the powerful.'[73]

Perhaps 'the law of equality' knows the difference, but do the politics and practices of hate censorship know the difference? To know the difference between the advantaged and the disadvantaged is not the same as knowing the public cognitive good or serving it by censorship. Determining the public cognitive good requires making socially subjective choices from politically boundless injuries. Who have the wisdom to do this? The courts, of course, have the legal authority to do so. But so too can the politicians, rival social groups, the police, customs officials, bookstore owners, librarians, the media, immigration authorities, and Internet service providers.[74] They are all censors, too, actual or potential.

'Hate censors' is a packaged idea. Unpacked, it splits into numerous actors, revealing many different censoring identities, official and unofficial, that can act, or threaten to act, for many different reasons besides the public good, including fear, political expedience, moral comfort, public approval, or even the 'bottom line.' Hate law misappropriates discursive public conflict, making it the 'property' of these actors.[75] They substitute their thinking for public thinking, turning supremely social and political disputes into police, administrative, customs, immigration, even business concerns. Why are these entities more expert in the public cognitive welfare than the public themselves? Bookstore owners, the police, customs and immigration officials, and the media possess no special skills for deciding the public cognitive good. Neither in knowledge, training, structure, nor institutional purposes are any of them well equipped to take on the job of protector and defender of the public psyche. Nor can they be. This is not their true function, but a function thrust upon them by those who trust in censorship. Progressive censors put extraordinary trust in the same deficient corporate and official structures (to act as expected) for the purposes of censorship that they so intensely distrust (to act as they should) for the purposes of freedom of speech.[76]

Bad faith on the part of these censors need not be assumed, although, given the 'establishment bias' of official ones and the corporate bias of entrepreneurial ones (as social activists point out), one can hardly foreclose it either.[77] The police, customs and immigration officers, library boards, the corporate media, and bookstores are not one entity with a singular public interest but a vast and disparate collection of public and private interests, professional values, and institutional purposes. How can they be of one mind, much less of the one socially correct mind expected of them by hate censorship theorists?[78] How are they to correctly protect the public psyche when even the 'experts' – scholars, social pundits, judges, even the censoring left – are not of one mind on the proper ambit of public silencing for the public good. MacKinnon's personified 'law of equality' is a politically vacuous, societally reductionist, 'theoretical' idea of censorship stripped of the practices and problems of repression of this kind of expression.

2 Chilling Effects

Trust in hate censorship assumes wrongful speakers rightfully silenced. Trust in the silencing decision depends on the decision's being right. If it did not, censorship would not be needed. Freedom of speech would do just fine. Even in ordinary civil disputes, a law that could, as a matter of course, punish those who ought not to be punished would be suspect. One that could do so by threat of criminal sanction would be more suspect still. But one that could do so on matters integral to the well-being of democratic society should be considered intolerable. Ordinarily, hate censorship theorists would be the first to distrust a law that could so mispunish – but this is not the case when it comes to hate speech law.

Wrongful punishment here takes two very different forms – one visible, the other invisible. The first kind, speakers silenced who ought not to have been quieted, is showcased by arbitrary, capricious, or self-serving applications of the law explored earlier in this chapter. But this is not the only wrong that censors accept. They accept a far larger one. The second kind – 'would-be' speakers who silence themselves when they need not, for fear of being punished for misspeaking – is also accepted. They, too, are punished. But it is not only they who are punished. By their unwarranted silence, democratic society is punished as well, and this is by far the larger and more important public wrong. Those wrongfully punished for misspeaking are only the tip of a far more chilling iceberg of public wrong. The danger of 'chill' is not the visible tip of ideas that are errantly suppressed. It is the much larger invisible base of unheard thoughts and unconsidered visions below that never get to see the light of day because of putative speakers' fear of financial ruin, professional blacklisting, collegial ostracism, embarrassment, family upheaval, detention, or even jail. Looking only at those wrongfully silenced (MacKinnon's 'misfiring of restrictions' point) misses what the U.S. Supreme Court long ago recognized as the far wider 'chilling effect' their silencing has on public discourse and political communication generally.[79]

Chilling effect, or public self-censorship for fear of misspeaking, incarcerates ideas. It is by far the greater societal punishment of errant public censorship, but it is also the one least talked about by hate censorship theorists. It is 'invisible' and unquantifiable. But it is no less harmful, to society and polity. Indeed, it is far more harmful, precisely because it is hidden and therefore easily missed or dismissed. As Borovoy observes,

> [t]he fact that those French-Canadian nationalists ultimately avoided conviction does not tell us what an ordeal it was to go through the criminal trial process. The fact that charges were withdrawn against those anti-American activists does not tell us what it was like to be arrested and to spend a couple of days in jail. The fact that the Jewish leader and the publisher were never charged does not tell us how potentially intimidating it would be for many

people to be the subject of government scrutiny. Nor does it guarantee that, in a very different political climate, charges would not be laid over the speech in question. Even if material is [only] temporarily detained [as was the case with the Mandela film] we do not know the extent to which the one-month delay might have undermined the anti-apartheid activities that had been planned. In the case of the Rushdie book, we can imagine how a different political climate might have produced a more serious consequence than a forty-eight hour delay.[80]

Hate censorship advocates do not always have difficulty recognizing the corrosive impact on public discourse of 'chilling effects.' They have great difficulty when it chills their opponents' speech but not when it chills their own speech. As an outraged Canadian Jewish Congress, speaking through its lawyer, Hal Joffe, said after a New Brunswick court 'unexpectedly' found for Malcolm Ross, '[h]ow are commentators to determine how something like this will impact them? As a result people who have appropriate comments to make may just shy away from them.'[81]

3 Accountability

Trustworthy censors should also be accountable censors. Accountability requires transparency and visibility. To borrow the words of a former U.S. president, 'trust but verify.'[82] To do less is to substitute faith for accountability in repression. That may be acceptable to theocracies and autocracies, but it should not be acceptable to a system premised on self-government and a cause intended to fortify rather than deny it.[83] It should especially not be acceptable in regard to public discourse on important public matters. Where the public impact of the message in contention depends on its currency, 'justice delayed' is truly public 'accountability denied.'

Even in the case of ordinary civil disputes, want of adjudicative transparency and accountability would be unacceptable. Ordinarily, hate censorship theorists would be the first to object to 'invisible reasons,' untimely redress, or no redress at all – except in the case of hate speech repression. Hate censorship's dilemma of unaccountability or delayed accountability is a function of speaker chill, deficient public knowledge, and want of public transparency. Chill wrongfully silences those who should speak. Deficient public knowledge and want of public transparency impair the public's ability to hold those censors answerable.

What is the public to verify in the case of hate censorship and how are they to do it? Those entrusted with the power to repress disagreeable public messages for 'wrong thinking' should be obliged to satisfactorily explain their own thinking in doing so. How else can their censorial actions be tested for propriety and their decisions verified as not capricious, arbitrary, or self-serving? In most cases, however, censors don't even have to consider the reasoning of those they censor, much less justify their own.[84] As Borovoy writes, '[w]hile judges and juries are required to hear both sides, cops and customs officials have no such obligation.'[85] Corporate censors (such as bookstores), unlike public sector employees, are not even required by a code of professional conduct, or burdened by a public service ethic, to answer to the general public for their decisions. They have to 'account' for the bottom line and their readership, not the public interest. This usually means avoiding problems with the law rather than safeguarding the public welfare. They can be charged for carrying the wrong materials. They cannot be charged for not carrying the right ones.[86] In case of doubt, the popular can be expected to trump the disagreeable. As Heather Reisman, CEO of Indigo Books, Canada's largest bookstore chain, said after the chain pulled Hitler's *Mein Kampf* from its shelves, 'With freedom of expression, the line is drawn on hate literature. It's a corporate decision. It's what we stand for.'[87] Corporate moral conviction is made easier when kowtowing to popular wisdom or fashionable elite thinking may be good for the bottom line.

It is not that gatekeepers of the public mind – newspapers, broadcasters, public libraries, or bookstores – would not presilence if there were no legal censorship. A bookstore, after all, cannot carry all materials. Even libraries must select what they carry. And selection, in matters of society and polity worth arguing about, invariably involves politically subjective discrimination. The difference here is public accountability. Where otherwise they may visibly silence of their own accord, hate law affords them moral cover and official protection to do so 'invisibly' in the name of the public interest. Outlawing hate is an idea of the public good that freely traverses social, political, legal, administrative, and even economic boundaries, generating multidimensional moral authority for its suppressions. Censors can hide behind not only their private and independent corporate status or administrative discretion but also an official censorial rectitude sanctioned by law, and thus more easily escape having to explain, much less convincingly defend, their actions to complainants. Can any of them be faulted – especially where repression by the authorities is threatened or public approval risked? Costly, belated, cumbersome, and uncertain *ex post facto* litigation is often the only recourse left to the aggrieved. Many legitimate and socially valuable works may thus end up being irreparably detained, morally blackened, or entirely lost in this way.

There is more reason to hide than not to – and much political latitude to do so. What *is* can be held to account. What is *feared* cannot so easily be. Administrators, politicians, and their enforcement arms – customs officials, retail inspectors, and the police – do not ordinarily volunteer their mistakes for correction or disciplinary action.[88] The veils of secrecy hiding mistakes or concealing outright bias are not easily pierced even in wrongful criminal repression of measurable, detectable *acts*.[89] Imagine censors acknowledging mistakes that cast doubt on their competence or good faith in regard to a public injury so socially pliable, politically boundless, and publicly exploitable as that embraced by 'hate propaganda.' How can anyone be singled out for fault, much less for discipline, for erring on the question of the public cognitive good here? There is much injurious content, many aspiring victims, and numerous possible victimizers to choose from. Complainants need not be heard. Decisions need not be justified to anyone's satisfaction. More often than not, it is the wrongfully censored who end up explaining themselves to the censor. If stamina and pocketbooks allow, they may enlist the public interest and appeal to the courts. But they may not. Nor do they have to. They may decide it is not worth the effort or the risk of loss. These are society's 'silent' losers. But it is not just they who lose. Society also loses. Material is lost that should be heard and that, but for censorship, would have been heard.

The ultimate victims in all this are the interested public and the public interest. But the most hurt are also the most powerless. The public has even less recourse than the author/publisher of the work seized. There is an asymmetry of rights between the public and the censor that is far more daunting than the one between the author/publisher of the work seized and the censor. The public would ordinarily depend on the resistance of the author or owner of the material seized for information about its content. Even then, the public cannot act on its own behalf. It has no legal claim of right to act in its own best interests. It is the author/owner of the work, not the public at large, who has the legal right to contest the seizure.[90]

Front-line censors' power of prior restraint – to suppress or discard 'wrongful' messages before their public expression – puts the public interest and public accountability in a 'catch-22' situation.[91] Those who cannot see and hear for themselves are unable to effectively challenge for error the judgment of those who can, and are prevented from acquiring the information they need by those same judges. If the author of the work seized accepts the seizure without much visible or virulent complaint, the public may not even be the wiser for it. Where public discourse is not public property, social disagreement can be officially confiscated and legally discarded without public knowledge. The public are silent losers because they are rightless and unknowing losers – a delightfully self-serving public dilemma for censors: one ideal for both perpetuating and claiming public support for censorship. So much for informed public consent!

Hate censorship is all about legal protection of the public interest. But it is the censors, especially front-line censors, who effectively are legally the better protected. The public must trust, for they cannot effectively verify. But then how can they know what public expression is legally permitted to them and what is not, without risking punishment for error? Safety requires that they err on the side of ignorance and silence, even when it is the censoring official who may be in error. How can it be otherwise? The public are not simply protected victims. They are feared potential victimizers. They are the ones who cannot be trusted. It is the public who must account to the censors, not the censors to the public. Public trust and public accountability are turned on their heads. Prejudging social discourse by preventive legal silencing is a right of official, not public, decision making – a repudiation of the public's right to think independently. But it is more than that. It is a morally transmutable claim of right to prejudge – a politically borderless assault on public discourse by most anyone with the power to decide. Even self- or profit-regarding information entrepreneurs can self-servingly substitute their thoughts on the public good for those of the public with the kind of moral immunity from effective public scrutiny that only a law against hate can give.

The problem here is that a great number and variety of actors can exercise or aspire to judicial-like powers to 'protect' the public cognition without judicial-like safeguards of accountability that protect the public interest. They are not just the front-line troops but often the last line of 'defence' in the protection of the public psyche – the public interest begins and often ends on their doorstep, not that of the courts.[92] It is not necessary for the courts to make bad censorial decisions to injure the public interest. It is enough if the front-line troops – acting as moral guardians of the public psyche under the cover of official claim of legal right, or from legitimate fear of hate law – do so. The censorship debate may be focused on the courts and the wisdom of their decisions, but the courts are only part, often the least revealing part, of the whole hate censorship picture. The more telling part is the part where the greatest chill is apt to come from – the 'wisdom' of these other, largely unaccountable, socially, professionally, structurally, or morally ill-equipped guardians of official right. Their interests in deciding the public cognitive good are diverse, distant, and often very different from the public-serving kind required of them by the courts or expected of them by trusting censorship theorists. It is here that public chill can more easily substitute for the public interest – where bad decisions are more likely to be made, to remain invisible, or to escape accountability. Those who are most likely to chill should be most accountable for the chill they cause. Paradoxically, they are the least accountable. This dilemma belies assumptions that a proactive regime of hate censorship can be trusted to function in a manner that is not arbitrary, capricious, self-serving, or contrary to the public interest.

Deficiencies of accountability, chilled speakers, and unknowing publics are self-reinforcive to the detriment of the public cause of repression – further belying censorship theorists' assumptions of a trustable censorship. Want of public accountability becomes a self-realizing, self-justifying censorial dilemma. Chilled speakers promote unknowing publics, and unknowing publics promote the chilling of speakers. Chilled speakers and unknowing publics are invitations for publicly unaccountable censorship. In turn, want of public accountability chills speakers, which promotes unknowing publics, which promotes want of public accountability. The public interest cannot be a winner here. Those who should speak, but do not, lose. Those who should hear, but cannot, lose. Those who should want, but will not get, more enlightened publics and accountable self-government – progressive censors themselves – lose. These are censorship's silent or unknowing losers and society's silent losses.

Public accountability is not simply a legal matter of judicial redress, as hate censorship theorists would have it, but a political one. Chilled speakers, silent losers, and unknowing publics – hate censors' accountability dilemma – are the least visible, tangible, or quantifiable and, therefore, one of the most under-appreciated public injuries of official silencing of disconcerting public discourse. But they are also, for that very reason, among the most important. Dilemmas like these may not be the 'law' of hate speech repression, but they *are* the politics of its practice. To turn a blind eye to them, as proponents of hate censorship do, is indeed to trust without seeing.

4 Conflict of Interest

Trustworthy hate censorship requires disinterested censors, following ascertainable standards, and acting in the public's best interests. Trust in the decision depends on trust in the independence of the decision maker. Even in ordinary civil litigation, where absolute winners and absolute losers are expected, it is considered improper for the parties to the dispute to be judges in their own case, either directly or indirectly.[93] Otherwise, the decision is seen as tainted and the decision-making process as self-serving not public serving. In the case of criminal law concerning the public good at its most basic, it should be especially important to eschew such conflict of interest, or even its mere appearance. Ordinarily, progressive theorists would be among the first to condemn such criminal justice – but not in the case of hate law.

The problem of conflict of interest in suppression of hate is not one of inadequate resources or administrative discretion.[94] It is not that discretion-wielding censors are too thinly spread to do a correct and consistent job. The problem is with the job itself – the character of the product and the nature of the process of repression of this kind of expression. Both are inherently political. Hate propaganda is, inescapably, 'political' speech, and participants in its repression are invariably politically tainted. In polities premised on self-government, self-interested publics can *legitimately* be hate censors. They can legally be judges in their own cause.[95] The more socially divisive the cause, however, the more politically tainted the choices and choosers of speech repression will be. What happens to censorship theorists' extraordinary assumptions of trust when self-interest and public interest collide where it counts the most?

Competing publics not only elect the politicians who make the censorship laws. They apply important political pressure that can effectively influence enforcement decisions. Whether, how, when, where, or which hate laws are enforced may often be more a function of such pressure than of the gravity of the social injury threatened. In apolitical hate censorship theory, politics may be a *non sequitur*, but in censorship practice it is central. There are winners and there are losers. Moreover, what is true for the politics of freedom of expression is no less true for the politics of its repression. Those with more political clout have better access to and influence over the decision-making process than those with less. Social discontent in a self-governing polity may be everybody's business. But whether or how it is publicly expressed is more the business of those with the power to silence – or to effectively threaten it. The winners are not necessarily those social activists who are 'right' but those who have the ear of the censors or enjoy the fear of their opponents.

Wise and well-intentioned hate censors there may be. But this is not enough. There must also be disinterested hate censors. Competing publics, however, cannot be disinterested publics. Competing politicians cannot be disinterested public servants.[96] Even wise and well-intentioned politicians, if they are to remain in office, must answer to self-interested publics applying self-serving political pressure, not just wise and fair publics applying pressure in the public interest. And that is the problem. To censor is one thing. To legally 'fix' the socially right and politically judicious censorship wanted and expected by trusting censorship theorists is not the same thing. Censorship purpose and censorship process may be indistinguishable in hate censorship theory but not in hate censorship practice.

In the end, who is muzzled may depend less on social right than on political, economic, even physical might – the very things hate censorship theorists distrust or condemn most.[97] Might and right may sometimes coincide, but they cannot be 'fixed' by law to do so. In a system premised on occasional governing majorities and changing social agendas, the self-interested and the self-serving can no more be denied social or political clout than the disinterested and the public serving can be granted a monopoly of it. Where conflicting social values and political interests compete for the censors' attention and protection, self-interested and self-serving politics of hate speech repression is likely to be the order of the day, not the exception. Consider the politics of repression of hate expression in the context of animosities between Serbs and Croats, religious fundamentalists and secular humanists, Arabs and Jews, Marxists and Fascists, gays and straights, feminists and traditionalists, Muslims and Christians.

In October 2000, following violent clashes in the Middle East, Arab demonstrators took to the streets in major Canadian cities. After reports that demonstrators had openly shouted 'death to the Jews,' urged on by Rashad Saleh, president of Palestine House, who compared Prime Minister Ehud Barak of Israel to Hitler, a scathing editorial appeared in the *Canadian Jewish News*. The piece condemned the demonstrations as a 'blood-lusting' display of 'hatred' and pointed an accusing finger at, among others, the Liberal government of Jean Chrétien.[98] The editorial suggested that the Government of Canada, succumbing to Arab pressure, had been complicit in the promotion of hate against Canadian Jews by voting to support UN Resolution 1322, a one-sided resolution that condemned Israel for the upsurge in violence in the Middle East. Even officially entrusted and legally empowered guardians of the public mind at the highest levels of public responsibility, it seems, cannot be trusted to be free from conflicts of interest in the politics of hate or the politicking of its repression.[99] How, then, can one trust those rival minority guardians of public right who are more answerable to their own local constituencies than to the general welfare? In the politics of public silencing, on important matters worth arguing about, there are no such things as ideologically disinterested censors, politically untainted trusts, or fixed trustees of the public good.

5 Fixability

A fifth problem in trusting the censors and their censorship is the 'unfixability' of all the problems discussed previously. I call censors' implicit assumptions to the contrary the 'fixability fallacy.'

Even in ordinary civil disputes, inability to correct even one of these problems would taint the integrity of the whole process. Imagine inability to correct of all of them! Hate censorship theorists would be the first to condemn trust in such a process as errantly irrational. But when it comes to hate censorship, no problem seems too great for proponents of hate censorship to overlook.

Fixability here is understood in two ways: one refers to correcting these problems; the other refers to guaranteeing that correction indefinitely into the future. Trust in hate censorship depends on both. When hate censorship theorists accord hate censorship its exceptional status of trust they speak not only to the present but also, far more importantly, to the future. Eradication, not respite from hate, is the goal.[100] The battle against hate is not to be won only to be later lost. Trust now, suspect later, is not what censors have in mind. Found truths and fixed meanings are about final triumphs, not transient ones. The dilemma, however, is that censorship's problems of trust cannot be 'fixed' (correction assured) for the future for the same reason that they cannot be 'fixed' (corrected) for the present – they are intrinsic. Trustworthy hate censorship would be publicly ascertainable, politically bounded, competently determined, discursively chill-free, and publicly accountable, not just for now but indefinitely. However, such censorship is not possible. A censorship free from political and social problems of application would be a censorship free of politics and problems. If this were possible, there would be no need for it in the first place. Society would already be free from intolerance, division, prejudice, ignorance, and injustice.

The fixability fallacy underscores a fundamental self-contradiction in the censorship position. It is odd that a cause premised on occasional governing majorities and changing social agendas could hold to its underlying assumptions. It is odder still for a cause that enlists a constitutionally entrenched charter of rights in its vision of the public good. As Madam Justice Beverley McLachlin, dissenting in *Keegstra*, said, '[t]o justify an invasion of a constitutional right on the ground that the public authorities can be trusted not to violate it unduly is to undermine the very premise upon which the *Charter* is predicated.'[101] To trust that the invasion will be judicious not just for now but indefinitely is to expect fixed not fluid self-government. If censorship 'misfirings,' spotlighted in this chapter, could happen in relatively left-friendly hate silencing climates in the recent past, what might one expect in more right-friendly hate silencing climates in the future? It is not only that we are required to trust current censoring majorities or influential minorities. We are also asked to trust future censoring majorities or influential minorities, rival victim groups, changing officialdom, and self- and profit-regarding information entrepreneurs. Even the least trustworthy have to be trusted – racist victimizers turned 'victim,' such as Malcolm Ross, who successfully sued cartoonist Beutel for depicting him as a Nazi. Anyone, and therefore everyone, can potentially be hate censors of the future – in a polity that trusts such censorship. Given a system of occasional governing majorities and changing social agendas – or, worse, a system as fundamentally structurally flawed as censorship theorists say the current one is – how can such extraordinary trust be justified?

History suggests it is not impossible to fix the trustees and the censorship expected at least for a time, perhaps a considerable time. But this would require fixing the assurances, definitions, defences, and defenders of current censorship. It would require censorship by political dictatorship, not by occasional governing majorities. In the former Soviet Union, censor, victim, victimizer, and content were fixed. Social politics

– its conflicts, divisions, and discords – was frozen in time. Publics had no difficulty knowing who were the trustees of the public good, what that trust embraced, and how it would be officially discharged. Self-appointed trustees of the public mind could be counted on to squelch all public expressions of social division, discord, and inegalitarian consciousness. Found truths, fixed meanings, and final triumphs were assured. But even Communism could not freeze the trustees or the system of trusteeship forever. Politics could only be put 'on ice.' Division, ignorance, and intolerance, masked and postponed by repression of public speech, festered and grew below the surface in the meantime, eventually exploding in more virulent and volatile form and in less propitious climates of public tolerance. The trusteeship dilemma of fixing social right illustrates well hate censors' politics of self-contradiction and self-defeat.

Conclusion

Hate speech law is an extraordinary remedy for a democracy in ordinary times. But hate, progressive censorship theorists argue, is no ordinary evil, and its repression no ordinary cause. Hate censorship, in this view, is an exception to what is ordinarily true. It is an extraordinary cause in a deficient system of choice, and it can be trusted to be limited and to serve the public interest as socially intended. But the case for extraordinary trust is precisely where hate censorship falls short.

How can censorship theorists trust in a legal prescription that cannot assure the competence of its prime enforcers, the integrity of their work, their independence from politically self-interested or self-serving publics, the social content of their repressions or political choice of victims – and that cannot hold them to timely account or avert the chilling effect of their labour? Hate censorship theorists say they neither ask for nor expect blind trust. But then what do they base their trust on – in a system that they intensely distrust? The reason for hate censorship is to assure indefinitely by law what censorship theorists say freedom of speech can only risk continuously by politics and public discourse – found truths, fixed meanings, and final triumphs on matters integral to the public well-being. But how can it guarantee for the 'foreseeable' future (much less for the 'unforeseeable' one) what it cannot 'fix' as needed and intended even for the present?

The law may artificially limit and fix hate propaganda by content, victim, and victimizer. But it cannot legally 'fix' the political nature of its subject matter or assure the 'right' politics of its repression. Either too much speech and too many speakers will be put at risk of being silenced or not the 'right' ones or enough of the 'right' ones will be quieted. Narrow and socially exclusive hate censorship inescapably lends itself to arbitrary, capricious, or politically self-serving applications in terms of the social messengers and public meanings it selects for repression or permits for expression, depending on prevailing social times and evolving political climates. But broad and socially inclusive hate censorship lends itself to political applications that are speech suffocating, victim patronizing, and injury trivializing, and is worse still.

These dilemmas may not be the *law* of hate censorship, as hate censorship theorists see it. But they are the politics of hate speech repression, as they fail to see it. Hate censorship is a legal 'answer' to an inescapably and intractably *political* problem – economistically grounded perspectives and their reductionist 'social character' approaches to freedom of speech notwithstanding. In the end, the case for extraordinary trust fails because it makes a legal promise it cannot politically keep. No official assurances of found truths, fixed meanings, and final triumphs on matters of society and polity worth arguing about can promise to be only publicly serving and not, over time, increasingly self-serving.

5

The Political Dilemma, Part II

The 'Slippery Slope'

History that has gone by can be judged. History that has still to be made and is yet to unfold cannot be. Contemplating the future is not risk free. There are many unforeseeables. Yet contemplation must avoid speculation. Speculation is 'unscholarly.' The line between speculation and scholarship is a difficult tightrope to walk. But in the debate over hate propaganda law, contemplating the future is unavoidable. Repressing hate is all about prevention, and prevention is all about the future. Opponents of hate censorship can no more avoid contemplating the future than proponents of hate censorship can. Over time, how is hate censorship likely to play out? Should we expect more or less intrusive censorship? Is hate censorship, once established, ever abandoned? What legacies might be left behind if or when it is abandoned? What processes are at work here? What drives them and how are they driven? If we are to understand not simply where we currently are with hate censorship but where we may be headed and why, it is important to address these questions. That is the focus of this chapter.

Censorship theorists' extraordinary trust in what they would otherwise suspect depends on two related assumptions: that the hate censorship practised will be the socially 'right' censorship; and that hate censorship is a politically limitable, stable, discursive balance. Chapter 4 focused on why the first assumption is most problematic. It can only be made if the law of hate silencing is stripped of the politics and hidden problems of hate silencing. The present chapter focuses on why the second assumption is also problematic. It can only be made if the discursive tendencies of hate silencing over an extended period of time are discounted. The politics of public silencing of intolerance is not just an ongoing process. It is also a slippery process – and a slippery politics.

Rather than affirm found truths, safeguard 'right' social meanings, and secure final public triumphs, as hate censors in Canada intend, hate censorship risks slipping, over time, into more rather than less corrosive public silencing in censors' attempts to do so.

The 'slippery slope' is a metaphor coined by free speech advocates to describe this risk. It describes a discursive tendency. It is not a prophecy. Social bumps, political detours, legal forks, and unforeseen public turns along the road of hate silencing may be expected.[1] Periodic pauses, even complete abandonment of silencing, are possible. There is nothing inevitable here. It is not necessarily the case that once the public silencing journey begins, there is no turning back. But turning back is apt to get harder before it can get easier as the journey progresses. That is a paradox of the slippery slope of hate silencing. The fears that drive it tend to be self-realizing, and the suppressions to satisfy them self-justifying. Over time, hate censors can no more warrant the politically stable and limited silencing balance expected than they can assure the right social answer wanted – one that can be fixed not just to serve only the public interest but also to serve it only as originally intended.

The slippery slope is a paradox in more ways than one. On the one hand, hate silencing is vulnerable to slippage because it tends to feed on itself – to the progressive detriment of the cause of repression. On the other hand, it is precisely this slippage that can grow the 'natural' seeds for its own self-correction. Part I of this chapter ferrets out the complex mix that can drive this tendency to slip, from four intersecting perspectives on the dilemma. Part II explores the dynamics of possible self-correction and the deleterious social legacies nourished by slippage if it is not arrested in good time.

Hate censorship law is hardly the only risk factor in the pressures for discursive decline in Canada. But it is a crucial officially legitimizing moral vehicle, spreading its silencing message into otherwise ordinary discursive contexts, as we shall see further in this and following chapters. It is a seminal and symbolic component of a comparatively seamless politico-legal culture of silencing (see the introduction), squeezing freedom of public discourse on public matters in Canada from diverse directions. The following discussion of its driving dynamics and possible social legacies should be understood in this larger context.

I The Drive to Slide

The slippery slope defies simple cause-and-effect explanations. It is a function of a complex web of dynamically interacting forces, contingent social and political factors, proactive and non-active participants, and fluid human perceptions.[2] It is both cause and effect in comparative symbiotic harmony. Its distinguishing feature is a paradox. Perceptions of the need for hate censorship tend not to reflect the reality of its work. But they shape it none the less – to the advantage of the 'need' and the detriment of the cause of repression.

1 Rival Groups and the Conduct of Silencing

I) THE CLUB OF SOCIAL CENSORSHIP RIVALRY

'Hate censor,' as used in this book, is a generic term. Those specifically entrusted with legal authority to silence or prevent hate are official hate censors. They can be political appointees,[3] administrative officials, censorship boards, or elected politicians and their enforcement arms, such as the police, customs, and immigration. But hate censorship does not depend only on official censors, as we have seen, or on silencing after the fact. Self-regarding communications entrepreneurs (print and broadcast) who fear official sanction or seek public favour can unofficially 'pre-censor' – silencing officially disagreeable speech before its expression. Public-regarding semi-official overseers of the public psyche that hold gate-keeping powers or first access to ideas – for example, schools, museums, or library boards – can also silence speech before its expression, in line with official wisdom. And as we saw in chapter 4, in a system premised on occasional governing majorities and changing social agendas most anyone can potentially, and legitimately, become a hate censor. Even more important, anyone can threaten to invoke hate censorship, or call upon its moral authority, in otherwise ordinary public discourse – often equally effectively. Those most likely to do so are rival offended groups.

The political dynamics that drive competitive or rival groups to prefer silencing over discourse are an important factor in making the censorship slope slippery for sliding. What I have called 'social censorship rivalry' elsewhere[4] describes a socially regressive discursive dynamic nourished by hate speech law. Social censorship rivalry can take limited legal censorship and, effectively, make it politically less limited. The distinguishing feature of this dynamic is the 'club' of official silencing – a seductive and infectious moral right and a powerful political implement in the hands of social rivals.

Talk, of course, is not the only kind of communication – silencing is communication also. Hate silencing speaks by doing. What it says is what it does. What it does, however, does not speak well for public discourse. The language of hate silencing in the hands of social rivals is a club that not only chills public discourse but also fuels division and polarizes politics. The politics of absolute victims and absolute victimizers allows for only absolute winners and absolute losers. As Epstein observes, such politics 'gets in the way of people talking with one another across divisions of race, gender, or ethnicity,' making it more difficult to transcend 'tribal loyalties.'[5] In a stable, multicultural democracy such as Canada, the more pressing social divisions are more likely to be rooted in the just causes and the multifaceted internecine squabbles of rival minority groups competing for political ascendancy than in the simplistic untruths of transparent, fringe racists. 'Answers' to these conflicts are socially elusive and politically slippery in the best of conditions. Finding the 'right' ones under the threat of silencing makes them more slippery not less so. Neither actual prosecution nor a favourable judicial decision is needed for the club of silencing to do its dirty divisive politics. The mere threat to wield the legal option can be enough.

In November 1989, a Muslim Student Association film was screened at the University of Toronto. David Satok, chair of the Joint Community Relations Committee of the Jewish Congress, Ontario Region, condemned the film as a 'racist act' for its portrayal of Jews as Christ-killers, conspirators, and controllers of the media and finance. The Jewish Congress asked that the status of the Muslim Student Association, as a recognized campus student organization, be withdrawn. But it did not stop there. Satok 'indicated as well' that the congress had 'informed the anti-hate unit of the police force of Metro and the O.P.P and the Ministry of the Attorney General' to 'ascertain whether the hate provisions of the Criminal Code have been violated.'[6] In April 1997, Jewish students at the University of Toronto tried to shut down a display put up by a Palestinian student group during Arab Culture Week by threatening to have those responsible charged with promoting hate propaganda.[7] The display included the sentence 'the SS were responsible for the majority of German war atrocities, comparable to those committed by the Zionists.' Where threats of campus expulsion or criminal silencing substitute for discourse, retaliation in kind may come to substitute for speech. If the answer to disconcerting speech is counter-speech, may not the preferred answer to the club be the counter-club? The progression from speaking to clubbing is a naturally slippery slope to begin with. Official right to silence hate tends to make it more so, not less.

At the University of Western Ontario, Professor Philippe Rushton, a psychology professor, published an offensive empirical study of highly dubious value on 'the differences between the races.' The Attorney General of Ontario, under pressure from a number of outraged groups, ordered the Ontario Provincial Police to conduct an investigation with a view to prosecuting him under the Criminal Code for promoting hate propaganda. Rushton promptly cancelled a speaking engagement.[8] When the possibility of criminal prosecution proved too problematic for his opponents, Rushton became the target of an official investigation for racism under the Ontario Human Rights Code.[9] From 1991 until 1995, his reputation in tatters, Rushton remained in limbo as to the merits of his case and the legality of his scholarship. As Borovoy writes, '[t]here are no reports that [Rushton] targeted minority students in his classes or behaved insensitively towards them as individuals. It was his scholarship that people found offensive.'[10]

The complaint was finally dropped because the outraged complainants had become unavailable. A decision on the merits of Rushton's claims, exposing the study's deficiencies, was never rendered. There was no need for it. The club had done its job without it. In the battle for the public mind, the message for opponents of the future is clear – clubbing works where talking may fail. Or, consider the 'creative' *quid pro quo* misuse of civil law against prejudice in the Desmond Ali case. Ali had been charged with criminal mischief arising from a school busing dispute. He succeeded in getting charges against him dropped after agreeing to withdraw a complaint to the Ontario Human Rights Commission alleging that the school principal blamed crowding on new immigrants.[11] If threat could be successfully misused as a club to procure favour in this instance, why should it not be self-servingly misused as a club to intimidate (silence) in others?

Clubbing is a proxy legal politics of competing public might substituting for the discursive public politics of communicating social right. Clubbing does not simply get in the way of enlightenment. It gets in the way of *wanting* to enlighten. The outcome of attempts to convince others of the rightness of one's social views can be too uncertain to risk one's political cause, but censorship, or its mere threat, can get results. Persuasion's success is rarely complete – some will always remain unconvinced. The persuader's own position may be put in doubt. Censorship's failures are invisible. Who can know how many remain unconvinced, even opposed, if they are afraid to speak? Disagreement can be socially disturbing, publicly disruptive, and personally offensive.

The silence that results from censorship is publicly soothing, orderly, and comforting. Persuasion is hard. It can be intellectually demanding as well as personally risky. Why should political rivals struggle to talk and risk their cause or their case when they think they can beat each other into submission through silencing and be assured of success? If the club can take the place of education even in the hallowed halls of higher learning, why should it be restrained elsewhere?

The personal costs of legal silencing (time, effort, uncertainty of outcome if legally challenged) may of course be prohibitive. But merely threatening it, or simply calling on its moral authority in otherwise ordinary discursive contexts, is often equally effective and corrosive. Moreover, the hidden costs of silencing can be spread across groups or diffused across society at large. The costs of persuasion are borne directly by the persuader. There are few disincentives to threatening silence 'against hate' but many 'good' reasons to forgo 'talking to hate.' Hate law affords political legitimacy and moral comfort to those who would substitute silencing for convincing. The language of hate silencing refuses to respect its legal limits. Its moral authority is politically transmutable, transcending the cognitively artificial boundaries legally set for it. It is socially seductive and politically infectious, subtly seeping, in one form or another, into otherwise ordinary discursive contexts – changing the tone and texture of public debate, corroding the language of public discourse with the intolerance of its own, conditioning social meanings in chilling or opportunistic ways, and giving succour to parallel cultures of extralegal silencing.

Clubbing opponents into silence risks becoming an ordinary rather than an exceptional feature of democratic discourse – the preferred way of dealing with political disagreement and society's many social ills. Suspicion can take the place of trust, cynicism the place of dialogue, and opportunism the place of conviction. A proactive political culture of rival silencing in place of talk can, in time, promote a passive and deceptive public culture of fear and quiet in place of discourse. What discursive message is sent to the rest of society when even the chief commissioner of the Ontario Human Rights Commission is threatened with an investigation under the hate provisions of the Ontario Human Rights Code – for comparing public funding of faith-based schools to South African apartheid?[12] Hate censorship theorists may dismiss all this, but rival groups cannot and, as their actions show, do not. As Bernie Farber (executive director of the Canadian Jewish Congress,

Ontario Region) himself said, following attempts to prevent *pro*-Israel academic, Daniel Pipes, from speaking at York University, 'If we cannot talk on campus, then where are we as a society?'[13]

It is a paradox of the silencing club that its discursive slipperiness is a self-inflicted dilemma. The more club and counter-club are used, or threatened, the more contending participants often find they 'need' to be used or threatened – to even the score. Clubbing tends to justify itself with every fresh use, feeding on itself. The appetite can grow with each 'successful' hit, polarizing public positions, eating up resistance to the club's future use, consuming what Robert Putnam has called 'social capital.'[14] Clubbing is a function of the political usefulness of the law of the club. Clubbing 'hate into submission' may be socially self-defeating, but its practitioners' fears are self-realizing and their suppressions self-justifying precisely because of it. Its slippery tendencies help explain how legal silencing can, paradoxically, outlive its socially 'useful' life.

II) THE CLUB OF THE CONDUCT OF THE CENSORSHIP DEBATE

On its merits, the case for freedom of speech is theoretically coherent, politically cogent, and, as I shall endeavour to show in chapter 6, pragmatically compelling. None the less, for numerous subtle and complex reasons, it is at a 'persuasive' disadvantage. The politically slippery slope of the rival silencing club is one. The abstract case for legally unfettered public discourse is a second. The club of the conduct of the censorship debate is a related third. These and other factors to be explored in this chapter can make for fertile censorship soil, nudging the language of public discourse along a seductive, slippery slope of silencing. Consider these issues in the matrix of the following dynamics.

First, there is a reductionist and moral asymmetry in arguing the respective cases – the advantage lies with those who would censor. Abstract reasoning in the cause of speech is hard to grasp – its subtle linkages to democracy hard to establish; its intangible public benefits hard to quantify. The case for a 'right to hate' is not self-evident. But opposing hate, like making love, as it were, speaks for itself. Freedom of expression offers choice not results. It cannot promise what censorship promises. Constitutional protection of a discursive right to fight cannot guarantee that the morally just cause will win. Nor that, once won, it cannot later be lost. Even a politically flawless regime of freedom of expression could not guarantee that. Freedom of expression can speak only in terms of political risks, social costs, hidden harms, foregone benefits, unknowing and silent losers, and lesser evils. The public, and censoring social activists, do not want to hear this.[15] The public, especially, want answers; quick fixes not abstract arguments for society's ills. Societally reductionist theorists promise what discursive choice cannot – found truths, fixed meanings, and final triumphs – because they are prepared to politically prejudge and legally pre-fix desired social outcomes. Who can argue with that – at least when it comes to hate? The harms of hate are everywhere obvious. The harms of hate repression 'obviously' are not.

There is a related problem here for freedom of expression. To make the case for expression requires not only much courage and thought but also, for these very reasons, much freedom to fully and fearlessly make that case. Asymmetry in debating advantage produces asymmetry in communication needs. But the conduct of the debate tends to be decided more by those who would silence than by those who would speak. And, as decided by them, it often allows little of either – thought, or the freedom to communicate it. Neither the intrinsic comparative merits of the two cases nor even the comparative persuasiveness of the respective sides in making their case is the primary force driving thinking on hate censorship in Canada today. The driving force can be found in the dynamics of the debate as it is *authoritatively* conducted by those who would and do censor.

The conduct of the debate involves words and may include persuasion but should not be confused with either. Persuasiveness and effectiveness in communicative outcomes are not synonymous. Effectiveness in making the hate censorship case is often more than simply the result of persuasion. It centrally includes pressure. It is important, however, to distinguish here between appropriate and inappropriate pressure. Hyperbole, like that coming from distinguished and influential thinkers such as MacKinnon, is not innocuous.[16] It clouds understanding of the complexities of the balancing issues, making it more difficult to put the brakes on slipping censorship. Such thinking may be misleading, misguided, and myopic. But it can be persuasive – in no small part precisely because of this. A progressively blinkered censorial mindset is taking hold of public discussions on intolerance – one that cannot see, much less see beyond, the limits and limitations of its own politically self-contradictory and socially self-defeating assumptions. If that were all there is to it, however, there could be no objection. After all, freedom of public expression on matters of society and polity worth arguing about centrally includes bad, misleading, or poorly thought-out ideas about freedom of expression itself, even from influential academia. Truth through choice accepts the possibility that bad ideas can, and sometimes do, win out. If censors' success in making more of their case than it is was the only thing driving the slide, no objection on free speech grounds could be made.

The problem of how the debate is conducted is not about how bad ideas, persuasively presented, may drive out good ideas, poorly presented, but about inappropriate conduct. It is about how a legal right to appropriate exclusive social meanings in one context can slip into moralistic assumptions and authoritative misuse of other rights to construct those meanings in other contexts. Social activists who censor do not just silence public expressions of hate. They corrode public discourse on thinking about hate, paralysing judgment and ending argument. The slope is slippery not simply because the *content* of hate is intellectually slippery. It is because the *right* to silence hate is politically slippery. Censors, who have 'found' the truth, not only need not search for it, they need not tolerate those who have not 'found' truth.

The problem here is one of more than just 'speech.' Recourse to shibboleths, sloganeering, shaming, and labelling may and sometimes does constrict the boundaries of considered public discourse.[17] But, in itself, the resort to strong speech, no less than the manipulations of misguided or misleading speech, is par for the course in a meaningful understanding of freedom of expression – one purposed to reflect who we truly are rather than to guarantee that only the right 'are.'[18] It is the *personal* consequences either directly threatened or subtly communicated by such strong language, or actions taken in furtherance of such language, that are the problem – and the driving force behind the slide. Often this is not simply strong *speech,* without more. They are veiled warnings. And what they warn of are *deeds* – injury to livelihoods, reputations, careers, or family for those deviating from the accepted line. Moralistic social slippage can all too easily translate into political and even legal slippage.

Consider the events surrounding the suspension of Professor Matin Yaqzan, a mathematics professor at the University of New Brunswick. Couched, implicitly, in the language of misogyny, a species of hate, they illustrate how legal rights to appropriate exclusively correct social meanings in one way can *slip* into a chilling assumption and misuse of other rights to construct those meanings in another way. Yaqzan was suspended under the university's sexual harassment code for an ill-considered article he authored on date rape. His mistake was to publicly express a most offensive (hateful?) view of women – that a late night invitation to a woman's room was an implicit invitation to sexual intercourse and that to 'promiscuous' women date rape was an 'inconvenience' rather than a 'moral outrage.'[19] When it was pointed out that no female student ever suggested that Yaqzan had, either verbally or physically, behaved improperly towards her, the student union went on a 'fishing expedition,' running ads in the campus newspaper soliciting testimony to the contrary, hoping to justify *ex post facto* the sexual harassment suspension.[20] The teachers' union, which had itself proposed a model sexual harassment code much like the one under which Professor Yaqzan had been suspended, found itself in the awkward position of calling such conduct a 'witch hunt.'[21]

There is a difference between losing one's battle for the public mind and losing one's job, hard-earned reputation – even, possibly, one's liberty – for daring to speak one's mind. Threatening communication – the language of hate silencing – may come packaged in the moralistic garb of tolerance. But when the sheep is unwrapped, it exposes the wolf of deeds hiding within. For non-conforming speakers who might not wish to share in the accepted social wisdom on matters in dispute, such communication speaks not of ideas but of acts. The putative speaker ignores the veiled warnings at his or her own risk. When conduct allied with public discourse slips from convincing to compelling and from debating to intimidating, the politics of sliding censorship becomes the practice of a slipping freedom of expression.

Bullying speakers into silence by threats, intimidation, or misuse of laws or codes of conduct designed for other ends is not a good example of the merits of the case for censorship. Nor, in a democratic society premised on freedom of public discourse on public matters, is it a good example of appropriate public communication. Most importantly, it is not a good example of the truer, more enlightened, and meaningful public discourse that progressive censors profess. But it is a good example of hate censorship in political practice. And it is effective – in more ways than one. Such conduct not only chills those who might think to question accepted wisdom; it also sends an ominous message of what can await those who might think to defend their right to do so. Quieting hate works to quiet thinking about quieting hate. The slope between the right to silence and silencing rights is slippery. Understanding its dynamics helps explain how hate speech law can successfully outlive its defensible merits.

2 Censors and Self-justification

A second ingredient making the censorship slope slippery for sliding involves a socially and politically regressive mix – immunity from failure and its demands for accountability. Those who censor hate, or threaten to, may have many reasons. True believers in the cause have one thing in common – an abiding faith that their weapon of choice is for the public good.[22] A preventive weapon is most successful the less it has to be used. The more it needs to be used the less successful it can be said to be. What distinguishes a preventive weapon such as hate propaganda law, however, is neither its success nor its failure, but its ability to justify itself in both. If hate is down, the law is needed, for this shows that the law is working. If hate is up, the law is needed even more. In either case, hate censorship justifies itself. It cannot fail.[23] How can a weapon that cannot fail be held accountable?

The accountability problem with hate censorship is not simply that failure need not be a deterrent to its use. The problem is that failure can be an incentive for more use. It can be an incentive to fail harder. If hate laws do not work as committed theorists want and expect them to, it is not because hate censorship is the wrong answer. It is because there is not enough of it. Failure is a problem of toothless silencing laws or weak-kneed politicians lacking the will to enforce them. The solution is not less censorship but a stronger, bigger, 'better' (and more divisive) silencing club by which social rivals can beat each other into submission. Following Malcolm Ross's successful suit against cartoonist Josh Beutel for depicting Ross as a Nazi, the CJC counsel proposed doing just that – strengthening the club. He recommended amending the Criminal Code so that groups like the CJC could take action against their tormentors directly, without first having to secure the consent of the attorney general.[24] Writes Borovoy, 'Incredibly ... [h]aving so correctly analyzed the problem, the CJC recommends making the situation even worse.'[25] Hate law cannot fail the public. It is the public that fails hate law.

Censoring social activists may stake their case for exceptional trust on a limited hate censorship. But all the while they push for its expansion. Proclaiming a limited law but advocating a more sweeping social and political embrace is not unusual in functionalist or teleological censorship thinking. As Mahoney writes, '[t]he law is not intended to prohibit anything but extreme forms of speech.' But then she says, 'an egalitarian society may be impossible to achieve when the dissemination of racist ideas is permitted ... if true equality is to be achieved between male and female persons, society must guard against misogynist materials.'[26] Self-justification, caught in self-contradiction, is made easy where failure is made impossible. Immunity from failure is a slippery self-propellant. It finds its fullest expression in the kind of public unaccountability that can only come from the moral authority of a law that vitally protects the public psyche – a law of found truths and officially correct meanings. Its slippery dynamics also help explain hate speech law's ability to outlive its claimed socially useful life.

3 The Public, the Politician, and the Paradox

A third ingredient making the slope slippery for sliding incorporates elements of the second. But the deciding discourse-depressing actors are not the same. The problem here is the paradoxical dynamic driving the perceptions of elected or appointed censors. This dynamic mixes dilemmas of failure immunity with the fuel of official political power to resist public accountability. Invariably, hate censorship begins with a call to suppress only transparent racists and marginal extremists.[27] That is how the Cohen Committee got started. But as we saw, particularly in chapter 1, conventional wisdom among influential social activists is that the Cohen Committee got it all wrong.

Hate censorship is an answer to an age-old problem that refuses to go away. Over time, two main public responses are possible. First, the public may demand stronger hate laws, more vigorous enforcement, or both. This would promote sliding. It may well be the most likely public response. Allowing hate 'free reign' hardly seems like a better response to the problem of failure to eradicate it. On the other hand, active public support for hate law is not inevitable. Ordinarily, in a consolidated democracy, mass enthusiasm for any cause is not easy to maintain forever.[28] Of course, fighting hate is not an ordinary cause, and the club of silencing is not an ordinary weapon. It is not inconceivable, however, that the public will lose their enthusiasm for hate censorship. The problem is, active public support for hate law is not necessary for the slope of censorship to be slippery.

Paradoxically, it is not only public enthusiasm that drives hate censorship. It is also faltering public enthusiasm that can itself be grist for the political mill of hate speech repression. The very elitism and distrust of the public that made their cognitive protection necessary in the first place seems corroborated by the public's failure to appreciate the need for their own protection. That failure proves to self-assured guardians of the public psyche what they claimed all along – that in not trusting the public they are right. The more members of the public question the need for the law, the more this shows their need for protection and the more protection it shows they are in need of. For censors who know the public better than the public know themselves, it cannot be that the law of silencing is failing. It is the public who are failing the law.

This is the closed mindset that can drive those with elected or appointed powers of censorship to push against tides of waning public enthusiasm for censorship. It is a function of a threefold mix: the belief of elected or appointed guardians of the public psyche in their own social infallibility; the kind of lack of accountability that can only come from the moral authority of a law vitally protecting the public psyche that cannot fail; and the political power of those occupying high office to hold on to their presumptions and protect their unaccountable assumptions. This mix can be a formidable obstacle standing in the way of changed public sentiments. It can help explain the potential of hate speech law to survive beyond even its politically useful life.

4 The Public, the Politician, and the Hatemonger

A fourth ingredient making hate censorship a slippery slope involves a complex mix of actions and perceptions driving the public, the hate-monger, and elected officials to go where only the hatemonger wants to be. It is a possible dynamic that begins with fear and political favour, but that can turn into something far worse. It is a dynamic that lends itself well to exploitation by the hatemonger, to hate's advantage. This dynamic can reverse waning public enthusiasm for an answer to a problem that refuses to go away.

The dynamic has its roots in the very existence of hate law. The problem is not simply that the longer hate law 'is on the books' the greater the risk that it will be used. The problem is, the longer it is on the books the greater the risk it will be misused or expanded in use. By misused, I mean used for the wrong reasons – for reasons other than its intended public good. By expanded, I mean extended beyond transparent messengers or obvious meanings of intolerance.[29] This dynamic combines a complex mixture of actions, reactions, and re-reactions to promote a regressive political climate that becomes increasingly tolerant of more onerous hate censorship.

One leg of this dynamic triad is the elected official. There is considerable political incentive for elected officials to retain even a counterproductive law with waning public support. Strong incentives exist for partisan political leaders, with discretionary powers of enforcement, to put a popular cause such as the eradication of hate into political play as part of their competitive bid to gain and hold power. This is a function of political opportunism. What politician wants to appear soft on (transparent) racism or sexism? How many want to hang their political credentials on how many hatemongers they did not try to silence?

The second leg of this paradoxical dynamic triad is the hatemonger. The dynamic may begin with the hatemonger's response to actual or threatened repression. But it need not. It may, equally, begin with his reaction to state failure to repress. If there is no law against hate, the hatemonger has no reason to hold his tongue. He can be bold. However, if the law is on the books but not used, he can be more than bold. He can be defiant. He thumbs his nose at the law. He thumbs his nose at hesitant politicians. He thumbs his nose at the public. But that is not all. If the law is on the books but not enforced, he can do something he could not do if there was no hate law. He can claim he is not a hate propagandist. He can legitimize his defiance.

This is where the third leg of the dynamic triad, the public, enters the picture. His defiance shocks the public conscience. His actions dare society to enforce the law. The politicians may resist. But if they do, public shock can turn into public anger. The more defiant the hatemonger becomes, the weaker politicians resisting repression look. Public anger can turn into public fear, then alarm. The mix of defiant racists, weak-looking politicians, and an angry, fearful, and alarmed public are a dangerous brew for political careers. The political incentive to play on public anger and pander to public fears grows. Judicious non-application of the law becomes more difficult. Hatemongers need to be stopped. The slide begins.

Transparent fanatics may be threatened with jail. But transparent fanatics are extremists. Out of sight is not the same as out of mind or the public out of danger. The hatemonger is more apt to become wiser than to give up the fight. One way is to substitute clandestine messages for the impermissible open ones. Another is to substitute hurtful acts such as synagogue desecration, vandalism, arson, bombings, and graffiti for the impermissible hurtful speech. The malevolent messenger and his evil message may simply take on different, more dangerous, forms. Of course, fanatics can and do commit criminal *acts* without censorship. But verbally frustrated ones have more 'reason' to do so and are apt to do more of them clandestinely. Repression of speech gives both more cause and more cover where before there was only opportunity. Events in Canada coinciding with and following hatemonger prosecutions suggest that cause for concern is not unfounded.[30] To the fearful, more hurtful acts are proof of the need for more suppression of hurtful speech. To the feared, more repression of hurtful speech is cause for yet more hurtful acts.[31] Speech repression and hurtful acts tend to feed on and justify each other.[32] All sides may call for less talk and more action.[33] Action calls for reaction, and reaction promotes counter-reaction.

Proactive prosecution can become crisis driven. Fear, suspicion, and cynicism can grow. Politicians can come to have real reason to act. It can become harder to turn back from silencing, to 'cut and run,' than to move 'forward,' to expand or 'strengthen' discursive repression. To cut one's losses may make practical but not political sense. Defying an alarmed public demanding 'action' in the face of racist defiance and growing danger may mean political suicide. Repression myopia may begin to set down firmer roots in both the public's and leaders' consciousness. Blinkered thinking may begin to take the place of wider horizons as the latest hate provocation encourages silencing advocates and discourages discursive ones that argue for alternatives to silencing. Paradoxically, what may have begun as waning public enthusiasm and lapsing enforcement of the law may, by that very combination, work in unexpected and unintended ways to continue and even expand censorship. In the long run, there can be no winners here – except the hatemonger and the cause of hate. The hatemonger cannot hope to succeed nearly as well without a law of hate speech repression as with it.

Regressive dynamics can arise from complex and paradoxical censorial mixes. The socially multifaceted and politically multidimensional dynamics driving public discourse down a slippery slope, actual and tendentious, explored in this section, help explain how legal silencing of hate can outlive its own 'useful' life – moral, social, and political.

II Changing Course: The Political Dynamics of Self-correction and the Legacies of Censorship's Slide

There is, however, nothing inevitable in these scenarios. These dynamics speak of various discursive tendencies over a period of time, not prophecies. Turning back from public silencing is not impossible. Discursively tolerant rival elites exist. Visionaries from the left, centre, and right may come together, courageously locking arms across the political divide, to reject legal silencing of socially disconcerting public discourse.

But one should not count on this happening. Unlike silencing hate, fighting for the right to express it openly is rarely personally rewarding and even less politically seductive.

Hate censorship's self-contradictions and self-defeats may well need first to take their 'natural' discursively corrosive course – to grow worse – before turning back is possible. That, as I argue below, is both reason to despair and reason to hope. The way in which such a turning back might occur and the shape and form it might take if or when it comes are discussed in the next two subsections.

1 The Political Dynamics of Self-correction

Slippage and slide contain the seeds of their own self-correction. A turning back can come from within the very dynamics of hate censorship itself. Public attitudes to hate speech repression in a self-governing polity such as Canada play a crucial role in censorship's ability to slide. Over time, public attitudes can play an equally critical role for reversing that slide. To understand how and why, it is helpful to elicit the reasons why they have not yet done so. Theories concerning public mobilization developed by public policy economists can be very helpful here.[34] These are broad theories helping to explain indicia for public mobilization generally and are not particular to censorship. However, they can broaden our understanding not only about why hate speech censorship can continue, even expand, despite socially invasive and politically insidious costs, but also how and why a reversal of that expansion may be possible.

Where the aggregate social and political costs to society of a public policy that is meant to benefit the public at large outweigh its aggregate social and political benefits, it would be self-contradictory and self-defeating for society to continue to pursue the policy. Yet political self-contradiction and social self-defeat do not seem to deter censors or rouse significant public outcry against censorship.[35] On the contrary, failure not just 'success' in silencing hate can propel hate censorship forward. This is the perplexing paradox of the slippery slope. Against a morally popular cause, the public cannot be expected to act as they should when they cannot connect public policy to any tangible personal loss. While beneficiaries of silencing are focused and well organized and the rewards are clear and immediate, the social and political costs to society are abstract, invisible, or distant and the losers are scattered, disorganized, unpopular, or simply unknowing and silent. As long as this 'disconnect' between benefits and costs remains, public mobilization is likely to be crippled. For now, this is the situation in Canada.

Politically, the social reach of hate censorship law may be growing, but 'officially' and 'legally' it is still relatively circumspect – to the chagrin of progressive censors. Current conditions bar mobilization against hate law primarily for two reasons. First, the public's awareness of public injury is not uniform because the costs of the repression of public expression are not uniformly felt. Marginal hatemongers are popular targets. But their opposition to the law is hardly public cause for abandoning it. It is more 'cause' for expanding it.[36] Second, the costs of *fighting* repression are not uniformly felt. Controversial speakers may well be personally more affected than the general public, and the risk of loss of their speech, many would agree, is not without social or political costs. Their opposition to the law might well be cause for reconsideration – but they are not quite the fuel for public mobilization that they seem. While they may be Canada's 'knowing' losers, there is much standing in the way of their being vocal and visible ones.

Openly controversial speakers or those advocating on their behalf are likely to be few and far between in an already discourse-depressed polity (see the introduction and chapters 1 and 2). Moreover, muckrakers bucking popular beliefs or standing up to conventional elite wisdom are more apt to be seen by the public as self-serving than publicly serving. Free speech advocates with a social conscience are not keen to risk charges of guilt by association – such as accusations of promoting racism[37] or, worse, such accusation's namesake (racist), levelled at the disagreeable by the suspicious. Personal costs of combating repression of expression, such as this, may not deter the true racist from speaking out for freedom of speech, but they are particularly devastating to the controversial speaker of conscience. Fear of speaking out is, of course, to be expected in any social climate of discursive intolerance. But when the subject is 'hate' and the climate is reinforced by threat of legal sanction or personal intimidation (see Part I above), even, or especially, the provocateur of conscience may be hesitant to challenge the societally deleterious but publicly soothing status quo. The most significant potential losers – future generations – have no voice of their own. Where connecting policy to loss counts most, the 'critical mass' needed for mobilization is most disconnected.

The public at large currently have little if any incentive to act against hate censorship of their own accord. Personally untouched by the social and political costs of repression, they remain scattered, unknowing, and silent losers. Public injury is diffuse and distant and the political case against it abstract. Publics fearful of risking existing social stability, good reputations, or tangible personal benefits that go to those who toe the official line are hardly likely to mobilize *en masse* for the right of others to 'speak hate.' Over time, cultural acclimatization to hate silencing tends to reinforce the public's sense of 'need' for the law and their resistance to its removal. The direct beneficiaries of hate law have no such problems in mobilizing for the right to silence. As favoured winners, they are not afraid, silent, invisible, or unknowing. The benefits to them are focused and tangible; their cause is just and popular; and their voices are organized and loud. In short, where the social and political costs of the hate law are scattered across time, space, and disconnected publics – invisible, intangible, thinly spread among many silent, afraid, or unknowing losers – the sense of concentrated public hurt required for public mobilization is unlikely to materialize. Public mobilization against hate censorship is asymmetrical. The forces of hate censorship hold a clear advantage over the forces of free speech.

But the advantage may not last. The imbalance against mobilization may inhere for a time, perhaps a long time, but be ultimately temporary none the less. Censorship's mobilization advantage over speech depends in very large measure on maintenance of a more or less *limited* public censorship. Failure to connect loss to policy depends on publics who do not see themselves as potential losers. If hate law is costly only to racists, ideologues, and idealists, why oppose it? Hate censorship can continue as a social and political failure – but an invisible and limited failure. This, by itself, would present an insurmountable obstacle to mobilization against it. The dilemma for hate censors and the paradox of hate censorship is that hate censorship is not easily limited or limitable.

Found truths, fixed meanings, and final triumphs on divisive issues of society and polity are not ideas about social progress and political democracy that lend themselves well to self-limits. A cause that is committed to the eradication of hate cannot be expected to resist the temptation to expand its repressive grasp to include an expanding list of offending publics and offensive meanings. Devout believers may preach limits but have exceptional difficulty practising what they preach. For reasons explored above, hate silencing is a slippery politics that subtly, slowly, and seductively works to fuel its own public expansion.

It is, paradoxically, these very tendencies towards slippage that can, over time, make it increasingly difficult to continue the policy of repression unchallenged. Politically exposed politicians tempted to exploit crises, event-driven censorship creating its own crises, the need to strengthen an ineffective law either to satisfy public frustrations or to counteract dwindling public support – all put more of the public at risk of being censured or censored. As Sniderman and colleagues observe, '[i]t is racists – or, perhaps more accurately, people charged with being racist, a potentially enormous group because it is ill-defined – whose basic rights are now subject to public challenge.'[38] Publics previously untouched by censorship who suddenly find themselves potential targets rather than simply protected subjects may begin to see more clearly the connection between policy and loss.

If enough of the public, though previously indisposed to identify with the targets of censorship, come to associate their own right to speak their mind with that of the racist to speak his mind, the stage may be ripe for public mobilization against censorship. Such associations are more apt to be made if repression of intolerant expression is felt to be personally invasive by touching the lives of the public in their daily routines – work, education, worship, leisure, or entertainment.[39] Previously unorganized, unknowing, or silent losers may become more knowing, less silent, and more organized objectors. The slippery slope of hate censorship is a dual paradox. Censors nourish the resentments to public silencing that they feed on to thrive.[40] The seeds of correction may be found in the very dynamics of the slide.

The possibility for correction, however, is no assurance that change, much less change for the better, will occur. The reach of official silencing must be more widely targeted in Canada, its hurt far more deeply publicly felt than it currently is, to form the 'critical mass' needed for change. Even then, dissenting elites must still be sufficiently moved to lead and opponents of change sufficiently weak to not block their progress. The public stage may be ripe for change but change, itself, may be checked. Or, it may exist in embryo but languish inactive indefinitely. A publicly driven turning back from censorship, if it is to occur, may well take several generations and many forms.

2 Political Backlash and Its Legacies

If the seeds of correction are likely to be found in the very dynamics of the slide, so too are the problems. The discursive conditions repression promotes must be bad enough to provoke mobilization against it but not bad enough to irretrievably injure the democratic quality of the mobilization it provokes. The 'dialectics' of the slippery slope, however, tend not to be evolutionary, as true dialectics should be.[41] The 'natural' end of progressive hate censorship is likely to leave society and democracy in a more fragile state of development than would be the case without such censorship.[42] An end belatedly disgorged from within the bowels of distended political self-contradiction and social self-defeat may not be the socially timely one needed or politically visionary one expected. The most likely outcome of a public surfeit of hate censorship is public disdain for the *cause* of hate censorship and not simply public disdain for the *club* of hate censorship.

Proactive progressive public silencing attempts to freeze politics into the desired forms. But it also tends to produce a politics it would rather freeze out. The more it tries to fix its desired politics, the more it tends to produce a backlash against the politics it imposes. Even the former Communist countries, in the end, could not freeze out dissentient backlash. Backlash against censorship works for both good and ill. It may break the back of sliding censorship, and that is good. But bad accompanies the good. The very suspicion, distrust, and resentment of public censorship that is *politically* good for the cause of self-government is *socially* bad for the cause against intolerance and ignorance and therefore that same self-government.

Backlash often begins with indifference that slips into resentment. When the public's fear for their own freedom to speak begins to prevail over their fear of hate or identification with the cause of rooting it out, resentment becomes the stuff of future change. If almost everyone is labelled 'guilty as suspected' because almost everything done or said can be interpreted as racism, sexism, homophobia, or xenophobia, then the view may grow (first privately) that perhaps these things are not so bad after all. Progressive censors seek deeper public appreciation of the evil of prejudice, but may find instead that the public price of censorial distention is dilution and trivialization of the cause against it.[43]

The backlash may be openly hostile. But it need not be. It can equally be 'chilled.' Bigotry can hide in fear, dishonesty, and self-righteous opportunism. The backlash may even have elements of both – different people expressing their fears and prejudices in different ways. Chilled backlash is less visible. Resentment, suspicion, and fear may be hidden beneath a deceptive public façade of tolerance and posturing. It is safer that way. That would seem to be the Canadian way. Canadians are less keen than Americans to risk open confrontation.[44] Chilled backlash is harder to recognize and harder to address than open hostility. Chilled backlashers are more likely to be deficient in self-knowledge and to hide from themselves and from others behind bigotry's self-denials than are open, exposed, and challenged ones.[45] Prejudice expressed in the form of chilled backlash may be self-comforting to the bigot and seem less threatening to society than open expressions of hostility, but it is socially more pernicious and can be politically more insidious.

Distrust, cynicism, and suspicion among social rivals are never a good thing. But they are especially bad in times of social crisis and political turmoil – the very conditions that may well describe the backlash-produced end of censorship. Community trust, or 'social capital,' as Robert Putnam has called it, is a current investment in future goodwill – that reservoir of community comity that sustains democracy in times of crisis.[46] Social capital cannot be cultivated by silencing or nurtured in crisis. It needs to be fostered by open and honest[47] public discourse during times of relative social harmony and political calm, for use in times of crisis. The multifaceted slippery politics of the club of hate censorship can contaminate this reservoir. Cynicism, suspicion, and distrust occasioned by political backlash deplete the social capital that society needs to draw on when it is most vulnerable – during bad times.

A backlash against hate censorship may, therefore, not be the end of censorship. It may only be the beginning – a calm before a worse storm to come. The censorship cycle may start anew, but from a backlash-tainted beginning.[48] Or the downward spiral may be halted. Conditions ripe for reversal can give courageous leaders and visionary elites a window of opportunity to harness public disillusionment with silencing to rebuild bridges of community trust and social understanding. Equally, however, opportunistic politicians, frustrated rival publics, and alarmist leaders aided by myopic theorists may use censorship's legacies of suspicion, cynicism, distrust, and opportunism to introduce a new and more onerous public censorship. This, too, is a possible legacy of backlash.

Conclusion

Hate censorship in politically consolidated representative democracies is a troubling paradox within a paradox. On the one hand, the perceived need for it may not reflect the reality of its work, but can shape it none the less, to the advantage of the 'need' and the detriment of the cause. Repression of expression can continue, even expand, in the face of political self-contradiction and social self-defeat. Failure need not curb the appetite for silencing. On the contrary, failure can feed it.

Silencing intolerance is a slippery slope. The moral authority of hate silencing is politically transmutable, transcending the cognitively artificial legal boundaries set for it. Its legitimating language is politically infectious and socially seductive, subtly seeping, in one form or another, into otherwise ordinary discursive contexts. It can erode the tone and texture of more honest public debate, corroding the language of public discourse with the intolerance of its own, conditioning public meanings in chilling or opportunistic ways, and giving succour to parallel cultures of extralegal silencing. Hate censorship is a self-realizing, self-justifying dilemma.

On the other hand, it is a dilemma that can sow the seeds of its own demise. Germination, however, is not inevitable. Censorship expansion, first, is apt to be the price of later contraction. Flowering may well depend on repression first taking its natural slippery course. Public frustration with and resentment of hate silencing must first grow and attain a 'critical mass' before they can coalesce into a broad but concentrated sense of public hurt that is ripe to effect discursive change. But by that time considerable injury may already have been done to society and polity. Public discourse freed from the shackles of public silencing is apt to be tainted and adulterated by the political backlash impelling the liberation.

Turning back is better than not turning back. But social progress without legal repression of disconcerting public expression in the first place is preferable to both. The alternative to turning back, continuing on, is the worst. The longer the club of silencing holds unsettling public discourse at bay – the more often, widely, or vigorously it is used or threatened in place of debate and dialogue – the harder it becomes for society to extricate itself from censorship's corrosive social-capital-depleting legacies – suspicion, cynicism, distrust, ignorance, intolerance, and opportunism. Openness alone can expose ignorance, dispel suspicion, and allay cynicism. Censorship invites them even when there are no secrets. Whether society can turn back is, therefore, not the only issue to consider. The timing of that turn is also critical.

The paradoxes of the slippery slope help explain why relinquishing the right to silence hate is so very difficult, why its political expansion is so hard to resist, and why its subtly corrosive legacies are so hard to recognize and avert in *good* time.

6

The Pragmatic Dilemma:

Hate Censorship That 'Works'

Politics contextualize the dilemma of hate repression. Politics is about the 'how' of silencing hate. But the 'how' of silencing hate is more than just politics. It is also a practical question. It is about not just what is or might be but also what can and cannot be. Defensible hate censorship needs to do two things. First, it must be *effective*. Second, it must be *successful*. Proponents of hate law use the two concepts interchangeably, but they are not interchangeable. Effective hate censorship would fully silence the message of intolerance. Successful hate censorship would further the deeper social goals of repression in the democratic context expected by censorship theorists. Hate law in Canada does neither. Nor can it do both. It cannot because effective silencing *and* successful promotion of the causes of repression are mutually exclusive. The more effective hate censorship is, the less successful it becomes. Hate propaganda law is fatally flawed at the point where censorship theory meets censorship practice.

This dilemma is not a problem of lack of social or political will in silencing intolerance. It resides in the very nature and limitations of hate censorship itself. This is, singularly, the most devastating blow to hate silencing law in Canada. It is 'pragmatic testimony' to the theoretical deficiencies and political and social self-contradictions in the censorship case explored in chapters 2 to 5. The dilemma of hate censorship is not that it is off balance as currently practised. The dilemma is that it cannot be practised any other way. It is irresolvably off balance because it is intrinsically self-defeating.

1 How Prosecution Misappropriates Discursive Public Conflict and Misshapes Public Perceptions to the Detriment of the Cause of Repression[1]

'The prosecution of hatemongers,' writes Manuel Prutschi, 'is the kind of dramatic action that meets head-on the concerns of victimized communities and helps keep our multicultural society intact.'[2] Experience with criminal prosecution of hatemongers in Canada, however, suggests quite the opposite. Criminal trials have several purposes.[3] They include general and specific deterrence, rehabilitation, healing or catharsis, retribution/justice (punishment), moral denunciation, and public education.[4] These are generic to all criminal trials. Goals often conflict. Trade-offs cannot be avoided. Rehabilitation and retribution or justice may conflict. More satisfaction of one goal may mean less satisfaction of another. But hate propaganda trials are not ordinary criminal trials. They present additional and unique problems.

Victory is apt to come at the cost of the deeper social and political values repression is intended to protect and promote in virtually every purposive area of criminal justice. Rehabilitation is a non-issue in a hate trial. Hate trials do not rehabilitate hatemongers.[5] On the other side, victim healing is apt to be more wounding than winning. Hate trials repunish the victims more than they punish their tormentors. Holocaust deniers end up feeling more important while their victims have ended up feeling even more emotionally bruised.[6] Even specific deterrence[7] has proved ineffective. Determined hatemongers do not just go away. They find other socially more pernicious and politically more problematic ways to get their message across (some of which I outline below). General deterrence is unlikely to be effective. Allies predisposed to make common cause with the unrepentant hatemonger are unlikely to be deterred from doing so by fear of prosecution. Instead, they too find 'better' ways to do so. Fear promotes opportunism.

The most important cost of a hate trial is the unintended cost to its most important purpose – moral denunciation and public education. The public is to think less of the message and the messenger of intolerance with prosecution than without prosecution. This is not just one more function of a hate trial but its *sine qua non*. It is *the* test of success. If it fails in this, all other purposes of prosecution come to naught. But, on balance, prosecution tends to be more hurtful than helpful to the state because it is more helpful than hurtful to the hatemonger. Given the divergence between the actual trial experience and what censors need and expect from a trial, there is no compelling reason to think that publics predisposed to think like the hatemonger are less likely to do so as a result of criminal prosecution,[8] nor that those not predisposed to do so are more likely to become solidified in their indisposition, nor that those who are unsure what to think will become 'more sure' to think what hate censors want them to think. Silencing the message of the hatemonger is the measure of censorship's effectiveness. Promoting right public thinking is the deciding measure of its success. Hate propaganda trials tend to fail themselves on both counts.

Publicity is key here. Censorship advocates argue that the free speech position is self-contradictory. On the one hand, opponents of censorship celebrate publicity: 'Let the hatemonger speak and he will expose himself for what he truly is.' On the other hand, they abjure publicity: 'Don't try him. Prosecution will just give him more publicity.' Framing the issue this way is terribly misleading. In either case, with or without prosecution, the hatemonger will stir up publicity. The question is not *whether* there is publicity but *what kind.* Is the publicity that filters through the medium of prosecution and trial better or worse for the cause against hate, ignorance, and prejudice than publicity without such prosecution and trial? The issue of publicity, in this case, is a comparative question, suggesting a qualitative answer.

To some degree, all criminal trials are a 'kind of public theatre in the round.'[9] But in ordinary criminal trials the theatre is quite different from that in hatemonger trials. Hatemonger trials are 'public show' trials *par excellence.*[10] But they are not just public show trials by design of the state but also by design of the hatemonger.[11] On balance, three things determine which side shows to better advantage: what each side needs to show; whom they must convince; and from where each side started.

The central problem for the state is that the 'show' is asymmetrical – it works to the comparative advantage of the hatemonger. Denunciation of this sort in a democracy depends on *educating* not just *notifying* the public.[12] This requires knowing publics not just 'nodding' ones.[13] In contrast, the hatemonger needs only to show his 'persecution' to deflect public attention from the hateful meaning of his message. The discursive forum may be legal, but the contest is supremely political. The prize is the public mind. For both sides, success hangs in the political balance. This, more than mere conviction for the state (or acquittal for the hatemonger), is the deciding test of censorship's success.[14]

In this battle, the public at large is important – but all its members are not equally important. Preaching to the converted cannot be the real test of the success of a hate trial.[15] Those more in need of cognitive protection – the impressionable, the uncertain, the latent doubters, the subconscious racists – are more vulnerable to being misled by a bad state show and are therefore more important. They are the swing voters. The courts may decide guilt or innocence. But it is the impact of trial on the thinking of the swing voters, not the decision of the court, that 'decides' whether the trial was a relative success or failure. It is the public mind, not the Supreme Court of Canada, that is the final court of appeal. It is the public who must be won over. But trial publicity is a two-edged sword, and unfortunately the hatemonger has the sharper edge. Before prosecution, the state in Canada starts the race for the public mind far ahead of marginal hatemongers and their transparently malevolent meanings. But it is apt to finish less far ahead than it likely would have without prosecution.

Prosecution of hate speech removes important discursive public conflict from the public forum and shifts it to the legal forum – appropriating its messages and reshaping their meanings in unintended ways. In focusing on the disconcerting substantive content of hate communication, censorship advocates miss the centrality of this shift in processing to its public meaning.[16] Prosecution-mediated public discourse serves the deeper interests and larger goals of the hatemonger better than it serves those of the state. Its unintended dynamics misshape public meanings of intolerance to the comparative advantage of the hatemonger.

First, defendants' rights and the requirements of due process bestow a kind of moral equivalency and dignity on the hatemonger that lend an aura of legitimacy to intolerant views. The trial forum protects the message of hate in ways that the public forum need not. The criminal trial process in Canada is not intended to be simply or solely a truth-seeking device. It is also designed to protect fundamental rights and safeguard the individual from abuse of powers by the disproportionate might and superior resources of the state. Presumptions of innocence, burdens of proof, legal defences, and rules of evidence are all central in a criminal trial. Due process is as important as the substantive merits of the case. The hatemonger is turned into the 'accused' – the oppressor transformed into the oppressed. In contrast, the public forum of legally unfettered expression need not presume the innocence of the accused, or prove beyond a reasonable doubt each and every element of his offence, his moral turpitude or malevolent intent. It need not give equal time to his defence or equal weight to morally unequal messages for fear of wrongful moral conviction in the forum of free public expression. In short, the public forum of free speech may confront and debate but it need not give procedural and evidentiary 'advantages' that the criminal trial process must accord to the 'defendant.'

Second, in the public forum of free expression, unlike the judicial forum of strict procedure, arguments to establish historical truth or social right are not prone to be side-swiped by accusations of procedural or evidentiary error. Zundel was charged under the 'false statements' section of the Criminal Code,[17] a section that was later held by the Supreme Court of Canada to be unconstitutional.[18] Keegstra was charged and convicted under the hate propaganda section of the Criminal Code. Though the two trials differed in the charges laid and their final result, they none the less illustrate similar problems for public perceptions. In trying the message of determined extremists, there are inescapable problems associated with procedural and evidentiary errors and rights of appeal, regardless of the language of the charge.[19]

If the defendant appeals conviction and succeeds on a procedural or evidentiary point of law, he will claim judicial vindication of his *views* – even though these legal safeguards are designed to protect the rights of criminal defendants generally and not speech defendants in show trials particularly.[20] In error-prone, if not error-driven, criminal trials, an aura of social legitimization may embellish the message of the defendant. If the defendant is granted a retrial because of defects in the first trial, he will claim moral victory and persecution.[21] The message of hate is turned into the message of the 'hated.'[22] The prosecution may feel it has 'no recourse' but to continue prosecution. To accept failure risks giving credibility to the defendant's message. If left in the public forum, both messenger and message could have been more squarely confronted on the merits in a *legally unprotected* clash and collision of viewpoints and emotions. Instead, the defendant, through his counsel, turns the trial process into a tool of lawyerly manipulation and a theatre of moral legitimization fed by evidentiary and procedural errors. Trial is turned into appeal, retrial, or reappeal, and the evil character of the defendant's message is subordinated or altogether lost in the tortuous legal processes required to deny his right to speak.

Third, prosecution shields the message of hate in still another way. Legal forums are specially prepared forums. They are particularly ill-suited for the state's purpose here. They are synthetic and artificial. The hatemonger is carefully groomed, his message rehearsed, and his meaning sanitized of its more unpleasant warts. Legal packaging dresses up the messenger and his meaning, putting the wolf into sheep's clothing. Since, in these things, 'the man' is as important as his message and presentation as significant as substance, an essential element alerting the public to the dangers of his meaning is lost. Hatemongers do not even have to speak to 'baa' at trial.[23] They may avail themselves of lawyers and 'expert' witnesses, more able and presentable than they, who may do so for them.[24] The medium becomes the message.

Fourth, prosecution spotlights inequality of power more than it highlights the threat posed by the hatemonger – to the relative benefit of the repressed. The image of a mighty state quieting a mere individual, the armed versus the unarmed, the weapon against the word, is especially bruising for the cause against intolerance. The defendant is turned into the underdog. If he loses, the underdog becomes the martyr. Suppression is turned into oppression, prosecution into persecution. The hatemonger wins even when he loses; the state loses even when it wins. In putting the speech of determined extremists on trial, the state puts the public interest and the cause against hate, ignorance, and prejudice in a no-win situation.

Fifth, as suggested by the Zundel and Keegstra trials, hate speech prosecutions do not lend themselves well to vindication – of the kind needed and expected by censors – even in the case of patent social and historical truths. The Holocaust may be reducible to legal truth. But the legally disprovable was only part, the less dangerous part, of the overall *political* message of these hatemongers. That message, seemingly given credibility by the very fact of prosecution, was old and clear. Canadian society and polity are in the pockets of an all-powerful Jewish lobby that controls the media, the courts, and the government. What can be better proof of this than the political power to decide who shall have freedom to speak as they think and who shall not – on fundamental matters of society and polity?[25] It is not transparently refutable facts, but these kinds of socially obfuscating political calumnies and their subtly insidious innuendoes and insinuations, broken off and magnified by prosecution, that are apt to *resonate* better with deeper public suspicions or subconscious prejudices. 'Successful' prosecution invites future hatemongers to shield their messages in the legally less prosecutable and play their meanings in the politically more creditable – in short, in the field of better hate resonance. The price of legally removing patently refutable social falsehoods from the public conscience is the elevation and implantation of subtler and socially more pernicious and politically more insidious meanings in their subconscious. The hatemonger could not have asked for more.

Societally reductionist censors want to criminalize and denounce hate, but they end up politicizing and announcing it more.[26] Legal victory is not synonymous with political, much less social, victory.[27] Hate prosecution should present a clearer not a murkier picture of good and evil. But where the defendant's case is so transparently without merit to start with, as is the case with the criminal hatemonger, the advantages offered up for him and his message by the unintended side-shows and by-products of prosecution are a 'plus,' not a 'minus,' for his cause – a political and social 'windfall,' relegitimating the man and resuscitating his message, that he could not get any other way. The lesson of prosecution is that if the hatemonger is 'behind' *before* trial, he is apt to be *less far* behind *after* trial. And, if he is 'ahead' before trial, he will likely be even *farther* ahead after trial. Wherever the legal race to win over vulnerable minds begins, the cause of the hatemonger will likely be farther ahead when it ends than before it began. On balance, prosecution is self-defeating because the public show is asymmetrical.

The risks of speech are the reason for hate censorship. But hate censorship can offer no assurances. Prosecution does nothing to correct systemic deficiencies in structures of public communication or human frailties in making the right choice. On the contrary, it resonates with them. In both defeat and 'success,' political show trials of this kind do more to rehabilitate and legitimate than debilitate the more intractable parts of the messages of intolerance. And they do so in subtle, subconscious, and ancillary ways that are harder for the public to identify and therefore more difficult for the censor to expose, counter, and correct. Censorship supporters readily find racist resonance in the 'dirty' politics of free speech.[28] To look only at the social resonance of hate's open expression is to overlook the worse social resonance in the even dirtier politics of its criminal repression. 'Social character' theorists of freedom of speech, such as Richard Moon, point out that it is not public identification with the *extreme* message itself but extremity's subtle resonance with deeper, subconscious, pre-existing public prejudices that is the real concern in prosecuting marginal hatemongers.[29] If so, should the greater concern not be with a legally mediated politics of public meaning construction that would tend to make this problem worse rather than better?

II Effective *and* Successful Censorship? Mutual Exclusivity and the Four False 'Faults'

Can the failure of official silencing to meet its expectations be attributed to deficiencies in censorial *method* not censorial *merit*? Can hate censorship be made more effective – more able to fully silence the message of intolerance? Can it be made more successful – more able to promote the underlying social causes of repression in the democratic political context premised? Can it be made *both* more effective and more successful? If so, the solution may be not to give up on legal censorship but to find better ways to do it – ways that silence what should be silenced without giving renewed life and legitimacy to what it should not.

The answers to these questions depend on where the locus of the public silencing dilemma is. Is it intrinsic within the very nature and limits of repression of this kind of discursive public conflict? If so, changing the means and methods of repression offers no answer. Or is the problem, as censors contend, everywhere except within hate censorship itself – in a deficient criminal trial process, irresponsible media, deficient coverage or targeting of hate, obstructive opponents, and technological change. If the latter, then society needs to find better ways of censoring – ways that address these problems.

1 Trial

If prosecution fails to meet censors' needs and expectations, is it the fault of a 'slanted' Canadian criminal justice system? 'Under our system of justice,' writes Prutschi, 'a painful lesson our community learned ... is that criminally charging a hatemonger does not automatically lead to *quiet*, immediate conviction and incarceration.'[30]

The adversarial system of the common law has been much criticized even with respect to *ordinary* criminal trials.[31] Protecting the rights of the accused, it is argued, often seems to take precedence over finding the truth and convicting the guilty in a timely fashion. Criminal denunciation is crucial to censors' cause against ignorance, prejudice, and hate. But the adversarial system of criminal denunciation is not a good way to successfully advance the cause; nor is it the only 'legitimate' way. There are different kinds of trial-mediated public discourse in representative democracies. They do not all shape the message and the messenger in the same way.[32]

Would a trial process less respecting of the rights of the accused more effectively silence the speech offender? Would it successfully secure only the desired public message? Asymmetry is intrinsic to hate speech repression – to the advantage of the determined hate messenger. Asymmetry is cause dependent not mode dependent. Decriminalization of open expression of hate propaganda, for example, could facilitate 'conviction' but what is gained is unlikely to make up for what is lost. The social and political price of decriminalization is threefold: the foregone expected moral denunciation in its most important sense (criminal); the provision of new opportunities allowing racist defendants to manipulate public perceptions within the context of relaxed procedures and loosened rules; the promotion of bad publicity for the political cause of repression, inescapable in these kinds of cases, associated with the abridgment of criminal rights to defend.

In ordinary civil disputes, relaxed procedures are not only possible but also often desirable. They are not meant to give an advantage to one side over the other. They affect the rights and prospects of the duelling parties equally. The purpose is to bring the parties closer together – to facilitate a 'meeting of minds' – and the cooperation of the disputants is expected. Victory is not seen as the most valuable outcome, much less the only socially desirable one.[33] Without give and take, without compromise, the system does not work. Silencing hate, however, is not an ordinary dispute between disputants equally interested in conciliation. Relaxed procedures are ill-suited to such cases and end up playing an unintended role.

Decriminalization fails because it attempts to force what is a supremely adversarial political dispute into a non-adversarial social context – to legally squeeze a square political peg into a round social hole. Compromising with hate is not socially desirable. Nor does the hatemonger seek to compromise. This makes for a paradoxical mix – to the detriment of the cause of the state. On the one hand, a more conciliatory civil forum affords the uncompromising hatemonger a more (directly) ideal context within which to legitimate and spread his message of intolerance.[34] On the other (same?) hand, relaxed prosecution affords him the opportunity to manipulate the symbols of persecution. Relaxed procedures under human rights codes may start with conciliation, but in the case of determined racists (what other kind is hate law meant for?) wind up in lengthy proceedings ending in punitive tribunal hearings or contempt charges for breach of court orders.[35] What may begin as expeditious state silencing of the message of hate is turned into slow airing of the hatemonger's message of persecution – for 'mere breaches of orders issued by biased commissions to be quiet.'

Relaxed procedures, intended for conciliation and compromise, are turned here into a means to secure easier victory. Dilemmas related to the abridgment of rights to effectively defend cannot, however, be successfully de-linked from dilemmas related to the repression of the message defended. The attempt to do so is artificial. And, for that very reason, it fails. Of course, victory can be made easier. But an easy victory is no more successful in the cause against ignorance, prejudice, and hate than a difficult victory. Hate propaganda, at bottom, is not a civil or criminal matter, nor can 'social character' theorists of 'free speech' successfully reduce it to either one. It is about the state of society and polity – and the public's right to openly express discontent about both. It is a political matter – *par excellence.*

The strength of the hatemonger's case lies not in the merits of the message but in the fact of its repression. In all forms of official silencing, the repressed can deflect attention from the merits of their message by presenting themselves as the underdog, the oppressed rather than the oppressor, the representative of right suppressed by far superior might. But in cases where defendants' due process rights are compromised to facilitate conviction, they can amplify these side resonances of repression by coding and clothing their malevolent meanings in the subtle language of abridged defence to more successfully taint and tarnish the cause against them.[36] They can convey the politically more insidious and difficult-to-challenge message that the reason why their oppressors need to proceed more abusively or expeditiously to silence the thoughts of those with whom they disagree is because they cannot defend their own thoughts. The more hatemongers' rights to effectively defend are compromised, the more credible their charge. If they lose, rights-abridging state victory rewards them and their cause by handing them even more ammunition to assert forum bias and reason to plead persecution and proclaim martyrdom. The evil content of the defendants' meaning is again dwarfed, this time by their added message of unfair trial. Again, they win even when they lose.

The state could silence effectively by abrogating all meaningful rights to defend. Presumptions of innocence, rights to an open trial, to a fair hearing, to an appeal – all could be effectively abridged. But the state would resemble a political tyranny in so doing. In an otherwise rights-conscious system of justice, this would be an exceedingly bruising public message for the cause against intolerance to have to bear. For it is the more important message of the repressed.[37] Trials and tribunals can be turned into nothing more than a transparent camouflage for a pre-ordained state victory. But without risking adverse publicity by respecting the rights of the accused, the state cannot garner good publicity for its cause either. In short, it is a 'lose-lose' situation for the state.

The dilemma of political show trials of this kind does not lie in the mode of the show but in the fact of repression. Repression politicizes prejudice – the very connection censors need least and hatemongers want most. The more it represses, the more it politicizes. The dilemma is irresolvable. The state must silence determined extremists expeditiously and effectively. But it must not do so unsuccessfully. It must repress with fairness and publicity to educate the public and avoid suspicion and martyrdom. But it must not repress with the kind of publicity that allows the hatemonger a 'show' through which he can manipulate the legal process to the advantage of his message. The state cannot do both. Public meaning construction mediated by prosecution cannot be legally fine-tuned to show *only* what is desired. It cannot assure that only the right message, its own message, will be communicated. It cannot 'stage' a show only for the benefit of the state. Suppressing hate speech is not an 'ordinary' case, civil or criminal. It is inescapably political and politically asymmetrical – to the comparative advantage of the cause of the repressed.

Denial of rights to defend is inextricably linked to denial of rights to speak and rights to hear. To effectively abridge one requires the effective abridgment of all the others. The former Communist countries knew all this. Their trials could not be faulted for ineffective or tardy silencing. But the price of such silencing was to sacrifice the success of the public cause of their repression. All repression-mediated modes of public discourse on disconcerting matters of society and polity are politically self-contradictory and socially self-defeating. It is not simply that official silencing does not do what censors want it and expect it to do, socially or politically. The problem is, it cannot. That's the irresolvable pragmatic dilemma.

2 Media Coverage

Is the failure of official silencing to meet the censors' needs and expectations a problem of an irresponsible media?[38] As Prutschi writes,

> [t]he media, in reporting the trial, all too frequently, shifted its attention away from the reality of the Holocaust to report uncritically on the Holocaust denial. Coverage ... tended to focus on efforts to cast doubt on survivor and expert testimony ... The mendacious, malicious, and bizarre testimony of defense witnesses was given equal time with that of survivors and recognized Holocaust scholars. The definition of Holocaust deniers of themselves as 'revisionists' was [uncritically] accepted ... [Zundel's lawyer was romanticized as a] 'maverick.' The story does not tell us much about the lawyer's past, his

political activity and views, or his motivation ... The Zundel trial was no ordinary criminal trial ... The media had to be clearly aware that the Holocaust deniers ... sought to have their poisonous views broadcast uncritically across the length and breadth of this country ... Holocaust deniers exploited the understandable bias of the fourth estate in favor of freedom of speech ... Any legitimate concern that the media might have had about the use of the criminal law to deal with hate propaganda would best have been left almost exclusively to the editorial pages. The media was also not sufficiently sensitive to the negative impact that their trial coverage had on the Jewish community ... The media had the opportunity to play a constructive educative function ... if its eyes and ears had been more open, its minds better prepared, and its hearts more properly attuned ... Cumulatively, [the media] provided the Holocaust deniers with totally undeserved legitimacy.[39]

So much for trusting state-independent media to do the extraordinary denunciatory and healing job officially expected of hate censorship.

The problems of trial, however, cannot be laid on the doorstep of the reportage, rather than the event. Media 'spin' is more than a problem of irresponsible and insensitive reporting. It is, more fundamentally, a dilemma of hate censorship itself – of repression-mediated public meaning construction for the public cognitive good. Blaming the media shifts the dilemma of censorship from where it belongs to where it does not. It ignores that what the media get first, even before their own spin, is the unintended spin of trial. It takes no media spin to see the hate-monger as trial, in fact, (mis)represents him – as the oppressed, the underdog, the voiceless. Media spin may embellish these deleterious by-products of trial, but the media do not *create* them. Trial does. Trial is a primary definer, framing the event for media and public consumption in a particular way. Was it media 'spin' to think that the Holocaust was 'not news' but its 'denial was'?[40] Was Holocaust denial not the reason for the trial? If, as Prutschi says, 'the Holocaust itself, rather than the accused, more often than not seemed on trial,'[41] can the 'fault' simply be laid on the doorstep of media manipulation? If there were no hate prosecution, there would be no media spin *of* hate prosecution.

Ideally, the media should have done a better job of covering the Zundel trial. Perhaps more background research, more context-sensitive reporting, more judicious editorial choices, even some voluntary self-censorship would have been helpful to the cause against hate.[42] But is it the job of the media to correct for the failures of trial? Is it their job to do what trial cannot? Have the media failed in doing *their* job if they do not make trial of hate censorship look better than trial itself does – or can? Or has the state failed? Has trial failed? Has repression of speech failed?

Moreover, can any state-independent, even well-intentioned, media be expected to be *only* 'subtle, sensitive and sensible,' as socially required by the cause – regardless of deadlines, circulation, commercial competition, political biases, and human frailties? And if they can't, or won't, what follows from this? Are wayward media to be legally required to 'properly' translate the message and meaning of the trial event as officially desired?[43] And if they were, would that be enough to ensure that *only* the officially right messages and socially correct meanings get out?

Public education in the causes of tolerance and democracy needs officially independent media more than it needs officially correct ones. Moreover, successful public causes need important 'friends.' Legal direction of the media on vital matters of society and polity that are put in public contention can only have 'accomplices.' This is not good even for self-serving political dictators fearing dissent for their own self-regarding ends. But it is especially bad for a cause that needs public support to succeed in a polity premised on self-government.

The media may often rightfully be faulted for incompetence, sloth, or bias, or even all three. But blaming 'irresponsible' reporting, like blaming a 'rights protective' trial, for bad publicity misses the point. State repression of disconcerting public discourse is a 'no-win' proposition for the *cause* of repression, in any event. This is not the 'fault' of the media, but rather a *fact* of repression of this kind of public expression. The media cannot be legally made to do *only* 'good' for the public cause against intolerance and ignorance. It can only be made to do bad, as political dictatorships that effectively silence disconcerting speech eventually discover. The dilemma for censorship success here lies not with media reporting but with hate silencing. Repression-mediated public discourse on important matters of state and society does not work for the public good as censorship theorists want and expect it to. Nor can it.

3 Opponents and Technology

Can the failure of official silencing to meet censors' needs and expectations be attributed to political opponents and new information technology? Consider the following, as reported by Anand: '[Deutsche Telekom, Germany's largest Internet provider] attempted to block access to a

Santa Cruz company that maintains certain well-known hate propagandists' World Wide Web sites. Within days, free speech proponents, such
as many American universities, duplicated these Web pages. To block
these mirror sites in Germany, Deutsche Telekom and other providers
would have to block access to everything on the internet from these
universities, a drastic step that many internet providers are not willing
to take.'[44]

Paul Lungen illustrates the problem posed by the Internet and its
hate links to more popular sites: '[M]usic is a key drawing card. Young
people who may not be interested in a Web site that adulates Adolf
Hitler can be drawn to such a location by a link from a site that offers
free music downloads.'[45] Others have noted how language can be exploited so that the forbidden can be hidden in the innocuous. The
'keyword Holocaust may well find the above garbage [racist and neo-
Nazi sites] listed along with the many legitimate, scholarly sites on the
subject.'[46] The American Civil Liberties Union has detailed the problem of automatic Internet links and the futility of trying to shut down
inappropriate sites without trespassing on appropriate ones.[47] The
Toronto Hate Crimes Unit has complained that it does not have the
resources to monitor the flow of hate propaganda on 2,500 Internet
websites.[48] The deputy minister of justice, Morris Rosenberg, has 'warned'
how easy it is to reproduce and how difficult it is to exclude and prove
racist speech in the communications age. Computers 'can be used to
create, copy and store' racially inflammatory material. Material can be
'downloaded and stored in formats that are difficult for law-enforcement officials to locate and use as evidence in criminal proceedings. It
can be electronically imported and exported out of reach of customs
controls.'[49] The *Canadian Jewish News* reports that 'Germany has given
up trying to bar its citizens from accessing foreign-based neo-Nazi sites
on the Internet. Germany, which has some of the world's toughest laws
banning hate speech, has decided that is unrealistic to try to shield
Germans from foreign Web sites. "You can't build a wall around Germany," one official said.'[50]

Can drastic steps compensate for the dilemmas posed by popular
sites, hidden meanings, and inextricable links? What does it take to
effectively protect Canadian minds from outside contamination by divisive, intolerant, and inegalitarian thoughts?[51] Can one close down the
Internet? Confiscate computers as well as books? One could try to jam
socially injurious signals from reaching vulnerable minds, shut down
movement to and from Canada, proscribe and punish hate propaganda

overheard in private conversation, or make socially correct re-education mandatory for all opponents of censorship – as was done under Communism. Censors may be right when they suggest that, in opposing censorship, speech advocates are 'free' to do *indirectly* what racists are not free to do *directly* – promote the cause of hate.[52] Do they not obstruct the effectiveness of hate law? Why tolerate the author of this book? If even *one link* in the chain binding the net of hate censorship is unsecured, the whole fabric of effective public protection is compromised.

Effectively policing hate is a 'geopolitical' problem. But its roots can be found in a practical dilemma. There is a functional *asymmetry* in how speech and censorship do their work that gives those who wish to communicate intolerance a comparative advantage over those who seek to silence them. Whether it would be better for democratic societies if all nations of the world agreed to shut down racist speech is, practically speaking, moot. If even one breaks ranks, effective silencing is threatened everywhere. The cry 'one hatemonger anywhere is one too many to tolerate everywhere' is not, from an effectiveness point of view, hyperbole. Functionally, hate censorship is geopolitically contained. Political communication is not. It is borderless. Silencing hate must be seamless to be effective.[53] Effective hate silencing can have no free speech gaps.[54] But effective hate speech can have censorship gaps. Silence, assured somewhere, does not *of itself* threaten thinking allowed elsewhere – silence does not convince. Speech allowed anywhere does threaten silencing everywhere – speech can convince. If this asymmetry cannot be resolved even within national censoring boundaries (because of variable domestic enforcement) how can it be resolved across them?[55] As Lawrence Lessig observes, '[i]magine ... a German court entering a judgment against Amazon.com ordering Amazon.com to stop selling *Mein Kampf* anywhere because someone in Germany had succeeded in accessing *Mein Kampf* from Amazon. Or, imagine a court in China ordering an American ISP to shut down its dissidents' site, because the speech at issue was illegal in China.'[56] Or imagine trying to shut down the UN's World Conference against Racism (WCAR) held in Durham, South Africa, because Syria engaged in 'explicit Holocaust denial'[57] and Third World delegates and NGOs 'demonized, de-legitimized and marginalized' Israel and Jews worldwide.[58] The greater the asymmetry in enforcement, the more the silencing country is disadvantaged. The more geopolitically dependent censorship is – either because the censoring country's fears are relatively 'too high' or the intruding country's fears are 'too low' – the more repressive the hate censoring country has to be to be 'free' of the intruding communication. How are 'vulner-able' adult minds to be effectively protected from undue social and political challenges consistent with the democratic premise of the cause of hate repression?

Cyberspace, where ideas flow in electronic 'bits' that transcend the physical boundaries of time and space, heightens the dilemma of rec-onciling effective silencing with successful promotion of the cause of hate repression by sharpening the asymmetry and raising the social and political costs to democracy of overcoming it. First, cyberspace can be a powerful 'disintermediator,' removing the gatekeepers and filters that stand in the way of political information exchange.[59] This 'works' the asymmetry to the further advantage of the dissident, the discontented, and the disgruntled. Universal access to ideas coupled with virtually costless decentralized production of them has given new meaning to the term 'mass communication.' One transmission can lead to any num-ber of direct or end-user reproductions. Messages can spread like a virus where anyone anywhere in the world can unload anything, at any time of the day or night, at virtually no personal cost, in the privacy of his or her own home.[60] As John Perry Barlow puts it, 'digitalized tech-nology is also erasing the legal jurisdictions of the physical world and replacing them with the unbounded and perhaps permanently lawless seas of Cyberspace [where] there are not only no national or local boundaries to contain the scene of the crime and determine the method of its prosecution, there are no clear cultural agreements on what a crime might be.'[61]

Second, cyberspace magnifies the dilemma of the democratically nec-essary but cognitively artificial private/public juridical distinction in silencing hate.[62] In cyberspace, public expression does not have to be made *in* public to *be* public; nor does it need to take material or perma-nent form in order to be publicly spread. As digitalization of informa-tion renders the physical or spatial containers of ideas increasingly obsolete, excluding 'creations of the mind' along the lines of the pub-lic/private distinction becomes ever more difficult.[63] As Barlow writes in his article 'Selling Wine without Bottles,' 'it is now possible to convey ideas from one mind to another without ever making them physical.'[64] What does effective policing of public expressions of hate mean for the success of the cause of hate repression in a communicative medium of electronic bits where the physical, temporal, and spatial distinctions – between expression and idea, message and messenger, public and pri-vate, speaker and listener – become increasingly blurred? Limited censorship to control hate, before the digital age, depended largely on two determinable things – *material* expression and *public* dissemination. In the digital age of cyberspace, hate censors must figure out some way to reconcile limited hate censorship with effective control of what, essentially, is private trade in immaterial forms of socially undesirable thinking.[65] And, they need to do so globally, as domestically required.

Effective control is not possible by limited or variable censorship. The links in the chain of public protection must *all* be effectively secured *everywhere*. Legal censorship is intended to provide the assurances and eliminate the risks that freedom of expression cannot. One weak link left unsecured, one hatemonger free to speak and proselytize in the age of cyberspace, is truly one too many for hate censors to tolerate. Plugging one hole in the matrix of public meaning construction does more harm than good if the wrong message can seep out, through other holes left open, in more defiant or subtly pernicious ways, as repressed political messages invariably do. But, given the interactive, socially multifaceted character and politically multidimensional flow of public meaning construction, how is this to be effectively, much less successfully, done?[66] The censorial dike standing in the way of determined divisive social messages is today a globally leaking sieve. The domestic price of truly effective hate silencing is the sacrifice of the democratic values of the cause of repression. And even then, censorship is unlikely to be effective, in silencing, for long.

History suggests that, in silencing determined political communication, effectively plugged communicative sieves are more vulnerable to sprout *worse* leaks later. Effective repression of socially divisive ideas was attempted by all former Communist countries. Few polities can claim the 'success' that Communist regimes could claim in effectively quieting inegalitarian public messages and their socially intolerant meanings, or in rooting out the dominant structures of private property and contract that ostensibly caused them. Family, school, work, worship, friends – even play – were all included in a seamless web of public silencing mixed with proactive official re-education – deconstructing and reconstructing public meanings in controlled contexts as needed. The only speech heard in public was the officially correct one. It required totalitarian dictatorships. But they all still failed to produce the enlightened and tolerant public cognition expected. Official silencing has not been successful in crafting the right social attitudes in any egalitarian experiment in effective hate silencing anywhere – Asian, Western, African, or Latin American. Quite the contrary; it has proved to be both socially and politically counter-productive. Over time, it has invariably failed even to effectively silence.[67]

'Censors' dilemma cannot be laid at the doorstep of new realities.' Communicative asymmetry is a function of the limits of hate censorship and the limitlessness of political communication – of old realities. It predates the Internet – even technology itself. It has existed since the time human beings discovered the power of political communication. The power of political silencing is only exceeded by the power of political communication. Witness the revolutionary influence of samizdat, second societies, and parallel economies in the former Communist systems of Eastern Europe.[68] They succeeded in nurturing and shaping minds to later launch new social and political orders, for good or ill, long before the global communications revolution made its mark. The dilemma of silencing is not a shortcoming of technology or variable enforcement. It is a fact of speech.

The dilemma is irresolvable. On balance, limited hate censorship is not just unsuccessful; it is also ineffective. It cannot silence 'as needed' – especially in the age of cyberspace. There can be no metastasizing leaks in the net of repression of this kind of infectious public expression. But unlimited hate censorship, censorship that can seamlessly silence as needed, is even less successful. It undermines even more the public cause of hate censorship. And, in time, it cannot even silence effectively. This dilemma is not the fault of misguided opponents or of new technology. It is a failure intrinsic to hate censorship.

4 Coverage or Targeting

Is the failure of official silencing to meet censors' needs and expectations a matter of deficient targeting? Theorists such as Anand and McKenna have suggested that the Cohen Committee failed to fully appreciate the depth and breadth of public prejudice. McKenna has argued that a limited conception of censorship misses its intended mark. Hate propaganda law, he complains, 'assumes that socially divisive and intolerant attitudes are confined to the domain of marginal extremists.'[69] But the embrace of prejudice, we know, is much wider. It can encompass even the respected, if not always the respectable – and is that not the deeper social problem, the real public danger? A weapon that excuses hate's most injurious messengers and more injurious meanings misses its socially correct mark. However, a weapon that does not excuse them but that cannot unerringly identify and reliably repress *only* the messages it seeks and ought to quiet risks catching the wrong ones. This describes the targeting dilemma of hate propaganda law. Limited hate censorship is guilty of the first problem. However, in avoiding the first problem it cannot avoid the second – and this is worse still.

Hate propaganda law has, indeed, targeted transparent racists such as Zundel. Their patently fraudulent fabrications are easier to catch. But for the same reason they are also easier to 'see through' and challenge and counter. Transparent untruths, rather than coerced silence or received truth without choice, can best rescue truth from its nemesis – irrelevance, overload, and atrophy.[70] The same cannot be said for more subtle, disguised, sophisticated, or clever messages and messengers of intolerance and division. They are far more able to cloud and to confuse so as to 'invisibly' influence unknowing and vulnerable minds. What is hidden or implied 'between the lines' may in the end be far more destructive of social harmony and political democracy than what is obvious within them. As Borovoy writes, 'in today's society, the veiled code word has much more impact than does naked invective.'[71]

The language of untransparent division may be intentional or unintentional. It can come clothed in scholarship,[72] 'coded' words,[73] abstract or general treatises, works of fiction, political caricature or cartoons,[74] artistic impressions, or hidden emphases; in inflection, tone, gesture, comedy, satire, or music.[75] Giuseppe Di Palma describes how, under Communism, the public invented a *private* language of coded communication to conceal non-conforming meanings, circumvent official 'socialist' dogma, and escape the censor's knife.[76] Hybrid forms of mass communication, such as the docudrama, increasingly blur the line between fact and fiction, news and entertainment. Hate may even include the bizarre and the bizarre include hate. 'New Age' mysticism has combined belief in flying saucers with belief in a world Jewish conspiracy.[77]

Both mode and medium of communication colour the impact of the message. The language of untransparent division can more effectively impart and imprint its meaning through those *popular* or *symbolic* forms that are most easily digested by the public – rallies, fiction, comedy, satire, and other forms of entertainment.[78] Appropriating and fixing officially correct meanings without trespassing on other rights is more difficult here. Jonathan Swift's classic political satire *Gulliver's Travels* used deceptively attractive children's imagery to evade the censor's knife and mock European society and monarchy. The condemnation by the Canadian Jewish Congress (Alberta Region) of the use of Nazi and

Holocaust imagery by gun lobbyists at a protest against gun controls is another illustration of the dilemma.[79] Jewish' outrage at the horrific juxtaposition of animals slaughtered for food alongside photographs of Nazi death camps by animal rights groups is still another.[80]

The meaning of speech is more than the bare message in still another way. It also includes the messenger. When presidential candidates (e.g., Pat Buchanan),[81] acclaimed novelists (e.g., Salman Rushdie),[82] university professors (e.g., Philippe Rushton or Hymie Rubenstein),[83] classic playwrights (e.g., William Shakespeare),[84] Nobel laureates (e.g., William Shockley),[85] or charismatic leaders (e.g., Louis Farrakhan)[86] speak, they do so with more authority than the likes of Zundel and Keegstra. Untransparent language spoken by respected figures and delivered in unconventional or popular forms can 'condition' thought in subtle ways. It is here that divisive social meanings can best hide.[87] If hate propaganda law is to be meaningfully effective, it cannot exempt hate's most influential messengers and excuse society's more injurious meanings. It needs to target the subtly harmful, not the transparently refutable and socially revitalizing. It cannot be a marginal censorship. It must be a more mainstream and main ideas censorship. But can a more mainstream and main ideas hate censorship be a more successful hate censorship?

On the one hand, marginal hate censorship misses the big fish for the easier catch. It nets the wrong speech (transparent fabrication) and the wrong speaker (social revitalizer). It elevates the politically more insidious messages and socially more opaque and pernicious meanings of marginal fanatics, those that resonate best with subconscious public prejudices, by quieting more readily refutable ones. It allows the more injurious speech (subtly divisive) and speaker (authoritatively influential) to escape. On the other hand, catching the more imjurious speech and speaker risks encroaching on vital public discourse and trespassing on the rights of legitimate discussants. The wider the net, the greater the risk.[88] The dilemma is irresolvable. Targeting and coverage cannot be fine-tuned to resolve the dilemma because insufficient coverage or deficient targeting is not the problem – hate censorship is. The medicine of silencing fails its own public cause in all doses, large and small. It is a dilemma for which censorship theories of equality, social harmony, and multiculturalism – found truths, fixed meanings, and final triumphs guaranteed by law – offer no workable answers.

At bottom, censors' problems of coverage and targeting reveal the impossibility of reconciling effective silencing with successful promotion of the social causes of repression in the democratic political context expected. Censorship theorists may dismiss this, but the dilemma is real. Indeed, it is far more real than they would like to think. Take extreme messages of intolerance. Successfully demarcating the line between hate repression and legitimate expression should not be difficult here. How invisible can the meaning of extremism be? If there is a targeting dilemma even here, where isn't there? But there is. Even extreme messages can come dressed in the garb of opaque meanings. There are three main reasons why: abstruse association; the changing face of racism, particularly of anti-Semitism; and signs that even hatemongers can learn from experience.

Part of the problem is that the politically multifaceted nature of hate readily lends itself to abstruse associations between the disreputable and the otherwise reputable. The result is to confer legitimacy on the otherwise distinctly contemptible, as Prutschi describes:

> ... Holocaust denial has brought about the convergence of the radical right and the radical left ... The most shocking association of all is that of the world-famous Jewish linguist and radical Noam Chomsky [with Pierre Guillaume who runs a Marxist publishing house that has published the 'works' of convicted hatemonger Robert Faurisson. Chomsky wrote a 'free speech' introduction to one of Faurisson's 'works']. As Professor Werner Cohn has pointed out in his pamphlet 'The Hidden Alliances of Noam Chomsky,' Guillaume's publishing house is a very obscure one and, if it has any credibility at all, it has it in good measure as a result of the connection with Chomsky.[89]

Hatred's abstruse associations have global political dimensions today, conferring legitimacy on the illegitimate in otherwise respected domestic organizations and international forums. Following a policy statement by the executive and council of the Canadian Labour Congress that compared Israel to South Africa under apartheid, former CLC president Dennis McDermott expressed deep concern that international anti-Semitism may be finding a new home in the Canadian labour movement.[90] The United Nations itself, as we have seen, provides a notable example of such abstruse association.[91]

Underscoring the dilemma of abstruse association is the changing face of racism, particularly anti-Semitism. Significant racists need not be intellectual lightweights. Some ten years ago, Paul Berman, in his extensive analysis of Holocaust denial, wrote that,

[It] has long been known that in times of acute social crisis anti-Semitism takes to the streets. The corollary now looming into focus is that in times of acute ideological crisis, anti-Semitism takes to the intellectual presses ... Our examination of Holocaust deniers in Europe and North America clearly indicates that ... anti-Semitism has not only infiltrated certain intellectual presses but has become the preserve of a portion of the western intelligentsia. Holocaust deniers are in the main university-educated teachers, academics, writers, professionals. They are not exactly like flat earthers. They are not mere kooks or inconsequential eccentrics dealing with a rather bizarre but harmless theory.[92]

Right-wing intellectualism's disposition to harbour virulent anti-Semitism is neither new nor surprising. Progressive left-wing intellectualism's growing tendency to do so, however, is. As reported in the *Canadian Jewish News*, 'Canadian leftists and liberals are aligning themselves with Islamic extremists to delegitimize Israel and promote an atmosphere of anti-Semitism, a leader of the World Jewish Congress said ... last week. "What is really shocking is that you have here today an unholy alliance between liberals, intellectuals from the left and the most extreme forces of Islam," Secretary General Avi Beker was quoted as saying at a WJC board meeting held in Ottawa.'[93] Within the progressive left's reduction of prejudice to a simplistic economistic equation – Western capitalism *equals* colonialism *equals* Zionism *equals* racism – anti-Semitism is finding a new but self-conflicting and problematic sanctuary.[94]

Finally, even some of the most transparent racists are not standing still for the convenience of hate censors (as described below). Hate censorship's assumed 'safe space' – between the socially unacceptable and the merely controversial, between the malevolent messenger and the controversial muckraker, between the merely obnoxious and the clearly abhorrent – is, in political practice, a line of demarcation that is becoming increasingly more, not less, blurred. Effective protection of the public psyche *and* successful promotion of social harmony, public enlightenment, and political democracy are becoming still more, not less, difficult to reconcile by means of censorship.

Hate censors, particularly progressive hate censors, lament the lack of political will to make hate censorship socially more effective. But they do not fully appreciate the dilemma of censorial success. Hate censorship is not unsuccessful because it is ineffective. It is unsuccessful because it represses. The more it represses, the more unsuccessful it becomes. Success by silencing is self-contradictory because effectiveness in silencing is self-defeating.

III Effectiveness and Success: The Dilemma of the Moving Target – the 'Slippery Slope' Revisited

To censorship theorists, the line demarcating the boundaries of hate proscription may be clear, but over time it can become unclear even where it should be crystal clear – silencing racist extremists. While the boundary can be fixed, the meanings proscribed and the mode of their conveyance cannot be. This is not a stable line of clarity, as hate censors like to think of it, but a shifting and elusive one. In an effective regime of hate silencing, a proactive one, the line is likely to become more not less elusive. Hate speech is a moving target, moved by prosecution itself – destabilizing hate censorship to the detriment of the cause of repression.

Censors want to succeed. For them, this means to effectively silence the message of intolerance. The drive to do so comes from both liberal egalitarians such as the Canadian Jewish Congress and illiberal egalitarians such as the structural transformers. But it comes especially from illiberal egalitarians. Time and again one hears their discontent with weak hate speech laws or want of political will enforcing them.[95] For committed censors, effective silencing of hate requires the 'strengthening' of the net of speech repression – to widen its reach or bolster its catch. But this is just one side pushing an expanding dynamic. The actions and reactions of the censored are the other side. The censored also wants to succeed. To do this requires making the censorial net set ineffective. To escape a net of limited reach it is necessary to step outside its limits. Once the censored is outside it, the censor must admit failure, abandon the cause, and look the worse off for it – or cast a wider net. If the net is cast still wider, the censored looks for (and finds) still other ways to step outside it. In short, the net must be continuously widened if effective silencing is to be regained. The censor's initial advantage is always made temporary by the determined censored's response. Paradoxically, it is not only pressures from failure to catch that can fuel a widening and more problematic net of repression. Successful catches also do – at the behest of the net-circumventing racist.

Consider this dynamic, beginning with proscription of transparently inflammatory speech. If only *incitement* to hatred is outlawed, the fearful or simply clever racist is invited to couch his intolerant message in permitted *advocacy*.[96] To regain effectiveness, the state is invited to ban intolerant advocacy. This invites the racist to shade his meaning in the subtler language of *promotion* of hate. The state, then, is invited to outlaw promotion of intolerance. If the law only prohibits promotion of hate by misstatement of fact,[97] then the racist is invited to camouflage his message in a still subtler language of hate – opinion, innuendo, code, and general or abstract speech. Again, the state can choose to pursue the next higher rung of speech repression. Or, it can admit failure, look the worse for it, and retreat to a marginal hate censorship – quieting only the most incorrigibly transparent racists – which, as explored above, serves the cause of such racists more than that of the state.

The dilemma of this dynamic is that it prevents a satisfactory censorship solution. There will always be insufficient fish caught. Censorship will always be less effective than it 'should' and 'needs to' be. Effectiveness breeds its own obsolescence. It is a never-ending, 'winless' battle. But it is more than that. It is, for a proactive public cause of hate censorship, a progressively more self-contradictory and self-defeating battle. It can breed a progressively more problematic censorship. With every toughening of the law, the racist is invited to hide his meanings in more socially pernicious and politically insidious forms – in subtle, symbolic, or coded messages of intolerance and prejudice. 'Social character' theorists of freedom of speech, such as Professor Richard Moon, are receptive to silencing 'extreme' but not 'ordinary' expressions of racism. Yet, at the same time, Moon argues that 'greater effort should be made ... to ensure that racist views are expressed in a context where they will be challenged ... where the racist character of certain discourse will be exposed and examined.'[98] Public silencing and public exposure, however, are self-contradictory. They cannot be made complementary. Marginal hate silencing 'works' to push transparent or extreme (impermissible) messages and meanings of intolerance into less not more transparent and easily challengeable (permissible) meaning contexts. More stringent public silencing works more to do so. Less stringent public silencing works less to do so. But all silencing works to do so. Worse, less stringent public silencing (ineffective hate law) invites more stringent public silencing (effective hate law). Hate censorship may be a reluctant player in a self-contradictory, self-defeating silencing dynamic, but it is a player none the less.

This dynamic may be described as hate censors' 'legal plumbing' dilemma. Failure to fully appreciate its slippery nature and the self-defeating tendencies of its flow can reduce censors to the role of 'legal plumbers' – reactively plugging progressively more problematic leaks 'as needed' in a failing cause. The dilemma of the moving target, moved by the targeting itself, deals a devastating blow to a successful hate censorship. Hate censors cannot solve the dilemma because hate censorship is the problem. The dynamic can only be propelled forward by a more proactive censorship. When awareness of the dilemma is masked by good legal plumbers, the social and political consequences are postponed to a later date.

'Real world' testimony to the legal plumbing dilemma is not wanting, nationally or internationally. As threats to rights to speak have grown in the last decade so, too, has the subtlety of racist messages and their meanings, in response.[99] Banned speakers of the determined kind have neither gone away nor given up the fight for fear of hate law. Instead, they have found camouflage in socially more problematic meanings and power in politically more elusive messaging forms that resonate better with deeper public prejudices and fears. Intolerance has nowhere been vanquished, let alone silenced by hate censorship laws – it has only become more problematized. In France, right-wing extremist Jean-Marie Le Pen appears to have learned that broadening his popular appeal requires that he successfully stave off the censor's knife. The result is a politically more sophisticated racist message shaded in more subtly pernicious political meanings.[100] Though France has some of the toughest laws against espousing hate, French prosecutors have long maintained that the country's criminal laws against inciting hatred are ineffective against increasingly subtle or 'vague' propaganda. France's justice minister vowed in 1996 to 'stiffen France's hate laws to punish "indirect provocation."'[101] Playing into the hands of the racists is hard not to do.[102]

Censorship, of course, is not the only explanation for hate's growing obfuscation. But it is more hurtful than helpful to the cause against it. Repression seems to have given even a transparent boor like Zundel a 'learning' experience. What he has learned, however, to the dismay of his censors, is neither silence nor tolerance but how to circumvent the censor's net better. When Parliament banned Canada's premier hatemonger from its precincts, he readily saw the opportunities to turn the ban into a circus, holding a 'media scrum' on the adjacent sidewalk and garnering twice as much (persecuted) publicity as before the ban. When prosecution banned him from uttering certain racist misstatements of fact he went on radio and conveyed much the same racist message, sheltered in forms of expression that resonate better with deep-seated or subconscious public prejudices – in innuendos and allusions. This not only made the message worse,[103] it also increased the risk of state trespass on legitimate speech while trying to catch illegitimate speech.

Zundel had suddenly become more difficult to prosecute for the same reason that he became more difficult to refute – his meaning was less transparent. Ontario's then attorney general found himself in the publicly awkward and politically shaky position of defending Zundel's radio comments as statements of belief and opinion: '[E]veryone is entitled to his opinion, however distasteful.' Canada's premier hate-monger was left thumbing his nose at the criminal law. In response, calls went out to toughen the law.[104] In hate censorship, cutting one's losses and getting out is not just hard to do. It is even harder to explain.[105] Zundel and his indefatigable ilk now appear to have found a more 'communication friendly' medium – cyberspace – through which to better express their defiance. Pressures to silence that medium are now growing.[106] Failure, it seems, is fodder for censorship.

Proponents of hate censorship would argue that, in the push and pull of this dynamic, the state is in the driver's seat. Anything less would be devastating to a cause making claim to success. But in a polity premised on self-government – sensitive to the need to protect vital public discourse, privacy rights, and other fundamental values – this is misleading. The state may, strictly speaking, be in the driver's seat. What moves this dynamic, however, is more a function of what the hatemonger does than what the state does. The state can set the rules of the game and invoke the vast legal and police machinery at its disposal to enforce them. But the state is never really in control of the directional tendency of the vehicle. The hatemonger is.

Paradoxically, the proactive censoring state is reduced to waging a reactive silencing fight – it must continuously 'prop up' its line of proscription to correct for the failing ones that the determined racist slipped out of – or look weak and helpless. Of course, it is not inevitable that the state will slide after the hatemonger to regain effectiveness. The state may resist, exercising self-restraint and holding off pursuit, consistent with the idea of limited censorship in a political democracy – as did Ontario's attorney general.[107] But the hatemonger will not. Indeed, the more restraint the state shows, the less restraint the emboldened hatemonger needs to show. In this cat-and-mouse game of competitive social message making and public meaning construction, the state can make all the rules. But it is the defiant and clever racist who can decide the next move. Whether by clever evasion in the face of pursuit or emboldened defiance in the face of restraint, the determined racist is the commanding energy, over which the censor, relentlessly tugging at the brittle strings of a self-defeating censorship dynamic, has no control.

The dilemma of this dynamic is irresolvable because the antagonists' social causes are politically asymmetrical. The advantage, in a democracy, will always lie with the determined extremist. Reconciling effectiveness *with* success is a dilemma only for the state not for the hatemonger. For a social cause espousing politically limited censorship in a polity premised on democracy, there is an irresolvable dilemma. Social and political needs conflict. Hate censors must not only *effectively* (seamlessly) silence. In doing so, they must also dutifully exercise restraint to avoid encroaching on vital public discourse and other fundamental democratic rights. They cannot do both successfully – they are self-contradictory demands. The censor in a democracy has limits. But the censored does not. Not only can the hatemonger be more effective the more he steps outside of the censor's limits. He can also be more successful. Indeed, he has *no* social expectations or political limits to restrain him. For the intolerant, effectiveness and success are not mutually exclusive but complementary. In a democracy, the advantage, driving the dynamic against the public cause of the censor, will always reside with the rule-circumventing extremist not the rule-making state.[108]

Notions of delimited found truths, fixed meanings, and final triumphs may work well in hate censorship theory. But in hate censorship practice, they are ongoing processes in a politically slippery, socially self-defeating dynamic. *Effective* hate silencing is not a one-time event but a continuous, and continually failing, process of widening the net – to a point that threatens to choke off vital public political discourse. Even devout proponents of social censorship would then no longer be able to speak simultaneously of effective silencing and successful promotion of the cause in terms that are interchangeable.

IV Differential Censorial Impact: The Final Blow

Hate propaganda law does its work as if the public of listeners and speakers were monolithic. But the domain of public cognition cannot be painted with such an indiscriminately broad brush. Audiences and speakers are not cognitively homogeneous. There are not one but many different kinds of listening publics. Their 'needs' for cognitive protection are not all the same. There are many different kinds of putative speakers. Society's 'needs,' in regard to their repression or expression are not the same. Hate propaganda does not have the same injurious impact on different listening audiences. Hate censorship does not have the same speech-preventive impact on different putative speakers.

Hate censorship is a blunt political instrument enlisted in the service of a refined social cause. Publics more in need of protection cannot successfully be more protected for the same reason that publics less in need of protection cannot successfully be less protected. More injurious speakers cannot successfully be silenced more effectively for the same reason that less injurious speakers cannot successfully be silenced less effectively. Indeed, hate censorship tends to have the very opposite effects to those intended and expected. A censorship that cannot differentiate speakers or audiences as needed cannot quiet or protect 'as needed.' Hate censors cannot divide the public impact of the law along the lines needed to be both more effective *and* more successful.

1 The Shield: Subjective Audience Impact

Even if hate censors knew which members of the public were vulnerable to be influenced by malevolent messages and which were not, they could not 'cost-effectively' tailor censorship as needed. What censors call 'hate propaganda' is what public policy economists would call 'public bads' or 'public goods' with negative 'externalities.'[109] 'Public bads' have certain 'public' features. Cleansing the public domain of the scourge of hate propaganda is much like assuring clean air and pristine water. Purity assured for some is purity assured for all. The problem is, all members of the public are not equally in need of cognitive purity. Hate speech law ought to provide public protection only 'as needed.' But it cannot do so, for both practical and political reasons. The political reasons are rooted in a practical quandary.

Practically, it is well-nigh near impossible to protect effectively 'as needed.' People 'talk' to one another. Ideas spread – with or without censorship. Private links binding the chain of determined publicly directed messages can be interrupted, but they cannot be effectively, much less selectively, severed forever. Shielding only some of the public from the malevolent message can be even more problematic than shielding all of the public. Unlike physically injurious acts, indiscriminate reproduction of 'publicly injurious' ideas is easy, but discriminating public exclusion is exceptionally hard. Hate propaganda law satisfies the consumptive properties and exhibits the segregative dilemmas of a 'public good' – non-rivalrous consumption and non-excludability.[110] Public protection is a leaking communicative sieve. The political and social cost this puts in the way of effective audience differentiation is highly prohibitive. To *effectively* insulate from cognitive harm *only* the morally incapable or cognitively vulnerable, 'as needed,' would require first correctly identifying, then physically, spatially, socially, or otherwise cognitively segregating or confining them.

Audience segregation 'to protect' is different from speaker incarceration to punish. Those found to be in need of protection would not be members of the public out to convert others to hate. They would be vulnerable members of the public found to be in danger of being converted *by* others to the cause of hate. Protection need not and ordinarily would not be based on anything specifically *done* or *said* against official wisdom but on an officially designated *state* of mental or moral social inadequacy. Vulnerability could be inferred from the 'socially intolerant' lifestyle or 'racially unenlightened' choices of subjects. The protected vulnerable would not be those who seek to change the system. They would not be candidates for the gulags, as were political dissidents in the former Soviet Union. They would be more like the morally or mentally deficient, confined to protective custody for their own good – to a kind of insular social ghetto, perhaps – as was done with Blacks under apartheid in South Africa.[111] Only it would be based on social right, not race. But could this be called a successful hate censorship? Indeed, how long would it be effective?

The protection hate censorship accords *all* Canadians today is governed by the needs of only *some*. But not just any some. It is governed by the needs of the *lowest* common denominator, the needs of the least able few – those whose social balance and moral public bearing are so low that they cannot handle the undue challenge posed by even a transparent fanatic like Zundel.[112] A law of silencing that cannot successfully differentiate between those who 'need' protection and those who do not cannot be called a well-balanced censorship. But a law of silencing that cannot differentiate even between the cognitive needs of the *least* socially able and the rest of society is more off balance still. This cannot be called a successful censorship in a self-governing polity and for a cause that requires self-knowing not simply right-nodding publics. The price of public equality in public protection is the forfeiture of the democratic needs of the cause of repression.

Well-balanced protection from proselytization, in heterogeneous social contexts housing cognitively diverse publics, cannot be a one-size-fits-all shield. It needs to effectively distinguish diverse publics and satisfy diverse cognitive needs. Successful shields effectively protect the needs of the cognitively incapable. But they do not do so at the cost of the needs of the cognitively capable and the underlying social values and democratic political expectations of the cause. Hate censors cannot successfully do both. The price of an indiscriminate public shield is suppression of everyone's rights to listen, learn, and grow based on the cognitive needs of the lowest social and moral common denominator.[113] But the price of an effective discriminating shield is to sacrifice social equality and, in time, public harmony itself. More discriminating shields pay a higher price. Less discriminating shields pay a lower price. But all discriminating shields pay a price.[114] To accept audience discrimination in the name of social equality and public harmony is deeply self-contradictory. No social cause that is committed to these goals can do so without fundamentally corrupting its cause.

The dilemma of the shield is irresolvable. Hate censors must shelter all the adult public, for they cannot effectively *and* successfully shield only some of the public. Neither option serves the cause of social progress or political democracy well. This dilemma is not the fault of new technologies. New technologies may worsen the dilemma, but they did not create it. Even before cyberspace, it was not possible to effectively *and* successfully tailor the elixir of quiet to protect only where and as needed. The dilemma is not the fault of a flawed socio-economic system of public choice. Real polities have diverse not uniform public needs. Real publics cannot be cognitively homogeneous. Most importantly, the dilemma is not the result of lack of censorial will. More discriminating public protection is no answer to the democratic dilemma of indiscriminate public protection. It is part of the problem. The dilemma of the shield is a failure of hate censorship. 'Successful' protection of the public psyche – where and as needed to achieve the social goals that are wanted in the democratic context expected – is beyond the power of legal silencing. Hate censorship is a blunt *shield* enlisted in the service of a refined cause.

2 The Sword: Subjective Speaker Impact

Hate censorship cannot effectively *and* successfully differentiate among putative speakers, either. Speakers, like audiences, are heterogeneous, not homogeneous. Speaker impact depends on the *subjective cognitions* of the speakers not the objective intent of the law. It depends especially on the degree of determination to speak, aversion to risk, integrity, and sophistication of the speakers. These dependencies decide how the law impacts. How they work determines how well hate propaganda law works. Unfortunately for censors, they do not work as they should.

The silencing impact of hate propaganda law may usefully be divided into four categories of affected speakers: the marginal fanatic; the social opportunist; the controversial but cautious and reflective thinker; and the sophisticated racist. Among the four, controversial but cautious and reflective thinkers are most 'valuable' to deliberative inquiry and robust but legitimate public discourse. But being more risk averse, such thinkers are more likely to have most regard for the possible costs of misspeaking. They are more apt than the others to exercise self-censorship for fear of inviting social opprobrium, financially ruinous litigation, or possible prosecution.

The sophisticated racist, the more subtle and, ultimately, greater threat in the long run to social tolerance in a consolidated democracy, can count on his sophistication to shield his message from official censure. He can more easily shroud the evil of his meaning behind the ambiguity of his sophistication and exploit to his advantage democratic reluctance to trespass on legitimate speech. The self-serving opportunist will be invited by career, social, political, economic, and other advantages to adjust his speech, kowtowing to official expectations, trimming his sails to the prevailing political winds, and exploiting conventional wisdom to his advantage.[115] The public at large, in its own interest, is invited by threat of official censure or opportunity for gain to engage in politically correct posturing and to substitute personally useful but socially deceitful pretensions in place of honest discourse when genuine belief may well be lacking.[116]

Finally, the determined racist has a number of options – all win-win for him but lose-lose for society. He can choose to benefit from being a defendant, an underdog, tried and judicially martyred. The rewards include a trial-filtered showcase for his cause – a better platform than he could otherwise hope to erect on his own. Or, if trial is too demanding and the possibility of conviction uninviting, he can go underground to do his dirty deeds. Or he may learn from the sophisticated racist and try to shelter his intolerance behind the veil of politically opaque but socially more insidious meanings. In every case, not only does he win even when he loses, he finds better (more injurious) ways to win.

The problem for hate censorship here is not that its speech-preventive impact differs widely from speaker to speaker but that none of these different impacts can be reconciled with a successful censorship. Most certainly, the dilemma is not that the impact on speakers is ineffective 'across the board.' In the case of some speakers, hate censorship can silence their messages very effectively. It is that it is unsuccessful across the board. It is, relatively, unsuccessful where success should be most obvious (with the transparent hatemonger), most effective where it should be least effective (with the controversial, thoughtful, but cautious speaker), least effective where it should be most effective (with the subtle, sophisticated racist), and socially concealing/falsifying when it should be socially revealing/clarifying (with the opportunist).[117]

The more encompassing (effective) hate censorship is in silencing, the greater is this dilemma of unintended speaker impact (of success). Differential impact on speakers depends on the subjective speaker not the objective intent of the law or the degree of political fortitude in applying it. Hate law cannot make opportunistic, self-serving speakers into honest public-serving speakers; thoughtful but risk-averse speakers into thoughtful but intrepid speakers; racist but refined speakers into racist but guileless speakers; or publicity-seeking fanatics into publicity-shy pussycats. 'Strengthening' hate censorship law by increasing punishment, widening the net, or lowering the *mens rea* threshold for conviction cannot eliminate, only accentuate, the self-defeating differential impact on speakers. Opportunistic speakers will pretend more. Cautious and thoughtful speakers will be more wary. Sophisticated racists will be subtler. And transparent racists will find other, more socially injurious or politically problematic (less easily challengeable) ways to get their message and meanings across. Hate censorship is a blunt *sword* enlisted in the service of a refined cause.

Conclusion

Hate censorship cannot advance the cause of social tolerance, public enlightenment, and political democracy in the way hate censors want and expect it to do. Legal silencing is a blunt political instrument enlisted in the service of a refined social cause. Differential impacts on audiences and speakers preclude a tailored censorship – one that protects 'where needed' or punishes 'as needed.' Marginal silencing is socially ineffective. Mainstream silencing is politically self-intrusive. Neither works to successfully promote the cause as needed. In turn, trying to succeed is a slippery and self-defeating process. Ineffective silencing invites more effective silencing. But more effective silencing promotes its opposite. It promotes its own obsolescence. Intolerance is a moving target, moved by censorship itself, to the detriment of the cause repression seeks to advance. Intolerance does not stand still for the convenience of censors. Hate censorship fails *itself* at all levels.

These dilemmas cannot be laid at the doorstep of the mode of repression, the media, the adequacy of coverage, technology, free speech advocates, or even a deficient system or a flawed public. They are not the result of a failure of censorial will. Censorial will cannot solve them because want of censorial will is not the problem. The 'fault' lies within the very nature and limits of hate speech repression itself. It is a dilemma intrinsic to hate silencing. Ultimately, it is a problem of hate law's inability to reconcile two needs – effective silencing of the message of intolerance with successful promotion of the cause repression seeks to advance.

Hate censorship in Canada can be made much more effective in silencing public expressions of intolerance. But it cannot be made less unsuccessful. More compelled and compliant media, more messengers and meanings targeted for repression, more attempts to chain or shackle technology, more muzzled or padlocked opponents, more rights-denying convictions, more onerous punishments, and, perhaps, even more socially discriminating public protection and proactive proscription are all possible. But the social and political costs of effectively quieting the message of intolerance would be devastating, on hate censors' own terms of social and political reference. Such costs could not possibly be called a successful censorship. But they do illustrate the pragmatic side of hate censorship's dilemma of political self-contradiction and social self-defeat. Hate censorship not only does not do what censors want and expect it to do – it cannot. Hate censors undermine their own cause in the very process of promoting it. The more effectively they silence the more they undermine it. No law compelling cognition but wanting enlightenment successfully does or can do what it is intended to do. The more effective it is, the more it fails. This is the irreconcilable practical dilemma of hate censorship.

7

The Jurisprudential Dilemma

The Exceptions Defence and Democratic Justification

This chapter explores the balancing dilemma from a defining jurisprudential perspective – that of the 'exceptions defence.' Censors argue that in no country in the world is freedom of expression absolute – even in the United States. There are many well-worn legal exceptions to freedom of public expression in consolidated representative democracies. Increasingly, hate propaganda law is defended not simply as a legal exception to freedom of expression consistent with other well-worn legal exceptions but as a particularly democratic one. But is it? A well-balanced jurisprudence of exceptions to freedom of expression should be both legally coherent and politically defensible. A legally coherent exceptions jurisprudence is one that is philosophically consistent. A politically defensible exceptions jurisprudence is one that is democratically defensible. Censors espouse both. However, the exceptions defence for hate propaganda law is neither. Nor can it be both simultaneously. The more philosophical coherence it gains, the less democratically defensible it becomes.

The exceptions defence for hate silencing is a 'packaged' defence – wrapped in unwieldy generalizations, contextual mischaracterizations, and self-contradictory assumptions. It is important to unpack it. I examine five of the most common or commonly touted 'public protecting' exceptions to freedom of expression: manner and form regulation; false public alarms and fighting words; obscenity; defamation of public officials (libel and slander); criminal group defamation; and seditious libel. I compare the reasons for these exceptions with those of hate propaganda law in terms of coherence and democratic defensibility.

I Manner and Form Regulation

Sometimes styled the 'police power,' manner and form limitations are designed not to prohibit the content of the expression but to regulate its method of conveyance – how, when, and where it is disseminated. The concern here is not with conversion to a feared cause, and so the message is not the issue. The concern is with trespass on other recognized rights by the manner and form of communication. The mode of communication may be proscribed as illegal, irrespective of the content of the message. This is regulation, not prohibition, because it still allows the message to be conveyed in other legal ways. In difficult cases, there may be some question of whether the message can be communicated effectively in alternative legal ways or is emasculated by the regulation.[1] If it is the latter, then, effectively, the right of expression is abrogated. In that case, the effect is prohibitory, not regulatory.[2]

The U.S. Supreme Court has struggled with problems of 'symbolic speech' and 'speech plus' modes of communication. In *Cox* v. *Louisiana*, the court held that 'we emphatically reject the notion that the First and Fourteenth Amendments afford the same kind of freedom to those who would communicate ideas by conduct such as patrolling, marching and picketing on streets and highways as these amendments afford to those who communicate ideas by pure speech.'[3] Illegal conduct can include blocking persons or thoroughfares or trespassing on private property,[4] harassing by repeated phone calls, or disturbing the public peace by shouting and screaming. If messengers were allowed to trespass on other recognized legal rights, without regard to the intrusiveness of the conduct of their communication, political voice and social victory would be by dint of physical compulsion or speaker demand not public volition or listener choice. Messengers no more have a right to a captive audience compelled to listen than the audience has a right to a captive speaker compelled to speak.

Since manner and form constraints are not concerned with the intrinsic merits of the content of the communication, truth, falsity, and political or social correctness are not at issue. The truthful may be limited, the falsifying allowed. 'Peaceniks' who persistently pester unwilling bystanders to 'make love not war' may have their message of tolerance abridged as surely as bigots who act likewise to preach hate. The point of contention here is not 'what' is said but 'how' it is said. The messenger is free to convey his message in less intrusive ways – say, by making one phone call, not repeated phone calls; by voicing his views during the day, not at all hours of the day or night; by not impeding persons (and their vehicles) who choose not to listen; by not committing private trespass. Manner and form regulation of speech, of one kind or another, can be found in all societies, irrespective of their political systems. It exists in a 'tyranny or a democracy, a monarchy or a society without a [formal] government at all.'[5] Without it, there would be public anarchy and even physical compulsion rather than public discourse. All societies accept some rules limiting the mode of conveyance of even acceptable expressions.

Manner and form regulation is an exception to freedom of speech that is sensitive to time, place, circumstances, other rights, and other values. It balances the foundational right on which other freedoms enjoyed in a democratic polity depend (right of public expression on public matters where it counts) against other important values (privacy, safety, tranquillity, property, mobility, etc.). Free speech advocates recognize and accept manner and form exceptions. They make no absolute claim of right against all other rights and values irrespective of circumstances.[6] Other values may sometimes take precedence over a public right to social and political communication – but not in all circumstances. In contrast, hate speech law takes precedence in all circumstances. It is content-conscious and circumstance-blind. Hate censors need do no balancing. Hate censorship is intended to be absolute against all other rights, at all times, in all places, and in every circumstance, existing and 'foreseeable.'[7] It is a blanket prohibition without public exception. It is a politically conscious but not politically self-conscious abrogation of public discourse on public matters. It is not anything like the democratic exception of manner and form regulation.

II False Alarms (Pranksterism) and Fighting Words

No one has the right to falsely yell 'Fire!' in a crowded theatre,[8] or to settle personal scores by deliberately provoking public fights. The exceptions to freedom of expression of pugilism and alarmism do not exist to protect the public from cognitive harm. We need not fear a socially and politically less enlightened polity from alarmists who falsely yell fire in a crowded theatre. We need not worry about becoming a nation of believers in the social and political virtues of vendettas from the venomous words of pugilists. We need not fear public corruption from the content of such expressions. Pugilists and alarmists make no social or political commentary. They are not out to convert society to a cause in any socially or politically meaningful sense of the word.[9] Silencing here is not political repression, for the same reason that speaking here is not political communication.

There is no risk here of competitive rival political silencing for there is no issue of competitive rival political speaking. What public interest in public discourse is legally misappropriated and officially misshapen here, to the detriment of the cause of repression? What public right to consider, choose, or decide between competing social or political points of view is abrogated? Martyrs are not made when the right to yell fire or to provoke fisticuffs to settle personal scores is abridged. Deeper appreciation of social, historical, or political truth is not undercut. Slide, slippage, or trespass on meaningful public discourse is not risked, nor is chill promoted. There is no danger here that if open communication is proscribed the message will be communicated surreptitiously in more publicly injurious forms. Silent or unknowing losers are not an issue.

Proscription here does have *regard* for content. But that regard is incidental to, not the purpose of, abridgment. The intrinsic merit of the content of the communication is irrelevant to official concern for the public consequence of its expression. The likelihood of greater public injury without proscription than with it is not socially subjective or politically speculative but virtually certain. Proximate cause is 'clear and present.' Publics hearing alarmists falsely yelling fire cannot choose to ignore the message – to search to their satisfaction for the truth.[10] There is no time. To disbelieve is to risk serious injury, even death. Nor can those fearing imminent bodily harm from pugilists ordinarily defend with words. Talk is no answer to force when force is what threatens talk. There is no freedom to talk when there is freedom to fight. In either case, targeted listeners are not *willing* publics denied their right to hear, in any meaningful sense of those words.

As communication, alarmism and pugilism are speech lines, not communicative triangles. There are listeners, but there is no third party. There is no public at large for conversion to a cause in any socially or politically meaningful sense of that term. Exceptions for provoking brawls or mass hysteria and deadly stampedes transcend politics and polities. They exist in all systems, dictatorial or democratic. It is no more acceptable to falsely yell fire in a crowded theatre, or to provoke public brawls, in a democracy than it is to do so in Communist China, corporatist

Singapore, monarchic Jordan, or theocratic Iran.[11] These apolitical exceptions to freedom of expression are not anything like the political exception of hate propaganda law.

III Defamation of Public Officials (Libel and Slander)

Laws against libel and slander can be found almost everywhere, in political democracies as well as in dictatorships. Unlike manner and form regulation, this exception *is* concerned with message content. And unlike proscriptions for pranksterism and pugilism, that concern is with conversion to the speaker's point of view. But does it buttress the case for hate propaganda law?

It is important first to distinguish defamation of 'private' individuals, or 'ordinary' libel, from defamation of public officials. Ordinary libel is concerned with harm to *personal* reputations. Proscription is protection of individuals *qua* individuals. This is not about matters of society, history, culture, or governance. In ordinary libel, if the individual is unsure of the limits of the permissible, she may hold her tongue when she need not or speak when she should not. But in either case, political society is not harmed – at worst, personal reputations are. What Jane Doe thinks about John Doe may be vitally important to Jane, John, and those who know or care to know them. But it is hardly vital to public discourse on consequential matters of society and polity. Ordinary libel law is not anything like hate propaganda law.

Can proponents of censorship find solace in a hybrid kind of libel exception, the right of public officials to sue citizens for defaming them?[12] Again, this exception can be found worldwide.[13] Even the U.S. Supreme Court has ruled that, in certain situations, public officials may have an action for libel against speakers for their public mispronouncements.[14] *New York Times* v. *Sullivan*[15] and *Garrison* v. *State of Louisiana*,[16] referred to by the prosecution early in Zundel for support but later abandoned, are directly on point.[17] The suggestion was that personal defamation of public officials often raises matters of public import. This is true. But these cases did not sanction proscription of communication of public import for personal hurt of the individual.

Sullivan sued the *New York Times* for publishing an advertisement containing falsehoods defaming him, in his role as chief of police, for putting down a civil rights demonstration in Montgomery. The court ruled that a newspaper could be held liable for defamation of a public official but only if the paper showed reckless disregard for the truth.

Even then, the recklessness had to be harmful to personal reputation rather than society at large. Repression of social or political falsehoods on behalf of particular groups or for the protection of society at large was *specifically* not sanctioned. As Justice Brennan wrote, '[t]he constitutional protection does not turn upon the "truth, popularity, or social utility of the ideas and beliefs which are offered." NAACP v. Button ... As Madison said, "some degree of abuse [of freedom of speech] is inseparable from the proper use of everything" ...'[18]

Sullivan tried to squeeze the claimed injury within the boundaries of the personal and the individual. The *Times* sought to put it outside them, into the realm of the public, the political, and the social. Sullivan argued that the words 'they' and 'the police' in the *Times* advertisement amounted to a personal attack on him in his official capacity as city commissioner in charge of the police. Rejecting personalization of political discourse, Justice Brennan declared that Sullivan had failed to 'establish that an impersonal attack on government operations was a libel of an official [Sullivan] responsible for those operations.'[19] In *Garrison*, a New Orleans attorney was charged with criminal contempt for his scathing comments against eight judges. Not even concern for the dignity and reputation of the courts, let alone for the personal reputations of the judges, could move the court to sustain repression of public expression: 'Concern for the dignity and reputation of the courts does not justify punishment as criminal contempt criticism of the judge or his decision ... This is true even though the utterance contains "half-truths" and "misinformation" ... Such repression can be justified, *if at all, only by a clear and present* [not subjective or speculative] danger of the obstruction of justice' (emphasis and parentheses mine).[20] Neither *Sullivan* nor *Garrison* buttresses censors' case that complainants can derive their offence by virtue only of belonging to a group disparaged for its group characteristics or by reason of falsification of historical facts distinct to that group. Neither case sanctioned repression of public discourse on important public matters for fear of public offence or to protect institutions from injury or publics from corruption by wrongful speakers.

Cases such as *Sullivan* and *Garrison* do not *lower* libel's threshold for public proscription to better protect offended groups or frail public psyches. They *raise* it, to better protect speech. They hoist the bar to a higher level (*reckless* disregard for truth, *clear and present* danger) precisely because the injuries to individual reputations in these cases also raise matters of social and political consequence. It is not that reckless disregard for truth is *sufficient* to find liability for public injuries that incidentally involve *personal* reputations. It is that reckless disregard for truth is *required* to find liability even for injuries to personal reputations if those injuries incidentally involve matters of *social and political* import. This, if anything, implicates rather than vindicates hate censors' case. Neither the exception of individual libel or libel of public officials is anything like the exception of hate propaganda law.

IV Obscenity

Some form of obscenity censorship has been recognized in virtually all Western democracies, including the United States. Obscenity is concerned not only with the content of the message but with protecting society *at large* from injury caused by exposure to that content. It would seem to be the 'democratic' exception that hate censors have been looking to for their philosophical coherence. Until recently, however, this was not a role that obscenity censorship could have aspired to. Even before the Charter, though constrained by the doctrine of parliamentary supremacy, the Supreme Court of Canada went to great lengths to find ways and means to strike down state proscriptions of obscenity that threatened public discourse on important public matters.[21] This may now be changing.

Historically, obscenity censorship was concerned with what may be called 'pornography' – material suppressed for sexual titillation and self-gratification. The more sexually explicit the material was, the more it stood to be repressed.[22] This was not just the 'traditional' Canadian understanding of obscenity. It was an understanding that traversed time, space, cultures, and polities – it was virtually universal. It could be found almost everywhere in the world, regardless of the system of government. And this is politically significant. Even in polities that came to have patently ideological understandings of obscenity, as the former Communist countries did, this was not to the exclusion of the traditional understanding. Repression of sexually explicit material for undue titillation was the *sine qua non* for suppression virtually everywhere where speech was repressed for obscenity. It was so in Canada – until now.

Historically, the danger for freedom of speech was that certain disagreeable sex-related meanings might be repressed for obscenity *despite* the fact that they were politically consequential. Today, the growing danger is that they might be suppressed *because of* this.[23] The Supreme

Court of Canada seems increasingly sympathetic to arguments that would treat obscenity not unlike the way it treats hate propaganda and, by inference, that would treat hate propaganda not unlike the way it treats obscenity. Unravelling the historical context, ideological nature, and political implications of this shift is critical to understanding its dangers. I begin by distinguishing 'pornography,' traditionally understood, from 'hate propaganda' in terms of the nature of the two products, the purposes of their messengers, and the respective consequences of their repression.

Hate propaganda, like pornography, may be repulsive to some, inviting to others. There are similarities – but the two are very different. Hate propaganda is speech with a political purpose. Pornography, in its *traditional* understanding, is not. Speech with a political purpose may sometimes be conveyed in pornographic form,[24] but the two are not synonymous. The public interest in sexual gratification is not the same as the public interest in social or political change. Nor is public fear of sexual arousal (the traditional objection to pornography) the same as public fear of social or political arousal.[25]

Nor are the purposes of the messengers the same. Pornography is a mercenary activity with a mercenary purpose. Remaking society and polity is not the pornographers' reason for working or the reason for public interest in their work. Pornographers, unlike hatemongers, are not political messengers, and pornography is not political speech in that sense. The oft-used 'merchants of hate' metaphor is misplaced and misleading – but illustrative.[26] Hate propagandists are in it not for the profit but for the politics. More often, they stand to lose rather than gain financially. Unlike pornographers, the job of professional hate propagandist in Canada is not especially well paid. Nor are their services and 'talents' in great public demand. Are these 'distinctions without a difference'? Or are they distinctions of consequence?

Compare the repression of explicit sexual depictions intended solely for physical gratification with the repression of transparent messages of intolerance intended for social proselytization and political transformation. Certain explicit appeals to sexual arousal may well be understood in 'political' terms, as incidentally sustaining structures of domination. But silencing for fear of public sexual arousal does not raise the democratic dilemmas for the purpose of repression that silencing for fear of public social and political arousal does for the cause of progressive hate censorship. Censors suppressing for the offence of explicit titillation do not aim to abridge contentious social or political commentary. Nor need they, to effectively silence. Historically, pornography censorship has managed to subsist side by side with some of the freest, most spirited, and dynamic cultural, scientific, social, and political eras of public discourse. As the U.S. Supreme Court observed in *Miller*, 'It is beyond question that the era following Thomas Jefferson to Theodore Roosevelt was an extraordinarily vigorous period not just in economics and politics but in *belles-lettres* and in the fields of social and political philosophies ... We do not see the harsh hand of censorship of ideas ... lurking in every state regulation of commercial exploitation of human interest in sex ...'[27]

Consider repression from the perspective of the politics of the club of social censorship rivalry discussed in chapter 5. All socially antagonistic groups (for example, Arabs, Jews, Blacks, Serbs, Croats, Muslims, Catholics) are political rivals, and all political rivals are, potentially, eager hate censors.[28] But pornography (traditionally understood) is not about political rivalry. Messengers of porn do not compete to silence opposing political messengers and social meanings, to lay claim to an officially correct history, or to tout their message of self-gratification as 'the one and only' correct meaning to the legal exclusion of contrary ones.[29] Hate speech repression excites the contentious politics of the silencing club by which rival political groups compete to officially appropriate exclusively correct public meanings. Hate censorship transforms a social politics of discursive public conflict into a legal politics of competitive public silencing – beating or threatening important public discourse into submission. Hate censorship, or its threat, saps public discourse of its vitality and drains community trust of its social capital. Pornography censorship does not.

Consider repression from the perspectives of more meaningful public discourse – the 'collision' thesis and information overload. In terms of intrinsic value, pornography and hate may, arguably, be comparable. But the value to society of their expression, or the loss to society from their repression, are not comparable. Can pornography renew and revitalize public understanding in the cause of moral progress? Hate propaganda can do so in the cause against ignorance, prejudice, and intolerance. The more explicit, raw, and repugnant the message of hate, the more it can renew and revitalize the message against it.[30] Can the suppression of open depictions of explicit sexual gratification risk information overload and meaning atrophy – to the detriment of moral self-enlightenment? Repression of open expressions of explicit hatemongering can do so – to the detriment of social self-enlightenment.[31] Repressing open expressions of explicit depictions of sex abridges freedom of public sexual self-gratification. Repressing open expressions of transparent messages of social intolerance abridges freedom of public self-enlightenment and more meaningful political discourse.

Consider repression from a pragmatic, 'working' perspective – the dilemma of reconciling effective silencing with successful promotion of the cause of repression. What important social message is misshapen or what insidious political meanings are publicly elevated and resonated by the prosecution of pornographers – to the detriment of the cause of moral enlightenment? How many purveyors of pornography hunger for public exposure and trial publicity, or care to profit more from martyrdom than money in the 'cause' of explicit sexual titillation? Can one seriously speak of *politically* unsafe repression in silencing the worst pornographers as one can in silencing the worst hatemongers? How many frustrated pornographers care to substitute hurtful acts such as vandalism, sabotage, and assault in place of proscribed speech in order to still get their message 'heard'? Can one meaningfully speak of a *political* threat to successful social adaptation and change in prosecuting pornographers?

Consider repression from the perspective of the slippery-slope dilemma. Just as effective prosecution of hate can move hatemongers into less transparent and more refined expressions of intolerance, so too effective prosecution of pornography may move pornographers into more restrained and refined depictions of human sexuality. But this is hardly counterproductive to the elevation of the human spirit. On the contrary, it promotes it. Where is the democratic dilemma between effective silencing and successful promotion of the cause of repression here? Dilemmas of slippage, slide, rivalry, trespass, transition, and trust – political self-contradiction, social self-defeat, pragmatic unworkability – are *intrinsic* to the repression of hate, but not to the repression of pornography. A law intended to prevent social division and its political discords cannot be otherwise. Profound implications for society, polity, and the respective causes flow from profound differences between the two in terms of the ends of the censors, the ends of the censored, the content of their meanings, and the consequences of their repression.[32]

It is appreciation for at least some of these socially important and politically consequential differences that allowed the U.S. Supreme Court in *Roth* v *U.S.*[33] to reject pornographic 'utterances' as 'speech' within the meaning of a meaningful constitutional protection: '[a]ll ideas having even the slightest redeeming social importance – unorthodox ideas, controversial ideas, even ideas hateful to the prevailing social climate – have the full protection of the First Amendment ... But ... such utterances (lewd and obscene) are no essential part of any exposition of ideas and are of such slight social value as a step to truth that any benefit ... is clearly outweighed by the social interest in order and morality.'[34] Effective repression of pornographic depictions, unlike effective repression of hate speech, need not fail even (or especially) when it 'succeeds.' Yet even here, as in all suppressions of socially unwanted public communication for the public good, unintended slippage cannot always be avoided in censorship practice.[35] Consider the following:

Police lay charges in the case of the widely acclaimed film *Last Tango in Paris*.[36]

Police lay charges in the case of the children's sex-education book *Show Me*.[37]

Alberta police department seizes material of an anti-pornography advocacy group.[38]

Toronto police 'investigation' targets a painting depicting the rape of a Mayan woman by Guatemalan soldiers. The painting is reported by those familiar with the work to be a political statement sympathetic to the plight of Guatemalan women.[39]

Canada Customs confiscates *Erotic Poems*, from a sixth-century B.C. anthology of Greek works.[40]

Canada Customs seizes an instructional film depicting the physiology of male masturbation headed for the University of Manitoba medical school.[41]

Imagine, then, the risks of slippage and trespass on legitimate public discourse when censors begin to treat obscenity and hate propaganda as one. At that point, titillation meets politics. The two can become almost indistinguishable.[42] Obscenity censorship crosses paths with hate speech censorship. But then, obscenity censorship is no longer repression of just sexual expression. It becomes also political repression. Political trespass and politicization begin at the point where repression of expression for moral fear of graphic sexual titillation ends and repression for political fear of social proselytization begins. At that point, dilemmas of political self-contradiction, social self-defeat, and pragamatic unworkabilty also begin.

For some, political trespass is not to be avoided but sought. This is, effectively, the 'world-view' of some feminist scholars today.[43] In this thinking, hate and obscenity become interchangeable – kindred spirits in a philosophically more coherent legal matrix of 'social' exceptions to freedom of expression. Interchangeability of language transmutes meanings. Transmutation cross-fertilizes censorship thinking, risking a socially more expansive and politically problematic speech repression. Progressive censors are expanding obscenity thinking to include socially disconcerting meanings on politically contentious matters of society and polity. But 'bootstrap' censorship thinking like this does not buttress the case for hate speech repression as a democratic exception to freedom of expression, much less as one that is consistent with other well-worn democratic exceptions. Rather, it shows the dangers of a sliding hate speech jurisprudence, one that would include ever more exceptions within the political clutches of its expansive social meaning. If 'progressive' meanings of hate swallow and enlarge more limited traditional meanings of obscenity, the problems of obscenity repression will also include the dilemmas of hate speech repression.

Recent developments suggest grounds for concern. Progressive thinking on obscenity is coalescing with a slippery thinking on hate. Today, sexual explicitness and sexual self-gratification are no longer what obscenity repression or the threat of it may turn on, but rather on social transformation and politically correct public beliefs.[44] In this thinking, sexually explicit material (the traditional concern of obscenity repression) ought not, by that fact alone, to be denied to willing adult consumers. But certain wrong social or political attitudes ought to be. Proponents of this shift have long sought to correct for the error of traditional obscenity law, which brought the 'morality play' of correct sexual mores into the cause of repression. Instead, however, they are bringing a far more politically problematic 'ideological play' into the cause of obscenity repression – socially correct attitudes on politically contentious matters of public consequence.[45]

It would be a grave mistake to characterize this shift as simply a 'moral crusade by a different name.' It is a different kind of crusade – a far more ideologically conscious and politically consequential crusade. Fear of open expressions of graphic sexual titillation (a still common social concern worldwide) can at least lend itself to relatively apolitical (legally ascertainable *and* philosophically delimitable) standards of review for error in censorship principle, if not always to error-free censorship practice.[46] Repression for fear of wrong social and political attitudes about society, women, and men does not lend itself well to such review, in either principle or practice.

Slippery politics in Canada is intersecting with slippery law. Charter jurisprudence has now broken with its pre-Charter past. Obscenity and hate propaganda are becoming increasingly indistinguishable in the minds of many on Canada's highest court.[47] Progressive obscenity thinking is proving to be transmutable between forums, cross-fertilizing its authors' expansive meaning across institutional boundaries. The Supreme Court of Canada now accepts that 'degrading or dehumanizing' sex or sex-related depictions, at least, may be suppressed as 'obscene' not for reasons of *explicit sexual titillation* but for sending the adult public the wrong social message.

What is as important as the words 'dehumanizing or degrading' is the far less well-articulated political justification – wrong social message – for suppressing such communications. What does it mean? The court offers, as a politically innocuous example of its current thinking, 'sex coupled with violence.' This 'will almost always' be 'obscene' because it sends a wrong, 'socially degrading' message about women.[48] But legally correct social meaning here cannot be so easily *politically* confined. The court itself is careful to leave open other possible constructions. What social shape and political form they might take is difficult to say when a right to abridge public meaning construction includes the right to ensure that the public gets *only* the right, socially elevating, message – the politically correct one. Over time, such constructions may take as many forms as there are future judges – with different social sympathies and political bents.

The price of separating, if not quite divorcing, sex from obscenity is the developing marriage of political ideology and obscenity. The court seems prepared to blur the prescriptive line between sexual titillation and social ideas, between self-gratification and public proselytization, between social mores and political disagreement. The problem is, if sex coupled with violence, to use the court's example, 'will almost always' be obscene because it sends the public the wrong message about women, it is not necessarily the only socially wrong message that may need to be repressed. There are other socially no less injurious messages and meanings that may need the censor's attention. As Borovoy asks, '[I]f we could suppress material merely because of its detrimental impact on male attitudes towards women, what about other potentially harmful attitudes? Could we suppress Communist propaganda for undermining our attitudes about the value of preserving democracy? Could we suppress certain feminist material because it might arguably create negative attitudes about the institution of marriage?'[49]

Not only 'real' feminists but REAL Women, many immigrant cultures, religious moralists, and even aggrieved men may also have to be consulted – or repressed – for political correctness. Progressive social censorship breeds politically expansive public censorship – extending official appropriation of public meaning construction into ever more contentious or unintended areas of public discourse.[50] If obscenity jurisprudence continues to expand in this direction, it will become increasingly entangled in the same problems as expansive hate propaganda censorship – growing political self-contradiction, social self-defeat, and pragmatic unworkability. Should we be moving closer to, or farther away from, this kind of 'coherent exceptions jurisprudence'?

V Group Defamation and Seditious Libel

1 *Group Defamation:* Beauharnais *v.* People of the State of Illinois[51]

Can proponents of hate propaganda law find juridical solace in U.S. experience with criminal group defamation statutes? In *Beauharnais*, decided over fifty years ago, the U.S. Supreme Court upheld the conviction of the accused under an Illinois criminal libel statute for distributing an *inflammatory* leaflet that vilified the 'Negro race.' Is this a true hate propaganda exception to freedom of speech that can be turned to by censors today?

The decision in *Beauharnais* turned not on judicial recognition of group libel but on the absence of political, social, and economic rights. It turned on recognition of conditions of exclusion of Blacks that were not much different from those during slavery, one hundred years earlier. These conditions were either state sponsored, state condoned, or both. Freedom of political expression itself and its corollary rights – of assembly, association, the right to vote or to run for office in order to change these appalling, oppressive conditions – were de facto denied to the Black community. The years immediately after the Second World War in the United States were still days of public lynching, property burning, and legal segregation of Blacks. This was before *Brown* v. *Board of Education of Topeka, Kansas.*[52] The 'separate but equal' doctrine of *Plessey* v. *Ferguson*[53] was still good constitutional law. It was more than a decade before the Civil Rights and Voting Rights acts began to accord Blacks the political rights and their legal incidents – necessary for public expression and self-representation – that were taken for granted by Whites.[54] In short, this was a period when fundamental freedoms and their legal incidents (freedom of speech, assembly, and association; equality rights) by which the targeted minority could challenge oppression, defend their rights, and advance their interests were still being denied to them by an oppressive majority.

The court noted both the political backdrop and the particular circumstances – mob hysteria, violence, and their historical context. Blacks and their families could not effectively 'answer' vilifying attacks without fear for life and limb. Incidents of beatings, burnings, rape, and even murder of Blacks – condoned, urged on, and sometimes even joined in by the local authorities themselves – were neither subjective nor speculative injuries at that time. They had not been so in the past, and there was no reason to think that conditions would change in the immediate future. Even then, the court made clear that abridgment of speech here was to be treated as a 'trial and error' experiment, until more effective means could be found for ensuring the safety and well-being of a community unable to defend itself.[55]

The court in *Beauharnais* was concerned with suppressing popular, not unpopular, expression – the vilifying speech of the majority, not a minority. This was not a case of a population at large that *might* be infected but of one that *already* was infected. All the combustible materials for grievous and irreparable physical injury were present and ready to burn. Only a spark was needed to light the fire – and this was not hard to find. If the courts wouldn't protect a threatened minority under these conditions, who would – the majority? *Beauharnais* was hardly a case of *fringe* hatemongering of the Zundelite kind.[56] These are not 'distinctions without a difference.' Canada at the beginning of the twenty-first century is not the United States of the middle of the twentieth. Indeed, the events in this case turned on social and political conditions that no longer exist even in the United States.

The case against the morally suasive value of *Beauharnais* need not, however, rest on distinctions of fact in the instant case. The problem with hate speech law in Canada is with the law itself. For one thing, the law is intended to be a permanent response to hate, not a stopgap remedy dependent for its application on *extraordinary* circumstances of imminent, grievous, or irreparable harm.[57] For another, the thinking underlying *Beauharnais*, prescient of future judicial directions as it turned out to be, does not stand for what censors today suggest it did. The court in *Beauharnais* did not sanction hate speech repression as an appropriate permanent answer to the problem of intolerance – one that was blind to the variables of place, time, and circumstance. This case stands for legal abridgment of socially *inflammatory* public messages *not* as an ordinary feature of democratic discourse but as an extraordinary answer to extraordinarily undemocratic social and political conditions. That, not censorship, is the 'exceptional' message and more meaningful legacy of *Beauharnais*. It is hardly one that buttresses the case for hate propaganda law in Canada today.

2 Seditious Libel: Boucher v. The King

Perhaps the best historical precedent for hate propaganda law can be found in what proponents of censorship would rather forget – British laws against seditious libel. The roots of these laws can be found in the ancient soil of European monarchies. Twentieth- and twenty-first century authoritarian and totalitarian polities have also expressed a particular fondness for such laws. The landmark Canadian case addressing them, *Boucher*,[58] is also one proponents of censorship would rather forget.

Interestingly, the *common law* did not proscribe vilification of a whole class of persons, only vilification of individuals.[59] Judicial thinking accepted that such vilification was a matter for society itself to deal with, not the law. But monarchical thinking disagreed – hence the creation of the various offences of seditious libel to fill the gap. The purpose, historically, of these laws was to ensure social harmony and public order among the king's obedient subjects. Compliant and pliant 'countrymen,' not critical and unruly ones, were needed by royal rule.

The formal legal marriage of 'sedition' (a political concern) to group 'libel' (a social concern) required no witness to harm. The injury feared was to established authority. But the threat did not have to be specifically directed against established authority to be found seditious. The feared political harm was assumed from the feared social disaffection, discontent, and ill will itself. Given monarchy's requirements for political stability – loyal faith in divine rule and uncritical subjects to ensure it – the assumption of threat to one (political stability) from a threat to the other (social harmony) was more often than not a well-founded fear.

For the authoritarian government of Maurice Duplessis in 1950s Quebec, ancient remedies for timeless ills proved hard to resist. Duplessis decided to deploy his legal arsenal, including the Criminal Code's proscription of seditious libel, against the ideas of Jehovah and Karl Marx.[60] Did these groups' aggressive campaign of proselytization not present as grave a danger of injuring the public interest in social harmony and political stability in Catholic Quebec as religious heretics had presented to such interests under British monarchy? Could group libel be brought in through the back door by way of criminal sedition? Until *Boucher*, the answers to these questions were arguably in some doubt. Absent a charter of rights and constrained by the doctrine (albeit federalized) of parliamentary supremacy, the ability of the court to address the issue head on was limited. None the less, most of the justices still found ways to do so.

The majority held that the seditious causal link must be demonstrated on the evidence, not presumed from the mere fact of promotion of social division, disaffection, or ill will.[61] The political fragility assumed for ancient royalty would not be presumed for established democracy. Most importantly, the *social* fragility assumed seemed to suffer a fatal blow. Justice Rand, as we saw, openly rejected as dated the presumptions underlying such laws.[62] In rejecting Duplessis's abridgment of Jehovah's Witnesses' proselytizing activities in a devoutly Catholic Quebec, he did so not because these activities were socially or politically innocuous but precisely because they were *not* innocuous.

The character of the public interest had changed. The needs of European monarchies would simply not do for the needs of a self-governing polity in the second half of the twentieth century. Public discourse that could not socially antagonize or politically proselytize was not politically meaningful discourse. Socially innocuous speakers preaching to the converted or soothing the fearful were appropriate, indeed necessary, for polities premised on the public good of uncritical subjects, kingly public order, and divine right to rule. But this was hardly appropriate for the fluid social and political needs of a consolidated democracy in the second half of the twentieth century. Canada was not in need of protection from itself.

One would have thought that *Boucher* laid the assumptions underlying such dated censorship thinking to rest. Unfortunately, hate propaganda law, underscored by the mushroom thesis, has effectively resurrected it. Progressive thinking is revitalizing and expanding it. 'Modern' justification for repression of socially disconcerting public discourse masks what is in fact an archaic sociopolitical understanding of the 'public good' in such repression. Hate propaganda law has much in common with ancient seditious libel laws.[63] But it is a coherence and a history that proponents of hate propaganda law would prefer to forget, or obscure, rather than espouse.

Conclusion

Hate propaganda law is better seen as an exception to well-worn democratic exceptions to freedom of speech than a better expression of them. Censors can build a philosophically more coherent exceptions jurisprudence to justify hate propaganda law. They can pretend that hate propaganda law is not unlike other democratic exceptions to freedom of expression. But this requires making other exceptions not unlike hate propaganda law.

The danger of jurisprudential indistinguishability is political interchangeability. Politically transmutable social meanings risk multidimensional censorship creep. If obscenity is not unlike hate propaganda, then obscenity can be hate propaganda. If group libel is not unlike hate propaganda, then group libel can be hate propaganda. If trespassing on privacy and public property rights is not unlike hate propaganda, then disturbances to private peace and public order can be hate propaganda. If unfair social criticism of public officials is not unlike hate propaganda, then criticisms of public policy can be hate propaganda. If public pugilism, hooliganism, and pranksterism are not unlike hate propaganda, then such offences to the public peace and tranquillity can be hate propaganda. This is not to depoliticize hate propaganda but to politicize and expand other exceptions to freedom of speech. It is to delegitimate meaningful public discourse and to turn otherwise apolitical, situational, or circumstantial social problems into ideological ones. It is to make hate propaganda a more total political instrument of social control.

To achieve a more total social control, Communist censorship did just that. Public communication – even music, comedy, and fiction – became political crimes if found to be contrary to social harmony, egalitarian social consciousness, or socialist public order.[64] Fighting, swearing, and pranksterism were 'hooliganism.' Hooliganism was not just a criminal offence against victimized publics, it was a political offence against *socialist* society. It was an attack on *socialist order*. The way hooligans thought was not just a *crime*, it was a *political* crime. Hooligans suffered from a bourgeois social consciousness.[65] Hooligans needed socialist re-education. Pornography was not just an affront to the sensibilities of the offended, it was a political offence. It was a crime against the *people*, an attack on *socialist equality*. Intemperate social criticism of public officials was not just a public libel, it was a *seditious* libel – a crime against the polity in the name of the people. Societal reductionism was meant to depoliticize society. Paradoxically, it served to politicize society still more.

Jurisprudential coherence cannot be found for hate propaganda law in apolitical exceptions to public discourse that are common to virtually all polities. Nor can it be defended in self-governing ones. To find legally suasive or germinal juridical precedent for the law, one has to go to places and polities one would rather avoid. One could go backwards in history to a different era, a different place, a world of colonies rather than autonomous nations, and of divine rulers rather than self-governing publics. But one could also go 'forward,' to a twentieth century populated, in part, by authoritarian publics not just tolerant ones, and totalitarian polities not just self-governing ones. Should exceptions jurisprudence be moving in these directions?

My case against hate speech law does not rest on lack of philosophical coherence but on the dangers of more of it. The worst thing defenders of censorship can do is to slide the moral authority, and politics and politicking, of hate propaganda law into ever more areas of public discourse through a more philosophically coherent but ideologized exceptions defence. They risk turning an *exception* to freedom of expression jurisprudence increasingly into an *abrogation* of freedom of expression jurisprudence – one that swallows up ever more exceptions to freedom of expression under the politically self-contradictory, socially self-defeating, and pragmatically unworkable banner of 'hate propaganda.' The cost of more jurisprudential coherence is less political defensibility. The exceptions defence for hate propaganda law can be made more philosophically coherent *or* more democratic – but not *both*. Such is the jurisprudential side of hate censorship's democratic dilemma.

8

Alternative Juridical Balances and Balancing Juridical Alternatives

Canadian courts have accepted the challenge to balance rights in the cause of tolerance, diversity, and social progress by legal silencing. Courts are practical institutions. Their task is not to bridge deficiencies of hate censorship in theory but to bridge them in working practice. The current balance struck in *Keegstra* and the thinking underlying it does not bridge these deficiencies very well either in theory or practice. Pressure for more expansive and expandable censorship threatens to widen the gap between what is, or can be, and what is expected and worsen the deficiencies further. How this will play out depends on how the court responds to the challenge. Not all balancing by legal silencing is equally deficient. Juridical misbalancing can vary widely. Different balancing attempts can injure in different ways or to different extents and be more, or less, stable in terms of holding to the initial balance struck. Can balancing by legal silencing ever serve society well? If so, when? Of what kind? This chapter explores possible answers to these questions by weighing the comparative strengths and weaknesses of four alternative juridical balancing 'options' from the perspectives of the insights developed in earlier chapters.[1]

These options may be expressed as follows:[2] (1) suppression of hatred against identifiable groups expressed through false facts on matters of society, history, or governance; (2) suppression of the promotion of hatred against identifiable groups; (3) suppression of advocacy or incitement to commit illegal acts of hatred against identifiable groups likely to cause such illegal acts; (4) temporary suppression of expressions of hatred in 'extraordinary' circumstances. I weight the relative strengths and weaknesses of each from three overlapping perspectives: (1) theoretical and functional balance – the rationality of the connection between the means and underlying ends of censorship; (2) political and pragmatic balance – how well democratic and practical dilemmas are addressed; (3) juridical balance – the role of the court as agent or object in appropriations of discursive public conflict.

I Suppression of Hatred against Identifiable Groups Expressed through False Facts on Matters of Society, History, or Governance[3]

One hate censorship option is to proscribe the use of false facts to express intolerance of identifiable groups. The court could give full judicial deference to the legislature's assumption that grievous social and political injury will follow in the absence of censorship of such expression. No proof of the feared harm to the public interest, on a case-by-case basis, would be required.[4] The court would be concerned only that the speech was in fact false and intolerant of identifiable groups, and that the degree of *mens rea* or moral turpitude required for conviction – knowledge, recklessness, or carelessness as to the truth or falsity of the assertions espoused – be proved.[5] This option is deficient from several perspectives on the balancing dilemma.

It is functionally deficient from a theoretical perspective. Means and ends are seriously disjointed. The distinguishing feature of the law here is that it represses only socially or politically divisive *false facts*. It exempts socially or politically divisive opinion, innuendo, abstract speech, fiction, or general treatises. The purpose of the exemption is to avoid trespass on legitimate speech. But the purpose of the protection is to ensure that the public thinks 'right.' The state would like to transform public thinking 'for good.'[6] But the circumspect statutory language 'works' only to protect it from transparent threat.[7] It offers only limited 'protection' against hatred. Given deeper underlying purposes of the law, the legal distinction between facts and non-facts is a highly problematic means for the desired end.

The distinction is artificial. Political communication cannot be successfully so divided because public cognition cannot be meaningfully so distinguished. Public meaning construction on divisive matters of society and polity is far too complex and multifaceted to allow for this kind of fine legal distinction. As a means of public protection it is self-crippled. How can publics who need to be shielded from even transparent falsehoods, such as Holocaust denial, be safely left exposed to more opaque messages of intolerance and prejudice? How can publics be freely trusted to see through disguised evil meanings, eschewing their subtly negative resonance with deep-seated prejudices, when they cannot be trusted to see through even transparent meanings of evil and undisguised malevolent motives? Subtle meanings and sophisticated messengers of intolerance are no less 'moulders and movers' of deep public sentiments than obvious ones. On the contrary, in a politically consolidated democracy such as Canada, socially and politically consequential choices are more apt to lurk in the meanings of subtly contentious messaging forms than in the proscriptively convenient discursive vessel of transparent falsehoods uttered by marginal fanatics. Indeed, how are self-governing publics to aquire the self-skills to make the enlightened distinctions (that democratic censors expect them to make) required by opaque expressions of social evil when they are denied the opportunity and *learning* experience to make those required by obvious ones? Speech paternalism may be legally divided in this way, but public meaning construction and self-government cannot be.

This option is also deficient from the perspective of the political and practical dilemmas of repression of this kind of expression. It is socially self-defeating and, ultimately, pragmatically unworkable. The distinguishing feature and strength of this option is that, by limiting coverage to false facts, it minimizes the possibilities for trespass on legitimate speech. But its 'strength' is also its 'working' weakness. Limiting coverage this way leaves the law underinclusive, in terms of its own underlying social goals and political expectations, in more ways than one. Fact-limited repression carries both generic and particular political and pragmatic dilemmas associated with repression of intolerant expression.[8] There is the generic dilemma of prosecution's negative resonance – the hatemonger's exploitation of his 'underdog' status and manipulation of repression's processes and procedures to his advantage. But there are also unintended dilemmas particular to this option.

First, in restricting the law's silencing reach to the quieting of transparent racists and marginal extremists only, censors do not simply exempt more subtle messengers and more problematic meanings from proscription – they *legitimate* them. In *officially* delegitimating *only* false facts as hate propaganda, the law would tend to *officially* legitimate more subtle expressions of prejudice as *not* hate propaganda. Second, fact censorship works to undermine its own best tool for raising public awareness – the patently refutable words of the transparent bigot himself. If the real problem is deep-seated prejudice, as social activists are at pains to point out, repression of the transparent and the refutable is more apt to hurt than help the goal of correcting false beliefs through public exposure and political challenge. Surface censorship that 'works' drives open public prejudice from the public 'face' and deep-seated prejudice still deeper into hiding.[9]

Third, fact censorship lends itself well to the dilemma of the 'slippery' target. If silencing transparent hatemongering 'works,' either or both of two consequences are possible. It will 'work' to turn openly hateful messengers into clandestinely hateful actors. Or it will work to push transparently hateful meanings into opaque discursive contexts, making them increasingly difficult to expose, challenge, or prosecute. It can even do both, driving the incorrigibly unrefined extremist underground to do more clandestine hurtful acts and pushing sophisticated ones into subtler and more insidious expressions of intolerant meanings. Out of public sight is not out of public mind, nor is the public out of danger, when it comes to answering *determined* hate.[10] Fact censorship, like all marginal censorship, undercuts its own proscriptive boundaries by the very limits of its repression – to the detriment of its underlying social and political purpose of enlightening the public, securing the safety of the polity, and delegitimizing the messenger. It resists attempts to create either a socially successful or a politically stable balance.

Finally, this option is deficient from a juridical perspective. First, it enlists the court in a purpose for which it was not intended. What can be more appropriate for publics in a polity premised on self-government than public debate about public 'facts' of social, political, and historical import? What can be less appropriate than to have lawyers, judges, customs officials, police, immigration officials, information entrepreneurs, or rival aspiring censors discard the public's right or substitute their own? The false facts suppressed would not have the special significance they do if they were only about personal or private matters. They concern the whole public. This is public property. It belongs to all of the public, not to the courts, the prosecutor, or their duly authorized accomplices or self-appointed proxies in discursive theft. In legally appropriating discursive public conflict, the court or its accomplices confiscate vital public politics. The judicial forum substitutes for the public forum. The legal process usurps the political process.[11]

Second, this option enlists the court in a cause for which it is ill-equipped. Fact determination is a role for which a court of law is ordinarily well suited. But legal assumptions of justiciability here can be politically deceptive.[12] The meaning of even patent facts of this sort can be socially multifaceted and politically multidimensional, as we have seen.[13] Facts that lend themselves to social division and public discord are inexorably politically interdependent. The public falsehoods the court was *not* asked to suppress may sometimes pose a greater threat to public truth and the public good than what it *was* asked to suppress. Demoting one socially disconcerting falsehood or half-truth may serve only to elevate a worse, politically interconnected, contending falsehood or half-truth in its place.[14] Censors cannot reduce socially multifaceted and politically multidimensional meanings to legally singular ones on the basis of their bare 'facts.'

Even when meanings are clear, public injuries from them may not be. Intolerant messengers openly proclaiming false facts are not punished for their inaccuracies *per se*, but for the public injuries feared therefrom. Not all are or can be punished. The messengers chosen to be suppressed are those messengers that censors find to be most important – those whose meanings are judged to be more injurious than others to society and polity. This inescapably involves making socially subjective and politically speculative silencing choices on contentious public matters in respect of which the court has no special 'apolitical' crystal ball.

Finally, judicial action comes not at the court's own initiative but at the behest of the prosecutorial majority or influential censoring minority. The court's selections for suppression are limited to the false social facts and feared public injuries it was given, not the ones it was denied. The politician's political choices for prosecution are primary definers and foremost deciders in the court's legal choices for judicial suppression. The court can, of course, second-guess the state. But this is easier said than done. The state cannot demonstrate, from any *one* case, that extremism's feared social resonance or political conflagration is more likely to occur without public silencing of the false facts selected for prosecution than with such silencing. The state's purpose is to prevent an 'at-large' harm that is, in its most important essence, prospective and boundless, not dependent on circumstance, time, or place.[15] Apprehended public harm, here, is not of a sort that lends itself to independent proof of injury on the ground of the *particular transgressor* or the facts of the *individual* case. Nor, therefore, can hate law be meaningfully so limited. Were the court, as a matter of course, to require case-by-case proof of what cannot be proven case by case, this option would, effectively, be rendered nugatory.

However one cuts it, the kinds of false facts suppressed under this option are the kinds that produce political trials, political spectacles, and politically selective and speculative public injuries. The legal questions may be whether the facts are false, whether they are about identifiable groups, and whether the accused has the *mens rea* required for conviction. But the deciding questions of proscription remain political – why *these* false social facts and not some others, why *this* public injury and not some other, why *this* offensive or offended group and not some other?[16] As a flustered Ray Girn, president of the University of Toronto's Objectivist Club asked, following Canada Customs' temporary detention of the newsletter *In Moral Defense of Israel*, on suspicion of promotion of hate propaganda, 'We have [received] other pamphlets attacking health care and multiculturalism, and those haven't been stopped or questioned [for hate propaganda]. So I don't know why these ones were.'[17] Under this option, censorship courts leave themselves vulnerable to entanglement in the partisan social messaging choices and political meaning constructions of others. This serves well neither the cause of judicial independence nor that of judicial integrity.

II Suppression of the Promotion of Hatred against Identifiable Groups[18]

A second hate censorship option is to proscribe *promotion* of hatred against identifiable groups. The main strength of this option is the functional weakness of the first – deficient coverage. The message feared is not confined to facts. The messenger feared is not confined to transparent racists. The 'promotion' of hatred option allows for more meaningful protection against intolerance than the option tied to dissemination of false facts. From a functional perspective of internal theoretical coherence this makes sense. As argued in option one, while hate censorship can be artificially legally divided along lines of fact, truth, and transparency for the convenience of repression, public thinking and self-government cannot be. This option is deficient from several perspectives on the balancing dilemma.

To begin with, its internal functional strength is also its democratic weakness. Its broadly worded proscription amplifies hate censorship's dilemmas of political self-contradiction and social self-defeat. Any message or messenger deemed to promote hatred against identifiable groups might be suspect and suppressible. More than just marginal fanatics can be quieted. More than just the transparent meanings of their hatred can be snatched from public discourse. Under this option, the suggestively unacceptable (or unacceptably suggestive) is also put at risk. Progressive censors are invited to appropriate and confiscate not only works such as Hitler's *Mein Kampf* from public discourse. They might also be tempted to grab Shakespeare's *Merchant of Venice*, Rushdie's *Satanic Verses* – maybe, one day, even Roberto Benigni's *Life Is Beautiful* or Professor Flanagan's *First Nations? Second Thoughts*. If trial of transparent racists such as Zundel can substitute for public discourse and public self-enlightenment, imagine what threats to prosecute a Salman Rushdie, a Philippe Rushton, a Pat Buchanan, or a Louis Farrakhan would do for public understanding and the cause of social tolerance. Indeed, imagine what front-line troops – the police, customs officials, and information entrepreneurs – could one day do.[19]

The problem, as this suggests, is that more open language of proscription is also socially more malleable and politically more pliable language of proscription. What socially disturbing and politically moving public discourse of public consequence does not harbour or harvest feelings of contempt by somebody, for someone or some things, sometimes? The requirement that proscription be limited to a category of 'identifiable' persons offers comfort more in legal theory than escape in fluid and evolving political practice.[20] What groups identifiable 'today,' to say nothing of those still to be identified 'tomorrow,' can *absolutely* not become maligned victims sometimes and in some ways or malevolent victimizers at other times and in other ways – as determined, from time to time, by rival occasional governing majorities or politically influential censoring minorities? If rival groups can threaten each other even with fact-dependent hate censorship 'today,' imagine what they can do to enlightened public discourse and social tolerance with promotion-dependent (opinion?) hate censorship 'tomorrow.' Whose found truths, fixed meanings, and final triumphs will be elevated? Whose denigrated? Who decides?

Finally, this option presents a more difficult dilemma than the first for the court. In the first option, the court could relatively easily and 'safely' ignore dilemmas of political self-contradiction and social self-defeat in state prosecutions. Who can argue with squelching the likes of Zundel or Keegstra? What can be wrong with suppressing transparently false claims such as the assertion that the Holocaust did not occur? But this option allows for proscriptive expansion, potentially catching less transparent messengers and meanings of intolerance. The politics and politicking of official hate repression would then become more visible and, therefore, more difficult for the court to ignore. True, message 'making' politicization in its own right is a publicly more visible and visibly problematic politicization of the court than is message 'taking' judicial politicization exercised in right of the fact censoring state. But amplified possibilities for state trespass on less obviously illegitimate meanings can in time make it more difficult for a reviewing court to guard against the first by hiding behind the second.

Where the language of proscription is not limited to determinable facts and transparent transgressors, the censorship-supporting court therefore leaves itself vulnerable to a moving politics that can end with an unenviable judicial choice. The court can become a message-making political 'top dog,' second-guessing more controversial speech-proscriptive state choices on a case-by-case basis and substituting, far more visibly, its own politically controversial position on correct social meanings for that of the appropriating state. Alternatively, it can defer to state choices as a matter of course and risk appearing over time like a message-'taking,' meaning-destructive, political 'lap-dog.' In short, it can risk independent politicization in its own right or it can risk dependent politicization in right of the state. Neither serves the public, the court, or the progressive cause well.

The role of top censorial dog may be difficult for censorship-supporting courts to avoid in any event. But it will become more difficult to avoid in the future if the court is faced with expansive state applications of an expandable hate censorship, as is possible under this option. On the other hand, the taint of politicization in its own right that might follow from a case-by-case reassessment of the state's politically more contentious silencing choices also has highly problematic and uninviting implications for the court. This risk is more likely to be unwittingly than willingly assumed. If assumed, it is more likely to be assumed later than earlier in the expansion. The greater threat to judicial integrity presented by this option, therefore, is not immediate but prospective. Its pliable language of repression, and a proactive political culture of hate censorship can, over time entrap even reluctant silencing courts in judicial message-making 'censorship creep.'

Judicial construction of correct social messages is not the same as judicial construction of correct social policy.[22] Message making is the public's means for policy making. In a democracy, social policy making is not intended to be final, but is an ongoing political process.[23] Judicial policy making does not raise the same questions of political legitimacy that judicial guarantees of right public speaking (found truths, fixed social meanings, and final political triumphs) do. Should the court appropriate the authority to politically fashion and officially fix exclusively correct public meanings on increasingly controversial matters of society and polity, it would not simply be making important social policy. It would be appropriating the public's discursive right to do so. No court of law can arrogate to itself the right to substitute its mind for that of the public as an ordinary feature of democratic discourse and retain its integrity as a neutral court of law. The more it finds itself doing so, the less it can proclaim its neutrality and safeguard its integrity.

By underappreciating this 'today,' the censorship-supporting Canadian court risks falling into a political legitimacy quagmire 'tomorrow,' from which extrication will be progressively more difficult but, for that very reason, increasingly necessary. Knopff and Morton warn that judges should avoid becoming unwitting pawns of left- or right-wing social activists.[24] Whether or not courts should heed that warning in the social *policy*-making field, in the social message-making field they ignore it at their own, and democracy's, cardinal risk.

III Suppression of Incitement to Illegal Acts of Hatred against Identifiable Groups Likely to Produce Such Illegal Acts[25]

A third hate-censorship option is to repress incitement to commit illegal *acts* of hatred where such expression is likely to produce those illegal acts. The distinguishing feature of this option is its narrow coverage and determinacy of feared harm. Only prescribed incitement is targeted. Only those likely to cause the illegal acts incited are proscribed.

This option could be defended on three grounds. First, such 'utterances are no essential part of any exposition of ideas and are of such slight social value as a step to truth that any benefit ... is clearly outweighed' by the public interest in social peace and public order.[26] Second, repression only of incitement does not trespass on general discourse, treatises, or abstract speech – the contending ideas can still be expressed in these more acceptable forms. Third, the assumed causal link between the wrongful speech (hate incitement) and the feared harm (*illegal acts* such as graffiti, assault, or homicide) is qualified and determinate, and the test of probability (likely to produce such acts) proximate.

This is an attractive option. On balance, it seems to do more good than ill for the cause of tolerance and democracy, preventing imminent harm without trespassing on vital discourse. For those subscribing to the value of 'some' – a much-circumscribed – hate censorship as an ordinary feature of democratic discourse, this option seems to offer the best of all possible worlds. But there are a number of problems even with this option.

First, it is functionally deficient from a theoretical perspective. The connection between means and ends may appear to succeed where all the other options fail. This option proscribes speech threatening imminent harm (urging the speaker *to do* before thinking) but exempts vital discourse (speech allowing the listener *to think* before doing). But this is not a saving grace but an artificial distinction. It assumes that people who cannot be trusted to govern themselves as they should (respect the law) when *inflamed* to hate, can be trusted to govern themselves as they should (respect the law) when exposed to hateful *suggestions*. Should the unthinking be provoked by inflammatory speech to act illegally, a myriad of *ordinary* laws targeting discriminatory practices, criminal conduct, illegal attempts or conspiracies, as well as surveillance and emergency preventive measures, are available to nip the problem in the bud, contain the harm, and punish the offenders. Moreover, some social division and political discord – even, on occasion, civil disobedience – born of anger and contempt, are par for the course in an adaptable, resilient, and strong democracy.

If the available measures are insufficient because so many people would ordinarily be provoked by inflammatory speech to 'unthinkingly' conduct themselves illegally, then such endemic social hatred is hardly likely to be effectively squelched by laws directed against inflammatory speech. A public unafraid to engage *en masse* in illegal conduct are not going to be deterred by laws against inflammatory speech. In that case, the law's assumption that people can be trusted to think as they should if given time to reflect – the reason for excluding from repression abstract, general, or ordinary expressions of intolerance – but not if incited, is flawed, and the law is irrational. In short, acceptance of the idea of self-government in one instance (*abstract, general,* intolerant speech) but not in the other (*inciteful* intolerant speech) is an artificial distinction. Hate censorship may be legally divided along lines of a to think–to do distinction for the convenience of repression, but self-government cannot be.

Censorship theorists counter that while the focus of proscription may be on the immediate and the measurable, the real injury feared is far more subtle and distant. Rational discourse, argument, and debate are essential to social progress and self-government. Incitement to illegal acts of intolerance is not. Indeed, it makes rational discourse more not less difficult. Incitement hardly qualifies as 'speech,' within the meaning of the noble public purposes of freedom of expression, to merit constitutional protection. It is comparable to fighting words or pornography.[27] As Catherine MacKinnon says of pornography, '[i]t is not ideas [men] are ejaculating over. Try arguing with an orgasm sometime.'[28] Equally, one may say, try arguing with incitement sometime. In short, incitement to illegal acts of public intolerance is socially and politically valueless, its deleterious public impact obvious, and counter-speech inapplicable or ineffective.

This kind of reasoning may seem persuasive, if not altogether novel. But it is neither. It has a long, and less than noble, historical pedigree. Its best expression recalls a social history that its current authors would rather forget. In 1925, the U.S. Supreme Court affirmed the conviction of Benjamin Gitlow for violating sections 160 and 161 of the *New York Penal Law*, which prohibited the crime of criminal anarchy. The accused had published a pamphlet titled 'The Left Wing Manifesto,' which called for the destruction of the bourgeoisie and the establishment of a social dictatorship of the proletariat. As the court wrote, 'Manifestly, the legislature has authority to forbid the advocacy of a doctrine designed and intended to overthrow the government without waiting until there is a present and imminent danger of success. If the state was compelled to wait until the apprehended danger became certain, then its right to protect itself would come into being simultaneously with the overthrow of the government, when there would be neither prosecuting officers nor courts for the enforcement of the law.'[29] With hindsight, we know that the answer of repression of expression was out of proportion to the magnitude of the threat. But more to the point, it was also seriously flawed in its understanding of the assumptions and functions of freedom of expression.

First, social incitement is not valueless to a democratic society. Self-government cannot exclude the emotive merely because the emotive is wrong. A meaningful understanding of self-government, one based on *who* we are rather than on how wise or how right we are, integrally assumes freedom of wrongful emotive expression.[30] Inflammatory social communication is an *essential part* of who we are – warts and all. It expresses the intensity of our feelings and the depth of our discontent. Wrongful feelings and intense emotions define us socially and politically as surely as do rightful feelings and dispassionate reason. Second, to suggest that incitement to illegal acts of public intolerance is valueless because it espouses no ideas of redeeming social merit confuses the public importance of the message with disagreement over its content.

Such speech would not be selected for special preventive criminal punishment if the ideas about society it espoused were socially or politically insignificant.

Third, freedom of expression not only assumes the right to hold ideas about society and polity. It assumes the right to *effectively* communicate them to others in the hope of converting like-minded people to the speaker's cause. The manner or form of communicative exchange, if it is not otherwise illegal, should not deny the right of exchange.[31] 'Ideas' about society and polity expressed through the medium of raw emotions are no less 'ideas' about society and polity than ones exchanged through the medium of reasoned debate. Indeed, inflammatory speech, symbolizing intensity of feelings and depth of beliefs, may often be the more important part of the message sought to be conveyed.

In *Cohen* v. *California*,[32] the essence of the defendant's transgression was to convey a socially divisive and politically disconcerting message without benefit of 'formal argument.' The defendant was charged and convicted for wearing attire with the inscription 'Fuck the Draft' in (of all places!) the corridor of a courthouse packed with proponents (and opponents) of the Vietnam War. Apart from objections to the obvious obscenity, there was also the fear (real in the circumstances) that the message, in the manner and place conveyed, might provoke a violent altercation. In overturning the conviction, the U.S. Supreme Court rejected the suggestion that the 'Constitution, while solicitous of the cognitive content of individual speech, has little or no regard for that emotive function which, practically speaking, may often be the more important element of the overall message sought to be communicated.'[33]

Some of the most important social and political ideas in human history have been communicated in inflammatory terms through emotions as varied as hatred, anger, laughter, tears, or awe. Historically, some emotive public communications have, indeed, caused grave social divisions and profound political change. Some changes have been good. Others have been bad.[34] Emotive speech *moves* messages.[35] As Borovoy says, 'try arguing with laughter sometime' or with 'awe or tears.'[36] Are we going to proscribe laughter, awe, tears, or anger because they may cause social and political change? Are we going to abridge freedom of speech where it is effective? Are we going to protect it when it is ineffective?

Fourth, the very assumption that incitement to illegal acts of hatred cannot be 'answered' or answered in time is itself highly problematic. Flawed comparisons to fighting words, pornography, or false alarms suggest that the two are analogous in character and illustrative in remedy. Such thinking fails to appreciate the political character of social incitement. Social incitements espouse a cause. They are about *changing* society and polity. A cause can be *directly* challenged and answered – with a contrary cause. Fighting words, false public alarms, or urges provoking orgasm cannot be. Proximate-cause assumptions of unanswerable harm (to-do–to-think distinction) are misplaced here. They put the cart of criminal 'doing' before the horse of public 'believing.' Social divisions, like social harmony, are neither set nor changed in a day merely because the medium of discursive exchange may sometimes be inflammatory. As Borovoy says, 'attitude formation is a slow process, allowing time for longer term measures ... to counteract the impugned messages.'[37]

Is the danger from socially inflammatory speech in Canada that this option apprehends so 'clear and present' that it may befall us before there is time to avert the evil by measures other than censorship?[38] Perhaps the fear is well founded for some fledgling, struggling, still-fragile representative democracies. For them, if stability is not somehow ensured in the short run, there may not be any democracy to speak of in the long run.[39] But the assumption is most questionable as an *ordinary* feature of democratic discourse in a consolidated representative democracy such as Canada.[40] The implicit assumption – that hate incitement is, *ordinarily*, more dangerous to society and polity than other, exempted forms of socially divisive communication – is specious. As, Justice Oliver Wendell Holmes said more than seventy-five years ago,

[i]t is said that their [Communist] manifesto was more than a theory, that it was an incitement. Every idea is an incitement. It offers itself for belief and if believed it is acted on unless some other belief outweighs it or some failure of energy stifles the movement at its birth. The only difference between the expression of an opinion and an incitement in the narrower sense is the speaker's enthusiasm for the result. Eloquence may set fire to reason ... [I]f in the long run the beliefs expressed in proletarian dictatorships are destined to be accepted by the dominant forces of the community, the only meaning of free speech is that they should be given their chance and have their way.[41]

This option also remains self-contradictory and self-defeating from a 'working' political and pragmatic perspective. Prosecution only of incitements to illegal acts of intolerance does not escape the dilemma of negative resonance. It only takes on a new, and in some ways more problematic, twist. First, it confers an aura of legitimacy on legally exempted, more subtly deleterious messengers and meanings of intolerance. Under such a law, one who promotes hate other than by incitement is not a hate propagandist. Second, it confers an aura of legitimacy on the incitative messenger and his meaning. Prosecuting only incitement to intolerance can suggest that if there is a problem with the message, it is not solely or mainly in the content of its meaning but in the speaker's *enthusiasm* in expressing it. Public focus is deflected from the impropriety of *what* the hatemonger says and intends to the impropriety of the *way* he says it. The larger cause of hate repression is again the loser. The public interest is again the ultimate victim.

Third, theorists' assumption that repressing only incitement is a stable balance, safeguarding legitimate speech from trespass while advantaging more reasoned discourse, ignores Canadian political realities and the slippery practical problems of repression of this kind of expression. Numerous problems of prejudice and hatred exist in Canada. But incitement to commit illegal acts of intolerance is hardly one of the major ones. Patently false facts may be difficult for racists to stay clear of (what is a devout hatemonger without them?), but incitement to illegal acts of hatred is less so. Even Canada's premier hatemongers, Zundel and Keegstra, have managed to stay well clear of charges of *inciting* hate. Alternative speech choices may be less appetizing to the discriminating palate but they are, ultimately, no less inviting to the hungry racist denied better ones. If true incitement is the *only* catch, there will be very few fish caught. But the slippery politics of trying to find some is not harmless in failure. Politics does not respect artificial legal boundaries set for it, even here.

When Eric Hafemann, lawyer for Helmut Oberlander, tried to convey the deep frustrations of some members of the German-Canadian community in Kitchener-Waterloo by saying that it would 'explode' if Ottawa attempted to deport his client (for lying about his Nazi past), the Canadian Jewish Congress (Ontario Region) not only filed a complaint with the Law Society, it also brought its 'concerns about potential violence' to the attention of the Kitchener-Waterloo police saying 'that the words stated by [Hafemann] pose a real threat to our community ...' Hafemann responded in kind, saying 'he would defend himself before the Law Society and is considering laying a complaint of his own, alleging an attempt by Congress to intimidate counsel.'[42] For the moralistic club of hate censorship to do its dirty, divisive politics, inciteful 'social dividers' need not, it seems, be marginal or transparent ones. In sum, the potential losses for the progressive cause and democratic society risked by a law against inciting intolerance are unlikely to be out-weighed by what is gained. This option does not solve the effectiveness-success dilemma of silencing hate. It is another illustration of it.

Finally, even this much-circumscribed proscription does not free the court from the creeping dilemma of message-making politicization. Censors here can prosecute incitements to illegal acts of hatred likely to produce such acts. But no such acts need occur.[43] In uncommonly volatile situations (a riot instigated by neo-Nazis), the question of harm prevention by speech repression can be an easy one for the court to answer correctly. But in these situations, other measures and laws exist to nip the harm in the bud (beefed-up surveillance, increased security, reading the riot act). In other, more ordinary circumstances, bald incitements (e.g., 'kill the Jews') may well do more in Canada to show-case the plight of the excoriated than to make converts or further the cause of the excoriater.[44]

Less obviously hateful meanings or more ambiguous messaging con-texts are no less problematic for the court than they are for the state. If they are atypical, in a proactive regime effectively suppressing incite-ment they are apt to become more typical. Is the owner of a social club guilty of inciting hatred and anti-Semitism for cancelling a Jewish char-ity event slated to feature the granddaughter of former Israeli prime minister Yitzhak Rabin? A German court thought so.[45] So too, in time, might a Canadian court looking for slippery racists. A neutral judicial 'watchdog' scrutinizing obvious state abuses may appear to be the ju-ridical strength of this option. But, over time, a judicial top dog con-structing social messages and political meanings is more likely to be-come its growing dilemma.[46]

Negative public resonance of repression, the potential for state abuse, the impairment of socially accurate and politically timely feedback, the danger of slippage and encroachment on legitimate public discourse, the dirty, divisive politics of social censorship rivalry, and the creeping risk of judicial entrapment in growing politicization may well be too high a price for Canadians to pay to quiet the odd incitement to illegal acts of hate.

IV Temporary Suppression of Expressions of Hatred in Extraordinary Conditions of Grave and Irreparable Harm

A fourth hate censorship option is to proscribe intolerant speech only if there is clear, cogent, and compelling evidence (1) of the likelihood of the feared harm; (2) of the likelihood of great and irreparable public harm; (3) that repression can likely prevent the harm; (4) that alternatives to speech prevention (ordinary laws, emergency and other measures) are inadequate to prevent the harm.

This option would not entirely preclude content-conscious abridgment of socially or politically disconcerting speech. However, hate censorship would change from a merit-conscious abridgment of public discourse as an ordinary feature of democratic discourse to a harm-conscious abridgement applicable only in circumstances of extraordinary social or political challenge. The operating assumption would be that, in the ordinary state of democratic discourse, these conditions would not be satisfied. Suppression of public expression would be a temporary measure, a last resort – an extraordinary, not an ordinary, feature of public parlance. It would last only as long as, and no longer than, the extraordinary circumstances justifying it. The court would monitor satisfaction of the conditions for the law's invocation. The monitoring would be continuous or regulated by a sunset clause.[47]

This option would involve rethinking not just the proper role of hate propaganda law *per se* but also its relationship to other laws concerned with threats to the polity at large.[48] Hate propaganda law would be concerned with intolerant public communication for fear of grievous public division or conversion to the cause of the speaker – in politically circumscribed situations to be outlined below. Other laws would continue to address grievous threats to established authority. For example, conspiratorial criminal communication (invariably confined to clandestine collaborators) even by hatemongers would not be punishable by hate propaganda law but by other laws or emergency measures.[49] Such communication is directed to established authority and threatens illegal conduct. The danger feared is from the (threatened) actions of the conspiratorial group itself, not from a presumably cognitively vulnerable public at risk of conversion at large to the cause of the conspirators.

A public call to arms by insurrectionists would, of course, be public communication with a socially divisive and politically proselytizing purpose. But in Canada, it would be a threat against, not of or by, the public at large. Insurrection or terrorism is not a *public* proselytization problem in a consolidated representative democracy. The public at large in Canada need not take up arms against the polity in order to change it – even to change it fundamentally. They can do so peacefully through the democratic process if they so wish.[50] This is not to say that such communication may not pose a *proselytization* danger in consolidated representative democracies – marginal extremists may convince other disgruntled extremists to take up arms against the majority. However, it is not a *public* proselytization or hate propaganda problem.

While hate propaganda would be a public proselytization problem, public proselytization would not, *ordinarily*, be a hate propaganda problem. Discursive public conflict on matters of society and polity would not, ordinarily, be proscribable under any law. Contemptuous social messages would have to be dealt with by the public themselves through speech measures such as education and remedies against illegal acts or discriminatory practices, rather than through enforced silence. Hate propaganda law would be concerned with such messages and their meanings only in extraordinary circumstances. What might these extraordinary circumstances be? War or threat of invasion might qualify. Insurrectionary or other public appeals to division, discord, or violence, *per se*, absent the extraordinary circumstances described below, would not qualify. Peacetime would not necessarily and in all cases be a disqualification. This option is preferable to all the other options, for the following reasons.

It is functionally least deficient from a democratic theoretical perspective. Exceptional remedies should require exceptional circumstances. Excepting extraordinary and temporary conditions, hate speech law, over time, is apt to be neither the socially more successful nor the politically least intrusive way to deal with the challenge of intolerance, division, and discord in a consolidated representative democracy. In the ordinary state of Canadian society, ordinary criminal laws prohibiting unlawful conduct, civil remedies against discriminatory practices, and social, community, and educative resources to combat ignorance and intolerance are more appropriate. This option is most at peace with the idea of public tolerance based on a deeper and less fragile basis of social progress – one premised on more transparent, accountable, and adaptable self-government. It assumes that in a polity premised on self-government, the public should ordinarily decide vital public matters for themselves and not have official censors or their duly authorized accomplices or unauthorized proxies in discursive theft do the thinking and deciding for them. And if they cannot do this, where it counts, even in ordinary times, then they are incapable of self-government.

Terrorists and insurrectionists may make public appeals to division and discord in the course of their conspiracies. But it is not their public appeals but their conspiracies that stand apart from freedom of political communication. Conspiracies are a planned assault on the democratic process of social and political choice by force of arms. Repression of acting terrorists represses force of arms.[51] Repression of their at-large public appeals for fear of public offence or public conversion to their cause represses political communication.[52] Other measures are ordinarily available to deal with the possibly harmful social and political effects of such appeals. And if these measures are not adequate because so many people would ordinarily be won over by their appeals, then no law directed against speech can prevent such endemic hate from taking its lawless course. To borrow, *mutatis mutandis*, the words of Mr Justice Holmes in *Gitlow*, 'if in the long run the beliefs expressed' by insurrectionists, terrorists, or hatemongers 'are destined to be accepted by the dominant forces of the community ... the only meaning of free speech is that they should be given their chance and have their way.'[53] Censorship cannot prevent it anyway.[54]

Under this option, at-large public appeals by insurrectionists, terrorists, or hatemongers, would not, *ipso facto*, be treated as an extraordinary condition in Canada justifying abridgment of political communication. Hate propaganda law would not and should not be misused, as was the *War Measures Act* during the Trudeau years, to repeat the self-serving civil rights abuses of that era.[55] One must be wary of 'bootstraps' arguments. Extraordinary conditions warranting abridgment of political communication must be demonstrated separate and apart from the proselytization threatened by the communication itself. They must not be assumed from the threat of public proselytization itself. It must be shown that proselytization in the cause of insurrection, terrorism, or hatemongering needs to be repressed in Canada because prevailing social or political conditions are extraordinary in the life of Canadian democracy. Censors should not be allowed to say that conditions are extraordinary in the life of Canadian democracy because society is threatened with proselytization by insurrectionists, terrorists, or hatemongers. The cart of intolerable social and political public appeals should not be put before the horse of extraordinary conditions justifying their repression.[56] A meaningful understanding of extraordinary conditions cannot be synonymous with the proselytization itself, threatened by political communication. Courts need to be conscious of how easily censorship thinking can slip from the first to the second in the moment of social crisis and the heat of political battle. When might such extraordinary conditions be demonstrated?

War, or threat of invasion, may constitute extraordinary conditions in the life of any democracy. External danger can sometimes change the character of internal threats. Exceptional, externally driven circumstances

may turn ordinary internal conditions of division and discord, otherwise tolerable as par for the course in a consolidated democracy, into
an extraordinary proselytic danger to the polity.[57] One example might
be where the 'turn' threatens irreparable injury to the public's freedom
of political choice. Where an external enemy making war or threatening invasion stands to successfully exploit or manipulate legally unfettered domestic rights to freedom of social and political communication
to irreparably injure the polity, the democratic premise for allowing
hate propaganda may no longer hold. In these cases, Canada might be
in a fragile position not unlike that of a fledgling democracy under
threat of internecine collapse. Unless the situation is stabilized in the
immediate run, there may be no long run to speak of. The difference,
however, and this is critical, is that if the external threat is defeated or
allayed so too is the *raison d'être* of the public censorship. Hate propaganda law here would be a temporary 'answer' to internal public divisions made exceptionally dangerous by extraordinary external conditions,
not a permanent remedy for ordinary internal divisions, as it now is.[58]

Peacetime would not necessarily and in all cases exclude application
of hate law. Even in a consolidated self-governing polity, extraordinary
internal conditions may arise that can turn otherwise legitimate intolerant public appeals into an irreparable danger to life and limb, avertable
only by temporary proscription of such public utterances. Consider a
small, isolated, ethnic community, inadequately policed, under siege,
in socially explosive circumstances.[59] Preventive intervention against
inflammatory speech may give some protection to the threatened
community. Ringleaders could be arrested (presumably by outside
law-enforcement authorities), enabling, perhaps, calmer heads to prevail or allowing time for more reliable outside policing to be put in
place.

Hate law here would provide a cooling-off period, not a permanent
solution. Permanently enforced public quiet cannot turn conditions of
extraordinary enmity into true social harmony in small, isolated communities any more than it can in large, cosmopolitan ones. Timeless,
placeless, and circumstanceless appropriation of discursive public conflict by censors for fear of public offence or public conversion to the
cause of the speaker is part of the problem, not part of the solution, to
deep-seated social divisions and the criminal acts of those who do not
fear to break the law. The ultimate goal here remains deeper social
harmony and public understanding through more, not less, dialogue.
While this may not always be possible, the least ideal answer is one that

would attempt to fabricate them from a permanent legalization of state appropriation of discursive public conflict.

˙ From a theoretical perspective, this option reflects best the needs of a socially vibrant postindustrial consolidated democratic polity and a cause intended to fortify not diminish it. It strikes a fine balance between appreciation of the ongoing discursive needs of such a polity and recognition that even such polities may, on rare occasions, need a temporary silencing crutch to get beyond an extraordinary proselytic public threat. It would not allow censors, as a matter of course, to misappropriate or discard public discourse on public matters. It would keep thieves of discursive public conflict out of where they do not regularly belong in a polity premised on self-government – the public mind. Silencing public discourse on public matters where it counts is an extraordinary remedy for a democracy. Extraordinary remedies should be reserved for extraordinary times.

This option is also least likely to promote a censorship politics of self-contradiction and self-defeat. Censors exercising this option would not promote what they condemn – clubbing, concealment, self-denial, opportunism, and political backlash. They would not trust, as a matter of course, in those whom they suspect – police, immigration and customs officials, media, politicians, courts, and self-regarding information entrepreneurs. Nor would they deny the public the tools they need to know themselves better and to hold their leaders more accountable. They would not try to legally immunize any ideology, social policy, or public agenda from political challenge by fixing it with official status. They would not abridge and impede the public's ability to do better what the public is supposed to do and then justify that abridgment by the public's impaired ability to do it. They would not pursue a better societal politics by attempting to legally freeze the politics of society.

Given its temporary duration, exacting preconditions, and extraordinary circumstances of application, effective silencing here should not come at the expense of successful promotion of the cause. It should not be unsuccessful where success should be most obvious – in exposing the dangers to society and polity of transparent hatemongers. It should not risk trespass on controversial but cautious speakers. It should not be publicly concealing or socially falsifying – endangering feedback and promoting politically correct posturing and public opportunism – when it should be socially clarifying. It should strike the most stable juridical balance – one that is least likely to slip, over time, in a direction its authors do not intend it to go.

Finally, this option best balances political legitimacy with judicial integrity. Public discourse on public matters, where it counts, is left in the hands of the public themselves, not some of the public, rival censoring elites, the courts, official censors, or their unofficial, self-interested, or self-regarding proxies. Excepting extraordinary circumstances of temporary, but grave and possibly irreparable danger, public ownership of public discourse is inviolable. Even the court cannot appropriate it. The court is allotted a legally much circumscribed but politically more appropriate role – protecting and promoting the process of public discourse on public matters rather than legally ensuring or politically constructing correct public meanings. This option allows the court, at one and the same time, to defy message 'taking' political capture at the hands of ideological rivals and to eschew ensnarement in message making politicization in its own right. The court here neither acts as a court of law in a democracy ought not to act nor leaves itself vulnerable to becoming what it ought not to become.

Not only should this option work as intended and expected. It best expresses what *can* work as intended and expected. It is a democratically sound and functionally coherent censorship balance. By returning discursive public conflict (except in extraordinary discursive circumstances) back to the public arena – where it originated, where it belongs in a system premised on self-government, and where it will ultimately end up in one form or another in any case – the court may better serve itself, the public interest, and the progressive cause of hate censors themselves.

9

Alternative Measures

Towards a Less Self-intrusive Balance

Censors' trust that hate speech law can do the social work expected in the democratic context premised, as an *ordinary* feature of democratic discourse, is theoretically deficient and functionally flawed. Excepting *extraordinary* conditions that may afflict even consolidated representative self-governments, hate censors undermine their own cause in the very process of promoting it through hate censorship. The more effectively they silence, the more they undermine their own cause. What, then, are the alternatives to censoring hate, in ordinary times?[1] Do the alternatives leave society ultimately 'defenseless' against public prejudice, social injustice, and 'abuses of power by the powerful,' as suggested by progressive censorship theorists such as Catherine MacKinnon?[2] Or are they apt to leave society better defended? That is the subject of this concluding chapter.

This chapter is a comparative and self-interrogatory thematic discussion of alternatives to legal silencing, drawing on the insights of earlier chapters. It is an exploration of alternative ways to advance today's progressive cause(s) of tolerance, social justice, and democracy – ways that eschew entrapment in censors' dilemmas of political self-contradiction, social self-defeat, and pragmatic unworkability. For, whatever else successful social progress and political democracy may mean, they cannot mean less than that which would eschew such entrapment. The alternatives may not satisfy censorship theorists and social activists working to 'eradicate' hate, but absolutism in victory has been part of the problem not part of the solution to intolerance and ignorance. The discussion of alternatives to legal silencing in this chapter is not intended to be comprehensive or exhaustive. My purpose is to explore and illustrate some less self-intrusive ways to advance the causes of tolerance, understanding, harmony, diversity, and democracy. There may be additional good ways to advance the cause without undermining it. My discussion should be taken as inclusive, not exclusive, of these other possibilities.[3]

Part I of this chapter begins with a brief historical account of what alternatives to hate censorship have been able to do to further the cause of tolerance and social progress in Canada and an exploration of why progressive censorship theorists have failed to adequately weigh the achievements of the alternatives into their 'balancing' equation. In Part II, I identify cause-specific alternatives to public silencing, explore the many complex and subtle ways they do their work, and discuss how and why they can do them better – without hate silencing.

I Progress and Prognosis: Alternatives to Legal Silencing Revisited

1 The Work of Alternatives in Canadian History

Progressive proponents of hate censorship such as Bakan, MacKinnon, McKenna, and others characterize freedom of expression as a paper or *de jure* right protecting the rich and the powerful. In this view, it is hate censorship that is the *de facto* leveller – a collective social right and a positive political freedom. In practice, however, discursive alternatives to hate silencing have not fitted well the theoretical individual-rights or 'negative'-freedoms mould into which progressive censors have tried to squeeze them. On the contrary, measures *inconsistent with public silencing* have been front-line public warriors advancing the 'positive' freedoms social activists themselves have defined as the test of social progress and enlightened political democracy – education, shelter, health, safety, equality, and justice.

What made social progress in these areas possible in Canada was not censorship but meaningful exercise of speech by or on behalf of those without an official voice. Some progress, of course, flowed from the threat or act of physical violence. But in the main, the history of social progress in Canada, of the more deep-seated, less fragile kind, has not been one of bloody revolution and violent revolutionaries but of peaceful evolution and reformative evolutionaries.[4] More to the point, the most dramatic progress by women and minorities,[5] gays,[6] labour,[7] farmers,[8] and the poor[9] has been a function of freedom to speak as they thought rather than of legal silencing of those who thought differently. From the historic introduction of universal health care to the establishing of occupational health and safety standards, to product liability laws and consumer protection acts, dramatic social progress far preceded acceptance of the idea of silencing in the cause of social progress.[10]

Legal entrenchment of minority voices in its many forms – whether through constitutional provisions mandating affirmative action and equality,[11] interpretive provisions speaking to community and multi-culturalism,[12] or constructive provisions like the one allowing for the carving out of the self-governing territory of Nunavut[13] – has depended on freedom of expression. Without meaningful freedom of expression, there would be no criminal law against public expressions of hate, much less a comprehensive network of provincial and federal civil and administrative measures to control it.[14] Most importantly – the claims of scholars like MacKinnon notwithstanding – freedom of expression has been the means for the powerless to penetrate and publicize institutional, structural, and systemic causes of injustice and abuses of power by the powerful.[15] Speech, of course, may not be the only way. Violence may be another. But freedom of speech is the only *peaceful* way.

Progressive censorship theorists say that the hungry need food, the ill need medicine, the homeless need shelter, the at-risk need safety, the exploited need dignity, and the oppressed need justice – and that they need them more than they need legal rights to complain. But the two need not be mutually exclusive. Certainly they have not been in Canada. Social progress in Canada has not been empty. Freedom to question, disturb, and disrupt has made social progress possible. This is hardly to rest content. The gap between the haves and the have-nots may be growing again,[16] but it was not hate censorship that narrowed it.[17] This is not to deny the advantages or the inequities of wealth, good fortune, connections, numbers, or influence. It is to recognize them.

Social progress, of course, has not been unmixed. Advancement has been relative and has helped some more than others. Gains have hardly always been equitably distributed, or linear.[18] Historically, as Banting suggests, two steps forward have sometimes meant one, two, or even three steps back.[19] After decades of fairly steady and sometimes dramatic social progress, recent comparative economic setbacks may portend an extended period of public reaction and political retrenchment.[20] That it now has global earmarks is significant for the idea of progress through public silencing.[21] The 'freeing up' of financial markets, fragmented production, and capital mobility (capital flight?) have made it much more difficult to develop and protect not just national labour but also national social and cultural strategies.[22] Internationalization and digitalization of mass communication present an even more formidable challenge to progressive censorship strategy than internationalization of production and markets does to progressive labour strategy.[23] Freedom of speech to disturb, disrupt, and transform is most valuable in times of retrenchment and reaction. Retrenchment is hardly the ideal time for progressive causes to urge a right to quiet such speech in the cause of tolerance – it can more easily be turned *against* them.[24]

Political reaction and economic retrenchment have gone hand in hand in Canada with socially expansive hate censorship. Dramatic social progress proved possible without hate censorship. Retrenchment has not been prevented with it. Reaction cannot be better exposed or answered by it. Social progress without self-contradiction and self-defeat cannot be better promoted with it.

2 Uses and Abuses of History: Missing and Mispackaging the Evidence

Prevention of public harm and transformation for social 'good' are both about the future.[25] But how can progressive censors speak to the future when they cannot satisfactorily account for the past? In an inegalitarian polity, where there are still rich and poor, what matters in the progressive view is not what progress there has been or what can be but only what need be or should be. When the comparative successes of alternatives to public silencing are tested against an ideal or absolute normative standard of social progress, gains can seem negligible or superficial. On the other hand, the losses can seem profound. Progressive 'presents' become largely irrelevant, but sordid pasts never are. Sordid pasts portend sordid futures. The more distant, and sordid, the more portentous they are.[26]

The problem with censorship theorists' normative standard of social success, however, is more than the standard itself. The problem is, it is a double standard. The 'should' standard is not used as it *should* be used. It *is* applied to freedom of expression – highlighting deficiencies of discursive alternatives in the cause of progress. But it is *not* applied to hate censorship – concealing deficiencies of official silencing in that same cause. Forget that hate censorship in Canada does not work, on censorship theorists' own terms of justifying reference, as it 'should.'[27] Or that it cannot successfully be *made* to work as it should.[28] Or that trying to make it work as it should is a self-defeating slippery political slope where fears become self-realizing and failure self-justifying.[29] In short, forget that hate censorship 'works' to undermine its own progressive cause in the very process of promoting it. A preventive weapon that cannot fail, that sees itself equally justified in failure as in success (or more so), will not submit itself to 'speculative' standards of success.

If there is a place for a normative standard of success, however, it is one that progressive censors would do better to apply to themselves. Eradication of, not simply respite from, hate is not a cause whereof the committed can accept feeble, fleeting, or fragile social and political victories. Found truths, fixed meanings, and final triumphs, to be assured by silencing law, are not an idea of social progress that can admit of error or risk public failure or political defeat – not and remain true to itself. If it could, censorship would not be needed. Freedom of speech would do just fine. To apply a normative standard of success to hate censorship is to apply only the standard implicit in censors' own terms of purposive reference. Yet no deficiencies in hate censorship practice – deficiencies otherwise intolerable in other social democratic contexts – seem too big to dismiss in hate censorship theory.

Such thinking may be derelict on its own terms of social and political reference. But it serves a useful purpose, albeit an ultimately self-defeating and self-deceptive one. Progressive censorship theorists can 'test' freedom of speech against a standard of public progress that no society has been able to live up to – to 'demonstrate' its social and political deficiencies, while moving the deficiencies of hate silencing beyond the reach of effective intellectual scrutiny or accountability. As a result, progressive censors can put their trust, for the purposes of hate censorship, in the same deficient institutions and structures they so intensely distrust for the purposes of freedom of speech. 'Double-think' like this is an intellectual luxury that only those who have already made meaningful social progress can afford to entertain. Social activists claim that it is voice not victory that they seek through public silencing. Voice denying voice is only possible where there already is a meaningful voice. The truly voiceless are invariably free speech advocates, as the progressive left in Canada themselves once were.

II The Case for Alternatives

At bottom, the dilemma of hate censorship is not that it is good public medicine with some bad side-effects but that it is the wrong medicine for the prescribed ailments. The side-effects *are* the treatment. Hate censorship is intrinsically self-intrusive – irreconcilably undermining its own cause in the very process of promoting it. Large dosages intrude more. Small dosages intrude less. But all dosages undermine censors' own cause. Marginal hate censorship is not just ineffective, it is unsuccessful. On balance it tends to help the cause of the marginal hatemonger rather than the cause against him. But less limited censorship is even more unsuccessful. Hate speech repression can be more effective or less unsuccessful, but it cannot be both. Worse, eradicating open expressions of intolerance is a slippery political slope. Restrained dosages of censorship mask the visibility of self-intrusion but highlight the failure to effectively silence. Less self-intrusive dosages, therefore, tend to 'call' for more self-intrusive ones in their place. Time is not on the side of public silencing. The price of extended treatment is the risk of a growing dependence on the elixir of public quiet – to the later greater detriment of tolerance, social progress, and political democracy.

These dilemmas are *intrinsic* to social progress that enlists repression of public discourse on public matters in the cause, for fear of public offence or conversion to the cause of the speaker. But the dilemmas are not intrinsic to the alternatives to silencing. Alternatives to public silencing can do what hate censorship cannot – advance the causes of community, tolerance, diversity, social progress, and political democracy without undercutting or undermining them in the very process of doing so.

1 Punishment and Command Alternatives

Punishment and command alternatives to public silencing are ordinarily of two kinds. They may punish unacceptable behaviour. Or they may (also) command desirable behaviour. The criminal law best illustrates the first. Civil actions and administrative remedies best illustrate the second. These are 'official' or legal remedies. Punishment and command measures of the social kind may be employed by *particular* communities for their *own* internal social needs. In either case, overuse of punishment and command measures is a sign of failing democracy.

Punishment and command alternatives may usefully be divided into two subcategories. They may be *society-directed*, or they may be *community self-directed*. Society-directed or 'at-large' measures consist of the larger society's laws, violations of which invoke some kind of official legal sanction. Self-directed community measures consist of the customs, norms, rules, or practices of a particular community, produced by and for that community. Violations invoke some kind of intracommunity sanction.

Punishment and command alternatives, society directed or community self-directed, play important roles in all four areas of concern to progressive censors – tolerance, community, diversity, and the safety of the citizenry and security of the polity.

1) SOCIETY-DIRECTED (OR AT-LARGE) ALTERNATIVES

One goal of hate censors is to secure general public safety, peace, and order – to protect society from relatively isolated criminal acts or threats of violence born of intolerant minds. Another is more fundamental – to protect the nation-state itself from the social conflagration and political self-destruction (the mushroom thesis) born of intolerant minds. A third is to prevent socially unacceptable but non-violent behaviour – civil practices of intolerance.

These three purposes of hate censorship are richly served by numerous punishment and command alternatives to hate speech repression. The first two are well served mostly by criminal laws, but also, in appropriate cases, by civil laws. Canadian criminal law today not only *punishes* criminal *behaviour* but also provides for *extra* punishment ('aggravating circumstance') if the behaviour is motivated by hate, bias, or prejudice.[30] It also includes tools of *prevention* (surveillance, investigation, detection)[31] and measures that combine prevention with punishment (laws related to criminal attempts, conspiracies, or accessories).[32]

These alternatives to silencing do not punish incorrect social beliefs or command change in social attitudes. They promote the cause of social tolerance and political democracy indirectly by detecting, preventing, or punishing illegal *conduct* that undermines the cause. Investigative and surveillance instruments are particularly important *preventive* weapons in the battle against hatemongers. In practice, prevention also involves far more than just the state and its official arms of law enforcement. Human rights groups and minorities themselves have become invaluable as unofficial resources in the battle against intolerance, providing information, monitoring illicit activities, and even creating teaching aids for time- and resource-strapped security forces. The Canadian representatives of the Simon Wiesenthal Center 'presented RCMP, Ontario Provincial Police and Metro Toronto Police officers with copies of a CD-ROM titled Digital Hate 2000 [which] contains the Web addresses of racist sites and is intended as a research and investigative tool for police. A second version of the CD-ROM is designed as a teaching aid for educators.'[33]

These weapons have been effective in deterring or controlling the only kind of physical threat to the public ever posed by hatemongers in Canada – minor or isolated threats to public order, social peace, and public safety. If isolated threats by marginal fanatics risk *mushrooming* uncontrollably into major conflagration, it will hardly be for want of adequate laws for the detection, prevention, and punishment of such threats. By 'working' to drive open threats into hiding, however, hate censorship would tend to undercut these laws. The more effective silencing is, the more it would tend to undercut them. Laws promoting concealment work at cross-purposes with laws encouraging detection and punishment. They counter-productively heighten the 'need' for more effective tools of detection, surveillance, and punishment, putting other civil liberties such as rights of freedom of association, privacy, and fair trial at greater risk. Detection, surveillance, and punishment should be last resorts in a democracy. Hate speech laws work more to impair than to promote that goal.

Criminal measures in consolidated democracies are a small part of the battle against hate and prejudice. Civil and administrative remedies play a far larger role. While criminal alternatives to silencing can 'negatively' punish illegal *acts* of intolerance, they cannot, ordinarily, command desirable acts of tolerance. Nor, ordinarily, can they require systemic or structural changes in furtherance of such behaviour, as can civil and administrative bodies. Both private- and public-sector practices of intolerance and social injustice are covered in Canada in an elaborate legal network of 'functioning' civil laws and regulations ranging from labour and housing codes to human rights and consumer protection acts.[34]

Some provisions proscribe discriminatory practices that are intentional or malevolently motivated. But systemic alternatives, such as affirmative action, can target discriminatory effects, correcting institutional and structural conditions that sustain them. Together they provide a wide range of remedies. Refusal to comply as directed can, in the last resort, be legally remedied by imposition of a penalty. But there are often other, far more creative and subtle ways to get the job done.[35] Withholding an expected benefit is sometimes equally or even more effective – a matter of turning a stick into a carrot. For example, Ottawa made an expected financial grant to the RCMP conditional on a change in the force's policy against the wearing of religious headgear by its officers.[36]

Civil and administrative measures targeting individual practices or systemic structures of discrimination have greatly widened the scope of alternatives to public silencing in the cause of tolerance and social progress. In the last two decades, the number, flexibility, range, and importance of these measures have grown immensely. Systemic alternatives have become particularly formidable weapons in the progressive arsenal of social progress, because intention to discriminate need not be shown to warrant legal redress. Where the problem is institutional or structural, they may be the only effective remedies. However, even *civil* weapons of punishment and command should ordinarily not be the remedies of first resort in a democracy. People populate institutions and structures. The ignorant, the prejudiced, or the resentful can frustrate even some of the best systemic remedies. In a proactive regime of hate censorship, however, one that criminally and civilly suppresses open expressions of intolerance at large, such thinking and feelings can be harder to ferret out for exposure and correction. Paradoxically, this counter-productively heightens the 'need' for more punishment and command, including systemic, alternatives in the cause of progress.

Conventional wisdom in Canada is to treat public silencing and the alternatives to it as if they were mutually complementary, not self-contradictory. It is a view that can argue for 'strengthening' *both* public silencing and its alternatives.[37] Yet, as suggested above, the assumed complementarity is false. Hate silencing undercuts the work of alternatives to silencing, making less measured or more intrusive punishment and command weapons more 'necessary.' This is not to say that alternatives do all they should. But public silencing cannot be made complementary to progress merely because the good work of particular alternatives is less than it should be. More effective silencing makes the 'job' of alternatives even harder, making more effective and democratically problematic measures against intolerance and injustice more 'necessary' still. This relationship should be reason to rethink rather than to redouble censorship. Hate silencing is a self-defeating, self-realizing, self-justifying dilemma in more ways than one.

II) SPILLOVER ALTERNATIVES

There is a category of civil and administrative measures abridging intolerant or unenlightened communication, applied in already spatially or cognitively regulated relations of social intercourse, that resembles hate law. But, both in *purpose* and social and political *consequence*, the two kinds of speech proscriptions are very different. Not all proscriptions of intolerant speech are democratically deficient, socially self-defeating, or functionally fatally flawed. Proscription that does not undermine self-government cannot be *politically* self-contradictory. Proscription that is not publicly purposed cannot be *socially* self-defeating.[38] This, of course, is no assurance of success. Nor does it guarantee legality.[39] But that is not my point. These measures are not objectionable *for the reason* that hate censorship is objectionable – namely that it promotes politically corrosive self-contradictions and is socially self-defeating. I call these measures 'spillover alternatives' to hate censorship because promoting public tolerance is not their purpose in abridging speech but an incidental effect of their work – a 'spillover' message.

Competency reviews and sexual harassment codes are illustrative. They can abridge the right to communicate socially intolerant messages, but they do so in apolitical contexts of social or commercial intercourse. They are not intended to regulate public discourse on public matters – they are speech abridgments designed to regulate work performance not protect the public. When applied for the specific, job-related purposes intended, they are not democratically deficient or functionally fatally flawed, as hate censorship is. Freedom of speech does not exempt bigots from competency reviews or misogynists from harassment codes. A right to public discourse on public matters is not intended to protect the jobs of incompetent workers or to absolve them of professional responsibility for their deficient work.[40] Academia and academic writing are not exempt. Incompetent teaching or substandard scholarship is no less incompetent or substandard because what is mistaught or miswritten is about state and society. Similarly, sexual harassers are no less enjoinable abusers because their *modus operandi* includes socially ignorant or prejudicial communication.

Legislating job performance to prevent incompetence or abuse is not the same as legislating public tolerance and enlightenment to prevent racist public proselytization. Harassment codes may not always catch abusive workers, and performance reviews may not correct all incompetent ones. But where they do, they are neither politically self-contradictory nor socially self-defeating *for effectively doing so*. The quality of employee work and working relations is a performance question, not a political dilemma. It is not about protecting vulnerable psyches of the public at large from undue social or political challenge. Sexual harassment codes protect persons ordinarily in a captive position of functional inferiority from unwanted performance-injuring communication by persons ordinarily in a position of authority. Hate speech law, by contrast, is especially keen to prevent *wanted* communication from being received by receptive publics at large.

Some kind of abridgment of speech related to work performance can be found in all productive-conscious societies, irrespective of their political system of governance. It can be found in a dictatorship or a democracy or even in a society without a formal government at all. Properly applied, for the job-performance purposes intended, abridgment of communication related to professional *incompetence or abuse* is neither democratically deficient nor functionally fatally flawed. Performance and competency reviews only raise dilemmas of democratic self-intrusion when they slip from protecting job performance to promoting desired public cognition on important matters of state and society.

One can, of course, be both a racist and incompetent at one's work. But incompetence and racism are neither synonymous nor mutually exclusive. One can be lazy or an intellectual lightweight without being a racist. And one can be industrious and intellectually able without being tolerant.[41] Depending on the requirements of the particular job, however, the source of one's performance incompetence may indeed be one's racism or sexism. Democratic and functional dilemmas of self-intrusion arise when job performance or professional competence are not the real reason for review but a mask for stifling public discourse on public matters for fear of public offence or social or political conversion to the cause of the speaker.[42] As the Philippe Rushton case would suggest, competency reviews of scholarship concerning matters of state and society must tread a thin but critical line to avoid slipping from concern for performance to a question of politics.[43] Sexual harassment reviews must tread equally carefully. It should be easier to do so. Sexually harassing speech is privately not publicly targeted communication. Hatemongers seek publicity and the largest audience possible for their message. Sexual harassers would prefer anonymity and the smallest audience possible. Their communication is not purposed to change state and society but to satisfy a private need. Yet, as the case of mathematics professor Yaqzan suggests, slippage into censorship is possible even here if the world-view of the speaker becomes more important to the reviewers than the speaker's performance of his job.[44]

Performance-related rules do not enjoin public communication on public matters outside the work environment for fear of public offence or conversion to the cause of the speakers.[45] They are not directed to protect the public psyche from its worst self. None the less, they can have important at-large spillover effects on the public pysche. The work environment is an important tool of public socialization. Most adults work, and much socialization takes place at work. Most can identify with the need to reject professionally substandard work or personally exploitive communications conveyed in coercive or confined contexts that would promote such substandard work. The underlying message against intolerance and ignorance such work-related abridgments 'teach' can spill-over or percolate into the larger public realm, incidentally enlightening and raising public awareness without the democratic dilemmas of self-intrusion and self-defeat posed by hate speech laws.[46]

III) SELF-DIRECTED COMMUNITY ALTERNATIVES

The repression of hate speech in Canada is also intended to promote a multicultural society. Multiculturalism depends on diversity of communities. But diversity of communities depends on continuity of communities – and the requirements of the two are not synonymous. Society-directed measures that punish illegal *acts* of public prejudice promote diversity, as do systemic weapons that command *practices* of equality and inclusion. But what promotes diversity need not necessarily further community continuity. Community continuity requires internal solidarity, a strong sense of community identity, and a distinctive sense of mission. A more just and tolerant society is not a substitute for these requirements. On the contrary, it can be a catalyst for assimilative flight rather than community continuity. It is a paradox of laws that successfully promote equality, tolerance, and inclusion that the more they succeed the more they can loosen the internal community bonds upon which diversity and multiculturalism depend. As Avner Shalev, director of the Holocaust memorial/museum in Jerusalem, said, 'The Holocaust ... is a unifying force among Jews, as well as a vehicle for combating assimilation.'[47] To recognize this is not to advocate injustice or intolerance, any more than Shalev is advocating genocide. Tolerating racist acts and discriminatory practices cannot be democracy's answer to community self-indifference or decay. It is to argue *against hate censorship*.[48]

A liberal polity that outlaws racist acts, energetically punishes discriminatory practices, and socially ostracizes intolerant speakers does not need a community-loosening law against intolerant *speech*; rather, it needs more effective, self-directed community measures against internal splintering, self-alienation, negative participation, or assimilative flight. The more welcoming or integrative the dominant culture, the more such community-sustaining measures are needed. Unlike hate censorship, community self-renewing measures are uplifting weapons that can effectively *and* successfully reconcile diversity with continuity in the cause of multiculturalism.

Self-directed punishment and command weapons play a role. Administered by communities themselves, they are *coercive* measures aiming to forge internal solidarity, inculcate community identity, and instil a distinctive sense of community purpose. Ordinarily, they require members to conform to certain codes of community conduct on pain of some sanction for violations. Penalties imposed on non-conforming members can range from reprimand to ostracism. Ostracism can take the form of formal exclusion from the community. Or it can take more restrained forms, such as partial exclusion or informal (but sometimes no less painful), tacit exclusion. The use and severity of these weapons varies from community to community along ethnic, cultural, and religious lines – depending on particular communities' tolerance for internal diversity and disagreement.

These are not preferred weapons of choice in the Jewish community. The Jewish community stresses tolerance and internal democracy as the glue to hold its diffuse membership together, favouring persuasion over fear, inclusion over exclusion, and reward over punishment.[49] Today, it is a community identified by immense pluralism, one that tolerates an enormous range of cultural variations, ideological forms, and religious practices – from Secular, Reform, and Reconstructionist to Traditional, Conservative, and Orthodox. There is room for almost every Jew – but not everyone. For a few, exclusion, even outright ostracism, may be the order of the day. Though rarely used to solidify, such tools of punishment cannot be entirely dispensed with either – no community can exist entirely without them. All communities must have some minimal requirements, some basic norms, violations of which call for a clear message to be sent to offenders.[50]

2 Discursive Alternatives

Punishment and command weapons, society directed or community self-directed, criminal, civil, or administrative, formal and informal, have played important roles in the progressive cause – promoting internal community solidarity, forging cultural diversity, preventing or punishing criminally intolerant conduct, and correcting private acts or public practices of intolerance in Canada. But such tools would not exist without the discursive weapons that made them possible – those that *utilize* freedom of speech or *depend* on its corollary rights – such as freedom of assembly and association – to do their work. Social progress, including the enactment of hate propaganda law itself and favourable judicial interpretations of it, would not have been possible without meaningful exercise of free speech by those without a 'formal voice.' But not all weapons of voice are the same, either in purpose or in consequence. Some seek to procure desired results, more than to change undesirable attitudes. Others seek to secure desired results *by* changing undesirable attitudes. It is important to understand both how these public communicative forms have done their work in Canada and the political nature and social consequences of their differences.

Discursive weapons may be usefully divided into four main categories, with further subdivisions within or across those categories. Depending on their targets and their means for accomplishing their goals, they may be either inward directed, outward directed, or both inward and outward directed. Inward- or self-directed discursive alternatives are communications by a community directed to itself. The purpose is to counter internal division, self-alienation, negative participation, or assimilation.[51] Outward-directed discursive alternatives are communications by a community (or its supporters) directed to selected targets outside of the community or to the public at large. The purpose is to change public attitudes or procure a tangible benefit for the community.

Discursive weapons may do their work in either or both of two ways – persuasion and pressure. The distinguishing feature of pressure communication is that it aims to 'win,' whereas persuasion communication seeks to 'win over.' Persuasion messaging seeks to enlighten the target of communication about the cause of the speaker. Tangible or material benefits may often follow, but need not. 'Winning over' may sometimes be an end in itself. Pressure speech ordinarily seeks to obtain tangible results. Enlightenment may sometimes follow, but need not. Pressure communication works by compelling. Persuasion communication works to convince. Both depend on a meaningful freedom of expression to do their work effectively. These categories are not mutually exclusive. In speech practice, modes of message making may be mixed, traversing between or across these categories. In the examples that follow, inclusion in one rather than another category is an analytical distillation aimed to illustrate the *predominant* 'working' features of particular forms of communication in particular contexts, not a general seal of categorical purity.

I) DISCURSIVE PRESSURE ALTERNATIVES

Outward-directed Pressure. Discursive public pressure may be defined as minority influence by exercise or threat of public voice. Influential minority voices may be singular. But more often they are plural – enlarged by liaising with or leveraging other voices, including influential ones, to speak on behalf of the cause. The target may be discriminatory governmental practices themselves. A multifaith coalition led by the Jewish community whittled down a constitutionally anchored, centuries-old agreement on the public financing of Catholic schools by joining with other minorities and by leveraging influential outside voices, such as the United Nations, on behalf of the cause.[52] Equally, the target may be prejudicial semi-public or even private-sector practices, and government the authoritative leverage. Affirmative-action programs restructuring hiring, firing, and promotions in education, employment, and finance would not have been possible without such leveraging.

Giving effective public voice to a minority cause is often a function of more than simply spoken, written, or broadcast communication. It includes the corollary freedoms of physical assembly and political association. These weapons are anathema to the public silencing of socially disconcerting discourse. They are relatively 'cost free' to the cause and therefore particularly important for the indigent or resource deprived. As described by Borovoy, they have played an important role in pressuring social progress in Canada: 'For these purposes, freedom of speech includes ... freedom of association, and freedom of assembly. Jews, blacks and other minorities began to protest publicly about racial and ethnic discrimination. They set up test cases, publicized incidents of discrimination, organized delegations to government, lobbied politicians, picketed, and demonstrated. These freedoms were exercised again and again to fight discriminatory practices.'[53] A sympathetic media can be a great asset to effective public pressure, and social activists' complaints that mainstream media have an establishment bias are hardly groundless. But minority influence need not be synonymous with a sympathetic media. Mainstream media bias did not stop minorities from effectively leveraging and enlisting the power of the media in the cause of meaningful social progress. Canadian broadcast and print media may not have led public protest, but they have invariably followed it – giving public voice and public exposure to causes that might otherwise not have been heard at all.

Social activists have come to appreciate the importance of leveraging voice in their political practices, even while ignoring it in their pro-censorship theories. Using one medium of communication (street protest, for example) as a lever to pressure progress through other media of communication (print and broadcast media) has greatly enlarged the scope of freedom of minority expression beyond the mere *de jure* right that progressive censors have alleged for it. Moreover, it is not only *public* voice that has been used to good effect. *Threatening* to go public has often been equally, if not more, effective. Given the often discreet nature of such pressure, much of it is difficult to document. And given the causal indeterminacy of its impact (without such threats, would the outcome have been different?) its value is difficult to quantify. It can be easily missed or dismissed. But it is no less important for that. Indeed, it is very important precisely because it can be so easily missed or dismissed. Evidence for it must often remain anecdotal. Borovoy describes 'threat's' strategic or tactical value: 'I am in a position to testify personally about the impact of freedom of the press. As Director of the Labour Committee for Human Rights, I invoked the press time and again to fight discriminatory practices. Even before some of our anti-discrimination laws were enacted, I was able, simply by *threatening* to go to the press, to obtain housing for blacks that had otherwise been denied them. Freedom of expression was critical, therefore, in the fight against discrimination [italics mine].'[54]

Public pressure has also been used to good effect to leverage what is becoming an increasingly important legitimating institution of social progress in Canada, the courts. Constitutional entrenchment of the Charter has promoted the intersection of law and politics. Minorities communicate the cause of social progress not just *to* the courts but also to the public *through* the courts.

Pressuring the courts in the cause of social progress has taken two messaging forms; one, pressuring to procure social justice; the other, pressuring to quiet voices standing in the way of it. The federally funded Court Challenges Program (CCP), References, wider acceptance of class action lawsuits, and liberalization of standing requirements (intervenor status) have greatly broadened access to the courts, heightened public awareness of progressive causes, and given legal teeth to challenges of the 'status quo.' Compensation claims by minority victims of past injustices are just the latest campaigns in the battle for the minds, hearts, and pocketbooks of the public.[55]

Legalization of social progress has not, however, been a politically exclusionary development, as suggested by some writers.[56] The Charter's unique non-obstante clause (legislative review of judicial review) itself suggests a politically interactive, rather than legally final, process of raising social awareness between and across forums.[57] Voices of progress have not so much been subtracted from the political forum and shifted to the legal forum, in a zero-sum game between forums, as subtly enlarged through a conjoined process of mutual leveraging. Progress pressured through the judicial forum has served to leverage voices of progress in the political arena, and progress pressured through the political arena has served to leverage voices of progress in the courts. In a politically interactive context of judicial review such as exists in Canada, each forum becomes an important strategic or tactical weapon of public communication, compounding and amplifying, rather than subtracting from, the voice of progress articulated in the others.[58] Opportunities for mutual leveraging have given a stronger voice (which is not synonymous with victory) to the voiceless than either forum would or could have given alone. Moreover, as with the media, leverage need not be synonymous with sympathy. The mere political threat to go to court may sometimes be enough to precipitate or procure social change.

The making of the Charter was foundational to the development of the minority politics of judicial leveraging. Voices of women, seniors, the disabled, visible minorities, and Native peoples were constitutionalized in several enumerated Charter provisions or in the process of Charter interpretation and application that has followed.[59] These 'Charter Canadians,' as Cairns calls them, were relied on heavily by the Trudeau government, which formed alliances with them to build the public support needed to get the Charter past anti-Charter provincial premiers.[60] They came to view the Charter as 'their' Charter – a means to achieving the kind of political influence and social justice they could not garner through the legislative process alone.

In turn, the court's perception of its role is changing – to one more receptive to such influence. As documented by Greene and his colleagues, Canada's highest court is now far more prepared to see itself as a forum for making social policy and promoting democracy than it once was.[61] A new judicial attitude to 'social information' has been a major part of this evolution. The collectivist requirements of social justice meant that the court's socially dismissive pre-Charter 'case and controversy' approach – narrow, particularistic, and individualistic – could never become much of a friend to the cause of social progress. This is now changing. 'Brandeis Briefs' referencing extrinsic social science evidence, once excluded, are now admitted and cited, as are scholarly opinions.[62] Legal literature is becoming more important.[63] This trend is significant because it is largely from academia, especially legal academia (to which one would expect judges to pay special heed), that some of the strongest voices for a progressive social agenda in Canada are communicated.[64] Today, progressive voices sit on the bench to hear those voices. Affirmative action has even found its way into that historic bastion of white, male, upper middle-class conservatism, the court itself.[65]

While all this testifies to the social evolution of the court, it tells only part of the story of the enlargement of minority voices – the more visible but not necessarily the most interesting part. If it were the whole story, social progress through the courts would undoubtedly be less than it has been. There is a subtler, less tangible, even perhaps immeasurable, but no less significant progressive influence acting on the judicial mindset. The left's attacks on racist, sexist, patriarchal domination has centrally included judges and their judging.[66] Judges may dismiss these scathing attacks. They may be loath to admit being moved, much less sometimes pushed, by such complaints. They may sometimes not even be aware that they are. But value-laden social policy making cannot be done in a political vacuum, particularly in a uniquely forum-interactive polity such as Canada.[67] It would be naïve to think that legal and political forums work in blissful disregard of each other when the same progressive voices are heard from both ends of the policy-making spectrum. Courts are not immune to being subtly moved, even while they may not be wholly convinced. Judicial social sensitivity may sometimes flow as much from self-consciousness (pressure) as from self-awareness (persuasion). Indeed, 'socially sensitizing' political pressure may often be the more important (deciding) part of the overall message of judicial social progress.

Finally, minority voices may take the form of public expression of economic pressure. This can be a double-edged sword. It can publicize the cause; but this alone is no guarantee of success. Much depends on the kind of publicity garnered, which in turn depends on the purpose of the pressure. Industrial action or withdrawal of productive services through strikes, to procure or secure labour interests, is a case in point. Unfavourable press coverage (calling for public censorship of bourgeois meanings?) has been more hurtful than helpful to the cause. But *socially* or *culturally* purposed economic pressure has done much better.

Such pressure can take many public messaging forms. The public boycott can be one of the more effective ones. Aggrieved minorities can sometimes offset their own inferior resources by pooling or leveraging the commercial voices of others on behalf of their cause – a kind of discursive pressure by public proxy. Black civil rights leader Rev. Al Sharpton's appeals for a public boycott of Burger King (pooled public purchasing power) to increase the company's business dealings with Afro-Americans is illustrative.[68] But even pooled public voices falling short of commercial boycotts have been used to good effect. The Jewish community led a successful public campaign, in combination with other religious minorities, to pressure Canada's premier charter airline to serve onboard kosher and other specialty meals at the same price as 'regular' meals.[69]

As with political or legal pressure, so too with economic pressure – the mere threat to go public may sometimes be enough. Moreover, here as there, pressure's impact is publicly diffuse, spilling its enlightening social, cultural, or religious messages far beyond their immediate commercial targets. Such messages may serve as a general public deterrent against socially or culturally insensitive behaviour or as a general public incentive for socially or culturally sensitive conduct. Commercial pressure in the cause of tolerance and diversity can be one of minorities' politically more effective means of publicly messaging their social cause. The diffuse public impact of these forms of messaging, however, can be subtle and unquantifiable and therefore easily missed or even dismissed from the silencing equation.

Pressure weapons in the progressive cause may not only influence behaviour but also prevent speech. Broadly, such weapons fall into two main categories of prevention – those that depend on legal means to do their silencing work and those that depend on extra-legal means. The first enlists official enforcement – including, if necessary, the policing machinery of the state – to quiet the feared message before its expression. Pressure may be applied to block socially or politically undesirable speakers from entering the country or, failing that, to prevent them from speaking once here. For example, political pressure was put on Immigration Canada by the Canadian Jewish Congress to bar Vladimir Zhirinovsky, Russian ultranationalist (and deputy speaker of Russia's lower house or Duma), from entering Canada. Failing that, the CJC wanted immigration officials to 'brief Zhirinovsky on Canada's anti-hate laws and the consequences of violating them.'[70] In rare cases, pressures for deportation or extradition – used ordinarily to expel untriable war criminals from Canada for their past heinous *acts* – may be leveraged to expel certain resident messengers who have voiced or intend to express heinous *beliefs*.[71] In all these cases, pressure communication works not as an *alternative* to hate censorship, but in the service of it.

In the second category, the offended community does or attempts to do the silencing for itself, officially and legally unaided. Amid fears of a spread of anti-Semitic violence following the breakdown of the Oslo Middle East peace accords, Jewish leaders launched a vigorous campaign to contest media representations of unfolding events. After repeatedly failing to convince the *Toronto Star* of the unfairness of its coverage, especially of its editorials, some Jewish leaders called publicly for a subscription boycott. At least two major advertisers pulled their full-page ads in supportive public protest.[72]

In the case of both categories, one public voice is used to attempt to deny another – either directly by preventing speech before its expression or indirectly by denying the conditions required to effectively do so. Reasons may include past failure to effectively contest the objectionable message on its merits or fear of giving it more credibility by attempting to do so. None are alternatives to censorship. However, all weapons used by one 'voice' to deny another are not the same, either for the cause of social progress or the cause of political democracy. It is important to distinguish extra-legal from legal abridgment of public discourse on public matters.

Extra-legal or non-official pressures to silence – public boycotts, for example – can be rejected or broken.[73] Laws cannot be – at least not with impunity. Boycotts are voluntary. Laws are not. Boycotts do not silence all of society. They can distinguish and discriminate 'as and where needed.' They are surgical swords that target selected messengers of political influence and public regard, such as the *Toronto Star*. Hate speech laws, even if selectively targeted, are not. They chill all of society, more than just marginal messengers of relative insignificance such as Zundel and Keegstra. They are blunt instruments enlisted in the service of a refined cause, as we have seen.[74] In seeking to be more effective, hate laws are also prone to political slippage, trespassing beyond their intended targets.[75] Boycotts are not.

Boycotts to silence can more easily be held to public account than hate laws that silence.[76] Boycotters make no official pronouncement on political correctness. They carry no public stamp of moral legitimacy, assert no claim of official infallibility, and have no power of institutional immunity. Boycotts to silence are transparent acts of political partisanship. Their impact is publicly visible and their authors are visibly political. They can be challenged. Boycotts often invite more discussion on the respective merits of the matter in dispute. Hate laws that silence promote less.[77] Boycotts can be difficult. They require much organization and can be broken by a few to the chagrin of the many. Legal silencing is easier. Many supporters are not needed, breaking ranks need not be fatal, and the mere threat of invoking the law can chill public discourse generally. Boycotts to silence are, ordinarily, a last not a first resort, following a failure of speech to convince. Hate laws that silence are, effectively, a first resort, a *fear* of failure to convince.

In short, boycotts to silence assert no social infallibility, invite public scrutiny, are comparatively easy to challenge and difficult to organize, need not slip or trespass where their authors do not intend them to go to be effective, and do not indiscriminately chill or punish public discourse on public matters. Both boycotting into silence and legal hate silencing are pressure communications in the service of less not more speech. But they are not just different forms of the same censorship. Neither in character, intended reach, nor consequential impact on public discourse and political democracy are the two the same. Extra-legal silencing is not an alternative to censorship – it is censorship. But it is preferable to *legal* censorship. It has been used to good public effect by minorities in the cause against hate and prejudice. A planned Canada Day rock concert by the White supremacist Heritage Front illustrates the point well. The group cancelled following massive adverse media coverage and threats by antiracist protesters to boycott and disrupt the event.[78]

II) PERSUASION ALTERNATIVES

Punishment and command alternatives to public silencing can address the *physical* expressions of intolerance and ignorance that stand in the way of social progress as well as the institutions and structures that sustain them. Criminal measures can punish criminally intolerant *behaviour*. Civil and administrative remedies can address discriminatory institutional *practices* and correct illegal *conduct*. In short, institutions may be legally prevented from discriminating and racists from openly practising racism. A meaningful right of pressure communication can make all this possible.

But punishment and command alternatives to legal silencing do not prevent a racist from remaining a racist or from secretly acting like one. Moreover, he may still speak to the public as he thinks and think as he speaks.[79] And, unenlightened publics may lawfully remain ignorant. Changing public thinking for the better may be the incidental hope but not the purpose of punishment and command alternatives to legal silencing. That is the function of persuasion alternatives.

a) ***Outward-directed Persuasion.*** Outward-directed persuasion can promote the cause of tolerance and social progress without self-intrusion in three ways. It can (1) counter public ignorance and prejudice by educating and enlightening; (2) bridge intercommunity divisions that threaten to drive rival communities apart or against each other; (3) transcend numerical, resource, and other disadvantages, forging common cause through political combination to more effectively press for public change.

Public-awareness Raising and Education. Political socialization is the glue that holds not simply societies but polities together.[80] Of course, polities can be held together by official fiat and public fear, not just public persuasion and social understanding. But getting along in polities premised on self-government and cultural diversity is not the same as getting along in polities premised on authoritarian governance and public order. Political dictatorships need publics that get along.[81] Self-governing multicultural polities need publics that *want* to get along.[82]

Pyrrhic social victories may be defined as public victories of the present obtained at the expense of social successes of the future. Those who *secure* their social victories through a politics of public persuasion cannot do what those who *procure* them through a legal politics of found truths, fixed meanings, and final triumphs can do – officially dismiss discursive conflicts, deny making wrong political choices, or fail to correct socially mistaken ones. In short, they cannot conceal the social costs or postpone the political consequences of pyrrhic public victories. While pyrrhic public victories are best avoided anywhere, they are not equally problematic everywhere. Political dictators can live (and often die) by them. But they are particularly problematic for causes dependent on deeper public understanding for their success, in systems of occasional majorities and changing social agendas. Silencing here can *win*. But avoiding pyrrhic public victories requires *winning over*. It requires public understanding – and the discursive tools that make deeper understanding possible.

Winning over involves the art of persuasion. Broadly, there are three discursive forms of persuasive public messaging – passive, interactive, or confrontational. Passive forms depend for their success on provoking public interest and promoting public access. Confrontational forms depend on message contestation or refutation as between rival messengers. Interactive forms depend on public or target participation.

Holocaust memorials in Canada and throughout the Western world are a good example of effective passive forms.[83] They pack a jarring counter-punch to the message of Holocaust revisionists. Made readily available, even 'inviting,' to the public, their archival resources, data banks, and visual, symbolic, and even tactile messaging forms provide more than just information. They provoke meaning through emotion. The one in Israel is particularly large but not atypical. Housing 55 million pages of documentation, some 150,000 photographs, an assortment of artifacts, and averaging 2 million pages of new documentation annually, it is set to include testimonials of Holocaust survivors taped by filmmaker Steven Spielberg's foundation, a definitive master list of Holocaust survivors, and a computerized database.[84]

Confrontational forms of public persuasion directly contest and refute the intolerant speaker – exposing prejudicial assumptions, taking to task irrational beliefs, and refuting contrived facts. They can counter the cause of hate and prejudice in two ways that more passive forms of counter-messaging cannot.

First, public confrontation can exact a *personal* price from the hatemonger as hiding him behind the veil of enforced silence or the camouflage of trial cannot. The more the hatemonger is exposed by his own unsheltered words of intolerance, the more the public can see him for the fool and the fiend that he really is – and treat him accordingly. The more the public came to know Zundel and Keegstra as they truly were, the more they became public pariahs – economically unemployable, socially outcast, and politically marginalized.[85] Second, public confrontation can exact a *public* price from the malevolent speaker as allowing him to shelter his message behind the veil of martyrdom or the camouflage of trial cannot. The more he freely defends the transparently indefensible, the more clearly the public can see his *message* as ignorant and his motives as malevolent and treat him and his public *cause* accordingly.

When hatemongers and their sympathizers in Canada were a more directly engageable public threat, instead of the surreptitious threat hate speech laws have made them today, daily protests in front of Zundel's headquarters in downtown Toronto were major media events. The juxtaposition of elderly, frail Holocaust survivors arrayed against a virtual 'army' of arrogant, steel-helmeted, leather-booted 'Zundelite storm troopers' painted a particularly poignant and persuasive picture against hatemongers and their message. Today, the prospect of arrest, detention, or seizure for openly espousing hate means that this kind of direct engagement with unveiled messages of evil is more likely to be publicly played out in the United States than in Canada.[86]

Functionally, confrontational and more passive ways of raising public awareness are not mutually exclusive but mutually reinforcing, packing a more convincing punch against intolerance together than either one could do alone. For one thing, there is no perfect substitute for live emotive confrontation as a way of drawing out and amplifying the deeper meanings of more passive discursive forms of raising public awareness.[87] This is especially true where the subject of contention concerns patently malevolent purposes and eminently refutable messages, such as those of Holocaust deniers. Only real-life confrontation can interactively and directly expose the wolf in sheep's clothing. Absent open public confrontation, more passive discursive alternatives in the cause against intolerance must contend with meaning atrophy and the socially and politically deleterious by-products of the silencing process itself. Substitutive or indirect forms of 'proxy confrontation' must therefore work publicly harder for socially less.[88]

Public education in Canada today shoulders a large part of the burden of more *meaningfully* raising public awareness – probably more than it otherwise would have to shoulder with freer rights of refutation by confrontation. The work performed by race relations committees, schools, public service boards, and the like is well known. But there are other public education forms and forums available – some more selective of their targets, others utilizing more subtle and symbolic media – to raise public awareness and advance the cause. One of the most important of these utilizes the third kind of messaging – interactive communication.

Interactive forms of raising public awareness enlist more personalized or 'hands on' ways of communicating the desired message. Consider the Inuit tour of Israel,[89] or the ten-day study visit to Israel by eighteen Canadian university presidents and the president of the Council of Ontario Universities.[90] Personalized discursive forms can pack a particularly strong messaging punch where they invoke the power of authoritative pronouncement and come clothed in official symbolism. The naming of seven Jewish Canadians to the Order of Canada for outstanding contributions to Canadian society, in a well-publicized ceremony on Parliament Hill, is an example.[91] Such tributes to Holocaust survivors were described by Jewish community activist Sigmund Reiser as having the joint purpose of 'trying to keep the memory of the Holocaust alive, and to recognize the many accomplishments of survivors' who 'rebuilt their lives, raised a family and helped make Canada a better place in any small way.'[92] State recognition, performed as part of the government's *official* functions, imprints awareness raising with the stamp of official legitimacy.

As this suggests, raising public awareness can even involve educating the public about awareness raising – a kind of self-reinforcement of the original message. *The Liberal* ran a feature story on Bisson Ramdewar, an ethnic Guyanese police detective awarded 'one of only a few Gold Medals of Excellence from Canada's Human Rights and Race Relations Center' not for his pursuit of offenders but for his sensitivity-raising community work as a policeman.[93] In Los Angeles, three Holocaust-related television programs won 2001 Emmy awards.[94] Community forms of self-recognition – such as the announcement by the *Canadian Jewish News* that for the sixth consecutive year it had received a Simon Rockower Award for the highest standards of journalism in Jewish publications – have subtle and symbolic *spillover* effects on public awareness.[95]

The definition of social progress itself has undergone profound expansion through the raising of public awareness. It has kept one pace ahead of success itself – which may help explain social activists' continuing frustrations with what they see as a failure of meaningful change. Today, social progress is an idea that goes far beyond simply the good race relations that the Cohen Committee saw as the proper goal of hate propaganda law. It can include the environment and social quality of life and enlist creative and subtle forms of public communication, such as design and architecture, by which to advance the cause. While Daniel Libeskind communicates the lessons of the Holocaust through architecture, Dan Burden communicates social consciousness by designing more livable cities. His environmentally sensitive, people-friendly designs involving space and transportation have brought new life and dignity to declining neighbourhoods and inner cities.[96]

Intercommunity Bridge Building. Bridge building may be defined as discourse *between* and *among* communities that fosters mutual trust, understanding, and confidence. Bridges of a sort may be laid across community divisions by silencing as well as discourse and by pressure as well as persuasion. All bridges, however, are not the same. Fear, force, or concealment make poor foundations for building bridges. Mutual trust, understanding, and confidence cannot be fashioned out of the cynicism, suspicion, or resentment that such frail foundations nurture. Less fragile community bridges require a better understanding of why bonds that unite outweigh differences that divide. Hiding the differences that divide makes it harder not easier to better understand the bonds that unite. Communities that must live together, at least in self-governing polities, need more than an external 'fix' that can come apart easily in crises. Bridges of tolerance and diversity erected on foundations of openness, honesty, and respect for disagreement can withstand the test of time better than can ones built on concealment or welded together by force.[97] Discourse 'clearing the air' may be sometimes be disconcerting, even divisive, but better bridges cannot be built without it. Today's investments in such discourse lay the cognitive foundations of mutual trust and confidence of the future – the social capital for bridging divides that rival communities who must live together need to be able to draw on in times of crisis.[98]

The most successful bridges are those that advance the needs of several or all minorities at the expense of none. They require large coalitions and large understandings, the kind constructed out of persuasion and openness rather than fear and concealment. This is not always possible. But working for it is critical in an increasingly multicultural society where the intercommunity conflicts of recognized minorities, as we have seen, may well be the most testing challenge to the social harmony of the future. Large understandings, especially, require deeper awareness of others' standpoint not just one's own. This may not always come without self-conflict. The price of putting aside differences may sometimes be to 'compromise' insistence on one's own unique hurt in order to acknowledge another's. This cannot be done by closing our minds to alternative or offensive meanings, but requires opening them up still more – to all meanings. The Museum of Tolerance in Los Angeles offers Holocaust instruction that includes lessons on other genocides.[99] The Canadian Council of Christians and Jews, an interfaith coalition created to bridge centuries of suspicion and fear between Jews and Christians, symbolically widened its bridge recently to include more political voices and social causes by changing its name to Canadian Council to Promote Equality and Respect.[100]

Emotive, symbolic, or interactive messaging forms play particularly powerful roles in raising intercommunity awareness, fostering understanding, and building mutual trust. In the cause against division, discord, and ignorance, the progressive arsenal of bridge-building alternatives to silencing is bottomless. They range from discursive forms of messaging – symposiums, theatre, poetry, music, prayer, healing circles, social education – to messaging by example. Indeed, racists and bigots may learn a thing or two about effective messaging of their meanings from bridge builders of tolerance.

In 'Voices of Change,' a play presented to students in grades five to eight in Toronto, the inspiration and symbolism of *drama* are used to convey the meaning of Canada's cultural mix in three ways: (1) through the three languages in the play; (2) through the author's theme – 'for Canadians of different backgrounds to be sensitive to the needs of others through the way they communicate'; and (3) through the play's unusual and innovative dialogue, described as 'based on the rhythm of the body emotions.'[101] Black History Month celebrations at a Toronto civic centre included the metaphorical messaging medium of joint (Black–Jewish) *poetry* reading.[102] Interfaith services, such as the nineteenth annual Christian Services in Memory of the Holocaust, held at Metropolitan United Church in Toronto, utilize the spiritual medium of *prayer* as an inspirational unifying form.[103]

Bridge-building *symposiums*, many aimed at early intervention to prevent intolerance before it can take root, are held regularly around the country. A day program organized by the Jewish Federation of Edmonton 'attracted 450 students' at Grande Prairie Regional College and included 'Grade 12 students from the city's three public and Catholic high schools, as well as six other schools from within a 120-kilometer radius of the city.'[104] The medium of discourse can include the universal language of *music*. It can be used to bridge intra and intercommunity divisions at the same time. The 'musical exchange' reported in the Canadian Jewish News is an example:

'When they are rehearsing, it's wonderful to see children from all streams of Jewish community [Orthodox, Conservative, Reform] working together,' said Adrienne Cohen, director of the Jewish *Koffler School of Music*. The School's Renanim Children's Choir recently performed with the Italian Columbus Centre and the Italian Cultural Institute. 'In this way,' says Cohen, 'the kids feel recognized and discover that music can provide a link between communities in the city.'[105]

Emotively intolerant speech can, effectively, be emotively answered.[106] Indeed, it can even be answered by emotive 'bridging by example,' not just 'speech.' Following a devastating earthquake in Nicaragua, the Canadian Jewish Humanitarian and Relief Committee joined forces with local Anglican and Catholic churches on a well-publicized 'transcontinental convoy, driving eight school buses packed with emergency supplies to an [impoverished] earthquake-ravaged region of El Salvador.'[107]

One of the most important preventive media of interactive communication for combating intolerance and ignorance is the one most taken for granted because it has been relatively so successful. The integrated public school system combines early intervention with pedagogy in a socializing context where it counts most – bridging divisions between today's generation of youngsters before they become the chasms of the next. The system has been far from perfect but, as Borovoy writes, 'By eating together in the cafeteria, working together in the classroom, and playing together in the school yard, [kids] were developing the habits of *enduring* respect.'[108] Arnold Auguste, publisher of *Share*, an influential magazine in the Black community, has said, 'We [Jews and Blacks] have so much in common, yet we are so far apart. We should build bridges with honesty and respect and we must be prepared for opposition. It's a risk worth taking.'[109]

Finally, even in the face of transparent expressions of extreme intolerance, bridge-building alternatives to legal silencing – talk, tact, and *legal* tolerance – may sometimes be the better 'answer.' When David Ahenakew (a former chief of the Assembly of First Nations) referred to Jews as a 'disease' and commended Hitler for 'frying' six million, shocked Jewish leaders called for prosecution under the Criminal Code. However, the collision here of good and evil also had the unexpected effect of drawing the two communities closer together. Quick Native condemnation of Ahenakew followed face-to-face meetings between Native and Jewish leaders. A tearful, publicly televized apology by Ahenakew, Native offers of a 'sentencing and healing circle' to make amends, Jewish offers of a 'study trip' to Israel for Native leaders, and vice-versa, all spoke of goodwill, reaching out, and confidence building that prosecution would threaten to undermine.[110] These are not exceptional 'remedies' in a culture of freedom of public discourse, but its very essence. However, they can become exceptional in a proactive culture of legal silencing that increasingly looks to hate law for its answers. Under pressure from Jewish leaders, Saskatchewan's Department of Public Prosecutions announced that Ahenakew would in fact be charged with promoting hate under the Criminal Code.[111] Public quiet, it seems, has become more important than the public cause. Far from being the complement to alternatives that progressive silencing theorists assume it to be or the last resort when all else has been tried but has failed, as expected by more liberal censors, the hate censorship option is a seductive slippery slope that can be an active player in that failure.

Political Combination and Comparative Political Edge. Effective bridge building is also central to political combination by which the excluded and the marginalized may gain the comparative political edge they need to move forward. Unequal material and communicative resources, subordinate social status, ethnic visibility, and unique legacies of oppression spotlighted by progressive censors help explain minority defeats and the disadvantages that caused them. But they cannot explain minority victories and what made them possible. Progressive censorship theorists' absolutist and normative focus on social gains that have been denied or that are still to be realized ignores comparative gains that have been achieved and constricts the scope of inquiry required to better understand how they were obtained.

Economic resources have not immunized Jews anywhere in the world from anti-Semitism. Visibility has not stopped the Chinese from sharing in the Canadian or American 'dream.' Unequal communicative resources have not prevented the political or legal assertion of Native rights and the idea of Native self-government. And uniquely vile historical forms of oppression, such as slavery and residential schools, have, over time, been vanquished. But as long as minority status remains, so too will vulnerability to exclusion and prejudice – whatever other minority-specific reasons for success or failure there may be.[112] To surmount, in some significant way, the disempowerment of minority status is to forge the single greatest defence to intolerance and exclusion in self-governing systems of majority rule.

Minority status cannot be surmounted by hate censorship. Nor can internal community solidarity, self-identity, or distinctive sense of purpose be better assured by it. But social progress requires somehow rising above the disadvantages of the first and constructing the advantages of the second. Implicit in the progressive censorship approach is the assumption that history, resources, and political clout are – like national origin, race, and skin colour – fixed for all time. This ignores the movement of history, the power of political combination based on mutual understanding and trust, and the importance of internal community purpose. Social progress in Canada has been a function not of public silencing but of these forces of empowerment. They are what has given even some of the most disadvantaged in Canada the 'comparative political edge' they need to move forward.

Political combination, for example, can multiply and amplify minority voices, in a common cause, far beyond what censors' assumptions of fixed resources, found victims, and static histories would suggest. It can pool and build not only political and economic resources but also, no less important, resources of social solidarity or *esprit de corps*. Political societies, social groups, formal and informal coalitions, tactical networks, and strategic alliances of every sort in Canada illustrate the power of freedom of association. As Borovoy writes,

> Those delegations that called upon cabinet ministers were composed of several groups, not just one. Blacks, Jews, unions, churches and others forged coalitions to fight discrimination. No one group could have had the impact that the coalitions made possible. Moreover, many of the organizations that fought for equality were themselves composed of diverse groups.
>
> One of the most remarkable of these organizations was the Labour Committee for Human Rights, a group officially sponsored by organized labour as a public service to fight racism in the community at large. The Labour Committee was a model of intergroup collaboration. It was administered by the Jewish Labour Committee, operated by union leaders drawn from the general labour movement, and buttressed by volunteers from the black community. This organization conducted the key campaigns that produced Canada's major human rights legislation and it set up test cases to ensure that the legislation functioned properly.[113]

The movement for gender equality depended on meaningful freedom of social and political combination to bridge numerous divisions. In Borovoy's words, '[T]he women's movement attracted significant allies from the liberal community: labour unions, churches, academics, writers and civil liberties organizations. The growing conglomeration of constituencies helped to overcome the resistance of various conservative establishments.'[114]

Pooling minority bodies, minds, and materials is not always easy. Voice (much less victory) is harder to come by when coalition building is difficult and individual communities are poor in both the numbers and the materials needed to advance independently. It is still harder where they also lack 'invisibility.' Natives and Blacks in Canada lack all three.[115] Progress has been uneven, and some communities have progressed far more than others. But uneven progress is hardly reason for more hate censorship. It is reason against it. Rival minorities and deprived communities need to talk freely and openly about their differences. They need to build the deeper understandings – the social capital – that can withstand the test of time.[116] Clubbing intolerance, and each other, into submission with politically slippery legal silencing builds the backlash, the resentments, and the hatreds of tomorrow.

Comparative political edge is also a function of particular communities' moral suasion in terms of the justice of their cause; their comparative internal cohesion, solidarity, and strength of purpose in advancing that cause; and their willingness to set aside intercommunity differences to join with other groups in pursuing causes held in common.[117] The first two (moral suasion and internal cohesion) may alone advance the cause – for particular communities. The three together advance it better – for all minorities. A dominant population, comparatively rich in numbers, material resources, or invisibility but poor in moral suasion, internal solidarity, or strength of prejudicial purpose, may be moved to make concessions to a population comparatively poor in numbers, resources, and invisibility but rich in moral suasion, internal solidarity, or willingness to set aside intercommunity differences. Nunavut, civil rights, affirmative action, and a host of other successes by numerically, resource-, and invisibility-deprived Natives and Blacks would have been impossible without comparative political edge. It is the key that explains social progress in Canada – the force that mitigates other disadvantages and moves communities forward in the face of otherwise insurmountable odds.

Comparative political edge is a force constructed out of a free-speech triad – discourse, assembly, and association. Communities that have internal solidarity and strength of purpose, or the wherewithal to combine to build them in common with others, are more likely to enjoy comparative political edge than those that do not. As this suggests, comparative political edge can be a double-edged sword. It can divide as well as unite. It can advance the cause of all minorities, but it can also advance the cause of some minorities at the expense of other minorities. It can promote social progress unevenly. Within communities it can advance multiple causes unevenly.

Jews have won some important victories, despite their paucity of numbers. The about-face by Canada Customs and Revenue Agency regarding its earlier decision to revoke the charitable status of Canadian Magen

David Adom for Israel is illustrative.[118] In other areas, however (changing Canada's pro-Palestinian U.N. voting record or the face of an increasingly unsympathetic media), it can be argued that neither comparative resource nor communicative edge has been sufficient to tip the scale.[119] In turn, materially and invisibility-disadvantaged Blacks have won impressive affirmative action victories in employment and competitive admissions to institutions of higher learning.[120] Natives, uniformly disadvantaged in every way, apart from the justice (moral suasion) of their cause, are winning impressive compensation, land, and constitutional claims from their numerically, materially, communicatively, and invisibility-advantaged historical oppressors. Of course, comparative political edge is no guarantee of victory, even for conjoined minorities, any more than it is for individual minorities, either on particular issues or across the policy board. That would be to confuse victory with voice. But then, what is? Indeed, as between rival minorities, where the most testing social divisions and future challenges to public tolerance in Canada are likely to come, for whom should it be?

As a force for progress, comparative political edge is an instrument of growth and change that is incompatible with official silencing of speech that offends or seeks to convert publics to the cause of the speaker. In the last three decades, the disadvantaged have patently gained far more through leveraging and bridge building that relied on *public* communication to *openly* promote their cause than sexists, racists, and homophobes have been able to gain through leveraging and 'bridge destroying' *public* communication to openly advance theirs. It is important to understand why.

Socially better minority combinations have two things in common – they promote the cause(s) of many minorities at the expense of few or none, and they do so on a more secure and enduring basis of social progress. Such combinations are more likely to be rooted in larger understandings and deeper foundations of mutual trust – facilitated by open and honest discourse – than purely tactical alliances and fleeting coalitions fabricated from concealment or bound together by pressure. There is good reason why bridge-builders of tolerance in Canada have been able to forge these larger social and political alliances using open and honest discourse, and why hatemongers have not been able to do so.[121] Coalition building in discursive freedom is asymmetrical. Tolerance needs openness and understanding to grow. Hate and ignorance do not. Those who hate gain a *comparative* political edge from concealment and secrecy, at least in consolidated democracies. But they are at a comparative political disadvantage where open and honest discourse prevails. Larger social alliances and political coalitions are preferable to smaller ones, especially in systems of majority rule. But the price of such combinations in Canada is understanding, tolerance, and even acceptance of differences. Those who incorrigibly hate are not good at understanding, much less tolerating, differences. They are especially not good at accepting differences. Those who hate most are least good at it. A house divided against itself cannot easily stand much less 'stand down' one that is united. The less tolerant the group, the smaller and more marginal it is therefore apt to be.

None of this is to suggest that the intolerant and the ignorant in Canada have been standing still. But if so, it is not for lack of hate censorship. On the contrary, it has been happening on censorship's *expanding* watch.[122] Moreover, the cause of tolerance and progress has not been standing still either. While the worst fanatics and fomenters of hate in Canada have long suffered from the numerical self-afflictions of their own intolerance – relegating their narrow agenda and singularly uncompromising cause to relative obscurity – diverse and large groups united in common cause against racism and intolerance are everywhere to be seen.[123] Open and honest bridge building is no assurance of success. But the alternative is less certain still.

b) Inward-directed Persuasion. Correcting extra-community prejudices and exposing concealed attitudes of ignorance can help remove public obstacles standing in the way of social progress. But this is not enough for group-distinctive success. Strong cultural self-identity, internal solidarity, and a distinctive sense of community purpose are quintessentially important. There is no good substitute for investment, nor silencing cure for underinvestment, in these internal resources. No community has progressed well as a community without them. But with them, many have beaten down outside barriers to inclusion built on prejudice and ignorance. The absence of open expressions of prejudice cannot 're-store' internal resources that are absent, nor can open expressions of prejudice displace those that are present. Legal speech protection is not what communities in Canada today need to effectively combat negative participation, self-alienation, withdrawal, or the forces of cultural disintegration and assimilative flight. Rather, they need freedom of self-directed community expression.

Community self-directed punishment and command weapons have played a role. So, too, have self-directed discursive weapons of pressure.

But, self-directed persuasion – speech intended to 'convince' or 'win over' – has played a far more constructive and democratic role. While self-administered community discipline may solder together internal solidarity, may moderate self-destructive behaviour, and may forge a contra-assimilative sense of distinctive community, it has serious drawbacks, especially in a democratic polity. First, commanded solidarity may be illegal, depending on the nature of the punishment meted out or threatened against violators. Second, commanded solidarity tends to weave a more fragile community bond. Self-destructive, other-destructive, or assimilative minds must be *won over*, not just *won*, or victory will be thin and fleeting in a socially and culturally free society. This is not something that can be done *for* a community from the outside with hate censorship; it needs to be done *by* the community itself from the inside with self-uplifting, self-inspiring speech. The fracturing of noble community traditions and distinctive self-identity is an affliction of liberal society that can strike any community. Of course, not all communities in Canada are equally vulnerable to social breakdown or cultural malaise, just as they are not equally vulnerable to invisible exclusion stemming from concealed prejudice.[124] But this is a reason not for more freedom of legal silencing but for more freedom of community self-awareness raising. It is precisely the communities that are most vulnerable to concealed prejudice and ignorance for which internal resilience and solidarity in the face of adversity are most important.

As in public-awareness raising, so too in community self-awareness raising – communication of desired meanings or refutation of undesired ones can be promoted better in a myriad of contextually sensitive and artistically creative ways, without public silencing. Consider self-directed confrontation and refutation by the Jewish community to counter the messianic message of 'Jews for Jesus.' A 'counter-missionary' handbook warns the community that 'These groups [Jews for Jesus] use three deceptive tactics to attract Jews. Firstly, they imply that a Jew can retain his Judaism even after converting. Secondly, they misquote, mistranslate and misrepresent ... Thirdly, they attempt to delegitimize Judaism ... In addition, many missionary groups employ scare tactics and intimidation [discouraging opposing viewpoints].'[125]

Or, consider the following 'news-ad' in the *Canadian Jewish News*:

> This summer Toronto will be the target of a major missionary crusade. Jews for Jesus has scheduled a two-week blitz in August that will employ the media, billboards and a street campaign that will flood our city with conversionary

tracts directed towards Jews. In response to this threat, JEWS FOR JUDAISM is organizing a counter-leafleting campaign to alert and educate the public. We are seeking to train volunteers who will distribute our counter-missionary literature in a non-confrontational manner.[126]

Non-confrontational forms of self-uplifting and self-solidifying ways of messaging the cause can range from the relatively passive to the highly interactive – from memorials and honorariums to book fairs, music, travel guides, homecoming tours, metaphorical field trips, dance, and even contests. The Chinese community has made a special point of *honouring* its entrepreneurs for their business accomplishments.[127] The *Globe and Mail* ran a half-page feature story on the late Gwendolyn Brooks, the first Black woman to win a Pulitzer Prize.[128] Jewish book fairs, catering to 'every age, every interest' within the Jewish community are now annual events.[129] The Friends of Simon Wiesenthal Center for Holocaust Studies, an international human rights organization dedicated to preserving the memory of the Holocaust, brought the meaning of the Holocaust alive through the *music* of four acclaimed Jewish composers who perished in the death camps.[130] The *Jewish Travel Guide 2000* (edited by Michael Zaidner) details the heritage of thousands of Jewish communities in some 110 countries from Albania to Zimbabwe. The guide includes capsule histories of each Jewish community, descriptions of synagogues, cultural organizations, libraries, hotels, kosher restaurants, and many other points of interest and information to the Jewish community.[131] 'Birthright Israel' is a program that offers an intensive, free, ten-day, self-awareness raising '*homecoming*' trip to Israel to eligible North American Jews aged eighteen to twenty-six.

Bob Moses, one of the chief Afro-American organizers of the Freedom Summer of 1964 civil rights march in Mississippi, today 'teaches about integers by leading students on a [metaphorical] tour of civil rights monuments. The kids draw pictures of the journey and create number lines in which each stop represents an integer, and use them to add and subtract positive and negative numbers.'[132] The School of Dance and Social Integration, based in Brazil, has become an international leader in using the expressive medium of *dance* to teach literacy and other essential life skills to the downtrodden and the disadvantaged. It has attracted funding from Ashkoda, a Washington-based non-profit organization that supports 1,100 'social entrepreneurs' in forty-one countries. The Kaplan Foundation of New York City was established to further humanitarian, scientific, and other public concerns, with a Jewish theme. Its annual *essay contest*, open to Jewish high school students around the world, has attracted entries from across the United States and Canada.[133]

Hate censors point to the Internet as one more reason, and way, to silence hate. However, as we saw in chapter 6, the information revolution has made 'cost-acceptable' social progress through public silencing even less feasible than before the revolution. At the same time, it has made social progress through speech more possible.[134] While the Internet has brought together both global voices of tolerance and dispersed voices of ignorance, it has also made self-uplifting discourse interactive, egalitarian, and even intergenerational in a way that 'meat space' never could.

> What can staffers at the United States Embassy in Moscow, a university student in Mexico and a housewife in Thornhill [a suburb of Toronto] possibly have in common? They are all taking for-credit courses from Bar-Ilan University. Started by Professor Mosh Kaveh, president of Bar Ilan University, who established the International Centre for Jewish Identity to look at different ways to promote Jewish identity world-wide ... [a] parent or grandparent can take a course together with a child or grandchild, even if they live in a different place.[135]

Leveraging both the government and the private sectors has helped here. A $150,000 government grant to Toronto's York University's Jewish Teacher Education Program 'will go towards developing three online courses during [a] two year pilot phase of the project – Serving Special Needs Students in the Jewish Classroom; Jewish Early Childhood Education; and Teaching Bible.'[136]

Self-uplifting ideas utilizing the Internet can not only revitalize self-identity and further continuity but also structure material social progress. Native leader and entrepreneur Gregg Bourland has referred to the Internet as 'something anyone can do anywhere.'[137] With no timber to sell, coal to mine, or wish to turn to casinos, the Cheyenne River Sioux have turned the Internet into their own business niche. The Cheyenne River Telephone Authority, owned and managed by the local Sioux, has dramatically reduced community poverty, despair, and hopelessness.[138]

3 Mixed Discursive Alternatives

Categories of discursive alternatives are not mutually exclusive. Desired public or community meaning construction can be effected in a myriad of integrative ways of messaging the cause – to take better account of diverse cognitive needs, changing social conditions, and evolving political contexts. Message-making may be expressively multifaceted and multi-directed. They may combine inward with outward direction or blend features of persuasion with features of pressure.

Outward-directed discursive pressure may leverage inward-directed persuasion. After months of pressure from Jewish leaders, Rogers Cable Company agreed to run a disclaimer to raise Jewish self-awareness before and after a locally produced television show featuring a 'Jews for Jesus type messianic "synagogue" in Toronto.'[139] Or, inward-directed persuasion may be blended with subtle pressure to pack a more meaningful self-awareness-raising punch. 'Birthright Israel,' the previously mentioned community self-awareness-raising carrot that offers eligible Canadian Jewish youth a free trip to Israel, may soon come with a 'Birthright Jewish Studies' prerequisite (for completion of a recognized university Jewish studies course) as a condition for taking the trip.[140]

Discursive alternatives to silencing can be artfully blended and judiciously calibrated in the interactive forms of messaging and ways of meaning that best promote deeper reflection, currency, and relevance. Students at Albert F. Ford Middle School in Massachusetts were asked to go on-line to do independent research into the meanings of the Holocaust from multifaceted perspectives. 'Health classes researched the minimum diet necessary for human survival compared to the diet of people hiding during the [Second World] war. And students in art classes drew images that symbolized their feelings about the Holocaust. In another moving exercise, students were asked to put themselves in Anne Frank's shoes and create new diary entries until her death at Bergen-Belsen.'[141]

Outward-directed discursive pressure can serve a mutually leveraging or dual inward-outward awareness-raising function. First, the mere exertion of public pressure can raise public awareness of the cause. Second, successful pressure can procure critical material resources – from research and cultural grants to tax breaks, tax credits, task forces, media blitzes, or even memorials – that can offset material or other disadvantages standing in the way of better self- and public messaging of the cause. The Montreal Holocaust Center's receipt of a $500,000 government pledge is one illustration.[142] Pressure to expand the mandate of the Aboriginal Healing Foundation, established in 1998 with $350 million in federal funding to pay for 'healing' and counselling programs in Native communities, is another.[143] The myriad women's organizations, with their interlocking networks and institutional contacts liaising official ears and eyes, are particularly good illustrations of discursive versatility and political creativity utilizing dual-purpose pressure speech. These pressure groups for raising self- and public awareness range from the Inuit Women's Association and Voice of Women to Media Watch, Women in Science and Engineering, and the Women's Legal Education and Action Fund.[144] Pressure exerted on officialdom by these groups may procure any number of dual-purpose awareness-raising benefits, from prioritized funding for women's studies programs to educational forums on domestic violence to print advertisements and broadcast public service announcements publicizing women's concerns.

Public persuasion, as we saw, can even be blended to serve a speech preventive pressure function comparable to legal censorship but without its social and democratic dilemmas.[145] When the White supremacist Heritage Front abruptly cancelled its Canada Day rock concert, it was not for fear of legal or other sanction but because they became convinced that their message would be so 'degraded' by antiracist voices of protest that it would not be worth publicly communicating it.[146] Losing the battle for the public ear to convert or simply to offend is hardly the same as losing one's job or liberty for daring to try.

Conclusion

Progressive social activists in Canada want community, diversity, tolerance, equality, and robust democracy. These are socially multifaceted causes housing politically multidimensional goals. They harbour many deep conflicts and self-conflicts that often require difficult policy trade-offs in 'working' practice. Societally reductionist theorists may work hard to package ever more of them into the one-size-fits-all language of 'hate,' for the convenience of censorship. But this only conceals the conflicts, delays their timely confrontation, and problematizes the day of public reckoning.

Socially multifaceted causes housing politically multidimensional goals need socially multifaceted approaches and politically flexible responses – approaches and responses that recognize and can balance conflicts and self-conflicts 'where and as needed.' Social progress and political democracy without self-intrusion depend on it. Discursive alternatives to legal silencing come in as many messaging shapes, meaning sizes, and 'working' styles as their social causes require and their political contexts demand. They are publicly transparent, circumstance conscious, target refinable, and error self-accountable. Discursive messengers of progress can promote their causes in a multitude of creative, sophisticated, subtle, or symbolic ways – artistically, poetically, musically, spiritually, even metaphorically. Of course, messengers of hate can do so too. But censors cannot.

Hate silencing is a blunt instrument enlisted in the service of refined causes. It is a singular answer to often plural questions, a legal response to a non-legal problem, a negative means employed for positive social ends, an absolute remedy and fixed assurance in the face of socially evolving and politically fluid maladies. Progressive censors cannot silence artistically, poetically, musically, spiritually, metaphorically, or with more sophistication. They cannot silence *better*. They can silence *less* or they can silence *more* – but either way they can only do so self-intrusively. Given the socially multifacted forms and politically multidimensional contexts of public meaning construction, hate censorship cannot be calibrated, mixed, or fine-tuned in the subtle messaging forms and nuanced meaning ways needed to balance conflicts and self-conflicts. Once a problem is successfully packaged in the language of hate, conflicts and self-conflicts vanish, discourse ends, and judgment becomes paralysed. There can be no compromise with 'hate.' Silencing hate is a zero-sum game. There can be only winners and losers, an absolutist public politics of legal might displacing a more nuanced and flexible discursive public politics of social right.[147] It is a politics of slash and burn where talk, tact, or even tolerance, may sometimes serve the cause better. A proactive legal regime of hate silencing is a poor way to raise self- or public awareness, eschew the pyrrhic public victories that endanger future social progress, forge the comparative political edge to surmount the obstacles standing in the way of such progress, or cultivate the social capital that rival minorities can draw on to bridge their divisions in the crises of the future. The more proactively such a regime silences, the less well it can do so. Reducing vital public discourse to found truths, absolute victims, fixed meanings, and final triumphs is not the better way for a multicultural society in a politically consolidated democracy to deal with ever more of its social divisions and political ills. But it is the way of progressive hate censorship.

In the final analysis, legal silencing cannot be successfully conjoined and calibrated with progressive alternatives to such silencing so as to create the all-purpose public cleanser in the cause of community, diversity, equality, social justice, and democracy that silencing theorists want and expect. The mix is mutually self-contradictory, and self-defeating, rather than complementary. Alternatives to silencing in Canada have an impressive track record of relative success in the progressive cause. But hate censors undercut the work of progressive alternatives with hate silencing, making more socially intrusive and democratically problematic alternatives more 'necessary' in their place. Hate censors do not simply undermine their own cause by the very means with which they promote it. Paradoxically, they 'work' to reproduce their own fears and redouble their own 'need' for more self-intrusive measures to satisfy them. Hate censorship is a self-realizing, self-justifying dilemma in more ways than one.

Conclusion

Thinking on hate censorship in Canada today enjoys a rather dubious distinction – an unplanned but no less unholy alliance between elite, popular, and juridical wisdom. Since the Cohen Committee came out with its limited remedy and its chary recommendations for protecting the polity from future harm, much has changed both in how hate is expressed and in thinking about its repression. Today, rival ethnic groups, social activists, influential academics, public institutions, and even racists and bigots look to the club of hate silencing as a legitimate substitute for the 'word.' The idea that a democracy can *successfully* safeguard the populace from public offence or the risk of conversion to the cause of the intolerant speaker by legally substituting officially correct meanings and official histories for publicly constructed ones appears to be comfortably embedded in the political culture. Freedom of expression is coming to count for less where it should count for more – in protecting socially disconcerting discourse that tests conventional or elite wisdoms and public faith in them. Freedom of public discourse on public matters is being squeezed from diverse directions, with the progressive left leading the way and the Canadian courts lending a sympathetic ear and a helping hand.

Silencing hate is a politically slippery slope and a double-edged social sword. It can move in unintended or unexpected ways, transcending and expanding the legal boundaries originally set for it. The law's moral authority and legitimating language are politically infectious and socially seductive, subtly seeping, in one form or another, into otherwise ordinary discursive contexts. They can erode the tone and texture of honest debate, corrode the language of public discourse with the intolerance of their own, condition public meanings in chilling or opportunistic ways and give succour to parallel cultures of extralegal silencing. Consider just a few *recent* examples of those cited in this book:

The chief commissioner of the Ontario Human Rights Commission is threatened with a hate investigation for comparing public funding of faith-based schools to South African apartheid.

Canada's largest bookstore takes a very public stand against 'trading in hate literature' by denying the public a historic work, Hitler's *Mein Kampf.*

Malcolm Ross, removed from his teaching duties for anti-Semitism, convinces a judge to fine a political cartoonist for depicting Ross as a Nazi.

Canada Customs detains a collection of thoughtful pro-Israel articles destined for a University of Toronto club, on suspicion of hate propaganda.

A lawyer defending his client against deportation for lying about his Nazi past is threatened with hate prosecution for saying that a frustrated German community may explode if his client is deported.

A psychology professor is threatened not with peer review on the competence of his scholarship but with criminal and civil hate prosecution for publishing his research.

A mathematics professor is suspended, hounded, and harassed into public silence not for anything he did or said to any woman but for what he publicly said *about* women.

A member of an identifiable minority group is *personally* compensated for hurt feelings and injury to his dignity after a newspaper publishes a series of articles disparaging the group.

Assorted rival campus, religious, and ethnic groups fighting over domestic agendas and international ills invoke the legitimating language and the moral and legal authority of hate law to try to shut each other up.

Despite a tearful, publicly televized apology by the speech offender, offers to make amends by his community, and the opening up of an educational and cultural dialogue between their communities, a much-decorated former Native leader is to be criminally prosecuted for uttering hate propaganda.

Jordan, Bahrain, Kuwait, and Saudi Arabia shut down Al-Jazeera, the 'Arab CNN' for being insufficiently pro-Arab. Meanwhile, the Canadian Jewish Congress aims to block CRTC approval of the news service in Canada on the grounds of expected violation of the hate propaganda provisions of the Criminal Code.

Today's progressive censoring theorists think not only that they can silence hate but also that they can educate the public against ignorance, renew democracy, and transform society 'for good' with found social truths, fixed public meanings, and final legal guarantees. As long as the social cause is good, victory can substitute for voice and final triumphs for ongoing political processes. This is an idea of tolerance, progress, and democracy that is theoretically deficient, politically self-contradictory, socially self-defeating, and pragmatically unworkable – on censors' own terms of justifying reference.

The progressive case for silencing open expressions of intolerance is a theoretically deficient legal end-run around the processes of social growth, public accountability, and political democracy in the name of those processes. Where self-government counts most – in affirming the public's right and duty to *learn* to coexist 'as they should' – hate censorship most denies self-government. Hate censorship theorists would substitute what is 'right' for knowing who we are. But knowing who we are is essential for knowing when and why we are wrong. More public self-enlightenment cannot come from public self-denial, and more elite accountability cannot come from assumptions of elite infallibility. If the public is to progress, it must *learn* to grow. If elites are to be accountable, they must be open to challenge. If society is to adapt, it must not fear to know its enemies or confront their challenges.

Progressive theorists, of the structuralist school of hate censorship thinking, see legal silencing as a legitimate and effective response to intolerance and ignorance in a deficient system of choice populated by a flawed or duped public. Hate silencing, however, does not address – much less redress – those deficiencies but simply masks their symptoms and postpones the day of public reckoning. Silencing substitutes public compliance for public comprehension, the camouflaged conflicts of the future for the open ones of today, and the artificial harmony of the moment for the social capital needed in the crises of tomorrow – to the later greater detriment of the public cause of progressive silencing. Over time, it is more likely that censors' fears will become self-realizing and their repressions self-justifying than that their remedy will become socially solidifying and politically satisfying.

Hate censorship is politically self-contradictory. Censors would legally assure official meanings and official histories but continue to subscribe to a political system of occasional governing majorities and changing social agendas. Progressive censors condemn the system, its structures, and its institutions as untrustworthy for the purposes of freedom of expression; but they then trust in those very same institutions and structures for the purposes of censorship. Politics is highlighted to underscore the congenital character of the disease but then denied to justify its repression. Ignorance and prejudice are public meanings *constructed* by structures of domination and patriarchy, but tolerance and understanding are public meanings that can be officially *given* by silencing fiat. Discursive chill is decried when censorship errantly detains or discards the agreeable, but is dismissed when it errantly retains or discards the disagreeable. Dearth of public discourse, lack of public accountability, and dirty politics are highlighted to enumerate the deficiencies of speech, but dismissed to shroud the deficiencies of official silencing. If the cause is right, politics can be legally frozen in time and social challenge and risks of change replaced with found truths, absolute historic victims, fixed public meanings, and final political triumphs.

Hate censorship is intrinsically unworkable. It cannot do for the progressive cause what hate censors want and expect it to do – delegitimate the messenger and depoliticize his message. Criminalizing intolerant thinking is socially artificial; prosecuting it is politically self-defeating. Public matters worth fighting about cannot be depoliticized. Repression distorts public discourse and politicizes and relegitimates intolerant messengers and problematizes their meanings for society still more. Effective silencing comes at the cost of success for the progressive cause(s) of censorship – in more ways than one. First, it invites opportunistic public posturing where genuine belief may be lacking. Second, by silencing transparent intolerant meanings, censors elevate and subtly resonate more socially pernicious and politically insidious ones in their place. Third, hate is a moving target, a chameleon. And it is silencing that moves it. Hate moves every time silencing finds it. It goes underground or it morphs above ground. Underground, it is harder to find and arrest. Above ground it becomes harder to expose and challenge. 'Found' truths, officially guaranteed by censors, tend to do this to 'unfound' ones, asserted by the censored. Devotees of final meanings and final triumphs tend not to see that it does. This is a slippery dynamic – and a self-realizing self-justifying dilemma. Paradoxically, in promoting its own obsolescence, hate censorship tends to reproduce its own 'need,' for more effective repression. This is a no-win proposition

– except for those who hate. Determined intolerance wins – even, indeed especially, when it loses. Hate censors decry weak-willed silencing. But they miss the dilemma of censorship success. Success by silencing is self-contradictory because effective silencing is self-defeating.

Successful repression of intolerant expression is not possible because it depends on forces beyond the control of progressive censors or on satisfaction of self-contradictory assumptions, especially assumptions inconsistent with the underlying social cause or democratic political premise of repression. These include unintended audience and speaker impacts which the censors cannot control; the self-defeating dynamics of the censorship process itself; the inexorable movement of time, history, demographics, social relations, politics, and modes of communication that censors cannot arrest; the innate asymmetries between speech and censorship (advantaging dissentient speech) that censors cannot 'correct'; a deficient system of public choice that censors do not otherwise trust; and a promise that they cannot keep, namely, that right public thinking can be 'fixed' by law in a system of occasional governing majorities and changeable social agendas. It is not a deficient system, a flawed or duped public, or weak-kneed politicians who fail hate censorship. It is hate censorship that fails itself. It cannot do for the cause of tolerance and democracy what censorship theorists want and expect it to do – advance it without undermining it in the very process of doing so. This dilemma is a failure not just on speech advocates' social and political terms of reference. It is an irreconcilable failure on censors' own terms of social and political reference. If, as Sniderman and his colleagues have said, 'the values of free expression and racial or religious tolerance remain in tension in Canadian society even though they both draw on the same underlying liberal principle,'[1] the dilemma resides not in the application of the principle but in its corruption – hate censorship is in irreconcilable tension with itself.

Societally reductionist theories – the 'social character' approach to freedom of public discourse – fashioned from economistic understandings of the balancing dilemma artificially strip hate silencing of political context, the movement of time, and the vicissitudes of history. This approach attempts to reduce socially multifaceted causes housing politically multidimensional conflicts into a purely legal and criminal issue, obscuring the overarching political dimensions, the diverse social contexts, and the intrinsic pragmatic dilemmas involved in enlisting public silencing in the service of these causes. Public meaning construction on public matters that count most cannot be successfully turned by hate censors into a one-time or final event of found social truths, fixed public meanings, and final political triumphs guaranteed by law. The human journey is a discursive work in progress, an ongoing voyage of conflicting public interests, evolving social conditions, and fluid political climates. Answers to conflicts packaged in the language of 'hate' may be self-evident for the convenience of repression – considered in the abstract, emptied of the movement of time, change, and political contestation, social ills are amenable to absolute remedies. But in practice, the answers to today's and tomorrow's problems of intolerance, community, diversity, equality, and democracy will need more flexible and nuanced responses. Principles worth fighting over invariably involve competing public choices and subjective policy trade-offs in socially evolving and politically fluid climates that do not lend themselves to simple or singular, much less fixed or final, legal answers. More of one good thing may mean less of another good thing. It may even mean legally tolerating some bad things, including the discursive tools needed to make better (less costly) choices. Social progress without pyrrhic public victories depends on it. Hate censorship allows, nay, encourages, its practitioners to ignore or dismiss such costs.

The idea that victory can ever be the *sine qua non* of freedom of public expression on public matters as an ordinary feature of democratic discourse is one that belongs in the discursive lexicon of polities founded on only right answers and right governments, not in the working vocabulary of polities premised on occasional governing majorities and changing social agendas. To prefer alternatives to legal public silencing in ordinary conditions of democratic discourse in a politically consolidated multicultural democracy in the twenty-first century is not to compromise the battle against injustice, intolerance, ignorance, and prejudice. It is to address it better. It is to appreciate the overarching *political* character of social progress and the importance of open, honest, and ongoing public discourse that makes less fragile social progress more possible.

For a law that is all about the future – how to protect democratic society from harm or transform it 'for good,' the test of time is its test of success. Time, however, is not on the side of hate speech law, much less on the side of the progressive case for more of it. Balancing social and political needs by hate silencing is not simply the wrong tool for the right cause. It will likely become 'more wrong' in the future. It is a politically blunt instrument enlisted in a social cause that will require ever more refined and flexible responses. History does not stand still for the convenience of censoring theorists. The danger to public harmony, community, diversity, and democracy posed by intolerance in Canada today is changing in three important ways.

First, to the degree that intolerance remains a problem of 'mainstream' thinking today, it is far more a problem of concealed prejudice than open expressions of hate.[2] What was once visible is now less visible and less challengeable – thanks especially to a criminal remedy that punishes visibility. Second, the more problematic challenge to tolerance in Canada no longer comes from an unenlightened 'dominant White society' as it once did, much less from fringe fanatics outside of any recognized community. It comes from the mainstream conflicts between historic rival ethnic communities themselves, asserting their 'just' causes – the new emerging, multicultural Canadian society. In a past era that proudly excluded 'Jew boys,' 'Niggers,' 'Chinks,' and dogs equally, it was easier for the diverse vulnerable to find common cause than risk mutual conflict.[3] There could be no doubt as to what constituted tolerance and social progress and what did not. This is more difficult in the age of Nunavut, affirmative action, and globally competing cultures – where the 'just' progress of one historically victimized community may come at the expense of another and where the domestic demands of multiculturalism intersect with international conflicts and clashes of civilizations. Third, historic ills have evolved as social progress has been made, becoming more complex and taking on new social and political forms. As Amanda Ripley writes, '[t]he problems of our time demand an especially crafty and determined breed of activist, because our enemies refuse to dress the part. Math illiteracy plagues black kids without wearing a hood or burning a cross. Urban sprawl doesn't need a gun to rob a community's quality of life and hunger can hide beneath a designer T-shirt.'[4] Hate censorship is a dated, failed, authoritarian relic of a pre-democratic past resuscitated by progressive censoring theorists for postmodern needs.

It would be good if progressive social theorists reconsidered their discursive devolution and returned to their historic role as moral guardians and public defenders of freedom of expression of social discontent – of the right of those, especially, with whom they most disagree. If they do not, it will fall to the courts to act. This is a daunting task for a progressive court. But it is hard to think of a more visionary or democratic one. Who but a rights-entrusted constitutional court is better equipped to shield and shelter the discursive foundations of democratic governance for the next generation from the popular mistakes of the previous one? The alternative is to risk entrapment in the dynamics of a politically self-contradictory and socially self-defeating 'slippery censorship slope' where fears become self-realizing, failure self-justifying, and the public quiet more important than the public cause and from which *timely* extrication becomes progressively more difficult but, for that very reason, increasingly important.

Appendix

Criminal Code (R.S.C. 1985, c. C-46) Hate Propaganda (Referenced Sections)

318. (1) Every one who advocates or promotes genocide is guilty of an indictable offence and liable to imprisonment for a term not exceeding five years.

(4) In this section, 'identifiable group' means any section of the public distinguished by colour, race, religion or ethnic origin.

319. (1) Every one who by communicating statements in any public place incites hatred against any identifiable group where such incitement is likely to lead to a breach of the peace is guilty of
   (a) an indictable offence and is liable to imprisonment for a term not exceeding two years; or
   (b) an offence punishable on summary conviction.

(2) Every one who, by communicating statements, other than in private conversation, wilfully promotes hatred against any identifiable group is guilty of
   (a) an indictable offence and is liable to imprisonment for a term not exceeding two years; or
   (b) an offence punishable on summary conviction.

(3) No person shall be convicted of an offence under subsection (2).
   (a) if he establishes that the statements communicated were true;
   (b) if, in good faith, he expressed or attempted to establish by argument an opinion on a religious subject;
   (c) if the statements were relevant to any subject of public interest, the discussion of which was for the public benefit, and if on reasonable grounds he believed them to be true; or

(d) if, in good faith, he intended to point out, for the purpose of removal, matters producing or tending to produce feelings of hatred toward an identifiable group in Canada.

(6) No proceeding for an offence under subsection (2) shall be instituted without the consent of the Attorney General.

(7) In this section,

'communicating' includes communicating by telephone, broadcasting or other audible or visible means;

'identifiable group' has the same meaning as in section 318;

'public place' includes any place to which the public have access as of right or by invitation, express or implied;

'statements' includes words spoken or written or recorded electronically or electro-magnetically or otherwise, and gestures, signs or other visible representations.

320.   (3) The owner and the author of the matter seized under subsection (1) and alleged to be hate propaganda may appear and be represented in the proceedings in order to oppose the making of an order for the forfeiture of the matter.

Table of Cases

Canadian Cases

American Cases

Table of Legislation

Notes

Introduction

1 See P.M. Sniderman, J.F. Fletcher, P.H. Russell, and P.E. Tetlock, *The Clash of Rights* (New Haven: Yale University Press, 1966).

2 A. Borovoy, *The New Anti-liberals* (Toronto: Canadian Scholars Press, 1999), esp. introduction and chapter 6. See also R. Epstein, 'The Harm Principle and How It Grew' (1995) 45 U.T.L.J. 369.

3 See articles by W. Schabas, 'Free Speech on Campus: Lessons from International and Comparative Law' (1995) 44 U.N.B.L.J. 11; B. Schrank, 'Academic Freedom and University Speech' (1995) 44 U.N.B.L.J. 75; K. Lamrock, 'Free Speech on Campus: The Principle beyond the Crucible' (1995) 44 U.N.B.L.J. 103; P. Hughes, 'Reconciling Valuable Interests; or Academic Freedom as Academic Responsibility' (1995) 44 U.N.B.L.J. 87; J. Bosnitch, 'Student Speech at UNB in the Early 1980s' (1995) 44 U.N.B.L.J. 93; A. Borovoy, 'When Rights Collide' (1995) 44 U.N.B.L.J. 49; J. Furedy, 'Academic Freedom, Opinions and Acts: The Voltaire–Mill Perspective Applied to Current Canadian Cases' (1995) 44 U.N.B.L.J. 131; and J. Grey, 'Freedom of Expression in a Canadian University Context' (1995) 44 U.N.B.L.J. 119. See also J. Macfarlane, 'Beyond a Right to Offend' (1997) 20 Dal. L.J. 78.

4 *Canada (Human Rights Commission)* v. *Taylor* [1990] 3 S.C.R. 892; *Ross* v. *New Brunswick School District No. 15* [1996] 1 S.C.R. 825.

5 *R.* v. *Keegstra* [1992] 3 S.C.R. 697; *R.* v. *Andrews and Smith* [1990] 3 S.C.R. 870.

6 Until the collapse of the 'Soviet Empire,' anti-Communist sentiment was the rallying point for many of these challenges. They included the now infamous attempts to outlaw the Canadian Communist Party in the union-

busting 1930s and the Duplessis 'padlock' law in Quebec in the 1950s. The American Palmer raids in the 1920s and the Senate witch-hunts for left-wing subversives in the 1950s (whose namesake, McCarthy, has come to signify right-wing persecution of social and political thought) are some of the more infamous examples from the United States. Refocused concerns of the right today include patriotism (U.S. – flag burning), business (Canada – labour picketing), and religious and moral issues (prayer, pornography).

7 Borovoy, *supra* note 2 at 7–12, 39–51, and 158–72.

8 See appendix: *Canadian Criminal Code*, R.S.C., 1985, c. C-46, ss 319.

9 See, generally, A. Dicey, *Introduction to the Study of the Law of the Constitution* 10th ed. (London: Macmillan, 1965).

10 See chapters 4, 5, and 6.

11 See especially chapter 4.

12 Chapters 1 and 2.

13 Chapters 1, 2, and 6.

14 See R. Bernstein, 'The Rising Hegemony of the Politically Correct,' *New York Times* (10 October 1990), 3–4.

15 See *Collin* v. *Smith*, 578 F.2d 1197 (1978) (where the court held that a neo-Nazi march could proceed through a Jewish neighbourhood in Skokie, Illinois). See also *American Booksellers Association, Inc.* v. *Hudnut*, 771 F.2d 323 (1985); *RAV* v. *City of St Paul*, 505 U.S. 377 (1992).

16 See, generally, L. Fisher, *The Politics of Shared Power: Congress and the Executive* 3d ed. (Washington, D.C.: Congressional Quarterly Press, 1993). See also R. Sherrill, *Why They Call It Politics: A Guide to America's Government* 4th ed. (New York: Harcourt Brace Jovanovich, 1984); S. Huntington, *American Politics: The Promise of Disharmony* (Cambridge, Mass.: Harvard University Press, 1981).

17 See B. Bailyn, *The Ideological Origins of the American Revolution* (Cambridge, Mass.: Harvard University Press, 1967); C. Rossiter, *The Political Thought of the American Revolution* (New York: Harcourt, Brace and World, 1963); A Hacker, *Two Nations: Black and White, Separate, Hostile, Unequal* (New York: Ballantine, 1993).

18 See T. White, *Breach of Faith: The Fall of Richard Nixon* (New York: Dell Publishers, 1976).

19 *New York Times* v. *Sullivan*, 376 U.S. 254 (1964).

20 See Bernstein, *supra* note 14. See also M. Rogin, 'The Countersubversive Tradition in American Politics' (1986) 31 Berkeley Journal of Sociology 1.

21 On judicial activism, differences in courts, and their significance, see M. Shapiro, *Courts: A Comparative and Political Analysis* rev. ed. (Chicago: University of Chicago Press, 1986).

22 *Supra*, note 1 at 64.

23 M. Minsky, *The Society of Mind*, quoted in M. Minsky, 'Will Robots Inherit the Earth?' (October 1994) Scientific American 108.

24 See chapter 1.

25 See chapter 4.

26 This has been a common and, more often than its targets might care to acknowledge, compelling 'radical' left-wing criticism of mainstream approaches to the social sciences generally, and I take it to heart. As Runciman wrote, 'The fact is, however, that what have been claimed as sciences of society have never turned out to be more than philosophies of history.' W. Runciman, *Social Science and Political Theory* (Cambridge: Cambridge University Press, 1965) at 2. See also D. Easton, J. Gunnell, and L. Graziano, eds, *The Development of Political Science: A Comparative Survey* (London: Routledge, 1991).

1 Foundations of the Imbalance

1 K. Dubick, 'Freedom to Hate: Do the *Criminal Code* Proscriptions against Hate Propaganda Infringe the *Charter*?' (1990) 54 Sask. L. Rev. 149.

2 The CJC appeared before a joint committee of the House of Commons and the Senate in 1953. See S. Cohen, 'Hate Propaganda – The Amendments to the *Criminal Code*' (1971) 17 McGill L.J. 740.

3 Canada, Special Committee on Hate Propaganda, *Report* (Ottawa: Queen's Printer, 1966) (Chair: M. Cohen; hereafter cited as *Cohen Report* or referred to as Cohen Committee).

4 Ibid. at 24–5 (hereafter cited as the 'mushroom thesis'). The 'clear and present' danger test comes from U.S. First Amendment jurisprudence. See *Schenck* v. *United States*, 249 U.S. 47 (1919) at 52.

5 Currently, *Canadian Criminal Code*, R.S.C., 1985, c. C-46, ss 319(1), 319(2), 319(3) (hereafter Criminal Code).

6 M. Cohen, 'The Hate Propaganda Amendments: Reflections on a Controversy' (1971) 9 Alta. L. Rev. 103 at 111.

7 *Canadian Charter of Rights and Freedoms*, Part I of the *Canada Act*, 1982, being schedule B to the *Canada Act 1982* (U.K.) 1982, c. 11 (hereafter Charter).

8 S. Anand, 'Expressions of Racial Hatred and Racism in Canada: An Historical Perspective' (1998) 77 Can. B. Rev. 181 at 187.

9 Ibid. at 196–7.

10 I. McKenna, 'Canada's Hate Propaganda Laws – A Critique' (1994) 26 Ottawa L. Rev. at 159.

11 Anand, *supra* note 8 at 196, quoting Canada, Canadian Human Rights Commission, *Annual Report 1989* (Ottawa: Minister of Supply and Services,

1990), 22. By 1998, the same year in which Anand's piece appeared, the *Canadian Jewish News* reported that the Canadian Human Rights Commission was highlighting human rights progress in a wide area, including employment equity, pay equity, and employers' willingness to accommodate minority groups. See P. Lungen, 'Report Documents Human Rights Progress in 1998,' *Canadian Jewish News* (31 March 1991), 5.

12 Anand, *supra* note 8 at 196, quoting A. Sunahara, *The Politics of Racism: The Uprooting of Japanese Canadians during the Second World War* (Toronto: J. Lorimer, 1981). Notice the date of Sunahara's conclusion and its unqualified use by Anand as evidence for today.

13 See Canada, Statistics Canada, 'Employment Equity Data Program; Housing, Family and Social Statistics Division' (Ottawa: Queen's Printer, 1991) at 177–99 and 223–32. The data show that Blacks, despite levels of education comparable to those of the total population, comprised 50 per cent more of the unemployed.

14 'Main characteristics are a general irrational and malicious abuse of certain identifiable minority groups in Canada.' *Cohen Report*, *supra* note 3 at 11.

15 Anand, *supra* note 8 at 182.

16 Ibid., 196.

17 McKenna, *supra* note 10 at 183–4. Is this the kind of 'balance' the Canadian Charter 'has in mind' when it restricts legislative abridgments of freedom of expression 'only to such reasonable limits prescribed by law as can be demonstrably justified in a free and democratic society?' See section 1 of the Charter. Both Anand and McKenna enlist the Charter's derogation clause in support of their expansive understanding of hate censorship.

18 Historically, Jews and Chinese have been grievously discriminated against. '[A]t McGill University ... Jewish students in arts ... are admitted only on an academic standing of 75% or over; other students are admitted on standing of 60% or over. This regulation is publicly known and seems to operate without any friction.' Queen's University Senate, *Statistics on Jewish Registration: Minutes of Queen's University* (Kingston, Ont.: 29 October 1943).

19 R. Csillag, 'Canada Offers to Open Doors to Palestinians,' *Canadian Jewish News* (18 January 2000), 6. As Csillag states, 'Reports that Canada has made a "secret" offer to accept potentially thousands of Palestinian refugees [in an attempt to help defuse the "right of return" issue in the Middle East] has raised the consternation and ire of many in the Jewish community.'

20 Even where there is agreement on social goals, there can be profound disagreement on how best to get there. Consider Borovoy, who has spent a lifetime fighting in the trenches for racial equality and women's rights. Agreeing in principle with affirmative action, he none the less asks, 'But

why should an entire generation of men be shut out of certain jobs because
of what happened to past generations of women?' A. Borovoy, *The New
Anti-liberals* (Toronto: Canadian Scholars Press, 1999) at 23.

21 Even something held so sacred to women's equality today as the abortion
right of choice could not have served quite the same social test of inequality a century ago, when the right was more apt to mean death at the hands
of inferior technology. Nor might it do so in the future to the same degree
as it does in the present if advances in prenatal and reproductive technology combine with depopulation and an aging population to reprioritize
current social values and economic needs. See L. Fenwick, *Private Choices,
Public Consequences: Reproductive Technology and the New Ethics of Conception,
Pregnancy, and Family* (Toronto: Dutton, 1998). See also P.M. Sniderman,
J.F. Fletcher, P.H. Russell, and P.E. Tetlock, *The Clash of Rights* (New
Haven: Yale University Press, 1996) at ch. 4, 'Equality: A Chameleon Right.'
See also 'The New Mosaic,' *Time* (7 May 2001), 20. Reporting on an aging
Canadian population, this article observes that, '[a]t current rates, popula-
tion growth would actually start declining in 2008 to 2010 without immi-
grants.' On the changing character of immigration needs in the knowledge
economy, it notes that '[a]ttracting highly skilled immigrants to Canada –
and keeping them – is perhaps the country's greatest challenge' (20).

22 For background, see Z. Eisenstein, *Capitalist Patriarchy and the Case for
Socialist Feminism* (New York: Monthly Review Press, 1979).

23 Anand, *supra* note 8; McKenna, *supra* note 10. While evidence, for example,
of the mainstream media's structural bias towards the status quo is not
wanting, there is considerable disagreement as to the character, extent,
and depth of their 'controlling' public impact even among 'left-wing'
critics. Compare M. Shudson, 'The Sociology of News Production Revisited,' in J. Curran and M. Gurevitch, eds, *Mass Media and Society* (New York:
Routledge, 1991); R. Ericson et al., *Representing Order* (Toronto: University
of Toronto Press, 1991); J. Downing, A. Sreberny, and A. Mohammadi,
Questioning the Media: A Critical Introduction 2nd ed. (Thousand Oaks, Calif.:
Sage Publications, 1995); R.A. Hackett, *News and Dissent: The Press and the
Politics of Peace in Canada* (Norwood, N.J.: Ablex Publication Corporation,
1991); S. Herman and N. Chomsky, *Manufacturing Consent: The Political
Economy of the Mass Media* (New York: Pantheon Books, 1988).

24 While Marx's idea of the dictatorship of the proletariat (theoretically
transitory but politically indefinite) is, arguably, quite consistent with the
idea of a broad-based public censorship, I doubt that Gramsci would have
approved of hate censorship. His insights may offer inspiration for those
subscribing to the progressive school of hate censorship thinking, but it is

unlikely that Gramsci would have shared their faith in hate censorship. See, generally, A. Gramsci, *Selections from the Prison Notebooks*, H. Quintin and N. Geoffrey, eds (New York: International, 1971).

25 On this idea of social engineering, see F.L. Morton and R. Knopff, *The Charter Revolution and the Court Party* (Peterborough, Ont.: Broadview Press, 2000).

26 To believe that freedom of expression in Canada has been little more than a tyrant or stooge in the service of racists, sexists, and right-wing ideologues is not only to ignore the considerable progress made through freedom of expression by women and minorities since the Cohen Committee report. It shows a rather poor understanding of how and why such progress could be made through freedom of expression despite inequalities of communicative resources. On this see chapter 9.

27 Nor would an equating of 'illegitimacies' – a 'pox on both your houses' response – be a satisfactory answer here. Legal censorship of this kind is not 'contra-democratic politics by another name.' It is the very antithesis, a denial, of politics. It may be difficult to overcome the 'psychological effects' of hegemonic structures of cognitive oppression. But it is neither illegal nor impossible to do so. Indeed, many have done so – social activists themselves being the best examples. It is only politically focused structures of legal censorship that would deny socially disagreeable politics altogether by quashing non-conforming expressions post facto – even of those speakers who do succeed in *cognitively* overcoming its strictures.

28 Anand, *supra* note 8 at 187–93.

29 The abstract to Anand's article, ibid., reads, 'The author examines the evidence of discrimination in Canadian society from government sanctioned discrimination, which forms part of our history, to modern evidence that shows the attitudes underlying this have not changed.' While all hate censors may agree on the need for hate speech law, even they do not agree on the assumed unchanged nature of the peril justifying it. Compare Anand's sweeping statements to a compilation of materials on anti-Jewish sentiments put out by the Joint Community Relations Committee of the Canadian Jewish Congress. Manuel Prutschi, one of the foremost advocates of hate propaganda law in Canada, could write in 1990 that although there is a 'significant minority pocket of intolerance' against Jews that must be kept 'in check,' the 'largest circle, constituting Canada's core, is healthy and solidly tolerant.' See M. Prutschi, 'A Jewish Perspective on Racism in Canada,' 'Anti-Semitism, Anti-Semites, the Community, the Media and the Law,' (Summer 1990) Canadian Jewish Congress, Joint Community Relations Committee, 6.

30 McKenna suggests that the committee's 'problem' stems from its definition of hatred – one that distinguishes hate from prejudice and focuses censorship only on hatred. McKenna, *supra* note 10. Anand suggests that the committee was empirically handicapped in that it was not privy to 'recent evidence' of the depth and breadth of racism in Canada. Anand, *supra* note 8 at 182.

31 Anand, *supra* note 8 at 185.

32 Cohen Committee, *supra* note 3 and note 4, and accompanying text.

33 From the context of university speech codes, Borovoy writes, 'Remarkably, the main impetus for these restrictions on speech was coming not from the right but from the left. This represented a virtually diametric reversal of roles ... This irony is further compounded by the extent to which the current advocates of censorship are beneficiaries of the very freedom they would curb.' Borovoy, *supra* note 20 at 81.

34 Canada, House of Commons, *Debates* (29 February 1964) at 132 (Mr G. Favreau).

35 I am indebted here to the seminal work of Jamie Cameron, whose more legally anchored analysis of the asymmetry need not concern us here but is the source of my title and the fabric from which I stitch my own conclusions. See J. Cameron, 'The Past, Present and Future of Expressive Freedom under the Charter' (1997) 35 Osgoode Hall L.J. 1.

36 In Canada, there was pressure on the CRTC to have radio talk show host Dr Laura Schlesinger taken off the air for calling homosexuality a 'biological error' and 'deviant behaviour.' In the United States, she was removed from an invitation list at an international conference on Jewish ethics, reportedly because of such statements. See 'Dr. Laura Uninvited,' *Canadian Jewish News* (31 August 2000), 2.

37 Human rights codes remain a primary instrument for protection of the general public. See, for example, *Ontario Human Rights Code,* R.S.O. 1970, c. 318 (as amended); *Canadian Human Rights Act,* R.S.C., 1985, c. H-6. Unlike the constitutionally entrenched Charter, which is limited to what may broadly be styled 'state action' and whose application is subject to ordinary review by the courts, the provisions of these statutory protections specifically apply to the private sector and are ordinarily interpreted and enforced by regulatory bodies, commissions, boards, or tribunals. Human rights codes have, arguably, acquired a quasi-constitutional status. See generally, P. Hogg, *Constitutional Law of Canada* 2000 Student Ed. (Scarborough, Ont.: Carswell, 2001).

38 Even here, some writers question whether legal proscription of speech is the better long-term remedy. See P. Hughes, 'Workplace Speech and

Conduct Models: Reconsidering the Legal Model' (1998) 77 Can. Bar Rev. 105 (questioning whether the legal model is effective and suggesting that it may be 'counter productive in changing the workplace culture') at 106.

39 *Canada (Human Rights Commission)* v. *Taylor* [1990] 3 S.C.R. 892.

40 *Canadian Human Rights Act*, R.S.C., 1985, c. H-6, s. 13 (proscribing telephonic communication of material that would expose a person or persons to hatred or contempt).

41 *Ross* v. *New Brunswick School District No. 15* [1996] 1 S.C.R. 825.

42 In Switzerland, seventy-nine-year-old Gaston-Armand Amaudruz went on trial on charges of 'racial discrimination' for denying that Nazi gas chambers existed. He faced a maximum sentence of three years in prison. See 'Holocaust Charges,' *Canadian Jewish News* (13 April 2000), 2.

43 S. 1 of the Charter. This allows state abridgment of enumerated freedoms only to such *reasonable limits prescribed by law as can be demonstrably justified in a free and democratic society.*

44 S. 28 of the Charter. This ensures that rights and freedoms are guaranteed equally to males and females; also ss 15(1) and, particularly, 15(2) (amelioration of conditions of disadvantage).

45 S. 27 of the Charter. This requires the 'interpretation' of rights to be 'consistent with the preservation and enhancement of the multicultural heritage of Canadians.'

46 Ss 16–22 of the Charter. These deal with the official languages of Canada. Section 23 of the Charter deals with minority language educational rights.

47 Ss 25, 35 of the Charter. These two sections refer to the protection of Aboriginal Rights.

48 S. 36 of the Charter. This speaks to economic and regional parity in Canada.

49 The U.S. Constitution also does not have a derogation clause like section 1 of the Charter. For some substantive implications of this textual distinction, see S. Braun, 'Should Commercial Speech Be Accorded Constitutional Recognition under the *Canadian Charter of Rights and Freedoms*?' (1986) 18 Ottawa L. Rev. 37.

50 I use the term 'Canadian constitution' broadly and in the plural sense, since, unlike the U.S. Constitution, the Canadian constitution depends heavily on constitutional conventions and cannot be so easily confined to a single or singular 'written' document. See R.J. Van Loom and M.S. Whittington, *The Canadian Political System* 4th ed. (Whitby, Ont.: McGraw-Hill, 1987) at 167–73.

51 It is not always clear what is and what is not promotive of that vision. Quebec's historic position, often presented as a cultural threatened French

island in a sea of English, could not sustain a 'cultural protecting' abridg-
ment of freedom of commercial speech – Quebec's infamous 'sign law.'
Bill 101 – *The Charter of the French Language*, R.S.Q., c. C-11, ss 1, 58. See also
Ford v. *A.G. Quebec* (1988) 54 D.L.R. (4th) 577 (S.C.C.).

52 P. Monaĥan, *Politics and the Constitution* (Toronto: Carswell, 1987) at 99.
See also 103–6.

53 The feature that made censorship in the former Communist countries so
all encompassing was the 'positive' requirement of active citizen participation in the 'official ideal.' It was not enough that the citizen refrained from
expressions contrary to that ideal.

To create socialist 'man' – one freed from the shackles of a false or
hegemonic self–regarding, materialistic consciousness – Communism, as
practised, found it necessary not just to shield its citizenry from the
corrupting effect of socially and politically divisive thoughts. It required
them to actively express themselves (self-inculcation) in the officially
sanctioned, correct ones. Messaging vehicles promotive of officially correct
public expression ranged from officially created and officially run state
unions to officially sanctioned associations of socialist youth such as
Komsomol. See V. Havel, 'The Power of the Powerless,' in A. Wilson, ed.,
Open Letters (London: Faber, 1991) (especially his most poignant insight
into the dilemma of the 'Greengrocers,' in which local produce merchants
were required, on pain of legal sanction, to prominently display a sign with
the inscription 'Workers of the World Unite! You Have Nothing to Lose
but Your Chains!').

54 Anand, *supra* note 8 at 187.

55 *R.* v. *Morgentaler* [1988] 1 S.C.R. 30.

56 Ibid. at 30.

57 *R.* v. *Keegstra* [1990] 3 S.C.R. 697 (hereafter *Keegstra*).

58 Ibid. at 697.

59 On problems with constructing public policy from test cases, see S. Braun,
'Judicial Apprehension of Violation of Legal Rights under the *Canadian
Charter of Rights and Freedoms*: Towards a Framework of Analysis' (1987) 24
U.W.O.L. Rev. 27 at 51–3.

60 *R.* v. *Zundel* [1992] 2 S.C.R. 731 (hereafter *Zundel*). Section 177 of the
Criminal Code R.S.C., 1985, c. C-46 (Spreading False News) made it a
criminal offence for anyone to 'wilfully publish a statement, tale or news
that he knows is false and that causes or is likely to cause injury or mischief
to a public interest.'

61 B. Elman and E. Nelson, 'Distinguishing *Zundel* and *Keegstra*' (1993) 4
Constit. Forum 71–8.

62 *Keegstra, supra* note 57. For a critical 'deconstruction' of the key assumptions underlying the court's decision in *Keegstra* see chapter 3 ('Functions
and Assumptions of Hate Propaganda Law') at 62.

63 The case made by the majority in *Keegstra.*

64 I have discussed this at some length, from different perspectives, elsewhere.
See Braun, *supra* note 59. See also P. Weiler, 'The Supreme Court and the
Law of Canadian Federalism' (1973) 23 U. of Toronto L.J. 307. Weiler
shows how federalism was used as a covert bill of rights to protect civil
liberties and political democracy, 342–52.

65 *Rocket* v. *Royal College of Dental Surgeons of Ontario* [1990] 2 S.C.R. 232
(hereafter *Rocket*). Invalidating a near-total prohibition on advertising by
dentists.

66 *Reference re ss 193 and 195.1(1)(c) of the Criminal Code* [1990] 1 S.C.R. 1123.

67 *R.* v. *Oakes* (1986) 26 D.L.R. (4th) 200 (S.C.C.).

68 Four requirements were set to justify a limit on a Charter right. First, the
state objective must be 'pressing and substantial.' The limit must then pass
a three-pronged proportionality test: it must be 'rationally connected' to
the objective; it must be the 'least intrusive' method of achieving the
objective; and the cost of abridgment must not be disproportionate to the
benefit secured by such abridgment. Failure on any one of these counts
can be grounds to strike down the state's case. Ibid. at 138–40.

69 *Singh* v. *Canada (Minister of Employment and Immigration)* [1985] 1 S.C.R. 177
(hereafter *Singh*).

70 J. Cameron, 'The Past, Present, and Future of Expressive Freedom under
the *Charter*' (1997) 35 Osgoode Hall L.J. 1.

71 *Irwin Toy* v. *Quebec* [1989] 1 S.C.R. 927.

72 Ibid. at 969. The court noted the 'We cannot ... exclude human activity
from the scope of guaranteed free expression on the basis of the content of
meaning being conveyed. Indeed, if the activity conveys or attempts to
convey a meaning, it has expressive content and prima facie falls within the
scope of the guarantee.'

73 Cameron, *supra* note 70 at 11.

74 *Rocket, supra* note 65 at 246–7.

75 *Keegstra, supra* note 57 at 697.

76 Ibid. at 759–60.

77 Ibid. at 760.

78 D. Greschner and E. Colvin, 'Expanding the Boundaries of Constitutional
Obligation: Lessons from the Canadian Experience' (1985) 22 Comp. Jur.
Rev. 1 at 18–21.

2 Functions and Assumptions of Freedom of Expression

1 See, for example, R. Dworkin, *Taking Rights Seriously* (Cambridge, Mass.: Harvard University Press, 1978), esp. 266–78, 364–8.

2 For a far more sweeping and still informative discussion of the functions and assumptions of freedom of speech see T. Emerson, 'Toward a General Theory of the First Amendment' (1962) 72 Yale L.J. 877.

3 *Re Allman* v. *Commissioner of Northwest Territories* (1984) 8 D.L.R. (4th) at 236.

4 A. Borovoy, *The New Anti-liberals* (Toronto: Canadian Scholars Press, 1999).

5 In much of the world, assemblies, parades, and other gatherings are permitted, even required, but only to 'demonstrate' support for officialdom. Soviet Communism was particularly skilled at orchestrated demonstrations.

6 'The right of association like the right of belief is more than the right to attend a meeting; it includes the right to express one's attitudes or philosophies by membership in a group or by affiliation with it or by other lawful means. Association in that context is a form of expression of opinion.' *Griswold* v. *Connecticut*, 381 U.S. 779 (1965) at 483.

7 Even if all of society were of one mind, 'freedom' to do the latter is not meaningful without the freedom to do the former.

8 *Whitney* v. *California*, 274 U.S. 357 (1927) at 377 (concerning a Marxist charged with threatening public peace and democracy for teaching criminal syndicalism). See also A. de Tocqueville, 'Majority Tyranny,' in *Democracy in America* (New York: Doubleday, 1969).

9 Who better fits this profile of the marginalized than the hatemonger?

10 Under the Canadian Criminal Code, the offence of incitement to hate is confined to utterances made in 'any public place' and of uttering statements promoting hatred to communications 'other than in private conversation.' See discussion chapter 6, at 11(3), 155.

11 Protection against injury to personal reputations has long been covered by ordinary laws against slander and defamation. For a good historical account, see: J. Williams, *The Law of Defamation in Canada* (Toronto: Butterworth, 1976).

12 Before their social message became publicly more palatable and officially more agreeable, the left rested their right to publicly disturb and socially transform not on official recognition of the merits of the content of their message but on the political importance of the right to its expression. Though they may say that their message is right while that of their opponents is wrong, they cannot now say that their opponents' message should be suppressed because it is politically unimportant.

13 They learned their trade from political mentors and political organizations. Keegstra can 'credit' his 'knowledge' and training in Holocaust denial to the 'Canadian League of Rights,' whose leader, Ron Gostick, was 'reared in the anti-Semitic strain of Alberta Social Credit.' Ross Taylor belonged to the Canadian Union of Fascists, then the White supremacist Western Guard. Don Andrews and Robert Smith, all activists in Zundel's trial, belong to the Nationalist Party, 'which, no doubt, echoes back to the fascist Ontario Nationalist Party of the 1930's.' The Citizens for Foreign Aid Reform (C-FAR) touts Paul Fromm as its organizational head. See M. Prutschi, 'Organized Anti-Semitism in Canada' (1985) 25(1) Orah 8.

14 J. Sartre, *Being and Nothingness* (New York: Philosophical Library, 1956) at 598.

15 M. Prutschi, 'Hate Groups and Bigotry's Fellow Travelers' (1990) 6 Currents 8–10.

16 But not the legal obligation. Unlike in Australia, even this minimal level of political participation is not legally required in Canada or the United States.

17 This includes all incidental rights, from the right to run for public office to rights of political assembly and association. See sections 2 and 3 of the *Canadian Charter of Rights and Freedoms*, Part I of the *Canada Act*, 1982, being schedule B to the *Canada Act 1982* (U.K.) 1982, c. 11 (hereafter Charter).

18 The Supreme Court of Canada ruled on 31 October 2002 that inmates of federal prisons cannot be denied the vote. See *http://cbc.ca/news/features/prison_vote.html.*

19 M. Walzer, 'Philosophy and Democracy' (1981) 9 Political Theory 379 at 384.

20 Mill gives a perhaps uncharacteristically non-instrumental justification: 'The best government has no more title to it [political censorship] than the worst. It is as noxious, or more noxious, when exerted in accordance with public opinion, than when in opposition to it. If all mankind minus one were of one opinion, and only one person were of the contrary opinion, mankind would be no more justified in silencing that one person, than he, if he had the power, would be justified in silencing mankind.' J.S. Mill, *On Liberty* (London: J.M. Dent and Sons, 1859) at 74.

21 There is a wealth of literature on some of the more deep-seated social, structural, and institutional causes. One of the most thoughtful and provocative remains R. Dahl, *Dilemmas of Pluralistic Democracy: Autonomy vs. Control* (New Haven: Yale University Press, 1982), especially chs 3, 5, and 6.

22 G. Woodcock, 'Voter's Block: What If They Called an Election and Nobody Came?' (1986) 65 The Canadian Forum 1 at 5–9.

23 For example, even Britain's prestigious conservative magazine *The Economist* has commented on Canada's 'duopolistic' cross-concentration of media outlets: 'The most visible impact of "cross-ownership," which is restricted in most developed countries, has been shameless promotion in the newspapers of their sister stations' programmes.' See *The Economist* (28 April–4 May 2001), 38.

24 P. Monahan, *Politics and the Constitution* (Toronto: Carswell, 1987) at 87.

25 I. McKenna, 'Canada's Hate Propaganda Laws – A Critique' (1994) 26 Ottawa L. Rev. 159. See also J. Bakan, 'Constitutional Interpretation and Social Change: You Can't Always Get What You Want (Nor What You Need)' (1991) 70 Can. Bar Rev. 305.

26 Take, for example, Manuel Prutschi's conclusion (national director, Community Relations Committee, Canadian Jewish Congress) that 'the largest circle, constituting Canada's core, is healthy and solidly tolerant.' None the less, 'there is a significant pocket of intolerance' that justifies censorship of hate propaganda 'to keep anti-Semitism and racism in check.' See M. Prutschi, 'A Jewish Perspective on Racism in Canada' (Summer 1990), Canadian Jewish Congress, Joint Community Relations Committee, 'Anti-Semitism, Anti-Semites, the Community, the Media and the Law,' 6.

27 How would progressive censorship structuralists like McKenna account for a mainstream corporate conglomerate such as Time-Warner carrying a feature story in *Time* showing, on its cover, a frying pan with the earth as the egg. See 'Global Warming,' *Time* (9 April 2001), 16–31.

28 Credibility of argument, however, should not be confused with viability of remedy. See chapter 6.

29 Quite the contrary. Sensitivity training and antiracism education are widespread in Canada today. See, for example, Part II *infra*.

30 M. Prutschi, 'Organized Anti-Semitism in Canada' (1985) 25 (1) Orah 8 at 9. 'They [hate groups] do not necessarily reflect popular sentiments about Jews nor the prevalent principles guiding mainstream Canada ... Canada's anti-Semitic groups in the post-war years have tended to be fragmented, and have held sway over very few people.'

31 Query whether this connection is implied in Meiklejohn. See A. Meiklejohn, *Political Freedom* (New York: Oxford University Press, 1965) and 'The First Amendment Is an Absolute,' in P.B. Kurland, ed., *Free Speech and Association: The Supreme Court and the First Amendment* (Chicago: University of Chicago Press, 1975).

32 For the opposite view, widely accepted under communism at one time and even holding some sway in the West, see V. Afanasyev, *Fundamentals of Scientific Communism* (Moscow: Progress, 1977).

33 As Justice Louis Brandeis said, 'It is the function of speech to free men from the bondage of irrational fears.' *Whitney* v. *California*, 274 U.S. 357 (1927) at 376.

34 As sustained by structures and institutions of hegemony. The Canadian Human Rights Commission has itself expressed this view ('The demons of racial and cultural prejudice have never been officially or unofficially exorcised from Canadian society ... instances of racism and intolerance are deeply etched in the historical record and, for that matter, not hard to find in the daily newspapers'). See chapter 1.

35 Ibid.

36 See H. Berman, *Justice in the U.S.S.R.* (Cambridge, Mass.: Harvard University Press, 1978), esp. ch. 1.

37 So impressed were some Western Soviet scholars with the comparably greater tranquillity of commanded social harmony and enforced political stability that, as late as 1990, with Communist satellites crumbling everywhere, one of the leading Soviet scholars could still dismiss warnings of collapse by 'Soviet radicals and American analysts [who] have talked about disintegration and chaos [in the Soviet Union].' See J. Hough, 'The Logic of Collective Action' (1990) Journal of Soviet Nationalities 61 – a roundtable discussion of M. Olson, *Logic of Collective Action* (Cambridge, Mass.: Harvard University Press, 1965).

38 'Only Communism (like Nazism and Fascism in the past) claims outright cognitive monopoly as the trustee of superior truth.' See G. Di Palma, 'Legitimation from the Top to Civil Society: Politico-Cultural Change in Eastern Europe' (1991) 44 World Politics 64.

39 See John Milton, *Areopagitica: A Speech for the Liberty of Unlicensed Printing to the Parliament of England* (London: 1664).

40 The requirement of *mens rea* for criminal offences generally has had the unfortunate effect of confusing the social requirements of conviction for criminal wrongs with the political purposes of freedom of expression. Honest belief, good faith, and truth defences in anti-hate legislation testify to this confusion. See *R.* v. *Zundel* (1987) 58 O.R. (2d) 129 (C.A.), where the learned trial judge observed, at 155, 'Spreading falsehoods knowingly is the antithesis of seeking truth through the free exchange of ideas.' See also s. 319(3) of the *Canadian Criminal Code*, R.S.C., 1985, c. C-46 (hereafter Criminal Code).

41 Depictions of ethnic slaughter in the evening newscasts may not intend stereotypical divisions and intolerance but may produce them none the less. Indeed, the proverbial 'road to hell' may be paved by the words of those with truthful intentions, as in so many Marxist revolutions worldwide.

42 The Ku Klux Klan did not intend truth, but the civil rights response to them in the 1960s and 1970s did produce truth, and the outpouring of outrage against the K.K.K. today also does so.

43 The 'chilling effect.' See *Dombrowski* v. *Pfister*, 380 U.S. 479 (1965) at 487.

44 J.S. Mill, *On Liberty*, *supra* note 20 at 74.

45 '[A]bsolute faith in a rational free marketplace of ideas [is] not only wrong-headed, but irresponsible.' K. Mahoney, 'Language as Violence v. Freedom of Expression: Canadian and American Perspectives on Group Defamation' (1988–9) 37 Buffalo Law Review 337 at 350.

46 Even Richard Moon, who expresses major reservations about hate censorship, misframes the case for freedom of speech, couching it not in relative and comparative terms of risk but in absolute terms of human rationality: 'Upon what is our commitment to freedom of expression based, if not on a belief in human reason and its power to recognize truth?' R. Moon, *The Constitutional Protection of Freedom of Expression* (Toronto: University of Toronto Press, 2000) at 135.

47 See M. Bakhtin, *Speech Genres and Other Late Essays*, translated by V. McGee (Austin: University of Texas Press, 1986) at 91. See also J. Thompson, *The Media and Modernity* (Stanford: Stanford University Press, 1995) at 39.

48 Moon touts such mind expansion for critical thinking but seems willing to reject its application where it is most testing and meaningful – 'extreme' hate. R. Moon, *supra* note 46 at 147. See my critique, chapter 6, at 166.

49 A common complaint, for example, of the declining generation of old civil rights and feminist advocates is that the younger generation do not, in the relative comforts won for them by the struggles of the past, fully appreciate the enormous sacrifices made and the lessons to be learned for the future.

50 S. Braun, 'Social and Racial Tolerance and Freedom of Expression in a Democratic Society: Friends or Foes? *Regina* v. *Zundel*' (1988) 11 Dal. L.J. 471, at 472, 474.

51 T. Tugend, 'Spielberg Foundation Shifts to Education,' *Canadian Jewish News* (30 August 2001), 39 (survivors of the Shoah Visual History Foundation, established in 1994).

52 A teachers' guide, put out by B'nai Brith Canada, which lists resources, tips, Internet websites, and bibliographies on the Holocaust, 'will be distributed across Ontario for the 2000–2001 school year.' R. Csillag, 'Holocaust's Victims Mourned, Survivors Honored,' *Canadian Jewish News* (11 May 2000), 6.

53 Ibid.

54 B. Rose, 'Christian Service Resists "forgetfulness" of Holocaust,' *Canadian Jewish News* (29 April 1999), 24 (nineteenth annual Christian Service in Memory of the Holocaust).

55 'Holocaust Education Week Begins,' *Canadian Jewish News* (21 October 1999), 7.

56 Ibid.

57 L. Anklewicz, 'Holocaust Movies Available on Video,' *Canadian Jewish News* (15 April 1999), 34.

58 One of the most recent to be funded is at the University of British Columbia. See 'Holocaust Course Funded,' *Canadian Jewish News* (6 May 1999), 2.

59 Overload is as much a subjective as an objective phenomenon. The less receptive the subject is to the message, the more likely she is to experience overload, to the detriment of the cause loaded.

60 See, generally, G. Ionescu, 'Political Undercomprehension or the Overload of Political Cognition' (1989) 24 Government and Opposition 413.

61 M. Weinfeld, 'Holocaust Overload in Fiction and Art,' *Canadian Jewish News* (11 March 1999), 10.

62 M. Love, 'Anti-Racism Education Experiencing "Backlash",' *Canadian Jewish News* (18 April 1996), 18.

63 *Whitney, supra* note 8 at 378.

64 Moon, while rejecting censorship of 'ordinary' prejudice, seems receptive to the idea of official truths and final triumphs in the case of 'extreme' messages of intolerance. See Moon, *supra* note 46 at 11.

65 See K. Griffin, 'Race Committee under Fire,' *The Liberal* (17 June 2001), 1, 10.

66 See K. Griffin, 'Board Faces Human Rights Complaint,' *The Liberal* (21 June 2001). The board did include a 'critical' statement of Zahra. See also '"Shame on You," 100 Chant at Board,' *The Liberal* (12 July 2001), 1, 6. (With both sides accusing each other of ulterior political motives, a hundred of Zahra's supporters disrupted a York Regional School Board meeting that day, demanding that the Race Relations Board retract its statement 'criticizing' Zahra.)

67 See R. Csillag, 'York Region Race Relations Dispute Heats Up,' *Canadian Jewish News* (26 July 2001), 3. (See also 'Are you telling me that if there are enough Palestinian children in class, they would hear about the Palestinian genocide?' Quoting Zafar Bangash, president of the Islamic Society of York Region, ibid.)

68 D. Lazarus and P. Lungen, 'Holocaust Museum May Be Derailed,' *Canadian Jewish News* (9 April 1999), 1.

69 Ibid.

70 G. Simcoe, 'Scene in Ottawa,' *Canadian Jewish News* (22 April 1999), 31. But see B. Rose, 'Fackenheim [renowned Jewish philosophy professor] Says Holocaust Museum Should Be Devoted to Jews Only,' *Canadian Jewish News* (22 April 1999), 13.

71 I. Cotler, 'Holocaust Imaging Disturbing,' *Canadian Jewish News* (13 May 1999), 1 and 34.

72 S. Kirshner, 'Historian Claims Misuse of Holocaust,' *Canadian Jewish News* (24 February 2000), 15.

73 H. Adelman, 'Hate Speech and Terrorism,' *Canadian Jewish News* (20 September 2001), 9.

74 See 'Shoe Name Outcry,' *Canadian Jewish News* (12 September 2002), 2.

75 H is the eighth letter of the alphabet, hence 'Heil Hitler.' See 'Clothes Removed,' *Canadian Jewish News* (12 September 2002), 2.

76 See 'Councillor Apologizes,' *Canadian Jewish News* (23 October 2001), 2.

77 R. Csillag, 'Missionaries Lose Menorah Logo Battle,' *Canadian Jewish News* (6 June 2002), 1 and 20.

78 Pluralistic pragmatists like Rabbi Haskel fear internal division from absolutist intracommunity meaning making more than they fear outside hostility. See L. Speisman, 'Orthodox Rabbi Calls for Mutual Respect among Jews,' *Canadian Jewish News* (3 June 1999), 18.

79 S. Kirshner, 'Not Your Ordinary Museum,' *Canadian Jewish News* (15 June 2000), 36.

80 Emphasis is mine. See *Canadian Jewish News* (17 October 2002), 35.

81 'Holocaust Bill Passes under Different Name,' *Canadian Jewish News* (23 November 2000), 2.

82 A. Segal, 'Making Holocaust Studies Relevant to Students,' *Canadian Jewish News* (29 June 2000), 15.

83 Ibid. Under Communism, all of society was turned into a controlled message-making, meaning-imposing 'classroom.'

84 The Shoah Foundation itself (documenting the eyewitness accounts of more than 50,000 Holocaust survivors) 'reversed its previous ban on making [their] testimony available on the Internet, which was intended to avoid misuse by hate groups and others.' Tugend, *supra* note 51.

85 See I. Greene and D. Shugarman, *Honest Politics: Seeking Integrity in Canadian Public Life* (Toronto: James Lorimer and Co., 1997).

86 Borovoy asks 'on what basis' would the 'mandatory truth', in university speech codes, of equality between the sexes and races be justified if, despite the weight of scientific evidence supporting it, 'additional scientific evidence emerges' that challenges it. To merely dismiss and suppress it, without 'subjecting it to the process of intelligent inquiry,' would be to forfeit any claim of a scientific basis for enforced equality as mandatory truth. To confront it would be to abandon acceptance of equality as a mandatory institutional truth. 'On what other basis, then, would the university declare equality to be an institutional truth? Religion? Ideology? Dogma?' See Borovoy, *supra* note 4 at 83.

87 Censored publics need only account for the right answers, not for understanding of the reasons why those answers are right. That requires freedom
of expression – and the right to be wrong.

88 E. Barendt, *Freedom of Speech* (Oxford: Oxford University Press, 1985), at 12.

89 Peace and order as ends in themselves, however, have not enjoyed much
political currency as justification for suppression of 'truthful' but socially
divisive speech. In Communism, the justifying 'public good' expected to
flow from an overriding concern for 'socialist peace and order' was the
promise of a more equal society, a society infused with true social (socialist?) harmony, social consciousness, and public self-insight. ASEAN
'performance legitimacy' justifications for censoriously enforced peace and
order have been more modest, promising only superior economic performance, not necessarily superior social consciousness or political performance. But see B. Kausikan, 'Asia's Different Standard' (1993) 92 Foreign
Policy 24–41, and the response by A. Neier, 'Asia's Unacceptable Standard'
(1993) 92 Foreign Policy 290–314.

90 As citizens of Communism used to joke of the two official Soviet dailies,
Pravda ('The Truth') and *Izvestia* ('The News'): 'There is no Pravda in
Izvestia and no Izvestia in Pravda.' See also U.S. Congress, House Committee on International Relations, 'Psychiatric Abuse of Political Prisoners
in the Soviet Union: Testimony of Leonia Plyusch' (Washington, D.C.:
30 March 1976).

91 The quoted phrase, representing the censorship critique of the free speech
position, is from Borovoy, *supra* note 4 at 167.

92 Of course, some end-of-history theories are more 'final' than others. Karl
Marx, a child of the Enlightenment and the age of rationalism, purported
to discover a scientific approach to the end of history – one culminating in
a classless society and a supremely self-enlightened public ('true consciousness'). In 'the end,' the evils of human irrationality, conflictual politics as
we know it, social discord, and economic exploitation would be replaced by
economic plenty, social peace, and the untrammelled elevation and
development of the human mind and spirit. Fukuyama sees a worldwide
tendency towards liberal democracy – where society's ills are not replaced
by a 'final solution' but managed within the framework of contentious
politics built on comparatively deeper foundations of social trust and public
tolerance than those which absolutist solutions will support. See F. Fukuyama,
The End of History and the Last Man (New York: Free Press, 1992).

93 Change may be self-generated, externally caused, or both. Rarely, if ever, at
least in an increasingly interconnected world, is major or revolutionary
change the product of only one of these forces.

94 On the welfare state as a form of 'social insurance' against social uncertainty, see H. Sinn, 'Social Insurance, Incentives, and Risk Taking,' *Working Paper Series, No. 5335*, National Bureau of Economic Research (Cambridge, Mass.: Nov. 1995), 2–12 and 29–31. See also E. Mackaay, *The Economics of Information and Law* (Boston: Kluwer-Nijhoff, 1982).

95 *Thornhill* v. *Alabama*, 310 U.S. 88 (1940) at 101, 102. I do not mean to suggest here that 'more successful' is necessarily synonymous with 'more ethical' – certainly if the whole of human history is considered. Some 'unsuccessful' preliterate societies, for example, may very well be considered to have been more ethical than postindustrial 'successful' ones today.

96 As learned by the former Communist countries.

97 Justice I.C. Rand, in *Boucher* v. *The King* [1951] S.C.R. 265 at 288.

98 Even in those polities suffering relative economic failure, research tends to confirm that freedom of speech provides a necessary feedback that increases governmental capacity to manage economic crises. See N. Sylvia, 'Political Causes of Famine: It's Never Fair to Just Blame the Weather,' *New York Times* (17 January 1993), 1 and 5. See also A. Sen, 'The Economics of Life and Death,' *Scientific American* (8 May 1993), 44. Sen notes that 'there has never been a famine in any country that's been a democracy with a relatively free press. I know of no exception. It applies to very poor countries with democratic systems as well as rich ones.'

99 S. Scott, *Dismantling Utopia: How Information Ended the Soviet Union* (Chicago: Irvin R. Dee, 1994). In Romania, for example, where pent-up hostilities became most acute because of Ceausescu's Stalinistic repression of social and political discontent, delayed eruption came with a particular vengeance. See A. Mark, *The Rise and Fall of Nicolae and Elana Ceausescu* (London: Chapman, 1992).

100 This is a critical function of freedom of expression in the context of hate censorship – but omitted from even some of the most thoughtful censorship discussions. See Moon, *supra* note 46 at 8–31 and 126–47.

101 The danger of chilled opportunism is well expressed in the proverb 'It is better to be insulted to one's face today than to be stabbed in the back tomorrow.'

102 *Whitney, supra* note 8 at 376–7.

103 Braun, *supra* note 50 at 481.

104 Ibid.

105 *New York Times* v. *Sullivan*, 376 U.S. 254 (1964) at 271. But speech, unlike silencing, allows for correction.

106 E.g., civil rights, Vietnam.

3 Functions and Assumptions of Hate Propaganda Law

1 M. Prutschi, 'Learning the Lessons of the Hatemonger Trials,' *Canadian Jewish News* (8 May 1986), 10.
2 'It is hard to imagine a more malevolent obscenity [than Holocaust denial] to inflict on those who had suffered so much.' A. Borovoy, *The New Anti-liberals* (Toronto: Canadian Scholars Press, 1999), at 39.
3 Historically, under the common law of civil defamation, while libel was actionable *per se*, slander was not – tangible and quantifiable injury to good reputation, apart from the hurt itself, had to be personally demonstrated. See J. Fleming, *The Law of Torts* 5th ed. (Sydney: Law Book, 1977) at 517–25. The law of criminal libel did protect certain kinds of hurt feelings but had a larger social and political purpose – public peace and order. It was grounded in principles of divine rule and obedient subjects, where even the most innocuous independent expressions (in an age when wounded self-honour, routinely felt, was equally routinely remedied by deadly duels, even war) could disturb divine peace and kingly public order. For a modern attempt at revival, see *R.* v. *Georgia Straight Publishing Co. et al.* (1970) 1 C.C.C. 94 (B.C. County Ct).
4 Despite warnings to that effect. 'Lack of action on hatemongers has also tended to lead some within the victimized communities to call for extra-legal action.' See M. Prutschi, *supra* note 1.
5 In many countries, the threat of serious interethnic and interracial conflict from 'victim retaliation' is very real. A very long ago time ago, Chief Justice Wilde said, 'You cannot ... form a correct judgement ... to establish the crime imputed to the defendant without ... a knowledge of the present state of society because the conduct of every individual in regard to the effect which that conduct is calculated to produce must depend upon the state of society in which he lives. This may be innocent in one state of society, because it may not tend to disturb the peace ... which at another time and in a different state of society, in consequence of its different tendency, may be open to just censure.' *Queen* v. *Russell* (1683) 9 State Tr. 577.
6 *Boucher* v. *The Queen* [1951] S.C.R. 265 at 288 (hereafter *Boucher*).
7 For Roman Catholics in Quebec, the social, political, religious, and cultural beliefs of Jehovah, aggressively promoted by its adherents, augured nothing less than a sword in the very heart of their 'way of life.' See also *Rex* v. *Kite* [1949] 2 W.W.R. 195 (B.C.S.C.).
8 The Duplessis government's intolerance of the activities of Marxists and Jehovah's Witnesses is now legendary. More remarkable, though, are the

imaginative ways the pre-Charter court struck down abridgment of sociopolitical expression in the absence of an entrenched bill of rights.

See *Roncarelli* v. *Duplessis* [1959] S.C.R. 121 ('vocational outlawry' – a statutory interpretation used to find that the discretion of the Quebec liquor licensing board to deny liquor licences to restaurateurs did not include a right to do so because the restaurateur was acting as a bondsman for a Jehovah's Witness); *Switzman* v. *Ebling* [1957] S.C.R. 285 ('padlock' law – a distribution of powers argument used to strike down a provincial law authorizing the padlocking of any house used to 'propagate Communism'; *Saumur* v. *City of Quebec* [1953] 2 S.C.R. 299 (a distribution of powers argument – but three justices also suggested or relied on the 'implied bill of rights' argument to strike down a municipal bylaw, aimed primarily at political undesirables such as the Witnesses and Communists that forbade the distribution of literature on the streets of Quebec City without prior inspection of the contents by the chief of police). See also Paul Weiler, 'The Supreme Court and the Law of Canadian Federalism' (1973) 23 U.T.L.J. 307 at 344 (detailing how 'implied' bill of rights and 'distribution of powers' arguments were used by the court as a kind of covert bill of rights before the charter).

9 *Boucher, supra* note 6 at 288.
10 On intolerance of public disturbances today, see M. Elliott, 'Death in Genoa (Mayhem Rules the streets as the G-8 Leaders Meet. Why Such Violent Protests?)' *Time* (30 July 2001), 17. As Elliott reports, 'Ask national police forces ... they will tell you they are baffled. The world today, after all, is not that of 1968. No young Americans are about to be drafted to fight in an unpopular war; no young Europeans have their rights and pleasures routinely stifled by a jackbooted state.'
11 *Whitney* v. *California* 274 U.S. 357 (1927).
12 Ibid. at 377.
13 See I. Berlin, 'Two Concepts of Liberty,' in *Four Essays on Liberty* (New York: Oxford, 1969) at 155 (cited with approval in *Keegstra*).
14 By 'negative participation,' I mean to include not only breaches of the law and commission of violence against others but also self-destructive behaviour such as alcoholism, drug abuse, and suicide.
15 M. Prutschi, 'There Ought to Be a Law Against Hate,' *Globe and Mail* (16 June 1988), A7.
16 For some illustrations of the concept of over- and underinclusion from a much different point of view, see J. Bakan, 'Constitutional Interpretation and Social Change: You Can't Always Get What You Want (Nor What You Need)' (1991) 70 Can. Bar. Rev. 305.

17 Canada, House of Commons, *Debates* (6 October 1971) at 8545–8 (Pierre Trudeau); *Canadian Multiculturalism Act*, SC 1988, c. 31.
18 See 'Shalom: Making a Difference,' *Toronto Star* (Special Supplement) (3 December 1992). This catalogues Jewish contributions to all areas of Canadian life from the arts and sciences to business, law, and medicine.
19 I. Abella, *A Coat of Many Colours: Two Centuries of Jewish Life in Canada* (Toronto: Lester and Orpen Dennys, 1990).
20 See G. Simcoe, 'Observations of a Lighter Kind,' *Canadian Jewish News* (15 June 2000), 28. (detailing the ubiquitous use of Yiddish terms and idioms in mainstream culture, including even in parliamentary debate).
21 This is intended not as a statement of contentment with the sufficiency of the progress made but only as an observation on the cogency of the claimed cognition-participation causal connection. Early statutes embryonic in the promotion of tolerance and equality were enacted by provincial legislatures at the end of the Second World War. In 1947, Saskatchewan enacted legislation outlawing discrimination in employment and housing and protecting freedom of expression. *Saskatchewan Bill of Rights*, SS 1947, c. 35. By 1962, with Ontario leading the way, most provinces began to consolidate their antidiscrimination laws in human rights acts or codes, to be separately administered by human rights commissions with powers of investigation, conciliation, and arbitration.
22 The infamous neo-Nazi march, allowed to proceed through Skokie, Illinois, exemplifies well the very different American legal approach. See *Collin* v. *Smith*, 578 F.2d 1197 (1978).
23 Ironically, Theodore Hertzl, considered to be the father of Zionism and the modern state of Israel, was himself an 'assimilated' Austrian Jew.
24 Karl Marx, himself a Jew by birth, is just one of many examples.
25 For example, Chinese, Japanese, Italian, Indian, and many other historically oppressed groups. In the case of Jews, examples range from scientist Einstein to San Francisco mayor Feinstein, and from philosopher Karl Marx to comedian Groucho Marx.
26 Even women and visible minorities are not immune to 'the threat.' 'Physical assimilation' is, obviously, either not an option (women) and therefore not a threat, or is not an immediate option (racial minorities – although it may become one over time through intermarriage) and therefore not a pressing threat. But loss of distinctive community identity and solidarity through social and cultural integration none the less is. A major concern of the aging generation of Black civil rights and feminist pioneers is that younger generations cannot, in the relative comfort and tolerance of the present, won for them by the struggles of the past,

appreciate those distinctive identities and safeguard those social solidarities that made it all possible. See 'Onward Women,' *Time* (4 December 1989), 54.

27 'What do you do with the increasingly powerful effects of pluralism, perceived by some as progress and by others as corrosive? That is the central question that faces Jewish education today, and as I have suggested previously, [it] has not been addressed in anything close to a satisfactory manner.' See E. Malamet, 'The Beast of Modernity,' *Canadian Jewish News* (10 June 1999), 12.

28 Abella, *supra* note 19. In the United States (which has the largest Jewish community), the intermarriage rate is around 50 per cent (most of whom after one generation are 'expected to become permanent losses to the community'). See also A. Dershowitz, *The Vanishing American Jew: In Search of the Jewish Identity in the Next Century* (Boston: Little Brown, 1997).

29 See S. Kirshner, 'Historian Claims Misuse of Holocaust,' *Canadian Jewish News* (24 February 2000), 15.

30 In *Muller* v. *State of Oregon*, 208 U.S. 412 (1908), a young Jewish lawyer by the name of Louis Brandeis introduced social science research into evidence in what became known as the 'Brandeis Brief.' In *Brown* v. *Board of Education of Topeka, Kansas*, 347 U.S. 483 (1954), reversing the separate-but-equal doctrine of *Plessey* v. *Ferguson*, 163 U.S. 537 (1896) and striking down segregation, the U.S. Supreme Court specifically referred to social science evidence of psychological harm to Black school children resulting from segregation as a deciding factor in its decision. Citing with approval, *inter alia*, Max Deutscher and Isidor Chein, 'The Psychological Effects of Enforced Segregation: A Survey of Social Science Opinion,' (1948) 26 Journal of Psychology 259; H. Witmer, *Personality in the Making: The Fact-finding Report of the Midcentury White House Conference on Children and Youth* (New York: Harper, 1952).

31 See A. Hacker, *Two Nations: Black and White, Separate, Hostile, Unequal* (New York: Ballantine, 1993). In Canada, writes Prutschi, 'It is true to say that the level of self-confidence among all of Canada's minorities is as high as it has ever been.' M. Prutschi, 'A Jewish Perspective on Racism in Canada' (Summer 1990), Canadian Jewish Congress: Joint Community Relations Committee, 'Anti-Semitism, Anti-Semites, the Community, the Media and the Law,' at 4(1).

32 Borovoy describes their translation into policy advances. *Supra* note 2 at 37.

33 This was learned by Toronto radio broadcasters Dick Smyth and Brian Henderson. Imagine, twenty or thirty years ago, two well-known 'mainstream' broadcasters like Smyth and Henderson apologizing for saying that

a disproportionate number of lawyers, doctors, and dentists are Jews. Borovoy, *supra* note 2 at 73 (28).

34 Some censors see the mere offence of racist speech as sufficient to abridge expression, ignoring the changing ability of the victim to set the record straight and enlighten society in so doing. 'The maker of a racist slur necessarily calls upon the entire history of slavery and racial discrimination in this country to injure the victim.' R. Delgado, 'Words That Wound: A Tort Action for Racist Insults, Epithets and Name Calling,' in M. Matsuda, C. Lawrence, R. Delgado, and K. Crenshaw eds, *Words That Wound* (Boulder, Colo.: Westview Press, 1993) at 105 . But see chapter 7 (part II, and the legitimate exception for 'fighting words') at 178.

35 Exclusion, or lesser protection, would present a more acute problem in Canada than in the United States because disproportionately positive participants make up a proportionately larger percentage of the historically vulnerable population in Canada than they do in the United States. In Canada, only a very few of the historically vulnerable would be protected, while the vast majority would be left out.

36 If it has any validity at all today, it is more apt be found within particular communities. Consider F. Williams, 'Beyond Stereotype Images,' *Canadian Jewish News* (15 June 2000), 12. Williams argues that Jewish stereotypes such as the 'Jewish American Princess' or 'JAP' and the smothering 'Jewish mother,' who puts her needs second to everyone else, injure in two ways. First, such stereotyping negates the good character and accomplishments of Jewish women. Second, by promoting ridicule or contempt, it reinforces outside prejudice against the community. Because self-generated stereotypes such as these are internal to the community, they are more accepted and acceptable, and therefore less easily confronted. Unfortunately, theories of legal censorship have no answer to this problem.

37 And 'outside' prejudice, in a changing multicultural society such as Canada, need no longer simply mean prejudice by a historically dominant White majority. Increasingly, it can mean prejudice between historically vulnerable minorities. As University of Toronto sociology professor Robert Brym recently observed, Muslims in Canada will eventually far outnumber Jews, and this is 'of concern' because 'a major source of anti-Semitism is in the Islamic community.' Quoted in R. Csillag, 'Is Jewish Population Declining?' *Canadian Jewish News* (30 January 2003), 28. On how this changes the character of the threat and the growing dilemma this poses for hate censorship in Canada, see chapter 4 ('II. Unwrapping the Politics of Victimhood: Absolute Victims and Absolute Victimizers').

38 'Outsider' includes both the infamous and the famous. Alexander examines the lives and careers not only of Justice Felix Frankfurter and entertainer Al Jolson (whose music virtually defined the 1920s) but also of mobster Arnold Rothstein. See M. Alexander, *Jazz Age Jews* (New York: Princeton University Press, 2000).

39 In Europe, Mideast tensions are once against spotlighting the 'Jew as not belonging.' See M. Ben-Dat, 'Anti-Semitism in Academia,' *Canadian Jewish News* (10 October 2002), 4. Professor Irwin Cotler argues that, while traditional anti-Semitism – the denial of the right of Jews to live openly in society – is in decline, it has been replaced by a new anti-Semitism that denies 'the rights of the Jewish people to live as equal members in the family of nations.' See 'Former premier [Bob Rae, Ontario] Warns against Rise of Anti-Semitism,' *Canadian Jewish News* (31 October 2002), 7.

40 M.E. Turpel, 'Aboriginal Peoples and the *Canadian Charter of Rights and Freedoms*' (1989) 10 Canadian Woman Studies 102 at 102–3. The 'majority' in a multicultural society might equally mean a larger, more powerful rival minority. See *supra* note 37. See also Joe Berkofsky, 'American Jewish Population Declining,' *Canadian Jewish News* (17 October 2002), at 1, 34 (suggesting good reason for Jewish alarm).

41 This thesis is also, unfortunately, one around which it is impossible to tie a politically manageable (justifiable?) hate censorship. See chapter 4 (discussion on the 'politics of victimhood') at 98.

42 See, for example, 'Between Two Worlds,' *Time* (13 March 1989), 149. This article reports that 'The Black middle class has everything the white middle class has, except a feeling that it really fits in.'

43 This is a point that needs repeating. Its importance, however, is not, as one would expect, in buttressing the case for censorship, but, as the following discussion will show, in illuminating what is wrong with it.

44 By the 1970s, for example, Bora Laskin, a Jew who as a young lawyer could not get a job with any law firm in Toronto, could take his place as the chief justice of the Supreme Court of Canada. See 'Laskin Obituary,' *Canadian Press* (26 March 1984).

45 See Canada, Special Committee on the Participation of Visible Minorities in Canadian Society, *Report* (Ottawa: Supply and Services, 1984).

46 Consider, for example, the experiences of Chassidim, or 'visible Jews' themselves – orthodox Jews with distinctive religious headdress and long black coats. In Montreal's Outremont community, 'many [Chassidim] claimed that it is extremely common to have coins thrown at them, or to have a passing car slow down for its passengers to hurl anti-Semitic

epithets, make references to Hitler, or give the Nazi salute.' Reported in J. Arnold, 'Anti-Semitic Incidents up in Montreal,' *Canadian Jewish News* (17 February 2000), 28.

47 Borovoy, *supra* note 2 at 192.

48 The residential schools can be viewed as a state-sponsored Keegstra-type problem ('captive audience of impressionable school-children subject to authority over them') multiplied tenfold. Seeking to 'free' Aboriginals of their 'superstition and ritual,' it was hoped that confinement and censorship would raise true consciousness among the next generation (read: realize the superiority of the White man's way of 'science and rationality'). The hope was that the next generation of Aboriginals would be 'no different' and Canadian society would 'see no difference.'

49 For their 'own good,' of course. Even certain sacred rituals were made a crime under the Criminal Code. See, for example, G. York, *The Dispossessed: Life and Death in Native Canada* (Toronto: Lester and Orpen Dennys, 1989).

50 Consider the results – crime, alcoholism, suicide. See M. Jackson, *Locking up Natives In Canada – A Report of the Committee of the Canadian Bar Association on Imprisonment and Release* (Ottawa: Canadian Bar Association, 1988).

51 See M. Boldt and J. Long, 'Tribal Traditions and the *Canadian Charter of Rights and Freedoms,*' in M. Boldt and J. Long, eds, *The Quest for Justice* (Toronto: University of Toronto Press, 1995).

52 One must be very careful about understanding equality and multiculturalism in this way. It can be a two-edged sword, discriminating as well as liberating. It needs to be carefully confined to a unique mix of particular historical circumstances (territorial-based cultures) and unbridgable social and cultural distinctions that warrant it. It must not be misused for racist designs, whether conciously, as illustrated by the discredited early-American juridical doctrine 'separate but equal' that segregated and kept American Blacks down – see *Plessey* v. *Ferguson*, 163 U.S. 537 (1896) – or unintentionally, as is now threatened by some Black activists themselves. See 'The End of Integration – Exhausted Courts and Frustrated Blacks Dust off Separate but Equal,' *Time* (29 April 1996), 27.

53 In the case of 'overachievers' like Jews, some members of the community privately advise less participatory visibility, accepting certain racist stereotypes of the Jew as 'too ambitious,' 'too clever,' or 'too ostentatious' for 'his own good.'

54 Borovoy, *supra* note 2 at 36.

55 Expressions of hate against 'visible' minorities, for example, may also be legislated as a more serious speech crime than expressions of hate against 'invisible' ones.

56 See chapter 1.

57 M. Prutschi, *supra* note 15.

58 One line of thinking is to equate hate propaganda law with prevention of anarchy. J. Rose, 'Total Freedom in Democratic Society Leads to Anarchy,' *Canadian Jewish News* (14 September 1990), 22.

59 In October 1993, the Federal Court 'ordered the Heritage Front, a white supremacist group, or anyone else associated with it to refrain from offering any [phone] messages that express an opinion on any racial, ethnic religious, social or political issues' [to anyone voluntarily choosing to call their line]. See P. Lungen, 'Court Shuts down Telephone Hotline,' *Canadian Jewish News* (21 October 1993), 3.

60 'It is far better for Canadians to come to grips with the problem now, before it attains unmanageable proportions, rather than deal with it at some future date in an atmosphere of urgency, of fear and perhaps even crisis.' Canada, Special Committee on Hate Propaganda, *Report* (Ottawa: Queen's Printer, 1966) (Chair M. Cohen), 24–5 (hereafter *Cohen Report*).

61 On this see, for example, M. Atkinson, 'What Kind of Democracy Do Canadians Want?' (1994) 27 Canadian Journal of Political Science 717.

62 '[M]ushroom into a real and monstrous threat to our way of life ...' *Cohen Report, supra* note 60 at 24–5.

63 Explicating this kind of thinking, see *People* v. *Lloyd* 35 [136 N.E. 505] (1922).

64 Or, euphemistically, 'foreseeable' future, which, not surprisingly, makes no provisions foreseeing the law's end.

65 Excerpted in W. Lacqueur and B. Ruben, eds, *The Human Rights Reader* (Philadelphia: Temple, 1979) at 85.

66 But, unlike hate propaganda law, even laws against seditious speech have traditionally been more narrowly confined by the court to those expressions specifically urging the violent overthrow of established authority. See S. Braun, 'Freedom of Expression v. Seditious Libel: Towards a Framework of Analysis' (1985) 22 Comp. Jur. Rev. 87.

67 W. Mayton, 'Seditious Libel and the Lost Guarantee of Freedom of Expression' (1984) 84 Columbia L. Rev. 91 at 103.

68 See, for example, Mahoney citing Hitler's Third Reich as evidence for Canada of how hate propaganda can 'drive reason from the field.' K. Mahoney, 'Language as Violence v. Freedom of Expression: Canadian and American Perspectives on Group Defamation' (1988–9) 37 Buffalo Law Review 337 at 350.

69 On the political roots of these totalitarian repressions, see I. Kershaw, *Hitler: 1889–1936, Hubris* and *Hitler: 1936–1945, Nemesis* (New York:

Norton, 1999 and 2000). See also R. Tucker, *Stalin in Power: The Revolution from Above* (New York: Norton, 1990); L. Rapoport, *Stalin's War against the Jews, the Doctor's Plot and the Soviet Solution* (New York: Free Press, 1990); and E. Radzinsky, *Stalin* (New York: Anchor, 1997). On political repression of disconcerting social expression as the single most important feature distinguishing a totalitarian regime from an 'ordinary' dictatorship, see Vaclav Havel, 'The Power of the Powerless,' in P. Wilson, ed., *Open Letters* (London: Faber and Faber, 1991).

70 See D. Goldhagen, *Hitler's Willing Executioners: Ordinary Germans and the Holocaust* (New York: Knopf, 1996). See also I. Kershaw, *supra* note 60. Both authors present compelling cases for the view that the roots of the Holocaust went far beyond the active Nazi faithful, reaching down to embrace ordinary Germans whose widespread paranoia of Jews far predated Weimar and was rooted in a political culture that did not just uncritically accept but venerated obedience, order, and authority.

71 Former Communist regimes were masters of public self-denial. Not only did they declare themselves free of prejudice and conflict, but in them planes did not crash, trains were never late, and leaders never got sick.

72 On the Milosevic mindset in Yugoslavia, see A. Freeman, 'Milosevic Moves to Maintain Power,' *Globe and Mail* (11 April 1997), A12.

73 S. Braun, 'Social and Racial Tolerance and Freedom of Expression in a Democratic Society: Friend or Foe: *Regina* v. *Zundel*' (1988) 11 Dal. L.J. 471 at 474–5.

74 See A. Doskow and S.B. Jacoby, 'Anti-Semitism and Law in Pre-Nazi Germany,' (1940) *Contemporary Jewish Record* 498 at 509.

75 Ibid.

76 For an incisive review of recent literature on transitional dangers and problems of 'democratic consolidation,' see S. Chull, 'On the Third Wave of Democratization: A Synthesis and Evaluation of Recent Theory and Research' (1994) 47 World Politics 135; see also R. Dankwart, 'Dictatorship to Democracy,' in K. Uner and L. Silk, eds, *A World Fit for People* (New York: New York University Press, 1994), 54–66.

77 Yeltsin may have outlawed the Communist Party, but he was not successful in outlawing its authoritarian ideas. If anything, attempts at repression seem to have reinvigorated both the 'Old Left' and the 'New Right' (e.g., Zhirinovsky), driving the faithful but fearful to reinvent themselves in publicly more palatable forms. Many new 'socialist parties' in the collapsed Communist empire of 'today' are but the former party faithful of the old Communist parties of 'yesterday.' In April 1997, Communists and Ultranationalists made up over half the members of the Russian Duma. They

rejected a nebulous new bill introduced to bar 'fascist propaganda.' See 'Moscow Rejects Bill,' *Canadian Jewish News* (3 April, 1997), 2.

78 See L. Krich, 'Anti-Semitism Promoting Unease in Russia,' *Canadian Jewish News* (25 February 1999), 44. Krich reports on bad economic times, scapegoating, and lawmakers themselves spreading anti-Semitism for political gain. See also 'No Prosecution of Communist Anti-Semite,' *Canadian Jewish News* (25 March 1999), 2. The better 'answer' here is not speech proscription (ineffective anyway in silencing the message of extremists) but better efforts at spreading economic improvement.

79 See chapter 2 (Part III, on feedback and adaptation to change).

80 Query whether 'emergency' or 'stop-gap' censorship could help carry socially unstable and politically fragile regimes over the 'hump' of the initial shock of transition from authoritarianism – 'just until they get their social and political bearings right.' The problem is that the right to silence disconcerting public discourse is too seductive to be easily relinquished and too socially selective and politically slippery to be used only as originally intended. See chapters 4 and 5. When even consolidated democracies in ordinary times feel compelled to rely on public censorship, it is hard to see how besieged, unstable, struggling democracies could feel secure enough to relinquish it. It is more likely that censorship would be expanded to silence political opponents as well as hate proponents (the line between the two being less than clear-cut, especially in states of perpetual crisis).

81 *Supra* note 65.

4 The Political Dilemma, Part I: Legally Definable *and* Politically Defensible Hate Censorship

1 Writes Moon, 'My hope is that making explicit the social character of freedom of expression will enable better understanding of the value and potential harm of expression and better judgment about the scope and limits of the freedom.' Unfortunately, writing out of the social character of freedom of expression the overarching politics and political dilemmas of its public repression does not seem to be the better way to do this. See R. Moon, *The Constitutional Protection of Freedom of Expression* (Toronto: University of Toronto Press, 2000) at 9. On the work that spawned so much debate on 'reductionist' approaches generally, see G. Almond and S. Verba, *The Civic Culture: Political Attitudes and Democracy in Five Nations* (Boston: Little, Brown 1965). See also G. Almond and S. Verba, *The Civic Culture Revisited* (Boston: Little, Brown, 1980).

2 See Canada, *Report of the Royal Commission on Newspapers* (Ottawa: Minister of Supply and Services, 1981). See also B. Bagdikian, *The Media Monopoly* 4th ed. (Boston: Beacon Press, 1992); C. Baker, *Advertising and a Democratic Press* (Princeton: Princeton University Press, 1994); J. Barron, *Freedom of the Press for Whom?* (Bloomington: Indiana University Press, 1973).

3 Chapters 1 and 2.

4 'Hate censors,' as used in this book, is a generic term. It embraces official structures and institutions (such as the police, customs, and immigration) that can legally silence. But it also includes 'unofficial' actors (such as the popular media, bookstores, and rival social groups) that can, for any number of reasons, suppress or effectively threaten to repress speech before its expression under claim or cover of legal right. In a system premised on occasional governing majorities and changing social agendas, most anyone can legitimately be or become a hate censor. See *infra* Parts II and III, and chapter 5.

5 *R. v. Keegstra* [1990] 3 S.C.R. 697 (hereafter *Keegstra*).

6 By arbitrary, I mean unascertainable, inconsistent, or unpredictable standards. By capricious, I mean on the personal whims of the decider. By politically self-serving, I mean for the self-advantage of the censors, not the intended publicly serving social purpose.

7 Extortion is not vital to self-government. The issue in murder is who did it, not if repression of its expression is right. The question in assault is not whether it should be punished, but how severely. Should there be a democratic right to engage in these crimes? Can anyone seriously ask 'Is it better to prevent these social wrongs or to allow and challenge them on the merits of their content or the motives of their actors?'

8 P.M. Sniderman, J.F. Fletcher, P.H. Russell, and P.E. Tetlock, *The Clash of Rights* (New Haven: Yale University Press, 1996). See especially, ch. 4, 'Equality: A Chameleon Right.'

9 S. Anand, 'Expression of Racial Hatred and Racism in Canada: An Historical Perspective' (1998) 77 Can. B. Rev. 187 at 196–7.

10 Indeed, to circumvent being silenced for racism, 'tenant' may substitute as an effective 'code' word in the arsenal of clever racists by which they may more safely denigrate Blacks, Hispanics, Natives, and other visible minorities. On the problem of coding see chapter 6 ('The Pragmatic Dilemma') at 161.

11 I. McKenna, 'Canada's Hate Propaganda Laws – A Critique' (1994) 26 Ottawa L. Rev. at 159.

12 See Canada, Canadian Human Rights Commission, *Annual Report 1989* (Ottawa: Minister of Supply and Services, 1990).

13 K. Davies, J. Dickey, and T. Stratford, eds, *Out of Focus: Writing in Women and the Media* (London: Women's Press, 1988) at 6.

14 P. Lungen, 'Collins Loses Human Rights Case,' *Canadian Jewish News* (11 February 1999), 3, 19.

15 McKenna, *supra* note 11 at 183–4.

16 Ibid.

17 'Among the "alarming trends" last year, said Kravitz-Morris [League co-chair] was the growing number of incidents involving messianic Christian organizations attempting to convert Jews.' See F. Kraft, 'Anti-Semitism, Hate on the Rise: League Audit,' *Canadian Jewish News* (17 February 2000), 3.

18 The Canadian Jewish Congress has called for a publication ban on certain of their advertisements because the 'hidden message' in them 'is that Judaism is no longer a religion that need be practiced and to be a complete Jew, one must accept Jesus.' See P. Lungen, 'CJC Seeks Ban on Offensive Religious Advertising,' *Canadian Jewish News* (11 April 1991), 6.

19 M. Landsberg, 'Porn Mutilates Women's Fight for Equality,' *Toronto Star* (11 June 1991), F1.

20 Quoted in B. Rose, 'Quotas Rejected,' *Canadian Jewish News* (27 March 1997), 13.

21 T. Flanagan, *First Nations: Second Thoughts* (Montreal: McGill-Queen's University Press, 2000).

22 From S. Fernandez, 'Academic Differences,' *Time* (15 May 2000), 24.

23 Ibid.

24 The Windsor Police Service's street crimes unit carried out a criminal investigation of the Windsor Public Library for this reason. See Ron Stang, 'Pro-Palestinian Library Exhibit Sparks Controversy in Windsor,' *Canadian Jewish News* (1 August 2002), 16.

25 See Paul Lungen, 'Complaint Filed over OHRC Chief's Remarks,' *Canadian Jewish News* (1 August 2002), 2, 6. The chief commissioner, of course, is bound by his adjudicative duties to be mindful of appearances of partiality. Public concern for adjudicative impartiality is one thing. Threats to have him investigated for breaking the law by promoting public intolerance, contrary to the *hate speech provisions* of the *Human Rights Code*, is quite another.

26 See chapter 2, subsection on 'Multiplicity of Social Truth and Public Division' at 49.

27 K. Griffin, 'Race Committee under Fire,' *The Liberal* (17 June 2001), 1, 10.

28 Borovoy relates the following conversation. '[I] remember encountering one of its [Ontario Human Rights Commission's] upper echelon officials at

a banquet. When I told him that the commission's position in this case [OHRC Complaints Nos 60-023, 24, 25, 26, 28] could logically support the forced removal of Salman Rushdie's *Satanic Verses* from libraries, his reply was nothing short of incredible: "How would you like it," he asked, "if libraries carried *Mein Kampf?*" A. Borovoy, *The New Anti-liberals* (Toronto: Canadian Scholars Press, 1999) at 147.

29 After receiving complaints from Jewish families, Nintendo of America pulled these cards when one of the Japanese-language cards, not meant for sale in the United States, depicted a red *manji*, or swastika. 'In Japan, where the symbol predates the Nazis by centuries, it means good fortune and can also represent a Buddhist temple.' See 'Pokeman Swastika,' *Canadian Jewish News* (16 December 1999), 2.

30 The interviews were part of a 'long list' of neo-Nazi and White supremacist books, pamphlets, magazines, newspapers, and audiocassettes condemned by Revenue Canada's customs officials. See M. Prutschi, 'Should Hate Merchants Be Silenced?' *Toronto Star* (28 February 1989), A21.

31 See R. Csillag, 'Jewish Groups Concerned about Anti-abortion Parlay,' *Canadian Jewish News* (18 March 1999), 3 (Morgentaler's Jewishness is made an issue – pro-life arguments couched in anti-Semitic terms).

32 M. Prutschi, 'Hate Groups and Bigotry's Fellow Travelers,' (1990) 6(2) Currents 9–10.

33 Ibid at 10.

34 Moon gives (qualified) support to censorship of 'extreme' but not 'ordinary' expressions of prejudice. Moon, *supra* note 1 at 142, 143.

35 Sniderman et al., *supra* note 8 at 71.

36 Ibid.

37 'The Vatican last week rejected what it described as ongoing attempts to depict all religions as equal. The idea that "one religion is as good as another" endangers the Roman Catholic Church's message, according to a declaration by the Holy See's Congregation for the Doctrine of the Faith.' See 'Faiths Not Equal,' *Canadian Jewish News* (14 September 2000), 2.

38 Sniderman et al., *supra* note 8 at 81.

39 See R. Boyle, 'Hate Literature Charges against 3 to Be Dropped,' *Globe and Mail* (4 July 1975), 1.

40 'Ottawa Halts "Satanic Verses" Imports,' *Canadian Press* (18 February 1989), 11.

41 M. Polanyi, 'Mandela Film Screened for Possible Hate Content,' *Globe and Mail* (24 December 1986), A14.

42 *Immigration Act*, R.S.C. 1985, c. I-2.

43 Ibid., s. 19(2)(a.1).

44 *Walker* v. *City of Birmingham*, 87 S. Ct. 1824 (1967).

45 *Criminal Code*, R.S.C. 1985, c. C-46, s. 319(2).

46 Ibid., s. 318(4).

47 Provincial human rights codes (variations in protection and enforcement themselves attesting to the subjective and political nature of defining the victim) have been leaders in victim expansion. The Ontario Human Rights Code now prohibits discrimination based on race, ancestry, place of origin, colour, ethnic origin, citizenship, creed, sex, age, marital or family status, handicap, sexual orientation, the receipt of public assistance, or record of offences. See *Ontario Human Rights Code*, S.O., 1971, c. 53 (as amended). Victim expansion for the purposes of material social protection (e.g., fair housing, services, employment) may well be defended. Victim expansion for the purposes of cognitive protection, however, is quite another thing. The former does not raise the democratic dilemmas for public discourse on public matters that the latter does.

48 None the less, it seems to stand still even for much-reserved censorship (free speech?) theorists. See Moon, *supra* note 1 at 143.

49 See *www.ummah.net/moa-on-line/*. P. Lungen, 'Police Asked to Investigate "Anti-Semitic" Web Site,' *Canadian Jewish News* (22 November 2001), 5. See also S. Stein, 'Suicide Bombings Political, Not Religious: Palestinian Prof,' *Canadian Jewish News* (24 October 2002), 7; and P. Lungen, 'Mideast Conflict Hits the Internet,' *Canadian Jewish News* (9 November 2000), 46.

50 'Arab-Language Newspapers Attack Jews,' *Canadian Jewish News* (22 March 2001), 2.

51 R. Csillag, 'Day's CJC Speech Brings Him Plaudits and Trouble,' *Canadian Jewish News* (17 May 2001), 1.

52 'Libraries Won't Ban Uris Book,' *Globe and Mail* (11 October 1984), 20. See Leon Uris, *The Haj* (London: Corgi Books, 1984).

52 Students' Federation of the University of Ottawa, 'News Release' (7 July 1982). See also Janice Arnold, 'Concordia Hillel Sues Student Union for $100,000,' *Canadian Jewish News* (2 January 2003), 3, 7. After the Concordia Student Union (CSU) withdrew its funding for Hillel, the Jewish student club, Hillel launched a civil action seeking punitive damages against the CSU (including Concordia University) accusing the pro-Palestinian CSU, *inter alia*, of trying to silence Hillel while promoting the views of those who distribute 'hate literature.'

54 'CPME Loses Ratification Bid,' *The Gazette* (10 December 1982); 'UWO Council Refuses Aid to Mideast Group,' *London Free Press* (10 December 1982); 'Taking the Blame for Opinions,' *The Gazette* (29 October 1982).

55 J. Korda, 'Slogans Conceal a Hateful Message,' *Canadian Jewish News* (6 March 1997), 10.

56 Borovoy, *supra* note 28 at 74 (at note 37). See also 'Mullins Returns,' *Canadian Jewish News* (17 May 2001), 2. Reporting on attempts to keep Eustace Mullins, New Age mystic and anti-Semite, from speaking at a New Age festival in British Columbia.

57 'Ironically,' writes Csillag, 'Al-Jazeera bureaus have been shut down in Jordan, Bahrain, Kuwait and Saudi Arabia,' for being insufficiently pro-Arab. See R. Csillag, 'BBC, CJC Aim to Bar Al-Jazeera from Canada,' *Canadian Jewish News* (16 April 2003), 3.

58 Following complaints by the Jewish Congress that Ahmad 'crosses the anti-Semitic line,' York's dean of arts responded that if Ahmad's talks or articles cross any legal line there are means at law to deal with it. 'Otherwise, it is my practice not to expect that I will agree with everything my colleagues write but to defend their freedom to write it.' See Anna Morgan, 'Israel, U.S. Blamed for World's Problems,' *Canadian Jewish News* (21 November 2002), at 3, 24. Compare the muted 'progressive' response to Professor Ahmad with the vocal and legal one to Professor Philippe Rushton – see chapter 5, Part I. See also R. Greene, 'In Britain, "Kill the Jews" Not Considered Incitement,' *Canadian Jewish News* (1 November 2001), 34. Reporting that British police refused to charge five Muslims, caught in the act of distributing pamphlets reading 'Kill the Jews' in an Orthodox Jewish section of London, with incitement of hatred because there was no one to incite. Citing inside sources, the real reason, Greene argues, is 'that the authorities are more reluctant to prosecute Muslims than far-right white extremists.'

59 R. Csillag, 'The Coverage of Israel in the Toronto Star,' *Canadian Jewish News* (27 March 1997), 9. Demographic trends showing an aging, declining Jewish population in the United States are further raising alarms. See Joe Berkofsky, 'American Jewish Population Declining,' *Canadian Jewish News* (17 October 2002), 1, 34.

60 Cited in Mordechai Ben-Dat, 'Anti-Semitism in Academia,' *Canadian Jewish News* (10 October 2002), 4. See also 'Special Report,' *Canadian Jewish News* (16 January 2003), 24.

61 P. Lungen, 'CLC Criticizes Israel,' *Canadian Jewish News* (20 June 2002), 2 22. Professor Zoloth of San Francisco State University reports similar sentiments among progressive circles on university campuses. See Sheldon Kirshner, 'Anti-Semitism Permeates: Scholar,' *Canadian Jewish News* (10 October 2002), 24. See also P. Lungen 'Workers Mull Leaving CUPE Ontario,' *Canadian Jewish News* (24 October 2002), 1, 5.

62 Finally releasing it under political pressure. P. Lungen, 'CCRA Seizes Pro-Israeli Literature,' *Canadian Jewish News* (10 October 2002), 1, 34. See *http://www.aynrand.org/israel/israel_sept_2002.pdf.*

63 Editorial: 'Do We Have Reason to Be Concerned?' *Canadian Jewish News* (10 October 2002), 8.

64 This is the same Malcolm Ross whose removal from his teaching position because of his off-duty anti-Semitic comments had earlier been upheld by the Supreme Court of Canada. See *Ross* v. *New Brunswick School District No. 15* [1996] 1 S.C.R. 825. Although the trial judge did not dispute the defendant's evidence of Ross's racist and anti-Semitic views, he found that depicting Ross as a Nazi 'goes too far.' *Ross* v. *New Brunswick Teachers' Association et al.* [1998], 199 N.B.R. (2d), 245. Illustrating the political uncertainty of judicial predictability in these matters, the New Brunswick Court of Appeal reversed the decision, finding Beutel's caricatures of Ross to be 'fair comment,' *Beutel* v. *Ross*, 2001 N.B.C.A. 62.

65 P. Lungen, 'Second Set of Charges against Zundel Dropped,' *Canadian Jewish News* (23 September 1987), 3. Littman had said that Nazi war criminals living in Canada 'may number up to 3000.'

66 P. Lungen, 'Zundel Lawsuit Includes P.M.,' *Canadian Jewish News* (19 November 1998), 1, 33.

67 J. Arnold, 'Defamation Charges Denied,' *Canadian Jewish News* (24 January 1991), 21. Irving lost a lawsuit in London, England, against Jewish historian Deborah Lipstadt, alleging she defamed him in her book *Denying the Holocaust: The Growing Assault on Truth and Memory* (New York: Free Press, 1993) when she 'called him a Holocaust denier who manipulates facts to suit his ideological bias.' This, however, has not deterred Irving from trying his luck against the London *Observer*. The newspaper spent $1 million preparing its defence against charges that it defamed Irving in an article 'Spin Time for Hitler,' by accusing him of using 'invention, omission or distortion to express an obsession.' See D. Davis, 'Another Lawsuit in Irving's Arsenal,' *Canadian Jewish News* (28 April 2000), 32. Recently losing this suit also has not, however, discouraged Irving from spreading his message in other ways. Although the Australian government banned him from entering the country on a speaking engagement, it could not prevent the screening of his film, *The Search for the Truth in History*, at the Melbourne Underground Film Festival. 'The film is believed to be the same speech he intended to make at that time.' *Canadian Jewish News* (17 July 2003), 2.

68 J. Arnold, 'Anti-Semitic Incidents Up in Montreal,' *Canadian Jewish News* (17 February 2000), 28.

69 Listing a history of war-era Jewish artists dismissed 'not for artistic reasons' but for being Jewish, the advertisement alleged that the failure to renew the contract of Kimberly Glasco was similarly motivated. 'The suit will proceed despite a full-page apology from *Now*. A lawyer for the ballet said the comparison to the Nazis was "extremely hurtful" to the ballet and to Kudelka [the ballet's artistic director who made the decision not to renew] personally.' See 'Nazis Ad Sparks Suit,' *Canadian Jewish News* (8 June 2000), 2.

70 B. Epstein, 'Political Correctness and Collective Powerlessness,' (1991) 21 Socialist Review 13, 24–5.

71 See Professor E. Lightman, 'Jewish and on the Left: A Tricky Place to Be,' *Canadian Jewish News* (14 November 2002), 9. See also S. Kirshner, 'Jewish Relations with Left "In Worst Shape Ever"' *Canadian Jewish News* (12 December 2002), 6 (citing Peter Beinart, editor of *The New Republic*).

72 See Carolyn Blackman, 'Anti-Semitism Greater Fear Than Sexism among Women,' Canadian Jewish News (14 November 2002), 48 (citing Gold, professor of women's studies at McMaster University).

73 C. MacKinnon, *Only Words* (Cambridge, Mass.: Harvard University Press, 1996), 103. In fact, there is much that can and has been fired against abuse of power by the powerful. These centrally include discursive tools that have none of the self-contradictory and self-defeating (self-intrusive) problems of hate propaganda censorship. Social progress made in Canada would not have been possible without them. See discussion chapter 3, Part III, 'Visible Exclusion,' at 73 and, especially, chapter 9.

74 There is growing pressure (and movement) to silence hate on the Internet. See chapter 6 at 168.

75 More generally see N. Christie, 'Conflicts as Property,' (1977) 17 British Journal of Criminology 1.

76 This intense distrust includes distrust of the courts. See *R.* v. *Kopyto* (1988), 62 O.R. (2d) 449 (C.A.). See also M. Mandel, *The Charter of Rights and the Legalization of Politics in Canada* (Toronto: Thompson Educational, 1994).

77 See, for example, 'Calls for IRB Probe,' *Canadian Jewish News* (29 October 1998), 2 (reporting that the 'chair of the immigration section of the Canadian Bar Association' has joined public calls for 'an independent and public inquiry into allegations of anti-Semitism, racism and homophobia at the Immigration and Refugee Board').

78 Even the same actors may be of different minds at different times. At first, Canada Post cut off Zundel's mail service (although it could not prevent him from sending mail). Then, under pressure, it reinstated his mail service. See *Canadian Press* (28 February 1985).

79 See *Dombrowski* v. *Pfister*, 380 U.S. 479 (1965) at 487.

80 Borovoy, *supra* note 28 at 42.

81 'Jewish Group Opposes Ruling on Cartoonist,' *Globe and Mail* (12 April 1998), A6.

82 This, of course, is not meant in any way to be a statement on the 'correctness' of Ronald Reagan's foreign policies.

83 Canadian parliamentary structure is characterized by party discipline, cabinet secrecy, fusion of executive and legislative branches of government, a relatively conservative media, a culture of relative risk aversion, and one-party domination at the federal level. Arguably, this has contributed to a political culture and a social setting that are less sensitive than they should be to problems of public accountability, transparency, and visibility. This is a problem whose institutional and political roots were recognized long ago. See J. McCamus, 'Freedom of Information in Canada,' (1983) 10 Government Publications Review 51.

84 Not just in repression but even its reversal. After Canada Post reinstated Zundel's mail service, the Crown corporation felt no obligation to give any reasons. See *Canadian Press* (28 February 1985).

85 Borovoy, *supra* note 28 at 10. Paul Lungen writes that Canada Customs did not explain why it chose to seize the newsletter *In Moral Defence of Israel* and a 'call to the office of CCRA [Canada Customs and Revenue Agency] Minister Elinor Caplan was not returned by The CJN's deadline ...' *Supra* note 62 at 34.

86 Consider in this regard the Toronto Women's Bookstore. It carried buttons reading 'End the Occupation' (designed with the Palestinian flag containing the logo WAO, for Women Against the Occupation, below the flag), but refused an offer from the Canadian Jewish Congress, Ontario Region, to supply the store with buttons reading, 'Stop the Homicide Bombings.' See Carolyn Blackman, 'Bookstore Says No to Jewish Buttons,' *Canadian Jewish News* (3 October 2002), 18.

87 See P. Lungen, 'Chapters, Indigo Pulls *Mein Kampf* from Their Bookstores,' *Canadian Jewish News* (6 December 2001), 22. See also CTV Evening News (29 November 2001).

88 See, generally, D. Rowat, 'Canada,' in D. Rowat, ed., *Administrative Secrecy in Developed Countries* (New York: Columbia University Press, 1979) at 279–308. This is a foundational book and the concerns expressed therein are every bit as relevant today as they were then.

89 See, for example, Nova Scotia, Royal Commission on the Donald Marshall, Jr, Prosecution, *Report* (Halifax: McCurdy's Printing and Typesetting, December 1989). See also Canada, Royal Commission on Aboriginal

Peoples, *Bridging the Cultural Divide: A Report on Aboriginal People and Criminal Justice in Canada* (Ottawa: Minister of Supply and Services, 1996).

90 It is the *accused*, not the public at large, who may claim the 'public interest' in their defence. See Criminal Code, s. 319(3) and s. 320(3).

91 See *Near* v. *Minnesota*, 283 U.S. 697 (1931).

92 Consider a letter to the chair of the Board of Trustees of the Canadian Museum of Civilization by Canadian Jewish Congress president Keith Landy which 'urged the museum to proceed with caution on elements of a Canadian art exhibit alleged to promote hatred against Americans and Israelis.' See 'Letter to museum,' *Canadian Jewish News* (11 October 2001), 2.

93 Exceptions can be found in the context of ongoing relationships such as labour, landlord and tenant, or family (e.g., divorce, custody) where absolute or 'one-time' winners and losers are not preferred. In these cases, interested parties are not only allowed to have a say (preferably an equal one); they are expected to have a more or less mutually equal input (preferably reaching compromise) into the final decision forged. This is hardly the case in censorship of hate. See chapter 6, Part II (1).

94 On administrative problems of discretion generally, see S. Blake, *Administrative Law in Canada* 3rd ed. (Markham, Ont.: Butterworth, 2001), esp. Introduction; Discretion and Bias.

95 On the censoring state as judge in its own cause, see McLachlin in *Keegstra* [1990] 3 S.C.R. 697 (citing, with approval, F. Schauer, *Free Speech: A Philosophical Enquiry* [Cambridge: Cambridge University Press, 1982].

96 While in opposition from 1990 to 1995, Charles Harnick regularly admonished the NDP government in Ontario for not charging Zundel under the hate propaganda provisions of the Criminal Code (upheld by the Supreme Court in *Keegstra*). As attorney general in the Conservative government of Mike Harris, however, he felt no need to do so.

97 'Success! ... Last week, students representing Network [North American Jewish Students' Union] staged their third sit-in in two months in the office of Attorney General Marion Boyd to protest' [the government's decision not to recharge Zundel after his two convictions under the false news section of the Criminal Code were quashed by the Supreme Court of Canada]. See 'Network to Press for Zundel Charges,' *Canadian Jewish News* (29 July 1993), 27. The expected victory, at least for now, has turned out to be premature.

98 See "J'accuse ...!" Canada's UN Vote Unconscionable,' *Canadian Jewish News* (19 October 2000), 1, 10. Following similar outbursts at demonstrations two years later in Calgary, Alberta, police were reported to be investigating the rallies and studying videotapes for 'possible charges of hatemongering.'

See 'Police Investigating,' *Canadian Jewish News* (2 May 2002), 2. In London, England, the Board of Deputies of British Jews had called for the criminal prosecution of 'Islamic Militants' distributing 'hate literature.' See 'London Attacks,' *Canadian Jewish News* (26 October 2000), 2.

99 See also chapter 2, the case of Abu-Zahra (discussed from the perspective of the political multiplicity of social truth and public division) at 49.

100 Chief Justice Brian Dickson in *Keegstra, supra* note 5, for example, refers, at 743, to the 'international commitment to eradicate hate propaganda.'

101 McLachlin in *Keegstra, supra* note 5 at 860.

5 The Political Dilemma, Part II: The 'Slippery Slope'

1 My phraseology is deliberate. The free speech perspective sees human development as an uncertain and ongoing project with comparative risks rather than as an officially fixable event with an assured or final desired outcome (chapter 2). The only certain thing in this project (the expected) is this element of uncertainty (the unexpected or unforeseen). I can, therefore, speak only in terms of tendencies not inevitabilities as to how this work in continuous progress may play out.

2 By non-active participants, I mean those who may not initiate social or political directions but whose beliefs, sentiments, reactions, and behaviour patterns may implicitly or explicitly be taken into account by those who do. In contemporary democracies, the largest non-active participants are the general public.

3 Political appointees, strictly speaking, would include judges of the high courts.

4 S. Braun, 'Social and Racial Tolerance and Freedom of Expression in a Democratic Society: Friend or Foe? *Regina* v. *Zundel*' (1988) 11 Dal. L.J. 471 at 478.

5 B. Epstein, 'Political Correctness and Collective Powerlessness' (1991) 21 Socialist Review 22.

6 'CJC Criticizes Anti-Semitic Film,' *Canadian Jewish News* (2 November 1989), 2.

7 See P. Lungen, 'Relations Deteriorate between Jewish, Arab Student Groups,' *Canadian Jewish News* (3 April 1997), 1, 17.

8 'Informed of Hate Probe, Rushton Cancels Speech,' *Globe and Mail* (13 March 1989), A1.

9 In Poland, professor Dariusz Ratajczak was banished from teaching for three years after being tried and found criminally guilty of 'spreading revisionism' contrary to a new law against the denial of Nazi and Communist-era hate

crimes. Ratajczak's crime was to author a book, *Dangerous Topics*, 'in which he wrote sympathetically about published materials that deny the Holocaust.' See 'Teacher Banned,' *Canadian Jewish News* (13 July 2000), 2.

10 A. Borovoy, *The New Anti-liberals* (Toronto: Canadian Scholars Press, 1999) at 105.

11 See K. Griffin, 'Charges Dropped against Protestor,' *The Liberal* (15 February 2000), 6.

12 See Paul Lungen, 'Complaint Filed over OHRC Chief's Remarks,' *Canadian Jewish News* (1 August 2002), 2, 6.

13 C. Blackman, 'Anti-Semitism Examined at CHAT Panel,' *Canadian Jewish News* (6 February 2003), 12. Alan Borovoy has said that Pipes was warned before he spoke, by a Toronto police officer, to be careful not to violate Canada's anti-hate law. See S. Kirshner, 'Jewish Interests Harmed by Anti-hate Law: Borovoy,' *Canadian Jewish News* (12 June 2003), 7.

14 See R. Putnam, *Making Democracy Work: Civic Traditions in Modern Italy* (Princeton: Princeton University Press, 1993); R. Putnam, 'Bowling Alone: America's Declining Social Capital' (1995) 61 Journal of Democracy; R. Putnam, 'Tuning In, Tuning Out: The Strange Disappearance of Social Capital in America' (1995) 28 Political Science and Politics 664. See also *infra*, Part II (2).

15 See J. Bakan, 'Constitutional Interpretation and Social Change: You Can't Always Get What You Want (Nor What You Need)' (1991) 70 Can. Bar Rev. 307.

16 Censors are more concerned with 'having nothing to fire against abuse of power by the powerful' than they are with the 'misfiring of restrictions against the powerless.' See C. MacKinnon, *Only Words* (Cambridge, Mass.: Harvard University Press, 1996) at 103.

17 Not all have the resources, public stature, or personal history of social activism of a Harry Arthurs, a Pierre Berton, or a June Callwood to speak their minds. See P. Berton, 'If [June] Callwood [celebrated social activist accused of making a racist remark] Is a Racist Then So Are We All,' *Toronto Star* (23 May 1992), H3. See also J. Kavanagh (quoting Callwood), 'Racism Charge the "Worst Thing Ever in My Life,"' *Toronto Star* (15 June 1992), A1. Arthurs, long an advocate for labour and women's causes, was accused by some feminists of sexism for defending his decision to appoint a male over a female for the deanship of Osgoode Hall Law School. See *Canadian Press* (2 June 1987).

18 Indeed, it is a very important part of it. See chapter 8: Part III, on incitement.

19 See 'Date Rape Comments Cause Campus Furor,' *Globe and Mail* (12 November 1993), A6.

20 See '[Teachers] Union to Grieve Ouster of Date-Rape Professor,' *Toronto Star* (17 November 1993), A14.

21 See S. Martin, 'When Free Speech and Equality Don't Mix,' *Toronto Star* (6 October 1994), A25.

22 Where the 'bottom line' and 'true belief' coincide, it may be difficult to know whether the deciding motivation is the first, the second, or both equally. Consider Indigo Books' decision to pull Hitler's *Mein Kampf* from its stores across Canada. CTV Evening News (29 November 2001). More on this in chapter 6.

23 Suggestions to the contrary can be ignored. See Institute for Jewish Policy Research, *Combating Holocaust Denial through Law in the United Kingdom* (2000). This long-awaited report on the British experience argues against expanding hate law prohibiting incitement to hatred to include denial of the Holocaust because such laws are 'ineffective' and an 'illegitimate infringement on freedom of expression,' and the problem is better addressed through 'education.' See *http://www.jpr.org.uk/publications/ reports/civil_society/No_3_200 0/indexhtm.*

24 K. Cox, 'Jewish Group Opposes Ruling on Cartoonist,' *Globe and Mail* (21 April 1998), A6. Currently, consent of the attorney general is expressly required to prosecute for promoting hate but not for inciting hate. Criminal Code, R.S.C. 1985, c. C-46, 319 (6).

25 Borovoy, *supra* note 10 at 51.

26 See K. Mahoney, 'Language as Violence v. Freedom of Expression: Canadian and American Perspectives on Group Defamation' (198–9) 37 Buffalo Law Review 337 at 348–50.

27 One might almost forget that hate propaganda law was a reaction to the disturbing rise of Nazi and neo-Nazi activities after the Second World War. Its purpose was defensive and its intended abridgment of social and political communication consciously limited. It was not meant to be an official tool for social transformation or for the furtherance of any particular political agenda to the legal exclusion of contrary ones.

28 Ordinarily true for any social cause generally. See, generally, M. Olson, 'The Logic of Collective Action,' excerpted in M. Olson, *The Rise and Decline of Nations* (New Haven: Yale University Press, 1982). See also roundtable discussion in (1990) Journal of Soviet Nationalities 61 at 5–65, especially J. Hough at 44–6.

29 See also chapter 6, Part II (4) at 160 and Part III at 165.

30 'Community officials are calling it [the defacing of six Montreal-area synagogues] the most serious anti-Semitic incident in over two years and the worst in memory for the level of co-ordination the crime must have

required. No arrests have been made as of press time and police reported
no leads in the case.' See J. Arnold, 'Shul Desecrations,' *Canadian Jewish
News* (7 January 1993), 1. In Winnipeg, 'some 300 headstones were
smashed a year ago in what was described as the worst incident of vandalism at a Jewish cemetery ever in North America.' See 'Headstones Buried,'
Canadian Jewish News (31 August 2000), 2. The 2000 annual audit of anti-
Semitic incidents by B'nai Brith Canada's League for Human Rights
reported a 'startling' 48 per cent increase in anti-Semitic vandalism
countrywide. See F. Kraft, 'Anti-Semitism, Hate on the Rise: League Audit,'
Canadian Jewish News (17 February 2000), 3.

31 P. Lungen, 'White Supremacist Incidents Become More Violent,'
   Canadian Jewish News (17 June 1993), 6 (on the heels of Keegstra's trial and
   conviction).

32 One of the key purposes of hate propaganda law, as the court noted in
   Keegstra, is 'to reduce racial, ethnic and religious tensions and perhaps even
   violence in Canada.' *R.* v. *Keegstra* [1990] 3 S.C.R. 697.

33 Csillag reports 'an escalation of violence among both racists and anti-
   racists.' See R. Csillag, 'Neo-Nazis Arrested in Ottawa Following Clash with
   Protestors,' *Canadian Jewish News* (17 June 1993), 6.

34 Such concepts, for example, as '*decoupling, focused benefits, scattered costs* and
   silent losers.' For a general discussion of these concepts, see C. Wolf, Jr,
   Markets or Government: Choosing between Imperfect Alternatives 2nd ed. (New
   York: MIT Press, 1995). See also D. Weimer and A. Vining, *Policy Analysis*
   (Englewood Cliffs: Prentice Hall, 1999).

35 On the foundational work on problems of public mobilization generally
   and the 'free rider' dilemma particularly, see M. Olson, *The Logic of
   Collective Action* (Cambridge, Mass.: Harvard University Press, 1965).

36 Moreover, hatemongers have many more options to get around their
   discursive loss besides *open* expressions of opposition to the law – a further
   reason for those who believe in hate censorship to expand the net. See
   below Part I (4) and chapter 6, Parts III and IV (2).

37 No less a figure than Helen Smolak for the Canadian Holocaust Remem-
   brance Association has suggested as much of the Canadian Civil Liberties
   Association itself. Cited in H. Levy, 'Should Hate Merchants Be Silenced?'
   Toronto Star (28 February 1989), A21.

38 P.M. Sniderman, J.F. Fletcher, P.H. Russell, and P.E. Tetlock, *The Clash of
   Rights* (New Haven: Yale University Press, 1996) at 61.

39 While the CRTC in Canada was contemplating pulling the plug on Dr
   Laura Schlesinger (one of radio's most popular talk show hosts) for her
   unenlightened comments on gays, an international conference in New

York unceremoniously dropped her for the same reason. See 'Dr. Laura Uninvited,' *Canadian Jewish News* (31 August 2000), 2.

40 See S. McIntyre, 'Backlash against Equality: The "Tyranny" of the Politically Correct' (1993) 38 McGill L.J. 1. McIntyre criticizes the 'right-wing political' backlash, while suggesting a censorship likely to expand it.

41 See K. Marx, *Marx's Capital*, C.J. Arthur ed. (London: Lawrence and Wishart, 1992).

42 Complete judicial reversal and a court-led timely turnback is not impossible. However, that would not be a 'natural' end, as it would come by legal fiat from without and against the public social and political processes rather than from within such processes' own dynamics.

43 As put by Pierre Berton, 'If [June] Callwood Is a Racist Then So Are We All,' *Toronto Star* (23 May 1992), H3.

44 See D. Baer, et al., 'National Character, Regional Culture, and the Values of Canadians and Americans' (1993) 30 The Canadian Review of Sociology and Anthropology 13.

45 An Environics Research poll done for the Association of Canadian Studies (ACS) found that while a majority of Canadians thought anti-Semitic sentiment was a problem in Canadian society, they did not consider themselves part of the problem. The discrepancy 'surprised' ACS director Jack Jedwab. See D. Lazarus 'Anti-Semitism Serious Problem: Poll,' *Canadian Jewish News* (10 April 2003), 1, 47.

46 R. Putnam, *supra* note 14.

47 'Honest' here refers to the expression of the true feelings of the speaker, not the truth of her speech.

48 On the reasons for asymmetry in successive cycles of protest generally, see S. Tarrow, 'Struggle, Politics and Reform: Collective Action, Social Movements and Cycles of Protest,' Center for International Relations, Cornell University, Western Societies Program, Occasional Paper No. 21 (Ithaca, N.Y.: 1989).

6 The Pragmatic Dilemma: Hate Censorship That 'Works'

1 This is a considerably revised version of part of my article 'Social and Racial Tolerance and Freedom of Expression in a Democratic Society: Friends or Foes? *Regina* v. *Zundel*' (1988) 11 Dal. L.J. 471.

2 M. Prutschi, 'There Ought to Be a Law against Hate' *Globe and Mail* (16 June 1988), A7.

3 See, generally, Canada, Law Reform Commission of Canada, *Our Criminal Law* (Ottawa: Law Reform Commission of Canada, 1997). See also

I. Primoratz, *Justifying Legal Punishment* (Atlantic Highlands, N.J.: Humanities Press International, 1998), at 7–13.

4 See R. Cross and A. Ashworth, *The English Sentencing System* (London: Butterworth, 1981), chapter 3 (2) 'Different Theories of Punishment' (aims of sentencing, 127; retributive theories, 128–34; utilitarian theories, 135–42.) See also Criminal Code, R.S.C., 1985, c. C-46, s. 718 ('Purpose and Principles of Sentencing').

5 This is not necessarily to say that once a hatemonger always a hatemonger, only that transformation is unlikely to be by dint of prosecution. See P. Lungen, 'Racists Use "Brainwashing" to Recruit Teens, Says Former White Supremacist,' *Canadian Jewish News* (17 February 2000), 16. (T.J. Leyden, a reformed former member of the Hammerskin Nation, attributes his transformation to demeaning personal experiences at his mentors' hands and jarring questions about his activities from his own young son.)

6 It is not the pain of reliving the past that is the problem here. It is the pain of reliving it as only the trial process allows. In *R. v. Keegstra* [1990] 3 S.C.R. 697 (hereafter *Keegstra*), for example, Holocaust victims had to 'listen calmly and wait patiently while an otherwise obscure "accused" was given a national forum to deny one of humanity's greatest atrocities and to lecture judge, jury and sitting public as if they were his high school students.' See 'Keegstra Lectures Courtroom on Jewish Conspiracy Theory,' *Globe and Mail* (30 May 1985), 3.

7 'Incapacitation was cited by the Law Reform Commission of Canada as one of the few justifiable reasons for sentencing.' Canada, *Sentencing, Canada* (Ottawa: Minister of Justice and Attorney General of Canada, 1984) at 7.

8 As McLachlin said, dissenting in *Keegstra*, 'listeners [gullible enough to believe Keegstra] might be just as likely to believe that there must be some truth in the racist expression because the government is trying to suppress it.' *Supra* note 6 at 853.

9 Canada, Law Reform Commission of Canada, *Our Criminal Law, supra* note 3 at 12.

10 Contrast this with ordinary libel actions between 'private' individuals where what society at large thinks about the matter in dispute, or how they come to think it, is irrelevant to the purpose of the lawsuits.

11 In ordinary criminal trials, the offenders shun the limelight and hide their guilt. In hate propaganda trials they relish publicity, flaunt their offence, and question the legitimacy of the law.

12 As the majority in *Keegstra* said, an essential purpose of a trial of hate is to make 'that kind of expression less attractive and hence decrease acceptance of its content.' *Supra* note 6 at 699. Hence, to simply silence is not enough.

13 See the discussion in chapter 2, Part II (2) ('Meaningful Public Discourse, Social Truth, and Social Division').

14 'Holocaust deniers, in the Zundel trial, sought more than an acquittal, they sought to have their poisonous views broadcast uncritically across the length and breadth of this country.' See M. Prutschi, 'Anti-Semitism on Trial: Zundel Convicted, Media Indicted' (1985) 27 Bulletin 13.

15 As Professor Deborah Lipstadt's lawyer said of his client's libel suit in Britain against Holocaust revisionist historian David Irving, 'The people who are impressed with Irving will continue to be, and those who are not will not be.' See R. Greene, 'BBC Eyes Holocaust Libel Case,' *Canadian Jewish News* (22 November 2001), 38.

16 On how process and forum shape the substance of public politics in Canada generally, see Keith Archer, et al., *Parameters of Power: Canada's Political Institutions* (Toronto: Nelson Canada (1995), esp. 1–23.

17 *Criminal Code*, R.S.C. 1970, c. 34. s. 177 (hereafter Criminal Code). Zundel succeeded on appeal, and a new trial was ordered on several 'technical' grounds involving defects in jury selection, misdirection as to the degree of *mens rea* required, and errors regarding the admissibility of certain histori- cal and other evidence.

18 *R.* v. *Zundel* [1992] 2 S.C.R, 731 (hereafter *Zundel*).

19 Some of the procedural and evidentiary problems in *Zundel* were peculiar to the particular statute, and these trials are still in their formative stages. Experience through precedent can obviate some, though hardly all or even most, of them. Moreover, statutes, interpretations, and courts can and do change, as do circumstances of prosecution, creating new opportunities for courtroom theatrics and fresh possibilities for procedural and evidentiary error.

20 'One cannot be happy at seeing a creep like him [Zundel] use a decision like this to portray himself as vindicated.' Alan Borovoy, head of the Canadian Civil Liberties Association, quoted in P. Small, 'Jewish Groups Demand New Criminal Charges Be Laid over Falsehoods,' *Toronto Star* (28 August 1992), A16. This article was written following the Supreme Court of Canada's reversal of Zundel's two convictions under the 'spreading false news' section of the Criminal Code. Contrast the public impact of legal error in repression of 'criminal' *social speech* with legal error in repression of criminal *acts*. The robber, the murderer, and the batterer may 'get off' on a 'technicality.' But none would or could claim by their acquittal vindication of stealing, killing, or beating others up. When the essence of the criminal 'act' (hatemongering) is the message (hate), no such easy separation of the offender from the offence is possible. Acquittal of the 'actor' risks 'acquittal' of his message.

21 Should the prosecutor decide to appeal an order for a new trial, rather than reprosecute the defendant, she not only risks losing the appeal but would, in the process, be diverting public attention from the evil content of the defendant's message to the finer points of evidentiary and procedural law.

22 Proving *mens rea* can present problems in any criminal trial. But failure to prove it presents a different kind of problem in hate speech trials. In non-speech criminal trials, where offensive act and guilty thought are separable, failure to prove the required *mens rea* (proving only the offensive *actus reus*) will 'acquit' the offender of moral guilt but not his act of its social harm. In hate propaganda prosecutions, where guilty mind and offensive 'act' are effectively synonymous, acquittal of the former tends to also acquit the defendant of the latter.

23 At his second trial, Zundel did not even take the stand but had his entire case of Holocaust denial played out on his behalf by his lawyer and 'expert' witnesses.

24 Wrote Prutschi, 'Zundel, for weeks, availed himself of his trial to provide a platform to internationally renowned Holocaust deniers. Likewise Keegstra, whose views could succinctly be summarized in an hour, remained on the stand for 26 seemingly endless days.' See M. Prutschi, 'Learning the Lessons of the Hatemonger Trials,' *Canadian Jewish News* (8 May 1986), 10.

25 Political discretion is hardly unusual in the exercise of prosecutorial powers, even in ordinary criminal trials. In the case of criminal prosecution of hate, however, it raises special problems for public perceptions by putting in political contention the very thing the state is trying to depoliticize. See P. Lungen, 'Ontario Court Asked to Rule if Gypsy, Roma Synonymous,' *Canadian Jewish News* (3 February 2000), 5. Lawyers applied to stay a case against anti-Gypsy skinhead demonstrators on the grounds of selective prosecution that ignored anti-Gypsy comments of city councillors.

26 Sniderman and colleagues have observed that the public has a 'disposition to respond to political issues in light of broader, vaguer, more emotional concerns than the issue has come to symbolize.' See, generally, P.M. Sniderman, et al., *The Clash of Rights* (New Haven: Yale University Press, 1996), at 57.

27 M. Prutschi, 'Zundel Verdict Validated Use of "False News" Law,' *Canadian Jewish News* (19 February 1987), 11. A premature observation at best.

28 See K. Jamieson, *Dirty Politics* (Oxford: Oxford University Press, 1992), at 42.

29 See R. Moon, *The Constitutional Protection of Freedom of Expression* (Toronto: University of Toronto Press, 2000), at 139.

30 Prutschi, *supra* note 24 at 10.

31 For some comparisons see M. Damaska, *The Faces of Justice and State Authority: A Comparative Approach to the Legal Process* (New Haven: Yale University Press, 1991).

32 Inquisitorial or investigatorial systems of continental Europe minimize a number of problems associated with the adversarial system's strict rules relating to admissibility of evidence, due process, proprietorship of witnesses, presumptions of guilt, and burden and onus of proof. See M. Damaska, 'Evidentiary Barriers to Conviction and Two Models of Criminal Procedure: A Comparative Study' (1973) 121 U. Pa. L. Rev. 505.

33 For a much fuller, practitioners' account, see A. Pirie, *Alternative Dispute Resolution* (Toronto: Irwin Law, 2001).

34 The problem here is not with any one factor alone but with all three taken together: relaxed procedure; context of repression; uncompromising hatemonger.

35 See E. Taylor, 'Hanging up on Hate: Contempt of Court as a Tool to Shut down Hatelines' (1995) 5 N.J. Con. L. 163 at 182. In 1996, the Canadian Human Rights Commission referred complaints about Zundel's U.S.-based Internet site to the Human Rights Tribunal for adjudication. See P. Lungen, 'Zundel Case Still Winding through Legal System,' *Canadian Jewish News* (6 April 2000), 17. But see *Zundel* v. *Canada (Human Rights Commission)* (2000-11-10) F.C.A. A-215-99 (finding against Zundel on the 'technical' ground that he had waived a legitimate charge of apprehension of bias by not objecting in time).

36 For more on clothing and coding, see below, Part II (4) ('Coverage or Targeting').

37 While accepting that 'no reasonable person could dispute the fact of the Holocaust,' the judge in Zundel's first trial refused to, effectively, abrogate Zundel's right to defend by granting the prosecution's request to take *judicial notice* of the Holocaust. See *R.* v. *Zundel* (1987), 58 O.R. (2d) 129 (C.A.).

38 For a 'radical left' view of the power of media misfiltering generally, see S. Herman and N. Chomsky, *Manufacturing Consent: The Political Economy of the Mass Media* (New York: Pantheon Books, 1988).

39 Prutschi, *supra* note 14 at 13–14.

40 Ibid. at 14. Prutschi writes, 'reporters had to avoid the temptation ... to be guided ... by the assumption that the Holocaust was not news and no Holocaust was news.'

41 M. Prutschi, 'Racist Expression and the Law in Canada,' *Sh'ma* (5 January 1990).

42 See, generally, J. Downing, A. Sreberny, and A. Mohammadi, *Questioning the Media: A Critical Introduction* 2nd ed. (Thousand Oaks, Calif.: Sage Publications, 1995).

43 Even manageable demands to speak as officially required can present democratic problems. See *West Virginia State Board of Education* v. *Barnette*, 319 U.S. 624 (1943). In this case, the U.S. Supreme Court invalidated the requirement to salute the flag.

44 S. Anand, 'Expression of Racial Hatred and Racism in Canada: An Historical Perspective' (1998) 77 Can. Bar. Rev. 181 at 194. See also S. Talty, 'Spinning Hate's World Wide Web,' *Edmonton Journal* (17 March 1996), 5.

45 P. Lungen, 'SWC Helping to Fight Hate on Internet,' *Canadian Jewish News* (17 June 1999), 3.

46 A. Schwarz, 'Holocaust Denial's a Tool for Pseudo-intellectuals,' *Canadian Jewish News* (28 April 2000), 20.

47 See *ACLU* v. *United States*, Nos CIV. A. 96–963, CIV. A. 96–1485; 1996 WL 311865 (E.D. Pa., 11 June 1996), 13–69.

48 B. Rose, 'Hate Propaganda on Web Can't Be Tracked, CJC Told,' *Canadian Jewish News* (14 September 2000), 5.

49 S. Kirshner, 'Deputy Minister Rosenberg Dispenses Justice,' *Canadian Jewish News* (28 September 2000), 13.

50 'Giving up on Web,' *Canadian Jewish News* (3 August 2000), 2.

51 Referring to Canadian extremists, Manuel Prutschi observes, 'I don't doubt they're incited by the inflammatory rhetoric that's been coming out of the Middle East.' See P. Lungen, 'Edmonton Synagogues Hit by Arson,' *Canadian Jewish News* (9 November 2000), 1, 36.

52 This charge was levelled against the Canadian Civil Liberties Association (despite its record of intervening on behalf of persecuted minorities) by none other than Helen Smolak for the Canadian Holocaust Remembrance Association. See H. Levy, 'Should Hate Merchants Be Silenced?' *Toronto Star* (28 February 1989), A21.

53 This is the 'prisoner's dilemma' with a profoundly practical 'communicative' twist. Aside from the difficulty of uniformly defining hate propaganda, even if every single country in the world were agreed to be of one mind and one defining understanding in banning it, variances in effective enforcement would still leave intrusive communication gaps through which hate could escape, 'free' to 'contaminate' whomever it touches and proselytize wherever it sets down roots. Given the differences among nations in policing, resources, and social, economic, and political structures, huge differences in enforcement could be expected even if worldwide cooperation were, in principle, possible.

54 While the Canadian Jewish Congress is trying to bar cable carriage of Al-Jazeera in Canada, 'many Canadians receive the 24-hour news network via the "grey market" U.S.-based DirecTV satellite service.' See R. Csillag, 'BBC,

CJC aim to bar Al-Jazeera from Canada,' *Canadian Jewish News* (16 April 2003), 3.

55 Are 'repeated games' eliciting the kind of *globally seamless* censorial cooperation required here really possible? See, generally, R. Jervis, 'Realism, Game Theory and Cooperation' (1998) 40 World Politics 371. See also R. Putnam, 'Diplomacy and Domestic Politics: The Logic of Two-Level Games' (1988) 42 International Organization 427.

56 L. Lessig, 'Cyberspace's Architectural Constitution.' Draft dated 12 June 2000, of a lecture given at Amsterdam, Netherlands. Available on the Web at *http://cyber.law.harvard.edu/works/lessig/www9.pdf.* His discussion is in the context of copyright and control of cultural content.

57 See E. Morgan, 'International Law Is the Problem, Not the Solution,' *Canadian Jewish News* (11 October 2001), 9.

58 See H. Adelman, 'Hate Speech and Terrorism,' *Canadian Jewish News* (20 September 2001), 9. Adelman lambastes the 'use and abuse of language to create a tissue of lies and a mountain of hate.'

59 On some views of this, in the context of the 'direct democracy' versus 'representative democracy' debate, see A. Shapiro, *The Control Revolution: How New Technology Is Putting Individuals in Charge and Changing the World We Know* (New York: Public Affairs, 1999), chapter 18, 'In Defense of Middlemen (Power and Delegation).'

60 Hardly the Habermasian public ideal of a full and free dialogical discourse in a shared space, but not a bad approximation of it, either, for complex modern societies. On Habermas, see P. Dahlgren, 'Introduction,' in P. Dahlgren and C. Sparks, eds, *Communication and Citizenship: Journalism and the Public Sphere in the New Media Age* (London: Routledge, 1991).

61 J. Barlow, 'Selling Wine without Bottles. The Economy of Mind on the Global Net,' in P. Hugenholtz, ed., *The Future of Copyright in a Digital Environment* (London: Kluwer Law International, 1996) at 169–74. The context of his discussion is intellectual property rights, but I use it here because his comments are particularly appropriate to the problem of prohibiting hate propaganda.

62 Under the Canadian Criminal Code, the offence of incitement to hate is confined to utterances made in 'any public place' and statements promoting hatred to communications 'other than in private conversation.' Criminal Code, R.S.C. 1985, c. C-46 s. 319 (1) and s. 319 (2).

63 Barlow, *supra* note 61.

64 Ibid. at 174.

65 Compare physical confiscation of a videotape of hatemongers openly denying the Holocaust with 'physical confiscation' of the same denial

appearing and disappearing in the form of instantaneous reprography of fleeting electronic bits across countless private screens. See 'Video Hoax,' *Canadian Jewish News* (3 May 2001), 2.

66 Public meaning construction is not a transmission belt. Silencing may be made seamless, but communication is multifaceted and interactive, not linear. See H. Anders, 'The Media and Social Construction of the Environment' (1991) 13 Media, Culture and Society 447. Communism recognized this early, ever vigilant to silence socially inappropriate thoughts whenever and wherever they were expressed. Private conversation was not exempt. The home enjoyed no immunity. Friends and neighbours were required to report on each other to the authorities for private expressions of socially inegalitarian thoughts. Even children were encouraged to report their socially errant parents.

67 See especially S. Scott, *Dismantling Utopia: How Information Ended the Soviet Union* (Chicago: Irvin R. Dee, 1994).

68 Samizdat – self-generated, discreetly disseminated, and selectively chain-distributed non-conforming expressions – helped bring down Communism. See G. Skilling and S. Precan, eds, 'Parallel Politics: Essays from Czechoslovakia from Czech and Slovak Samizdat' (1981) 3 International Journal of Politics 3. See also G. Skilling, *Samizdat and an Independent Society in Central and Eastern Europe* (Columbus: Ohio University Press, 1989).

69 I. McKenna, 'Canada's Hate Propaganda Laws – A Critique' (1994) 26 Ottawa L. Rev. 159.

70 See chapter 2: II (2) ('Meaningful Public Discourse, Social Truth, and Social Division').

71 A. Borovoy, *The New Anti-liberals* (Toronto: Canadian Scholars Press, 1999) at 159.

72 Compare the work of David Irving, Holocaust revisionist, author of over twenty history books, and 'expert' witness for Zundel, to that of Professor Philippe Rushton, at the University of Western Ontario.

73 E.g., when a Canadian lawyer, defending his client against deportation for lying about his Nazi past, stated that Ottawa was catering to 'special interest groups,' the chair of the CJCs Ontario Region, complained that the lawyer was using a 'code word' for the Jewish community. See P. Lungen, 'Oberlander's Lawyer Subject of Law Society Complaint,' *Canadian Jewish News* (23 March 2000), 6.

74 History is replete with cartoon caricatures of the Jew as the grotesque, hooked-nose, money-monger.

75 Anand gives the example of George Burdi, 'lead singer for the rock band Rahowa, an acronym for Racial Holy War. As its name implies, it is a white

supremacist rock band whose lyrics constitute hate propaganda.' S. Anand, *supra* note 44 at 194. Burdi was later convicted of promoting hate. See F. Kraft, 'Burdi Gets Sentence for Promoting Hate,' *Canadian Jewish News* (7 October 1999), 32. The Jewish Anti-Defamation League, in its list *Bigots Who Rock: An ADL List of Hate Music Groups*, 'identifies 541 rock bands, primarily based in the United States and Europe, that use hate-filled lyrics or have active links to organized hate groups.' See 'ADL Issues List of Hate Music Groups,' *Canadian Jewish News* (1 November 2001), 2. And, see *http:/ /www.adl.org.along*. Under the Criminal Code, hate 'statements includes words spoken or written or recorded electronically or electromagnetically or otherwise and gestures, signs or other visible representations.' Criminal Code ss. 319 (7). In Israel, a petition before the Supreme Court asks the court to block any financial support for the performance of works by the renowned German composer (and anti-Semite) Richard Wagner.

76 See G. di Palma, 'Legitimation from the Top to Civil Society: Politico-Cultural Change in Eastern Europe' (1991) 44 World Politics 64.

77 P. Lungen, 'Conspiracy for a New Age,' *Canadian Jewish News* (15 March 1999), 27 (reporting on British writer David Icke, a former spokesperson for Britain's Green party and author of *And the Truth Will Set You Free* and *The Robots' Rebellion*). Writes Lungen, 'Serta [who operates the Learning Annex where Icke spoke] suggested Icke is popular in the New Age community because of his "entertainment value," although he acknowledges "some people take it seriously."'

78 See, for example, J. Fiske, *Television Culture* (London: Routledge, 1987).

79 'CJC spokesperson Ron Sorokin said he was disturbed to see protestors wearing Star of David badges and comparing themselves to Jewish victims of the Holocaust.' See 'Nazis Imagery Condemned,' *Canadian Jewish News* (1 October 1998), 2.

80 See P. Lungen, 'Rights Group Compares Animal Slaughter to Holocaust,' *Canadian Jewish News* (6 March 2003) 1, 34.

81 'I believe he is more dangerous than David Duke [former Grand Wizard of the Ku Klux Klan, successful candidate for the Louisiana legislature, and unsuccessful candidate for the U.S. Senate]. He espouses Duke's positions, but in disguise. Buchanan has never carried a Nazi party card, or been a member of the Ku Klux Klan. But, many of his views are identical with Duke's.' A. Weiss, 'Buchanan Candidacy a Dangerous Sign,' *Canadian Jewish News* (5 March 1992), 15.

82 His first 'post death threat' work is a noticeably safer, 'non-political' effort. See S. Rushdie, *The Moor's Last Sigh* (Toronto: Vintage Canada, 1996).

83 'We are most concerned that Dr. Rubenstein is presenting his own
   subjective opinions as fact and that because he has a Ph.D. and is a
   professor, people will take his views as facts' (University of Manitoba
   Students' Union, explaining its human rights complaint against Professor
   Rubenstein, charging him with distributing 'hate literature' for a pamphlet
   he authored entitled 'homosexual myths and reality' and for his public
   statements questioning conventional psychiatric views on sexual predisposi-
   tions). See M. Love, 'Prof. Draws Fire for Views on Anti-homophobic
   Education,' *Canadian Jewish News* (13 May 1999), 30.
84 McLachlin, dissenting in *Keegstra*, noted heightened public concern over
   Shakespeare's stereotypical portrayal of the Jewish character Shylock in the
   Merchant of Venice. Supra note 6 at 680.
85 Developer of the transistor, he became better known for his infamous
   'dysgenics' theories on intellectual differences between the races. See
   G. Moore, 'Solid-State Physicist: William Shockley,' *Time* (29 March 1999),
   122.
86 *Toronto Star* columnist Cecil Foster writes how Farrakhan 'spread his
   charm, using his charisma to strongly connect with blacks living in this
   country.' See C. Foster, 'Farrakhan's Charm Has West Indian Flavor,'
   Toronto Star (23 September 1996), A13. Dudley Laws, executive director of
   the Black Action Defense Committee, describes Farrakhan as a 'great man.'
   See D. Laws, 'Nothing Wrong with Farrakhan,' *Share* (19 September 1996),
   1. Outside the convention room where he was speaking, Farrakhan's
   organization was busy selling booklets entitled 'The Jewish Onslaught and
   the Jews and their Lies.' See 'Thousands Attend Farrakhan Speech,' *Globe
   and Mail* (16 September 1996), A12.
87 'Can life be beautiful in a concentration camp?' asks a letter to the editor
   criticizing Roberto Benigni's Oscar-winning 1997 movie as subtle fodder
   for Holocaust deniers because of its 'light-hearted' take on the Holocaust.
   See 'Letter to the Editors,' *Canadian Jewish News* (11 March 1999), 8. Or
   consider the Jewish–Black divisions over the Toronto production of the
   musical *Showboat.* See R. Fuller, 'When Indignation Obscures Truth,' *Globe
   and Mail* (2 June 1993), 3. See also J. Korda, 'Slogans Conceal a Hateful
   Message,' *Canadian Jewish News* (6 March 1997), 10. Korda writes 'The
   Nation of Islam disguises its wicked and hateful message behind slogans of
   pride and education, many followers are disillusioned and tend to overlook
   the significance of the hidden bigotry. This type of racism perpetrates the
   violent vilification of many peoples, while those spreading the rhetoric
   often think they are acting in the best interests of their community.'

88 'Father Christmas' was removed from a Roman Catholic school in Ontario because of allegations that it promoted a negative image of Santa Claus. See M. Lucow, 'B.C. Group Denies Anti-Semitism,' *Canadian Jewish News* (11 April 1991), 6. In 1991, the Toronto Board of Education recommended that Mary Poppins and Doctor Dolittle be removed from elementary schools because of their 'racist and sexist biases.' See R. Landes, *The Canadian Polity* 5th ed. (Scarborough, Ont.: Prentice Hall, 1998) at 272.

89 M. Prutschi, 'Holocaust Denial Today,' in E. Lipsitz, ed., *Canadian Jewry Today: Who's Who in Canadian Jewry* (Downsview, Ont.: J.E.S.L. Education Products, 1989).

90 See P. Lungen, 'CLC Criticizes Israel.' *Canadian Jewish News* (20 June 2002), 22.

91 *Supra* note 58 and accompanying text.

92 Ibid.

93 See 'WJC Knocks Leftist,' *Canadian Jewish News* (28 November 2002), 2.

94 'This is the new thing,' observes Professor Morton Weinfeld. 'There is a growing tie between anti-Americanism, anti-Semitism and anti-Zionism.' See S. Kirshner, 'Anti-Semitism Worries Canadian Jews: Sociologists,' *Canadian Jewish News* (20 February 2003), 5 (paper given at conference Antisemitism: The Politicization of Prejudice in the Contemporary World).

95 See chapter 1.

96 The U.S. Supreme Court has distinguished advocacy from incitement in the context of the *Smith Act*. The *Smith Act*, which prohibited incitement to lawless acts endangering the government, was used in the 1950s by McCarthyites against 'Communists,' real and imagined. To constitute incitement, the court held, the language must urge the listener 'to do' rather than simply 'to believe.' See *Yates* v. *U.S.*, 354 U.S. 298 (1957), at 318. In *Noto* v. *U.S.*, 367 U.S. 290 (1960), at 297–8, the court refined this further, stating that 'the mere abstract teaching ... of the moral propriety or even moral necessity for a resort to force and violence, is not the same as preparing a group for violent action and steering it to such action.'

97 The 'false news' section of the Criminal Code (C-34, s. 177) under which Zundel was charged, and which the Supreme Court of Canada struck down for vagueness/overbreadth, proscribed public dissemination of 'false news that causes or is likely to cause injury or mischief to a public interest.'

98 See R. Moon, *supra* note 29 at 142 and 143.

99 See A. Schwartz, 'Holocaust Denial's a Tool for Pseudo-intellectuals,' *Canadian Jewish News* (28 April 2000), 18 and 20. Citing growing sophistication of hate, Schwartz reports on, among others, Arthur Butz, a professor

of electrical engineering at Northwestern University whose innocuous-sounding but virulently anti-Semitic Institute for Historical Review would do even the most transparent racist proud.

100 In 1987 he said, 'I don't say they [the gas chambers] never existed but I have never seen any myself. Moreover, I think this [whole question] is a mere detail in the history of the Second World War.' See C. Gasner, 'The Year 5747 Saw Release of Descheney,' *Canadian Jewish News* (23 September 1987), 13. (Notice here the irony of the *Canadian Jewish News* reporting such racist comments in detail.) By 2002, following Le Pen's second-place showing in the opening round of the French presidential elections, John Gray could write, 'The political genius of Mr. Le Pen is his capacity to touch every source of discomfort within French society and to link them all together – immigration, crime, AIDS, Islamic fundamentalism, taxes ... the weakening of France, the ascendancy of Europe.' J. Gray, 'France's Long Romance with Le Pen,' *Globe and Mail* (26 April 2002), A21.

101 See L. Yanowitch, 'France up in Arms over Le Pen,' *Canadian Jewish News* (26 September 1996), 35.

102 See P. Lungen, 'Internet Site Offers Nazi Items,' *Canadian Jewish News* (29 March 2001), 1, 50. A French appellate court upheld an earlier ruling that ordered Internet giant Yahoo! to bar French users from visiting sites that sold Nazi memorabilia and other collectibles. A search of e-Bay using the search word 'Nazi' turned up 3,768 items for sale.

103 As pointed out by an angry Sabina Citron, a central figure in having Zundel charged under the false news provision of the Criminal Code.

104 Reported in S. Birnbaun, 'New Foundation to Honor Righteous Christian,' *Canadian Jewish News* (23 September 1987), 23.

105 What politician will risk his career and come out openly and honestly to brand hate propaganda law a failure that should be abandoned?

106 In its report *Promoting Equality: A New Vision 2000*, a review panel headed by former Supreme Court of Canada Justice La Forest has recommended widening the scope of the *Canadian Human Rights Act* to hold Internet servers with 'knowledge, actual or constructive,' of promotion of hate on the Internet liable. Notice the word 'constructive.' Meanwhile, a 'new media working group' studying 'the issue of hate and bias on the internet' (under the auspices, no less, of the Secretary of State for Multiculturalism) is looking to make censorship on the Internet easier with the 'concept of a hotline, similar to Crime Stoppers, that would give the public a central location to complain about internet hate propaganda.' See P. Lungen, 'Panel Recommends Tackling Hate on the

Internet,' *Canadian Jewish News* (6 July 2000), 7. Bill C-36, the federal government's new anti-terrorism bill, would amend the *Canadian Human Rights Act* to prohibit the distribution of hate materials through the Internet or any interconnected computer network, including a private network.

107 Though I suspect this restraint had more to do with politics and a change of government than an abiding respect for limited censorship and political democracy. While in opposition from 1990 to 1995, Charles Harnick regularly admonished the NDP government in Ontario for not charging Zundel under the hate propaganda provisions of the Criminal Code. As attorney general in the Conservative government of Mike Harris, however, he had a sudden change of heart.

108 In a self-serving dictatorship, or a 'totalitarian' one such as the Soviet Union under Stalin, the opposite is true. Stalin was not limited by *his cause* from doing whatever was necessary to effectively silence. For his purposes, effectiveness and success were complementary, not self-contradictory. The locus of control was and could be set exclusively at his initiative. In such cases, the dynamic of censorship is literally driven by the side with the bigger gun. Under Stalin, speech repression became virtually 'total,' and there was no silencing *dynamic* left to speak of.

109 On these concepts, see I. Kaul, I. Grunberg, and M. Stern, eds, *Global Public Goods: International Cooperation in the 21st Century* (New York: Oxford University Press, 1999), at 2–19.

110 Ibid. at 2–5.

111 Maybe a formal apartheid system of social right would not be needed. Perhaps censors could simply *regulate* 'exposure' of vulnerable adults to socially intolerant thinking – the way parents regulate the activities of wayward children. Require ID, set curfew, require periodic 'reporting in,' restrict where to go, what to see, whom to associate with? Developing DNA, sensor, and communicative technologies offer many new and 'exciting' possibilities here for the state to protect where and as needed. But even the mentally ill and inmates of prison cannot be totally shielded from unwanted outside messages.

112 That the price of protecting the 'cognitively needy' few may be the public growth and politically discursive needs of the great many (Canadian society) seems not to trouble 'democratic' censors. Some scholars look to public resonance theory to justify discriminatory admission to the club of independent thinking. See R. Moon, *supra* note 29 at 142–3. Moon suggests that at the subconscious level of public prejudice there is no

meaningful difference between the lowest and the general common denominator. Unfortunately, this view does not address the democratic problem of hate silencing – it illustrates it.

113 Consider P. Lungen, 'Anti-Semitic Books Found on Indigo's Web Site,' *Canadian Jewish News* (29 March 2001), 7. Indigo Books Music and More, which no longer stocks or sells *The Protocols of the Elders of Zion* and *The Hoax of the Twentieth Century)* has promised to remove the titles and any references to them from its website.

114 Keith Landy, president of the Canadian Jewish Congress, has suggested that *Mein Kampf* be restricted to 'scholars.' See report, CTV Evening News (29 November 2001). Manuel Prutschi, chair of the CJC's Community Relations Committee, 'acknowledged' that the book should be available to 'students of history' but spoke against its availability 'in your neighbourhood bookstore.' See P. Lungen, 'Chapters, Indigo Pulls *Mein Kampf* from Their Bookstores,' *Canadian Jewish News* (6 December 2001), 22. Crude 'baby steps' towards audience apartheid? Would (vulnerable?) academics such as Philippe Rushton qualify for admittance into this privileged circle of 'scholar' or 'student of history,' or be banned?

115 Chill and opportunism are not mutually exclusive. Chill can house opportunism by the very silence of the speech that is not uttered but ought to be as well as by speech that is uttered but ought not to be. Historically, chill mixed with opportunism has made for some lethal combinations. In China, millions of peasants died of starvation in part because Mao Tse Tung's faithful were afraid to tell him the true extent to which his policies were causing widespread famine. To gain personal favour, some self-servingly told him only what he wanted to hear. Some held their tongues for fear of reprisals; still others, for fear of giving ammunition to opponents of the cause. See J. Becker, *Hungry Ghosts: Mao's Secret Famine* (New York: Henry Holt, 1998), esp. Introduction and chapter 6.

116 Illustrating how 'self-intimidation' can produce *chilling opportunism* that gets in the way of people talking honestly with one another, consider the following from Epstein: 'For years I have used Clayborne Carson's book ... It has become more and more difficult for me to induce ... what are always predominantly white classes to discuss this book ... The last time this happened, students acknowledged – under my prodding – that they could not talk about the book without entertaining criticisms of a black movement, which would raise the possibility of racism.' See B. Epstein, 'Political Correctness and Collective Powerlessness' (1991), 21 Socialist Review 21 at 21–2.

117 This might be seen as a problem of both underinclusiveness and overinclusiveness. But it is much worse than that. There is *no* (intended) inclusiveness. Means and ends are not rationally connected to do the job intended with respect to *any* category of speaker.

7 The Jurisprudential Dilemma: The Exceptions Defence and Democratic Justification

1 For example, British Columbia enacted legislation enjoining anti-abortion protestors from showing 'any act of disapproval ... with respect to ... abortion services by any means, including ... graphic, verbal or written ...' within fifty metres of certain abortion clinics: Bill 48, *Access to Abortion Services Act*, S.B. 1995, s. 2(1)(b). Noting that access to health services and privacy issues needed to be considered in the balance, Borovoy suggests that the regulations went *beyond* what was necessary to protect these interests and were in fact concerned with prohibiting the content of the message. 'To re-route picket lines in this way is to transform freedom of communication into freedom of soliloquy.' See A Borovoy, *The New Anti-liberals* (Toronto: Canadian Scholars Press, 1999) at 142.

2 Courts are not unaware that states may try to hide behind their right of regulation when their real purpose is to prohibit content. The Canadian court struck down such an attempt as early as 1953, albeit having to resort, in the absence of a charter of rights, to such means as the distribution of powers argument. See *Saumur* v. *Quebec* [1953] 2 S.C.R. 299, especially Justice Rand, at 333 (Rand held that the *unfettered discretion* of the chief of police to inspect the *contents* of pamphlets intended for distribution on the streets revealed a *prohibitory* purpose based on the content of the ideas contained therein. It was not a reasonable regulation concerned only with the safe and orderly regulation of the streets and was therefore *ultra vires* the municipality and the province).

3 *Cox* v. *Louisiana*, 379 U.S. 536 (1965) at 555.

4 See L. Loader, 'Trespass to Property: Shopping Centres' (1992) 8 J.L. and Soc. Pol. 254–81.

5 I merely adapt here the words of the Ontario Divisional Court in *Re Klein and Law Society of Upper Canada* (1985), 16 D.L.R. (4th), 524 at 534, used in the context of regulation of commercial speech. However, I do not agree with its characterization of commercial speech and its conclusion. See S. Braun, 'Should Commercial Speech Be Accorded Constitutional Recognition under the Canadian Charter of Rights and Freedoms?' (1986) 18 Ottawa L. Rev. 37.

6 Even the political right to convince and convert is not absolute. See chapter 8, Part IV, 'Temporary Suppression of Expressions of Hatred in Extraordinary Conditions ...' at 209.

7 On the law's timeless and placeless quality, see chapter 3, Part IV (the mushroom thesis) at 78.

8 See Criminal Code, R.S.C., 1985, c. C-46, s. 437.

9 *Both* proselytic purpose and intolerant social content should be present to warrant hate speech proscription. There is a category of communication that 'mimics' these requirements but that can be proscribed for other reasons. *Incidentally* racially intolerant communication – utterances not *purposed* to convert to a social or political cause but made in furtherance of an illegal act – need not be a saving grace on free speech grounds. 'Thus it has long been regarded as unlawful for businesses to advertise that "no blacks need apply."' See Borovoy, *supra* note 1 at 144.

10 The idea of allowing listeners time to 'consider' the message, thereby exposing messengers and their meanings to refutation (counter-speech), has been fundamental to U.S. First Amendment jurisprudence. See *Yates* v. *U.S.*, 354 U.S. 298 (1957) at 325, drawing a distinction between expressions urging the listener 'to believe' (valid) and urging him 'to do' (invalid). This was further refined by the Ku Klux Klan case *Brandenburg* v. *Ohio*, 395 U.S. 444 (1969) at 448. The U.S. Supreme Court held that even advocacy 'inciting lawless action' is permissible unless the state can demonstrate that the advocacy was 'likely to cause or produce such action.' The requirement of 'proximate cause' helps to obviate the problem of 'subjective and speculative' injuries. But, in an earlier case, Justice Oliver Wendell Holmes had rejected the validity, in a self-governing society, of the 'to think–to do' distinction in the case of *socially or politically purposed* speech. *Gitlow* v. *New York*, 268 U.S. 652 (1925) at 673 (regarding a Marxist charged with a form of seditious incitement).

11 See *Chaplinsky* v. *New Hampshire*, 315 U.S. 568 (1942). In the more than half-century since it was decided, *Chaplinsky*'s application beyond fighting words is no longer credible. See *Collin* v. *Smith*, 578 F.2d 1197 (7th Circuit) (1978) (on a Nazi march that was allowed to proceed through a Jewish neighbourhood in Skokie, Illinois). See also *American Booksellers Ass'n, Inc.* v. *Hudnut*, 771 F.2d 323 (7th Circuit) (1985).

12 See generally, R.E. Brown, *The Law of Defamation in Canada* 2nd ed. (Toronto: Carswell, 1999), esp. 15–7 to 15–8.

13 So, too, examples of its political misuse are worldwide. In Israel, cabinet minister Ariel Sharon, in a blatant attempt to intimidate the press, brought a libel suit against the Israeli daily newspaper *Ha'aretz* over a scathing article it wrote about Sharon's role in the 1982 Lebanon war. See

R. Gruber, 'Sharon, Pope Hold Talks,' *Canadian Jewish News* (6 May 1999),
53. In Canada, Quebec premier Lucien Bouchard and former premier
Jacques Parizeau sued Richard Lafferty, a senior partner in a stock brokerage firm, for $300,000 for 'incendiary, injurious and defamatory' com-
ments. Lafferty had likened their political conduct to 'demoguery [sic] ...
no different from what Hitler did.' The offensive comments, made more
than six years earlier, were not even intended for the public at large. They
appeared in a brokerage newsletter directed only to the firm's clients, with
the words 'confidential' printed on the top but leaked to *Le Devoir*. See J.
Arnold, 'Bouchard, Parizeau Launch Libel Suit,' *Canadian Jewish News* (2
December 1999), 31. See also *Vander Zalm v. Times Publishers et al.* (1980)
109 D.L.R. (3d) 531 (British Columbia Supreme Court finding against the
premier of British Columbia, who sued a political cartoonist for depicting
the premier as a cruel tyrant pulling the wings off a fly).

14 See D.A. Alderson, 'The Constitutionalization of Defamation: American and
Canadian Approaches to the Constitutional Regulation of Speech' (1993)
15 Advocates' Q. 385.

15 *New York Times v. Sullivan*, 376 U.S. 254 (1964) (hereafter *Sullivan*).

16 *Garrison v. State of Louisiana*, 379 U.S. 364 (1964).

17 On the use of American cases in Canada generally, see I. Bushnell, 'The
Use of American Cases' (1986) 35 U.N.B.L.J. 15.

18 *Sullivan, supra* note 15 at 271. Correction itself requires free speech.

19 Ibid. at 292.

20 *Supra* note 16 at 272–3.

21 See S. Braun, 'Freedom of Expression v. Obscenity Censorship: The
Developing Canadian Jurisprudence' in (1985–6) 50 Sask. L. Rev. 39. For
the United States, see *Cohen v. California*, 403 U.S. 15, 26, (1971) (hereafter
Cohen). The court held that the state, could not prohibit the accused from
wearing a cap inscribed with the insignia 'Fuck the Draft' in the corridor of
a courthouse.

22 Braun, ibid, at 53–7.

23 Some early doubts of a change of course notwithstanding. See R. Kramar,
'Obscenity: Return to Old Morality Play or New Approach?' (1992) 35
Crim. L.Q. 77.

24 See *Cohen, supra* note 21.

25 This, of course, is not to say that consuming 'sleaze' may not 'impact' to
modify society, for good or ill. See H. Clor, ed., *Censorship and Freedom of
Expression* (Chicago: Rand McNally, 1971) at 17.

26 See M. Prutschi, 'Should Hate Merchants Be Silenced?' *Toronto Star*
(28 February 1989), A21.

27 *Miller v. California*, 413 U.S. 15 (1973) at 35–6.

28 This potentiality is borne out by actual attempts and threats by rival groups to silence each other. See discussion, cases, and examples, especially chapter 4, Part I, at 90 'Unwrapping the Politics of Content' and Part II, at 98, 'Unwrapping the Politics of Victimhood'; and chapter 5, Part I (1), 'Rival Groups and the Conduct of the Debate,' at 123.

29 Recall from chapter 4 how even racists and revisionists such as Zundel and Irving have taken legal action to try to silence their opponents.

30 See chapters 2 and 6.

31 See chapter 2.

32 The court considered the question of sexually explicit depictions of children in *R. v. Sharpe* [2001] 1 S.C.R. 45, upholding the universally recognized *parens patriae* rights of the state to protect children from exploitation and harm (see esp. 52). The state's purpose raised no issue of abridgment of contentious public communication on matters of state and society by rival political actors. The court severed two offending and incidental sections of the impugned statute (which raised issues of social and political import different from that raised by hate propaganda), to give less intrusive effect to the state's legitimate *parens patriae* purpose.

33 *Roth v. U.S.*, 354 U.S. 476 (1957).

34 Ibid. at 484.

35 In what I have called 'mixed works' – public communication coupling explicit sexual titillation with larger social and political meanings – it may sometimes be difficult to disentangle the illegitimate from the legitimate. See Braun, *supra* note 21 at 46–52 ('mixed works and the internal necessities test'). See also J. McLaren, 'Now You See It, Now You Don't: The Historical Record and the Elusive Task of Defining the Obscene,' in D. Schneiderman, ed., *Freedom of Expression and the Charter* (Toronto: Carswell, 1991).

36 *R. v. Odeon Morton Theatres Ltd. and United Artists Corp.* (1974), CCC (2d) 185 (Man. CA).

37 *R. v. Macmillan of Canada Ltd.* (1976), 31 CCC (2d) 286 (Ont. Co. Ct.).

38 'Anti-porn Group Target of Seizure,' *Globe and Mail* (17 October 1987), A6.

39 L. King, 'Censorship and Law Reform: Will Changing the Laws Mean a Change for the Better?' in V. Burstyn ed., *Women against Censorship* (Vancouver: Douglas and McIntyre, 1985) at 87.

40 See 'Erotic Poems,' *Canadian Press* (19 December 1986).

41 *Re University of Manitoba and Deputy Minister, Revenue Canada* (1984), 4 D.L.R. (4th) 659. See also Braun, *supra* note 21 at 49.

42 Obscenity, as a metaphor for hate propaganda, is becoming increasingly common. Following the destruction of the World Trade Center in New York, Keith Landy, national president of the CJC said, 'There have been

accusations, which can be characterized as nothing else than *obscene hate propaganda*, that Israel knew and did not warn of the atrocity or actually was behind it.' See K. Landy, 'No Moral Relativism in the Battle against International Terrorism,' *Canadian Jewish News* (18 October 2001), 32. An architecture professor for the defence, in Holocaust revisionist David Irving's failed lawsuit against Professor Lipstadt, later said of the trial in London, England, 'there was a real sense that this was a completely *obscene* issue we'd been involved in.' See F. Kraft, 'Quite a Bitter Victory,' *Canadian Jewish News* (28 April 2000), 1. See also, 'This year's is the third annual festival sponsored by Hammerskin Nations, a neo-Nazi group that uses *hardcore* music as a vehicle to disseminate white supremacist beliefs.' See 'ADL Issues List of Hate Music Groups,' *Canadian Jewish News* (1 November 2001), 2 (emphasis mine).

43 See K. Mahoney, '*R. v. Keegstra*: A Rationale for Regulating Pornography' (1992) 37 McGill L.J. 242.

44 This can mean that even the most graphic depiction of sexual activity may no longer necessarily be obscene, while more sexually innocuous ones might be. In 1993, the Ontario Human Rights Commission found 'sufficient evidence' to recommend investigating two complaints against certain convenience stores in Toronto that were selling *Penthouse* and *Playboy* magazines on the grounds that they might be creating a 'hostile environment for women' in Ontario. What other public messages might create a 'hostile environment' for women in Ontario, sufficient to invoke the threat of repression? See Ontario Human Rights Commission Complaints Nos. 60–023, 60–024, 60–025 (the 'Findlay' complaints), and 60–026, 60–028 (the 'McKay' complaints). See also 'The Centerfold War: Do Skin Magazines Violate Human Rights?' *Maclean's* (10 May 1993), 14, 16. Three years after the suit was first brought, the HRC finally dropped it.

45 See K. Mahoney, 'Obscenity, Morals and the Law: A Feminist Critique' (1985) 17 Ottawa L. Rev. 1.

46 This is true even if, as Moon suggests, the criterion of sexual explicitness goes much deeper, sustaining traditional social norms of male domination. See R. Moon, *The Constitutional Protection of Freedom of Expression* (Toronto: University of Toronto Press, 2000) at 113.

47 See *R. v. Butler* (1992) 89 D.L.R. (4th) 449. 'The message of obscenity which degrades and dehumanizes is analogous to that of hate propaganda,' per Sopinka at 501.

48 Ibid., 471, per Sopinka.

49 A. Borovoy, *When Freedoms Collide* (Toronto: Lester and Orpen Dennys, 1988) at 63.

50 See, for example, B. Walsh, 'Canadian Dissident' (1993) 59 Quill and Quire 9 (on a Canada Customs seizure of a comic magazine deemed degrading to *men*). See 'Police Raid Gay Bookstore,' *Globe and Mail* (1 May 1992), D1.

51 *Beauharnais* v. *Illinois*, 343 U.S. 250 (1952) (hereafter *Beauharnais*). This case can no longer be considered good law. See, for example, *Collin* v. *Smith*, 578 F.2d 1197 (1978); *American Booksellers Association, Inc.* v. *Hudnut*, 771 F.2d 323 (1985).

52 *Brown* v. *Board of Education of Topeka, Kansas*, 347 U.S. 483 (1954).

53 *Plessey* v. *Ferguson*, 163 U.S. 537 (1896).

54 The U.S. Supreme Court's reluctance, articulated in *Colgrove* v. *Green*, 328 U.S. 549 (1946), on the need to scrutinize gerrymandering of voting districts that often resulted in the exclusion of racial minorities from effective political representation, only began to wane in the 1960s. See *Baker* v. *Carr*, 369 U.S. 186 (1962) (malapportionment of voting districts may violate Equal Protection Clause). See also *Gray* v. *Sanders*, 372 U.S. 368 (1963) ('one man one vote' principle invalidates Georgia County unit system of primary elections in state-wide offices). See also *Wesberry* v. *Sanders*, 376 U.S. 1 (1964) (principle extended to congressional districts), and see *Reynolds* v. *Sims*, 377 U.S. 533 (1964) (principle challenges constitutionality of at least forty state legislatures).

55 *Beauharnais, supra* note 51 at 259–63.

56 Progressive resort to *Beauharnais* is meant to be legally *suasive*, not legally *obligatory*. Canadian courts are not bound to follow U.S. law.

57 The progenitor for the offence of 'hate propaganda' was a series of postwar historical studies of oppression and genocide. See Canada, The Special Committee on Hate Propaganda, *Report* (Ottawa: Queen's Printer 1966). The context for concluding that there was a compelling need for the law reflected concern with the oppressive conditions that still existed in the Canada of the 1950s. Human rights developments since then – particularly the promulgation of human rights codes, housing and employment acts, and expanded opportunities for public vocalization of minority rights – have dramatically changed the social and political landscape but not the legal permanence or ubiquitous moral presence of hate speech law, in the battle for minority rights in Canada. See Canada, Law Reform Commission of Canada, *Hate Propaganda Working Paper* 50 (Ottawa: Law Reform Commission of Canada, 1986). Current thinking pushing for hate censorship expansion relies heavily for its justification, as we saw, on discounting noticeably improved social and political conditions. Such thinking is

possible when the expectations from change grow faster than the pace of change itself.

58 *Boucher* v. *The King*, [1951] S.C.R. 265.

59 J. Fleming, *The Law of Torts* (Sidney: Law Book Co., 1977) at 536.

60 See also *Roncarelli* v. *Duplessis* [1959] S.C.R. 95, and *Switzman* v. *Elbling* [1957] S.C.R. 285.

61 See S. Braun, 'Freedom of Expression v. Seditious Libel: Towards a Framework of Analysis' (1985) 22 Comp. Jur. Rev. 87. The law of seditious libel now expressly requires that the threat be specifically directed to the forcible overthrow of government. See Criminal Code, R.S.C., 1985, c. C-46, s. 59 (2).

62 Chapter 3, Part I, note 9 and accompanying text.

63 Observes Borovoy, 'I shudder to think of what would have happened to the Jehovah's Witnesses in the early 1950's if the anti-hate law had been enacted then.' See Borovoy, *supra* note 1 at 42.

64 See, for example, H. Skilling, 'Charter 77 and the Musical Underground' (1990) 22 Can. Slav. Papers 20.

65 See for example Article 206 (1) R.S.F.S. Criminal Code (1964) (as amended). See also, generally, H. Berman and J. Spindler, *Soviet Criminal Law and Procedure: The R.S.R.S.R. Codes* 2nd ed. (Cambridge, Mass.: Harvard University Press, 1972) at 77–81, and S. Butler (rev. ed) 4 Collected Legislation of the U.S.S.R., (Fundamental Principles) Part VII, s. 8, 19–20; Article 32 (Socialist Legal Consciousness); Article 1 (Tasks of Soviet Criminal Legislation); Article 7 (3–5) (Concept of Crime and Crimes against the State); Article 6 (Wrecking); Article 7 (Anti-Soviet Agitation and Propaganda).

8 Alternative Juridical Balances and Balancing Juridical Alternatives

1 The four do not exhaust all juridical balancing possibilities. They represent a politico-legal spectrum within and along which most possibilities, practised, proposed, or contemplated, would fall.

2 It is neither necessary, nor particularly useful, for me to address all possible issues raised by each option. I will focus *only* on the *distinguishing* features of each balancing scenario. The phrase 'alternative juridical balances' in the title of this chapter refers to my discussion of the comparative merits of the four balancing alternatives. The words 'balancing juridical alternatives' refers to my discussion of the stability of each balance – the comparative difficulties (slippery slope) of holding the line where initially drawn.

3 My wording corrects for some 'errors' in the 'False News' section of the Criminal Code, struck down in *R. v. Zundel* [1992] 2 S.C.R. 731. That section made the mistake of proscribing mere 'mischief or injury to the public interest' and failed to specify a category of 'identifiable' groups as the victims through which such injury was feared. It therefore risked trespass on 'legitimate' speech by its very words of insignificance ('mischief') and victim/society indeterminacy ('or injury to a public interest').

4 Sometimes referred to as proscription in the 'air' in American jurisprudence, the doctrine would allow the state to legislate against words, not just their effects. Where it is held that the gravity of the threatened harm is great and possibly irreparable but that evidence of it cannot feasibly be established before its occurrence, the harm may be assumed from the mere fact of expression itself.

5 The lower the *mens rea* threshold for conviction, the greater the risk of chill. If, for example, careless, not just intentional or reckless, speech is caught, fewer of the public will risk speaking. See S. Braun, 'Social and Racial Hatred and Freedom of Expression in a Democratic Society: Friends or Foes?' (1988) 11 Dal. L.J. 471 at 499. If the state sets the *mens rea* threshold for conviction too low, the court might well strike down the legislation for this reason. However, this would be mere judicial 'technical tinkering' with the dilemma of hate law. A *mens rea* focus fails to address the broader political, social, and pragmatic problems of repression of this kind of expression. See especially chapter 2, Part II (2), 'Meaningful Public Discourse, Social Truth, and Social Division.' For the purposes of this option, assume that the threshold is not set too low and the legislation is upheld. If hate law cannot be convincingly defended even in a *less* rights-invasive version of *mens rea*, it most assuredly cannot be defended in a *more* rights-invasive version.

6 By 'for good,' I intend both meanings, *better* and *final.*

7 By 'work,' I mean function, not success.

8 For elaboration on the discussion following see especially chapter 6.

9 See chapters 2, 3, and 6.

10 See chapters 2, Part III at 57; 5, Part I (4) at 133; and 6, Part II (4) and III at 160, 165.

11 See, generally, J. Agresto, *The Supreme Court and Constitutional Democracy* (Ithaca, N.Y.: Cornell University Press, 1984).

12 Illustrating the struggle for justiciability in more obvious political contexts, see *Operation Dismantle Inc. v. R.* [1985] 1 S.C.R. 441 (on maintaining a distinction between law and politics).

13 See chapters 2 and 4.

14 As, for example, Palestinian Canadians would argue should comparisons equating the Jewish state's treatment of Palestinians with the Nazi treatment of Jews be singled out for proscription. Illustrating the point from the other side, from a non-legal silencing context, see Carolyn Blackman, 'Bookstore Says No to Jewish Buttons,' *Canadian Jewish News* (3 October 2002), 18. Toronto Women's Bookstore carried buttons reading 'End the Occupation' (designed with the Palestinian flag containing the logo WAO, for Women Against the Occupation, below the flag) but refused an offer from the Canadian Jewish Congress, Ontario Region, to carry buttons reading, 'Stop the Homicide Bombings.'

15 See chapter 3, especially Part IV (mushroom thesis) at 78.

16 See chapter 4.

17 See chapter 4, Part II, 'Unwrapping the Politics of Victimhood,' at 98. See also 'CCRA Seizes Pro-Israel Literature,' *Canadian Jewish News* (10 October 2002), 34.

18 The gist of this language is comparable to the first, and most resorted to, branch of hate propaganda law, which punishes '[e]veryone who, by communicating statements, other than in private conversation, wilfully promotes hatred against any identifiable group.' *Criminal Code*, R.S.C., 1985, c. C-46, s. 319(2), (hereafter Criminal Code).

19 See chapter 4, Part III: 'The Politics of Fixing Social Right,' (1) Competence, and (3) Accountability, at 107, 110

20 See chapter 4, Part II, 'Unwrapping the Politics of Victimhood,' at 98.

21 See also chapters 5 and 6.

22 On judicial policy making, see C. Manfredi, *Judicial Power and the Charter: Canada and the Paradox of Liberal Constitutionalism* (Toronto: McClelland and Stewart, 1993).

23 For scepticism that courts have the wisdom to engage in 'social engineering,' see R. Knopff, *Human Rights and Social Technology: The New War on Discrimination* (Ottawa: Carleton University Press, 1990).

24 R. Knopff and F.L. Morton, *Charter Politics* (Scarborough, Ont.: Nelson, 1992).

25 This language, reflects a much less common mode of promotion of hatred in Canada. It is, except in one very important respect, comparable to the language of the first branch of hate propaganda law, which punishes '[e]veryone who by communicating statements in any public place, incites hatred against any identifiable group where such incitement is likely to lead to a breach of the peace.' Criminal Code, s. 319(1). I correct for the words 'breach of the peace' by leaving them out. Those words can allow for abridgment of speech for relatively minor injuries to society. For the

purposes of this option, assume that the courts find that the statute proscribes only serious, not trivial, injury. I prefer an understanding that is easier for proponents of censorship to defend; for if they cannot defend the easier claims, they can hardly defend the more difficult ones.

26 I am here adapting, *mutatis mutandis,* the words of the U.S. Supreme Court, formulated in the context of obscenity censorship in *Roth* v. *U.S.,* 354 U.S. 476 (1957).

27 See discussion, D. Dyzenhaus, 'Pornography and Public Reason' (1994) 9 Can J. of Jurisprudence 261.

28 C. MacKinnon, *Only Words* (Cambridge, Mass.: Harvard University Press, 1996) at 17.

29 See *Gitlow* v. *New York,* 268 U.S. 625 (1925) at 665 and 669–70. See also S. Braun, 'Freedom of Expression v. Seditious Libel: Towards a Framework of Analysis' (1985) 22 Comp. Jur. Rev. 87 at 90–7.

30 See chapter 2, Part I. See also M. Walzer, 'Philosophy and Democracy' (1981) 9 Political Theory 379 at 384.

31 See chapter 7, Part I, 'Manner and Form Regulation,' at 177.

32 *Cohen* v. *California,* 403 U.S. 15 (1971).

33 Ibid. at 26.

34 One of the best examples, historically, of well-intentioned change gone sour everywhere is Marxism itself. Recall the revolutionary cry 'Workers of the world unite, you have nothing to lose but your chains!'

35 For the root of 'emotive,' see *Webster's New World Dictionary* 4th ed. (New York: Warner Books, 1990).

36 A. Borovoy, *The New Anti-liberals* (Toronto: Canadian Scholars Press, 1999) at 162.

37 Ibid. at 164.

38 Justice Brandeis's classic test, articulated in *Whitney* v. *California,* 274 U.S. 357 (1927) at 377. It was first adumbrated by Mr Justice Holmes in *Schenck* v. *U.S.,* 249 U.S. 47 (1919) at 52.

39 Though even for fledgling democracies, procuring a more democratic future with hate silencing, much less securing it, is highly problematic. See chapter 3, especially Part IV, at 78.

40 I say 'as an ordinary feature' because hate censorship is not intended as a temporary or emergency measure, dependent on extraordinary times or exceptional circumstances. See discussion chapter 3, Part IV (the mushroom thesis) at 78.

41 *Gitlow, supra* note 29 at 673.

42 See P. Lungen, 'Oberlander's Lawyer Subject of Law Society Complaint,' *Canadian Jewish News* (23 March 2000), 6. These are hardly the type of

issues involved in the prevention of street hooliganism (fighting words) or public alarms (falsely yelling fire in a crowded theatre).

43 See T. Mayton, 'Seditious Libel and the Lost Guarantee of Freedom of Expression' (1984) 84 Columbia. L. Rev. 91 at 112.

44 In August 1997, a group of skinheads were charged and several later convicted of inciting hatred for parading with offensive signs reading 'Honk if you hate Gypsies' in front of the Lido Motel in Ottawa where Gypsies had been temporarily put up by immigration authorities. See 'Skinheads Plead Guilty,' *Canadian Jewish News* (29 April 1999), 6. Under the hate propaganda provisions of the Criminal Code, 'statements includes words spoken or written or recorded electronically or electromagnetically or otherwise and gestures, signs or other visible representations.' Canadian Criminal Code ss. 319 (7).

45 The club owner was tried and convicted in Germany on 4 September 2002 for this reason. He defended, unsuccessfully, that he didn't want to host political events. See 'Owner Convicted,' *Canadian Jewish News* (19 September 2002), 2.

46 There seems to be a worldwide trend towards 'judicial top dog' in both policy and message making. See N. Tate and T. Vallinder, eds, *The Global Expansion of Judicial Power* (New York: New York University Press, 1995). See also M. Volcansek, ed., *Judicial Politics and Policymaking in Western Europe* (London: Frank Cass and Co., 1992).

47 A 'sunset' clause requires the state to redemonstrate the exceptional need for the law after a set period of time. Monitoring promotes political visibility, public transparency, and accountability.

48 See P. Peppin, 'Emergency Legislation and Rights in Canada: The War Measures Act and Civil Liberties' (1993) 18 Queen's L.J. 129.

49 An inchoate offence, conspiracy's gravamen is the *agreement* to commit an illegal act. See R. Cross and A. Ashworth, *The English Sentencing System* (London: Butterworth, 1981) at 156–7.

50 Under the *Canadian Charter of Rights and Freedoms*, Part I, of the *Canada Act, 1982*, being schedule B to the *Canada Act 1982* (U.K.) 1982, c. 11 (hereafter Charter), for example, no provision appears to be immune from amendment by a sufficiently large majority. And, even if it were, no court of law or its judges could stop a sufficiently large majority from having its way. Hitler's rise to power would suggest that, in some social and political circumstances, this may be true even in the case of only a determined plurality.

51 Examples of 'acting' insurrection or terrorism, properly falling within the purview of 'force of arms' and criminal (but not hate propaganda) law

might include activities such as *fund-raising* and *procurement*, not just planning and preparing terrorist acts. See Bill C-36, the federal government's anti-terrorism bill, addressing the 'money trail.' On international terrorism, the Canadian connection and the role of the Canadian Security Intelligence Service (CSIS) following the terrorist attacks on the World Trade Center in New York, see R. Csillag, 'The Canadian Connection,' *Canadian Jewish News* (20 September 2001), 4.

52 Consider two 'incendiary' websites in Canada operated by Islamic terrorist groups, 'which openly plan, execute and celebrate the murder of Jews in Israel and abroad.' Should they be shut down by Canada's security agencies for subverting Canadian 'public values founded on principles' that 'recognize the supremacy of God' and loyalty to 'equality, democracy and the rule of law' – even if no terrorist acts are actually planned, executed, or even counselled by the site in Canada? See 'A Matter of Obligation,' *Canadian Jewish News* (23 August 2001), 8. See also 'Web Sites Praising "Jihad" Worry Jewish Groups: Message Board Spreads "Vicious Anti-Semitic Material,"' *Canadian Jewish News*, (23 August 2001), 3. Reporting on the Montreal registered *www.Islamway.com*, '[b]oth BBC and Canadian Jewish Congress say the site itself [discussion board with postings that glorify holy war and describe Jews as treacherous and enemies of Islam] does not incite hatred or violence against Jews.' But, said CJC, Ontario Region's Len Rudner, 'We find it offensive that discussion so wild and intemperate is allowed.' The other site, *www.qudscall.com*, is more problematic, possibly crossing the line between at-large public appeals and conspiratorial or other illegal action in furtherance of the cause. It not only suggests a public call to arms ('our struggle with the sons of Israel in Palestine is on civilization, ideology, history and existence') and glorifies suicide bombers. It also calls for attacks on Jewish and American targets and actively solicits donations 'for the military Jihad.'

53 *Gitlow, supra* note 29 at 673. (Holmes, of course, was referring specifically to Marxist calls for a bloody revolution like the one in the Soviet Union, and installation of a proletariat dictatorship in the United States.) Query, therefore, the relevance, in themselves, of a terrorist's 'ideological, political or religious' views. See definition section, Bill C-36, the government's proposed anti-terrorism bill.

54 But it can, in the long run, make it more likely, for all the reasons discussed in this book.

55 'War Measures'-type acts are intended as *temporary* measures to meet *transitory* threats, not permanent ones. The problem is not with the principle behind such acts, but with the scope of the language and the

justification for their political invocation, as in 1970. This 'constitutional dictatorship,' or Canada's 'other constitution,' as Smiley called it, was used by then Prime Minister Trudeau to suspend the most fundamental rights and liberties of *all* Canadians across the country to answer a relatively impotent and geographically confined threat to public security posed by the FLQ terrorist group operating in the province of Quebec. See D. Smiley, *Canada in Question: Federalism in the Eighties* 3rd ed. (Toronto: McGraw-Hill Ryerson, 1980) at 49.

The circumstances of its invocation would not have satisfied the test of extraordinary circumstances laid out by me for abridgment of political communication here. Not only was the threat *internal*, but less rights-invasive measures would have been more than adequate to meet it. In fact, the kidnapping of British trade commissioner James Cross and the kidnapping-murder of Quebec cabinet minister Pierre Laporte caused widespread public disgust. *Wholesale* suspension of fundamental civil liberties of *all* Canadians was disproportionate to the legitimate purposes of public and national security. It was more designed to make Trudeau's political *point* than it was needed by the country to meet the threat. See I. Peritz, 'October Crisis Hit Unknowns the Hardest: Majority Detained by War Measures Act Were Street Activists, Students, Intellectuals,' *Globe and Mail* (16 October 2000), A3.

56 A series of tests should be employed to prevent this. Does the danger of harm stem from a fear that the general public will be converted to the cause of the speakers? Or does it stem from a conspiracy or other threat to commit illegal acts? If the latter, criminal laws against illegal threats, attempts, and conspiracies to commit illegal acts are ordinarily available and appropriate to deal with the danger. If the former, a further question needs be asked. Are the circumstances sufficiently extraordinary to justify turning an otherwise fundamental public right to political communication into an irreparable threat to the life and well-being of the polity? It is very doubtful that this last test would have been satisfied in the following example. Following the terrorist attacks on the World Trade Center in New York, one thousand neo-Nazis took to the streets in Berlin to publicly celebrate and propagandize the attacks. 'In banners and speeches, members of the far-right National Democratic Party called the attacks against the United States a justified response to American policies, and protested Germany's support for a war on terrorism.' See 'Neo-Nazis Celebrate Sept. 11 Attacks,' *Canadian Jewish News* (18 October 2001), 2.

57 Consider the White House request, following the attack on the World Trade Center and the American military response against Afghanistan, that

the media refrain from running in full the statements of Osama bin Laden, allegedly for fear of hidden messages designed to trigger terrorist acts. But other statements suggested that the administration was more concerned that a full airing of bin Laden's reasons for Islamic fundamentalists' hatred of the United States (e.g., U.S. support of Israel) would garner public sympathy for his political cause. It is most doubtful that the criteria of extraordinary circumstances had been met that would have justified the White House request based on the latter reason. See 'White House Seeks to Limit Transcripts,' *New York Times* (12 October 2001), B7.

58 Even legitimate trespass on discourse on public matters for fear of divisive content must not be more intrusive than is necessary to meet the externally conditioned threat. In some cases, a curfew may suffice. In others, a blanket restriction may be necessary. It all depends on the particular threat and the specific circumstances. The court ought not to countenance a *carte blanche* right to arrest, detain, or interrogate people as a matter of course.

59 I am unaware of any *Canadian* community that would currently fit this profile. A community that might have is a Jewish community, numbering just 200, in the Russian village of Borovichi, a town of 90,000 people. Rising anti-Semitic speech daily fanned the flames of neo-Nazi harassment and attacks against this tiny community. See L. Krichevsky, 'Russian Court Bans Moscow Neo-Nazis Group,' *Canadian Jewish News* (29 April 1999), 34.

9 Alternative Measures: Towards a Less Self-intrusive Balance

1 By 'alternative' to hate censorship, I mean any peaceful measure aimed to promote one or more of hate censorship theorists' goals (public safety, political stability, community solidarity, tolerance, diversity, equality, and democracy) that does not, on pain of legal sanction, abridge contentious public discourse on matters of state and society for fear of public offence or conversion (proselytization) to the cause of the speaker.

2 Catherine A. MacKinnon, *Only Words* (Cambridge, Mass.: Harvard University Press, 1996), 103.

3 For example, my thesis is not inconsistent with measures reducing media concentration where, on balance, the 'net' effect would be to enlarge rather than restrict discourse. Much has been written elsewhere on this, so I will not discuss it here. See, for example, B. Bagdikian, *The Media Monopoly*, 4th ed. (Boston: Beacon Press, 1992).

4 See, generally, Norman Penner, *From Protest to Power: Social Democracy in Canada, 1900 – Present* (Toronto: James Lorimer and Co, 1992).

5 See A. Alan Borovoy, *The New Anti-liberals* (Toronto: Canadian Scholars' Press, 1999), 3–7.

6 Following recognition by the Supreme Court of Canada of the entitlement of same-sex couples to social benefits in *M.* v. *H.*, the federal government responded with Bill C-23, which is expected to amend sixty-eight federal statutes to extend benefits to same-sex couples. 'The past year may well come to be regarded as a watershed in the recognition of [gay and lesbian] rights,' said Michelle Falardeau-Ramsay of the Canadian Human Rights Commission. Reported in *Canadian Jewish News* (6 April 2000), 17.

7 Early labour codes governing hours, wages, and conditions of work followed sometimes violent expressions of social discontent because peaceful expressions were often legally (and sometimes illegally) denied – hardly an argument for more censorship.

8 Who can forget those egg or manure protests? See 'Farmers Make Point in Street Procession,' *The Liberal* (28 January 2001), 3. See also J. Strict, *The Economics of Government Regulation* (Toronto: Thompson Educational Publishing 1993).

9 From publicizing their plight, to rent control and building safety codes, to protecting the food supply from contamination and the public from disease. See, for example, *Canadian General Standards Board, Standards* 32-GP-110M and 32-237M (reprinted in K. Archer, et al., *Parameters of Power* [Toronto: Nelson Canada, 1995], 274; describing how five accredited standards-writing organizations submit their detailed recommendations on food labelling and handling and safety regulations to the Standards Council of Canada). See also 'Tent City Slated for Forced Eviction,' *Sunday Star* (26 November 2000), 1, 4.

10 See also chapter 3, Part III (1) 'Visible Exclusion,' at 73. Product liability laws have gone from *caveat emptor* to almost strict seller liability, dramatically rebalancing the inequality of bargaining power under the common law of torts. See Dean F. Edgell, *Product Liability Law in Canada* (Toronto: Butterworth, 2000) (includes discussion of liability in negligence and contract, regulatory standards, and class-action lawsuits).

11 *Constitution Act, 1982*, Part I, *Canadian Charter of Rights and Freedoms*, ss 15(1) and (2) (hereafter Charter).

12 Ibid. s. 27.

13 Native culture is now official Canadian currency (see the 1999 Canadian two-dollar coin with a Native scene and the word 'Nunavut' boldly inscribed). Natives now also have their own separate Nunavut Court of Justice. See Canadian Criminal Code, R.S.C., 1985, c. C-46, Part XIX.1, ss 573-573.2 (3).

14 Discussed in Part II, below.

15 See Nova Scotia, Royal Commission on the Donald Marshall, Jr, Prosecution, *Report* (Halifax: McCurdy's Printing and Typesetting, December 1989); Canada, Royal Commission on Aboriginal Peoples, *Bridging the Cultural Divide: A Report on Aboriginal People and Criminal Justice in Canada* (Ottawa: Minister of Supply and Services, 1996).

16 See Canada, National Council of Welfare, *Another Look at Welfare Reform: Report by the National Council of Welfare* (Canada): Minister of Public Works and Government Services (1997).

17 As the documentation of progressive thinkers itself shows, for example, the federal government initially failed to exempt health care in NAFTA. But public pressure, led by the Canadian Health Coalition, forced Ottawa's hand to secure an agreement that 'considerably increased the ability of provincial governments to protect health and social services.' See Stephen McBride and John Shields, *Dismantling a Nation* (Halifax: Fernwood Publishing, 1997) at 87.

18 'Social progress' has been more 'linear' than 'pure' economic advancement has been (see, e.g., the fate of pay-equity legislation in Ontario under the Mike Harris government). None the less, 1999 was also the year when an approximately $3.5-billion pay-equity settlement was reached by the Treasury Board and the Public Service Alliance of Canada (PSAC), affecting 230,0000 former and current federal government employees, 85 per cent of whom were women. See Guy Dixon and Bruce Little, 'Pay Equity Settlement Could Enhance Economy,' *Globe and Mail* (11 September 2000), B1.

19 See Keith G. Banting, *The Welfare State and Canadian Federalism* (Kingston: McGill-Queen's University Press, 1982), 171.

20 Or worse. See generally Stephen McBride and John Shields, *supra*, note 17.

21 See Jane Pulkingham and Gordon Ternowetsky, eds, *Remaking Canadian Social Policy (Social Security in the Late 1990's)* (Halifax: Fernwood Publishing, 1996). See also Hans Werner Sinn, 'Social Insurance, Incentives, and Risk Taking,' *Working Paper Series, No. 5335*, National Bureau of Economic Research (Cambridge, Mass.: Nov. 1995), 29–31.

22 See John Wiseman, 'National Social Policy in an Age of Global Power: Lessons from Canada and Australia,' in Pulkingham and Ternowetsky eds, *supra* note 21, 114. See also Gordon Betcherman, 'Globalization and Labour Markets,' in Robert Boyer and Daniel Drache, eds, *States against Markets: The Limits of Globalization* (New York: Routledge, 1996), 256–69.

23 See chapter 6, Part II (3) and Part IV (1) at 155, 170.

24 See Gay Abbate, 'Mounties Assailed for APEC Bungling,' *Globe and Mail* (7 August 2001), 1, 4. Abbate details the report of former judge Ted Hughes who found, *inter alia*, that the police had violated left-wing protesters' rights during demonstrations that turned violent at the 1997 APEC summit in Vancouver. Illustrating the narrow mind-set of retrenchment and reaction, see Michael Elliott, 'Death in Genoa: Mayhem Rules the Streets as the G-8 Leaders Meet. Why Such Violent Protests?' *Time* (30 July 2001), 17. 'Ask national police forces ... they will tell you they are baffled. The world today, after all, is not that of 1968. No young Americans are about to be drafted to fight in an unpopular war; no young Europeans have their rights and pleasures routinely stifled by a jackbooted state.'

25 'For good' here is used in both censorial senses, 'better' and 'final.'

26 See chapter 1, Part II, especially 19–20.

27 See chapters 2, 3, and 4.

28 See especially chapter 6.

29 See chapters 5 and 6.

30 See *Criminal Code*, R.S.C. 1985, c. C-46 (hereafter Criminal Code), s. 718.2 (a) (i) (sentencing) and s. 430 (4) (wilful damage to religious property). Most likely offences are ss 264–9 (assault); s. 430 (mischief); ss 63–9 (unlawful assemblies and riots); s. 433 (arson); s. 231 (murder); part III (firearms and other weapons offences).

31 See for example *Crown Liability and Proceedings Act*, R.S.C., 1985, c. 50, ss 16–19 ('wiretapping').

32 Criminal Code, R.S.C., c. C-46, part XIII (Attempts, Conspiracies, Accessories).

33 Paul Lungen, 'SWC Helping to Fight Hate on the Internet,' *Canadian Jewish News* (17 June 1999), 3.

34 Provincial and the federal human rights acts are the anchors. See, for example, Paul Lungen, 'Report Documents Human Rights Progress in 1998,' *Canadian Jewish News* (31 March 1999), 5 (excerpts from report of the Canadian Human Rights Commission).

35 On the relative merits of the penalty versus compliance models of law enforcement generally, see Keith Hawkins and John Thomas, eds, *Enforcing Regulation* (Boston: Kluwer, 1984).

36 See 'Headgear Policy Reversed,' *Canadian Jewish News* (18 March 1999), 2.

37 See, for example, Morris Rosenberg, Deputy Attorney General of Canada, responding favourably to calls to strengthen the Criminal Code provisions against both acts and expressions of hate. See Sheldon Kirshner, 'Deputy Minister Rosenburg Dispenses Justice,' *Canadian Jewish News* (28 September 2000), 13.

38 Defeat is not the same as self-defeat. A law that does not work as intended in one set of circumstances is defeating. A law that cannot work as intended in any circumstances is self-defeating.

39 The law may be overbroad or improperly enacted, may violate other rights, et cetera.

40 See also Elizabeth Shilton and Karen Schucher, *Education Labour and Employment Law in Ontario* 2d ed. (Aurora, Ont.: Canada Law Book Inc., 2000) (contains an extensive discussion of the recently enacted Education Quality Improvement Act, 1997).

41 See chapter 6, Part II (4) ('intellectualization' of prejudice) at 163–4.

42 General disapproval of gay teachers, for example, can mask a larger political agenda than simply the educational one of good teaching in reading, writing, and arithmetic. This illustrates political correctness, clothed in competency review, from the right-wing side of discursive public conflict.

43 There was no shortage of voices suggesting that his work fell well below acceptable standards of scholarship. But no serious challenge advocating dismissal for academic incompetence was ever mounted. Moves to prosecute him under the publicly purposed hate propaganda provisions of the Criminal Code and actions taken against him under the equally publicly purposed antidiscrimination provisions of the *Ontario Human Rights Act* left no doubt as to his offence. It was the public offensiveness of his ideas and the fear of proselytization to a racist cause that concerned his outraged community rather than collegial concern for scholarly standards or teaching performance.

44 See 'Date Rape Comments Cause Campus Furor,' *Globe and Mail* (9 November 1993), A6, and discussion, chapter 5, Part I (1) (ii) at 127. Categorizing the distinction, see J. Furedy, 'Academic Freedom, Opinions and Acts: The Voltaire–Mill Perspective Applied to Current Canadian Cases' (1995) 44 U.N.B.L.J. at 131–4.

45 They may, in some cases, however, prevent speaking out publicly for other performance-related reasons, as is the case with judges, for example. In these cases, good performance is a function of public confidence in the integrity and ability of the performer.

46 A wealth of formal (institutionalized) as well as informal awareness-raising mechanisms exist that can promote this spillover effect. For example, the Canadian Jewish Congress, Ontario Region, has 'offered its assistance [its 'bias and sensitivity training program, "Understanding our Differences"'] to the Ontario Provincial Police following recent allegations of pornogra-

phy and racist joke trading by OPP employees.' See 'Offers Help to OPP,' *Canadian Jewish News* (26 July 2001), 2.

47 S. Kirshner, 'Yad Vashem Set to Undergo Major Expansion,' *Canadian Jewish News* (18 November 1999), 5.

48 See Leila Speisman, 'Assimilation Threatens Jewry: Chief Rabbi [Israel],' *Canadian Jewish News* (21 June 2001), 1, 19 and chapter 3: Part II.

49 See, generally, M. Walzer, M. Lorberbaum, Y. Lorberbaum, and N.J. Zohar, eds, *The Jewish Political Tradition (Volume 1: Authority)* (New Haven: Yale University Press, 2001).

50 One of the more morbid examples, from the Jewish community, is the case of Malvern Jacobs, a Jew by birth, who later became an ordained Christian minister and dean of the Department of Jewish Studies at Canada Christian College. Jacobs was denied burial in a Jewish cemetery in a surreal stand-off that saw his funeral procession stopped and his coffin turned back from the cemetery gates. See Ben Rose, 'Cemetery Bars Burial of Christian Minister,' *Canadian Jewish News* (8 July 1999), 3. See also Francis Kraft, 'Intermarriage May Preclude Membership at Shul,' *Canadian Jewish News* (12 September 2002), 5; and see *supra* note 49, (Volume II: Membership).

51 See chapter 3, Part II, at 66.

52 See 'UN Slams Ontario,' *Canadian Jewish News* (13 July 2000), 2.

53 A. Borovoy, *supra* note 5 at 36.

54 Ibid, 37.

55 See Erin Anderson: 'Class Actions Expected to Grow with Residential School Claims: Group Suits Make It Easier for the "Little Guy" to Take on Government,' *Globe and Mail* (10 July 1999), A7. See also Lindsey Arkley, 'Wounded Society Needs Tribunal: Residential School Abuse – Law Commission President Favors Australian Proposal for Reparations,' *National Post* (17 August 2001), 1, 8.

56 See Michael Mandel, *The Charter of Rights and the Legalization of Politics in Canada* (Toronto: Thompson Educational Publishing, 1994).

57 Canadian Charter of Rights and Freedoms, *supra* note 11, s. 33.

58 Consider Ron and Natalie Pollack, Winnipeg brother and sister, 'famous locally for launching lawsuits and human rights complaints.' Recent politico-legal activity finds them 'seeking unspecified damages from the University of Manitoba and its campus radio station CJUM' on the grounds that 'programmers discriminated against them by rejecting their proposal for a Jewish program, while allowing a Christian broadcast.' Reported in 'Siblings Sue,' *Canadian Jewish News* (19 April 2001), 2.

59 See chapter 1, Part III, at 23.

60 See Alan Cairns, *Reconfigurations: Canadian Citizenship and Constitutional Change* (Toronto: McClelland and Stewart, 1995).

61 I. Greene et al., *Final Appeal* (Toronto: James Lorimer and Co., 1998), 30, 33–4.

62 Ibid. at 30.

63 See Gordon Bale, 'W.R. Lederman and the Citation of Legal Periodicals by the Supreme Court of Canada' (1994) 19 Queen's L.J. 36.

64 See, for example, A Petter, 'The Politics of the *Charter*' (1986) Sup. Ct. L. Rev. 473. J. Fudge, 'The Public/Private Distinction: The Possibilities and the Limits to the Use of *Charter* Litigation to Further Feminist Struggles,' (1987) 25 Osgoode Hall L.J. 485. Multidisciplinary journals, such as the *Journal of Law and Social Policy*, have been proliferating in North America, and even 'traditional' legal journals now devote more space to social issues.

65 An advertisement soliciting applications for a judicial vacancy reads 'The Judiciary of the Ontario Court of Justice should reasonably reflect the diversity of the population its serves.' See Law Society of Upper Canada, *Careers: Ontario Reports* (11 October 2002) at lxvi.

66 See, for example, P. Brest, 'Interpretation and Interest' (1982) 34 Stan. L. Rev. 765. See also Joel Bakan, 'Partiality and Legitimacy in Constitutional Theory' (1989) 4 Legal Theory Workshop Series.

67 See Patrick Monahan, *Politics and the Constitution* (Toronto: Carswell, 1987), 51–72.

68 It was given 'teeth' with the promise of picketing of the giant chain's New York City establishments. See Toronto Star Wire Service, 'Burger King Faces Boycott,' *Toronto Star* (11 October 2000), E2.

69 See Paul Lungen, 'Canada 3000 Grounds Charge for Special Meals,' *Canadian Jewish News* (1 July 1999), 5. 'Congress [CJC] had been in the forefront of a broad-based campaign by community and religious organizations that called on Canada 3000 to rescind the special meal charge [$10 extra for kosher, vegetarian, diabetic, halal, and other special meals]. The coalition included Seventh Day Adventists and the Vietnamese Buddhist Association, whose members require vegetarian meals, as well as the Canadian Islamic Congress ... "It is a heartening sign that when groups work together in a principled cause, the ultimate result is success [said Manuel Prutschi]."'

70 'If at any point during his visit he offends Canadian legislation, he should be removed summarily,' CJC stated. See Ron Csillag, 'Coming or Not, Community Girds for Zhirinovsky,' *Canadian Jewish News* (28 September 2000), 5.

71 See 'Zundel Windfall,' *Canadian Jewish News* (21 December 2000), 2
   (reporting, *inter alia*, that the Supreme Court has ruled that the Security
   Intelligence Review Committee can review a Canadian Security Intelligence
   Service recommendation that Ernst Zundel be refused citizenship). Zundel
   entered Canada in 1958 and first applied for citizenship in 1993.

72 Paul Lungen, 'Angry Readers, Advertisers Boycott the *Star*,' *Canadian Jewish
   News* (23 November 2000), 3. See also Paul Lungen, 'Toronto *Star* under
   Fire for Mideast Ad,' *Canadian Jewish News* (21 December 2000), 5 (report-
   ing the 'outrage' of Canadian Islamic Congress at what appeared to be the
   Star's decision to 'cave in' and 'censor' one of their 'anti-Semitic' advertisements. The *Star* quickly backtracked, citing an 'administrative foul up' and
   offered to run the advertisement at a discount). See also P. Lungen,
   'Health Group Pulls Anti-Semitic Books – Again,' *Canadian Jewish News* (16
   January 2003), 5 (reporting interrupted success in CJC's public pressure on
   the Consumer Health Organization of Canada to have works such as those
   of Eustace Mullins, David Icke, and William Cooper pulled from its sales
   list on the Web).

73 See David Lazarus, 'Quebec Scholar Decries Academic Boycott of Israel,'
   Canadian Jewish News (19 September 2002), 23 (reporting growing voices
   against those joining a boycott of Jewish scholars).

74 See chapter 6, Part IV, at 169.

75 See chapter 6, Part II (4) at 160, 165, and Part III.

76 See chapter 2, Part II (4) at 54, and chapter 4, Part III (3) at 110.

77 See chapter 5, Part I (1) and (2) at 123, 131.

78 See 'Concert Cancelled,' *Canadian Jewish News* (13 July 2000), 2.

79 I say 'think as he speaks' to contrast with hate censorship, which promotes
   deceptive public posturing and public dishonesty. See chapter 2: Part II (2)
   and (4) and Part III, at 43, 54, 57; chapter 6, Part IV (2) at 172.

80 See Ronald G. Landes, 'Political Education and Political Socialization,' in
   Jon H. Pammett and Jean-Luc Pepin, eds, *Political Education in Canada*
   (Halifax: Institute for Research on Public Policy, 1988), 15–20; Richard E.
   Dawson, et al, *Political Socialization* 2nd ed. (Boston: Little, Brown, 1977).

81 Compare George Avis, ed., *The Making of the Soviet Citizen: Character Formation
   and Civic Training in Soviet Education* (London: Croom Helm, 1987).

82 Distinguishing between 'subject political culture' and 'participant political
   culture,' see Ronald G. Landes, *The Canadian Polity: A Comparative Introduction* 5th ed. (Scarborough, Ont.: Prentice Hall, 1998), 247.

83 And now also in a growing number of Eastern European (former Communist) countries such as Hungary and Poland.

84 S. Kirshner, *supra*, note 47.

85 Until recently, Zundel was self-employed in the United States in the hate propaganda publishing business (from where he sent his message of hate electronically into Canada). Zundel is now back in Canada (following the overstaying of his U.S. visa) and awaiting deportation proceedings back to his native Germany. Keegstra now repairs cars in Alberta. Prosecution made knowing these hatemongers, as they *truly* are more, not less, difficult. See chapter 6, Part I (1) at 144.

86 For, example, the march by Nazis through a Jewish neighbourhood in Skokie, Illinois. See *Collin* v. *Smith*, 578 F.2d 1197 (1978). In another example, in 1995, Jewish groups 'shadowed' Russian ultranationalist Vladimir Zhirinovsky, confronting him in protests everywhere he went on his visit to the United States. See Csillag, *supra* note 70.

87 Indirectly confronting discursive proxies, such as Steven Spielberg's filmed survivor testimonials, notwithstanding. See chapter 2, Part II (2).

88 Forms of proxy confrontation are becoming ever more creative as a substitute for living, interactive, contestation and refutation. See Anna Morgan, 'Artist Uses Pop Culture in Exhibit on Holocaust,' *Canadian Jewish News* (14 November 2002), 15. Morgan describes the work of pop artists who try to solicit a deeper meaning of the Holocaust by 'exchanging clear war lessons with conflicting messages.' The idea is to reach a better understanding of the event by 'getting closer to the source.' One video has Hitler speaking Hebrew, falsely saying he is 'deeply sorry.' Artists try to conflate 'cool cerebral strategies' with 'emotionally loaded subject matter.' Photos of Nazis as Hollywood stars and sculptures of Mengele as a handsome man 'are meant to shock the viewer and explore the paradox between appearance and reality.' On the problems with attempts to impart deeper meanings by substituting ever more subtle messaging forms for real-life real-time confrontation, see chapter 2: Part II (2) (note reference to Morton Weinfeld and accompanying discussion on problems of meaning atrophy and message overload) at 47–8.

89 See Myron Love, 'First Nations and Inuit Tour Israel,' *Canadian Jewish News* (14 November 2002), 1, 32.

90 As Moshe Ronen, CJC president, said, 'Study visits like these present an invaluable opportunity for discourse, exchange and learning that could set the stage for future joint activity between Canadian and Israeli universities.' See 'University Presidents Join Study Visit to Israel,' *Canadian Jewish News* (1 July 1999), 16.

91 See 'Order of Canada,' *Canadian Jewish News* (19 July 1999), 2.

92 See 'Ottawa to Honor Holocaust Survivors,' *Canadian Jewish News* (13 July 2000), 21.

93 See 'Cop Wins Human Rights Award: Bisson Ramdewar Helped Form Community Council,' *The Liberal* (2 April 2001), 7.

94 See 'Winning Programs,' *Canadian Jewish News* (15 November 2001), 2.

95 See 'The CJN Wins Award,' *Canadian Jewish News* (14 June 2001), 1.

96 See 'New Agents of Change (He Takes Back the Streets for Walking),' *Time* (18 June 2001), 50. A. Segal, 'Architect Communicates Lessons of Holocaust,' *Canadian Jewish News* (13 November 2003), 3.

97 On the centrality of 'honesty' and 'mutual respect' to a democratic society, see Ian Greene and David Shugarman, *Honest Politics: Seeking Integrity in Canadian Public Life* (Toronto: James Lorimer and Co., 1997).

98 On 'social capital,' see Robert Putnam, 'Bowling Alone: America's Declining Social Capital,' (1995) 61 Journal of Democracy 138.

99 See chapter 2, Part II (3) at 48.

100 See 'Name Change,' *Canadian Jewish News* (26 October 2000), 2.

101 See Ben Rose, 'Voices of Change Highlights Rights of Minorities to Kids,' *Canadian Jewish News* (1 June 2000), 25.

102 See photo feature, 'Black–Jewish Relations,' *Canadian Jewish News* (8 February 2000), 1, 6.

103 See Ben Rose 'Christian Service Resists "Forgetfulness" of Holocaust,' *Canadian Jewish News* (29 April 1999), 24.

104 See 'Holocaust Symposium,' *Canadian Jewish News* (1 July 1999), 2.

105 Bridging both intra and intercommunity divisions. See Frances Kraft, 'York U's JSK to Be Refurbished under Jewish Toronto Tomorrow,' *Canadian Jewish News* (22 June 2000), 19.

106 See chapter 8, Part III ('Incitement), especially 205–7.

107 See 'Interfaith Mission,' *Canadian Jewish News* (26 July 2001), 2.

108 Borovoy, *supra* note 5 at 37 (emphasis mine). See also Robin Williams, Jr, *Strangers Next Door: Ethnic Relations in American Communities* (Englewood Cliffs: Prentice-Hall, 1964). 'Out of hundreds of tabulations, there emerges the major finding that *in all the surveys in all communities and for all groups, majority and minorities, the greater the frequency of interaction, the lower the prevalence of ethnic prejudice*' (quoted in Borovoy).

109 See Ben Rose, 'Blacks and Jews Urged to Work Together,' *Canadian Jewish News* (21 December 2000), 7.

110 See Carolyn Blackman, 'Jewish and Aboriginal Leaders Meet,' *Canadian Jewish News* (16 January 2003), 3, 5. In a Native 'sentencing circle,' [also known as peace making circles] elders lead a process of 'restorative justice' where the purpose of punishment is to 'restore balance and harmony in a relationship.' In a 'healing circle,' the 'offender speaks directly with the victims,' which in this case 'could mean Holocaust survivors and Jewish leaders.' See Sarah Schmidt, 'Native Justice Proposed

for Ahenakew,' *National Post* (9 January 2002), at A1, A7. See also J. Rudin and D. Russell, *Native Alternative Dispute Resolution* (Toronto: Ontario Native Council on Justice, 1993), esp. 38–42.

111 See P. Lungen, 'Ahenakew Charged with Promoting Hate,' *Canadian Jewish News* (19 June 2003) at 3. Cutting off one's nose to spite one's face, perhaps?

112 Hence, growing concern over evidence of the declining U.S. Jewish population. See chapter 3, Part II, especially at 72.

113 Borovoy, *supra* note 5 at 37.

114 Ibid, 6.

115 Though, in the United States, at least, Afro-Americans are comparatively 'richer' than Jews in numbers.

116 See Robert Putnam, *Making Democracy Work* (Princeton: Princeton University Press, 1993), and chapter 5 at 124–7.

117 A most profound illustration of the latter has been the campaign to secure provincial funding for faith-based schools in Ontario, which saw the Islamic Society of North America join in common cause with the Jewish community. Reported in Ron Csillag, 'Missionaries Launch New Conversion Offensive,' *Canadian Jewish News* (14 December 2001), 14.

118 Following a massive media blitz, CCRA agreed to allow CMDA to keep its charitable status (despite a ruling by the Federal Court of Appeal sustaining CCRA's revocation because CMDA operations in Israel included the 'occupied territories.') See J. Arnold, 'Magen David Adom, CCRA Cut a Deal,' *Canadian Jewish News* (21 November 2002), 1, 40.

119 See D. Goldberg, 'Canada's Vote at the 57 UN General Assembly,' *Canadian Jewish News* (16 January 2003), at 9.

120 In the United States, the next battleground may be reparations for slavery. See Jack E. White, 'Dividing Line: An Impossible Dream,' *Time* (2 April 2001), 27.

121 Honesty, here, refers not to the truth of the content of the message but to the true feelings of the messenger in expressing them.

122 See chapters 1, 3, 4, 5, amd 6.

123 The endemic tendency of intolerant groups to fall victim to factionalism and internal splintering has been observed by leading advocates of hate censorship themselves. M. Prutschi, 'Organized Anti-Semitism in Canada,' (1985) 25 (1) *Orah* 9. 'They [hate groups] do not necessarily reflect popular sentiments about Jews nor the prevalent principles guiding mainstream Canada ... Canada's anti-Semitic groups in the post-war years have tended to be fragmented, and have held sway over very few people.'

Observing the same phenomenon in Germany, see S. Kirshner, 'Right-wing Extremists Torn by Disunity,' *Canadian Jewish News* (17 August 2000), 11.

124 See chapter 3, Part III (2) at 66.

125 See Jews for Judaism, *The Jewish Response to Missionaries: Counter-missionary Handbook* (Toronto: 1996), 5.

126 See *Canadian Jewish News* (13 July 2000), 14.

127 See 'Chinese Business Awards Accepting Nominations,' *The Liberal* (28 November 2000), 7.

128 See Herbert McCann, 'Poet Was First Black Woman to Win a Pulitzer,' *Globe and Mail* (5 December 2000), R10.

129 See Carolyn Blackman 'Jewish Book Fair Caters to All Ages,' *Canadian Jewish News* (24 October 2002), 6.

130 See Cynthia Gasner, 'Music of Holocaust Victims to Come to Life,' *Canadian Jewish News* (31 May 2001), 41.

131 Bill Gladstone, 'New Edition for Handy Jewish Guide,' *Canadian Jewish News* (15 June 2000), 36.

132 See Jack White, 'Radical Equations,' *Time* (18 June 2001), 56–7.

133 See 'Quebec Wins,' *Canadian Jewish News* (1 July 1999), 2.

134 See, generally, Andrew J. Shapiro, 'The Control Revolution: How New Technology Is Putting Individuals in Charge and Changing the World We Know,' (1999) Public Affairs, 180–93. See also, generally, Lawrence Lessig, 'Innovation, Regulation, and the Internet,' *The American Prospect* 11 (27 March–10 April 2000), 1–6 (arguing that the proper role of government in cyberspace is not to try to regulate message content but to prohibit big business and big money from doing so – as media conglomerates have done in 'meatspace' – through discriminatory access). What the public needs is not a *Big Brother* of *Cyberspace* to somehow guarantee *right* thinking but a *Neutral Brother* of *Openspace* to allow *free thinking*.

135 See Leila Speisman, 'Bar-Ilan Offers University Course on the Internet,' *Canadian Jewish News* (28 April 2000), 5.

136 See 'Jewish Teacher Program Awarded $150,000 Grant,' *Canadian Jewish News* (12 April 2001), 17.

137 See Marguerite Michaels and Eagle Butte, 'New Agents of Change: Winning Big without Casinos,' *Time* (18 June 2001), 53.

138 Ibid. Unemployment, for example, plummeted from 75 per cent to 25 per cent.

139 The disclaimer made clear that 'Jews for Jesus' was neither a group nor a synagogue representative of the Jewish faith. Reported in *Canadian Jewish News* (8 February 2002), 8.

140 See Morton Weinfeld, 'A New Birthright Jewish Studies Program,'
    Canadian Jewish News (13 July 2000), 10.
141 See Mark Miefkiewicz, 'Teaching Kids about Anne Frank,' *Canadian Jewish
    News* (17 June 1999), 12.
142 David Lazarus, 'Montreal Holocaust Center Gets $500,000 Pledge,'
    Canadian Jewish News (21 September 2000), 49.
143 See Lindsey Askley, 'Residential School Abuse,' *National Post* (17 August
    2001), 1, 8.
144 See Susan D. Phillips, 'Meaning and Structure in Social Movements:
    Mapping the Network of National Canadian Woman's Organizations'
    (1991) 24 Canadian Journal of Political Science, 781–2.
145 A pure persuasion speech function is one that converts not by pressure
    but by 'convincing' the listener of the incorrectness of his position.
146 See *supra* note 78.
147 For a powerful critique against such politics generally, see Loren E.
    Lomasky, *Persons, Rights, and the Moral Community* (Oxford: Oxford
    University Press, 1987).

Conclusion

1 P.M. Sniderman, J.F. Fletcher, P.H. Russell, and P.E. Tetlock, *The Clash of
  Rights* (New Haven: Yale University Press, 1996) at 64.
2 Borovoy writes, 'on racial and ethnic matters, the more effective anti-
  egalitarian talk is not about the inferiority of racial minorities but rather
  about the potential disharmony caused by Third World immigration.' See
  A. Borovoy, *The new Anti-liberals* (Toronto: Canadian Scholars Press, 1999)
  at 159.
3 In the U.S., see 'Race Relations: Browns vs Blacks,' *Time* (29 July 1991)
  (reporting that, 'Once solidly united in the fight for equality, America's
  largest minority groups have turned on each other in a fight for power').
4 See 'New Agents of Change,' *Time* (18 June 2000), 50.

Select Bibliography

Government Reports and Publications

Canada, Canadian Human Rights Commission, *Annual Report 1989* (Ottawa: Minister of Supply and Services, 1990).

Canada, House of Commons, *Debates* (6 October 1971) at 8545–8 (Mr P. Trudeau).

Canada, House of Commons, *Debates* (29 February 1964) at 132 (Mr G. Favreau).

Canada, Law Reform Commission, *Hate Propaganda Working Paper 50* (Ottawa: Law Reform Commission, 1986).

Canada, Law Reform Commission of Canada, *Our Criminal Law* (Ottawa: Law Reform Commission of Canada, 1997).

Canada, National Council of Welfare, *Another Look at Welfare Reform: A Report by the National Council of Welfare* (Ottawa: Minister of Public Works and Government Services of Canada, 1997).

Canada, *Report of the Royal Commission on Newspapers* (Ottawa: Minister of Supply and Services, 1981).

Canada, Royal Commission on Aboriginal Peoples, *Bridging the Cultural Divide: A Report on Aboriginal People and Criminal Justice in Canada* (Ottawa: Minister of Supply and Services, 1996).

Canada, Special Committee on Hate Propaganda, *Report* (Ottawa: Queen's Printer, 1966).

Canada, Special Committee on the Participation of Visible Minorities in Canadian Society, *Report* (Ottawa: Minister of Supply and Services, 1984).

Canada, Statistics Canada, 'Employment Equity Data Program; Housing, Family and Social Statistics Division' (Ottawa: Queen's Printer, 1991).

Nova Scotia, Royal Commission on the Donald Marshall, Jr, Prosecution, *Report* (Halifax: McCurdy's Printing and Typesetting, December 1989).

U.S. Congress, House Committee on International Relations, 'Psychiatric Abuse of Political Prisoners in the Soviet Union: Testimony of Leonia Plyusch' (Washington, D.C.: 30 March 1976).

Books

Abella, I., *A Coat of Many Colours, Two Centuries of Jewish Life in Canada* (Toronto: Lester and Orpen Dennys, 1990).

Afanasyev, V., *Fundamentals of Scientific Communism* (Moscow: Progress, 1977).

Agresto, J., *The Supreme Court and Constitutional Democracy* (Ithaca, N.Y.: Cornell University Press, 1984).

Alexander, M., *Jazz Age Jews* (New York: Princeton University Press, 2000).

Almond, G., and S. Verba, *The Civic Culture: Political Attitudes and Democracy in Five Nations* (Boston: Little, Brown, 1965).

Almond, G., and S. Verba, *The Civic Culture Revisited* (Boston: Little, Brown, 1980).

Archer, K., et al., *Parameters of Power: Canada's Political Institutions* (Toronto: Nelson Canada, 1995).

Avis G., ed., *The Making of the Soviet Citizen: Character Formation and Civic Training in Soviet Education* (London: Croom Helm, 1987).

Bagdikian, B., *The Media Monopoly* 4th ed. (Boston: Beacon Press, 1992).

Bailyn, B., *The Ideological Origins of the American Revolution* (Cambridge, Mass.: Harvard University Press, 1967).

Baker, C., *Advertising and a Democratic Press* (Princeton: Princeton University Press, 1994).

Bakhtin, M., *Speech Genres and Other Late Essays*, translated by V. McGee (Austin: University of Texas Press, 1986).

Banting, K., *The Welfare State and Canadian Federalism* (Kingston, Ont.: McGill-Queen's University Press, 1982).

Barendt, E., *Freedom of Speech* (Oxford: Oxford University Press, 1985).

Barron, J., *Freedom of the Press for Whom?* (Bloomington: Indiana University Press, 1973).

Becker, J., *Hungry Ghosts: Mao's Secret Famine* (New York: Henry Holt, 1998).

Berman, H., *Justice in the U.S.S.R.* (Cambridge, Mass.: Harvard University Press, 1978).

Berman, H., and J. Spindler, *Soviet Criminal Law and Procedure: The R.S.R.S.R. Codes* 2nd ed. (Cambridge, Mass.: Harvard University Press, 1972).

Blake, S., *Administrative Law in Canada* 3rd ed. (Markham, Ont.: Butterworth, 2001).

Boldt, M., and J. Long, eds, *The Quest for Justice* (Toronto: University of Toronto Press, 1995).

Borovy, A., *When Freedoms Collide* (Toronto: Lester and Orpen Dennys, 1988).

Borovoy, A., *The New Anti-liberals* (Toronto: Canadian Scholars Press, 1999).

Boyer, R., and D. Drache, eds, *States against Markets: The Limits of Globalization* (New York: Routledge, 1996).

Brown, R., *The Law of Defamation in Canada* 2nd ed. (Toronto: Carswell, 1999).

Burstyn, V., ed., *Women against Censorship* (Vancouver: Douglas and McIntyre, 1985).

Cairns, A., *Reconfigurations: Canadian Citizenship and Constitutional Change* (Toronto: McClelland and Stewart, 1995).

Clor, H., ed., *Censorship and Freedom of Expression* (Chicago: Rand McNally, 1971).

Cross, R., and A. Ashworth, *The English Sentencing System* (London: Butterworth, 1981).

Curran, J., and M. Gurevitch, eds, *Mass Media and Society* (New York: Routledge, 1991).

Dahl, R., *Dilemmas of Pluralistic Democracy: Autonomy vs. Control* (New Haven: Yale University Press, 1982).

Dahlgren, P., and C. Sparks, eds, *Communication and Citizenship: Journalism and the Public Sphere in the New Media Age* (London: Routledge, 1991).

Damaska, M., *The Faces of Justice and State Authority: A Comparative Approach to the Legal Process* (New Haven: Yale University Press, 1991).

Davies, K., J. Dickey, and T. Stratford, eds, *Out of Focus: Writing in Women and the Media* (London: Women's Press, 1988).

Dawson, R.E., *Political Socialization* 2nd ed. (Boston: Little, Brown, 1977).

Dershowitz, A., *The Vanishing American Jew: In Search of the Jewish Identity in the Next Century* (Boston: Little Brown, 1997).

Dicey, A., *Introduction to the Study of the Law of the Constitution* 10th ed. (London: Macmillan, 1965).

Downing, J., A. Sreberny, and A. Mohammadi, *Questioning the Media: A Critical Introduction* 2nd ed. (Thousand Oaks, Calif.: Sage Publications, 1995).

Dworkin, R., *Taking Rights Seriously* (Cambridge, Mass.: Harvard University Press, 1978).

Easton, D., J. Gunnell, and L. Graziano, eds, *The Development of Political Science: A Comparative Survey* (London: Routledge, 1991).

Edgell, D., *Product Liability Law in Canada* (Toronto: Butterworth, 2000).

Eisenstein, Z., *Capitalist Patriarchy and the Case for Socialist Feminism* (New York: Monthly Review Press, 1979).

Ericson, R., et al., *Representing Order* (Toronto: University of Toronto Press, 1991).

Fenwick, L., *Private Choices, Public Consequences: Reproductive Technology and the New Ethics of Conception, Pregnancy, and Family* (Toronto: Dutton, 1998).

Fisher, L., *The Politics of Shared Power: Congress and the Executive* 3rd ed. (Washington, D.C.: Congressional Quarterly Press, 1993).

Fiske, J., *Television Culture* (London: Routledge, 1987).

Flanagan, T., *First Nations: Second Thoughts* (Montreal: McGill-Queen's University Press, 2000).

Fleming, J., *The Law of Torts* 5th ed. (Sydney: Law Book, 1977).

Fukuyama, F., *The End of History and the Last Man* (New York: Free Press, 1992).

Goldhagen, D., *Hitler's Willing Executioners: Ordinary Germans and the Holocaust* (New York: Knopf, 1996).

Gramsci, A. *Selections from the Prison Notebooks.* H. Quintin and N. Geoffrey, eds (New York: International, 1971).

Greene, I., et al., *Final Appeal* (Toronto: James Lorimer and Co., 1998).

Greene, I., and D. Shugarman, *Honest Politics: Seeking Integrity in Canadian Public Life* (Toronto: James Lorimer and Co., 1997).

Hacker, A., *Two Nations: Black and White, Separate, Hostile, Unequal* (New York: Ballantine, 1993).

Hackett R.A., *News and Dissent: The Press and the Politics of Peace in Canada* (Norwood, N.J.: Ablex Publication Corporation, 1991).

Hawkins, K., and J. Thomas, eds, *Enforcing Regulation* (Boston: Kluwer, 1984).

Herman, S., and N. Chomsky, *Manufacturing Consent: The Political Economy of the Mass Media* (New York: Pantheon Books, 1988).

Hogg, P., *Constitutional Law of Canada* 2000 Student Ed. (Scarborough, Ont.: Carswell, 2001).

Hugenholtz, P., ed., *The Future of Copyright in a Digital Environment* (London: Kluwer Law International, 1996).

Huntington, S., *American Politics: The Promise of Disharmony* (Cambridge, Mass.: Harvard University Press, 1981).

Institute for Jewish Policy Research (JPR) Law Panel, *Combating Holocaust Denial through Law in the United Kingdom.* JPR Report No. 3, 2000. *http://www.jpr.org.uk/publication/reports/civilsociety/No_3_2000/indexhtm.*

Jackson, M., *Locking up Natives in Canada – A Report of the Committee of the Canadian Bar Association on Imprisonment and Release* (Ottawa: Canadian Bar Association, 1988).

Jamieson, K., *Dirty Politics* (Oxford: Oxford University Press, 1992).

Jews for Judaism, *The Jewish Response to Missionaries: Counter-missionary Handbook* (Toronto: 1996).

Kaul, I., I. Grunberg, and M. Stern, eds, *Global Public Goods: International Cooperation in the 21st Century* (New York: Oxford University Press, 1999).

Kershaw, I., *Hitler: 1889–1936, Hubris* (New York: Norton, 1999).

Kershaw, I., *Hitler: 1936–1945, Nemesis* (New York: Norton, 2000).

Knopff, R., *Human Rights and Social Technology: The New War on Discrimination* (Ottawa: Carleton University Press, 1990).

Knopff, R., and F.L. Morton, *Charter Politics* (Scarborough, Ont.: Nelson, 1992).

Krause, K., and M. Williams, eds., *Critical Security Studies: Concepts and Cases* (Minneapolis: University of Minnesota Press, 1997).

Lacqueur, W., and B. Ruben, eds, *The Human Rights Reader* (Philadelphia: Temple, 1979).

Landes, R.G., *The Canadian Polity* 5th ed. (Scarborough, Ont.: Prentice Hall, 1998).

Law Society of Upper Canada, *Careers: Ontario Reports* (Toronto: Law Society of Upper Canada, 11 October 2002), lxvi.

Lipsitz, E., ed., *Canadian Jewry Today: Who's Who in Canadian Jewry* (Downsview, Ont.: J.E.S.L. Education Products, 1989).

Lipstadt, D., *Denying the Holocaust: The Growing Assault on Truth and Memory* (New York: Free Press, 1993).

Lomasky, L., *Persons, Rights, and the Moral Community* (Oxford: Oxford University Press, 1987).

Macaulay, H., and Bruce Yandle, *Environmental Use and the Market* (Lexington, Mass.: Lexington Books, 1977).

McBride, S., and J. Shields, *Dismantling a Nation* (Halifax: Fernwood Publishing, 1997).

Mackaay, E., *The Economics of Information and Law* (Boston: Kluwer-Nijhoff, 1982).

MacKinnon, C., *Only Words* (Cambridge, Mass.: Harvard University Press, 1996).

Mandel, M., *The Charter of Rights and the Legalization of Politics in Canada* (Toronto: Thompson Educational Publishing, 1994).

Mar.fredi, C., *Judicial Power and the Charter: Canada and the Paradox of Liberal Constitutionalism* (Toronto: McClelland and Stewart, 1993).

Mark, A., *The Rise and Fall of Nicolae and Elana Ceausescu* (London: Chapman, 1992).

Marx, K., *Marx's Capital*, ed. C. Arthur (London: Lawrence and Wishart, 1992).

Matsuda, M., C. Lawrence, R. Delgado, and K. Crenshaw, eds, *Words That Wound* (Boulder, Colo.: Westview Press, 1993).

Meiklejohn, A., *Political Freedom* (New York: Oxford University Press, 1965).

Mill, J.S., *On Liberty* (London: J.M. Dent and Sons, 1859).

Milton, J., *Areopagitica: A Speech for the Liberty of Unlicensed Printing to the Parliament of England* (London: 1664).

Monahan, P., *Politics and the Constitution* (Toronto: Carswell, 1987).

Moon, R., *The Constitutional Protection of Freedom of Expression* (Toronto: University of Toronto Press, 2000).

Morton, F.L., and R. Knopff, *The Charter Revolution and the Court Party* (Peterborough, Ont.: Broadview Press, 2000).

Olson, M., *Logic of Collective Action* (Cambridge, Mass.: Harvard University Press, 1965).

Olson, M., *The Rise and Decline of Nations* (New Haven: Yale University Press, 1982).

Penner, N., *From Protest to Power: Social Democracy in Canada, 1900–Present* (Toronto: James Lorimer and Co, 1992).

Pirie, A., *Alternative Dispute Resolution* (Toronto: Irwin Law, 2001).

Primoratz, I., *Justifying Legal Punishment* (Atlantic Highlands, N.J.: Humanities Press International, 1998).

Pulkingham, J., and G. Ternowetsky, eds, *Remaking Canadian Social Policy (Social Security in the Late 1990's)* (Halifax: Fernwood Publishing, 1996).

Putnam, R., *Making Democracy Work: Civic Traditions in Modern Italy* (Princeton: Princeton University Press, 1993).

Queen's University Senate, *Statistics on Jewish Registration: Minutes of Queen's University* (Kingston, Ont.: 29 October 1943).

Radzinsky, E., *Stalin: The First In-depth Biography Based on Explosive New Documents from Russia's Archives* (New York: Anchor, 1997).

Rapoport, L., *Stalin's War against the Jews, the Doctor's Plot and the Soviet Solution* (New York: Free Press, 1990).

Rhoads, S., *Incomparable Worth: Pay Equity Meets the Market* (Cambridge: Cambridge University Press, 1993).

Rossiter, C., *The Political Thought of the American Revolution* (New York: Harcourt, Brace and World, 1963).

Rowat, D., ed., *Administrative Secrecy in Developed Countries* (New York: Columbia University Press, 1979).

Rudin, J., and D. Russell, *Native Alternative Dispute Resolution* (Toronto: Ontario Native Council on Justice, 1993).

Runciman, W., *Social Science and Political Theory* (Cambridge: Cambridge University Press, 1965).

Rushdie, S., *The Moor's Last Sigh* (Toronto: Vintage Canada, 1996).

Sartre, J., *Being and Nothingness* (New York: Philosophical Library, 1956).

Schauer, F., *Free Speech: A Philosophical Enquiry* (Cambridge: Cambridge University Press, 1982).

Schneiderman, D., ed., *Freedom of Expression and the Charter* (Toronto: Carswell, 1991).

Scott, S., *Dismantling Utopia: How Information Ended the Soviet Union* (Chicago: Irvin R. Dee, 1994).

Shapiro, A., *The Control Revolution: How New Technology Is Putting Individuals in Charge and Changing the World We Know* (New York: Public Affairs, 1999).

Shapiro, M., *Courts: A Comparative and Political Analysis* rev. ed. (Chicago: University of Chicago Press, 1986).

Sherrill, R., *Why They Call It Politics: A Guide to America's Government* 4th ed. (New York: Harcourt Brace Jovanovich, 1984).

Shilton, E., and K. Schucher, *Education, Labour and Employment Law in Ontario* 2nd ed. (Aurora, Ont.: Canada Law Book Inc., 2000).

Skilling G., *Samizdat and an Independent Society in Central and Eastern Europe* (Columbus: Ohio University Press, 1989).

Smiley, D., *Canada in Question: Federalism in the Eighties* 3rd ed. (Toronto: McGraw-Hill Ryerson, 1980).

Sniderman, P.M., J.F. Fletcher, P.H. Russell, and P.E. Tetlock, *The Clash of Rights* (New Haven: Yale University Press, 1996).

Sowell, T., *Knowledge and Decisions* (New York: Basic Books, 1980).

Strict, J., *The Economics of Government Regulation* (Toronto: Thompson Educational Publishing, 1993).

Sunahara, A., *The Politics of Racism: The Uprooting of Japanese Canadians during the Second World War* (Toronto: J. Lorimer, 1981).

Tate, N., and T. Vallinder, eds, *The Global Expansion of Judicial Power* (New York: New York University Press, 1995).

Thompson, J., *The Media and Modernity* (Stanford: Stanford University Press, 1995).

Tocqueville, A. de, *Democracy in America* (New York: Doubleday, 1969).

Tucker, R., *Stalin in Power: The Revolution from Above* (New York: Norton, 1990).

Uner, K., and L. Silk, eds, *A World Fit for People* (New York: New York University Press, 1994).

Uris, L., *The Haj* (London: Corgi Books, 1984).

Van Loom, R.J., and M.S. Whittington, *The Canadian Political System* 4th ed. (Whitby, Ont.: McGraw-Hill, 1987).

Volcansek, M., ed., *Judicial Politics and Policymaking in Western Europe* (London: Frank Cass and Co., 1992).

Walzer, M., M. Lorberbaum, Y. Lorberbaum, and N.J. Zohar, eds, *The Jewish Political Tradition (Volume 1: Authority); Volume II: Membership)* (New Haven: Yale University Press, 2001).

Webster's New World Dictionary 4th ed. (New York: Warner Books, 1990).

Weimer D., and A. Vining, *Policy Analysis* (Englewood Cliffs: Prentice-Hall, 1999).

White, T., *Breach of Faith: The Fall of Richard Nixon* (New York: Dell Publishers, 1976).

Williams, J., *The Law of Defamation in Canada* (Toronto: Butterworth, 1976).

Williams, R., Jr, *Strangers Next Door: Ethnic Relations in American Communities* (Englewood Cliffs: Prentice-Hall, 1964).

Wilson, P., ed., *Open Letters* (London: Faber and Faber, 1991).

Witmer, H., *Personality in the Making: The Fact-Finding Report of the Midcentury White House Conference on Children and Youth* (New York: Harper, 1952).

Wolf, C., Jr, *Markets or Government: Choosing between Imperfect Alternatives* 2nd ed. (New York: MIT Press, 1995).

York, G., *The Dispossessed: Life and Death in Native Canada* (Toronto: Lester and Orpen Dennys, 1989).

Articles

Acharya, A., 'Ideas, Identity and Institution-Building' (1997) 10 Pacific Review 10.

Alderson, D., 'The Constitutionalization of Defamation: American and Canadian Approaches to the Constitutional Regulation of Speech' (1993) 15 Advocates' Q. 385.

Anand, S., 'Expressions of Racial Hatred and Racism in Canada: An Historical Perspective' (1998) 77 Can. B. Rev. 181.

Anders, H., 'The Media and Social Construction of the Environment' (1991) 13 Media, Culture and Society 447.

Atkinson, M., 'What Kind of Democracy Do Canadians Want?' (1994) 27 Canadian Journal of Political Science 717.

Baer, D., et al., 'National Character, Regional Culture, and the Values of Canadians and Americans' (1993) 30 The Canadian Review of Sociology and Anthropology 13.

Bakan, J., 'Constitutional Interpretation and Social Change: You Can't Always Get What You Want (Nor What You Need)' (1991) 70 Can. Bar Rev. 305.

Bakan, J. 'Partiality and Legitimacy in Constitutional Theory' (1989) 4 Legal Theory Workshop Series.

Bale, G., 'W.R. Lederman and the Citation of Legal Periodicals by the Supreme Court of Canada' (1994) 19 Queen's Law Journal 36.

Borovoy, A., 'When Rights Collide' (1995) 44 U.N.B.L.J. 49.

Bosnitch, J., 'Student Speech at UNB in the Early 1980s' (1995) 44 U.N.B.L.J. 93.

Braun, S., 'Freedom of Expression v. Obscenity Censorship: The Developing Canadian Jurisprudence' (1985–6) 50 Sask. L. Rev. 39.

Braun, S., 'Freedom of Expression v. Seditious Libel: Towards a Framework of Analysis' (1985) 22 Comp. Jur. Rev. 87.

Braun, S., 'Judicial Apprehension of Violation of Legal Rights under the *Canadian Charter of Rights and Freedoms*: Towards a Framework of Analysis' (1987) 24 U.W.O.L. Rev. 27.

Braun, S., 'Should Commercial Speech Be Accorded Constitutional Recognition under the *Canadian Charter of Rights and Freedoms?*' (1986) 18 Ottawa L. Rev. 37.

Braun, S., 'Social and Racial Tolerance and Freedom of Expression in a Democratic Society: Friends or Foes? *Regina* v. *Zundel*' (1988) 11 Dal. L.J. 471.

Brest, J.P., 'Interpretation and Interest' (1982) 34 Stan. L. Rev. 765.

Bushnell, I., 'The Use of American Cases' (1986) 35 U.N.B.L.J. 15.

Cameron, J., 'The Past, Present, and Future of Expressive Freedom under the *Charter*' (1997) 35 Osgoode Hall L.J. 1.

Christie, N., 'Conflicts as Property' (1977) 17 British Journal of Criminology 1.

Chull, S., 'On the Third Wave of Democratization: A Synthesis and Evaluation of Recent Theory and Research' (1994) 47 World Politics 135.

Cohen, M., 'The Hate Propaganda Amendments: Reflections on a Controversy' (1971) 9 Alta L. Rev. 103.

Cohen, S., 'Hate Propaganda – The Amendments to the *Criminal Code*' (1971) 17 McGill L.J. 740.

Damaska, M., 'Evidentiary Barriers to Conviction and Two Models of Criminal Procedure: A Comparative Study' (1973) 121 U. Pa. L. Rev. 505.

Di Palma, G., 'Legitimation from the Top to Civil Society: Politico-Cultural Change in Eastern Europe' (1991) 44 World Politics 64.

Deutscher, M., and J. Chein, 'The Psychological Effects of Enforced Segregation: A Survey of Social Science Opinion' (1948) 26 Journal of Psychology 259.

Doskow, A., and S.B. Jacoby. 'Anti-Semitism and Law in Pre-Nazi Germany.' (1940) Contemporary Jewish Record 509.

Dubick, K., 'Freedom to Hate: Do the *Criminal Code* Proscriptions against Hate Propaganda Infringe the *Charter?*' (1990) 54 Sask. L. Rev. 149.

Dyzenhaus, D., 'Pornography and Public Reason' (1994) 9 Can J. of Jurisprudence 261.

Elman, B., and E. Nelson, 'Distinguishing *Zundel* and *Keegstra*' (1993) 4 Constit. Forum 71–8.

Emerson, T., 'Toward a General Theory of the First Amendment' (1962) 72 Yale L.J. 877.

Epstein, B., 'Political Correctness and Collective Powerlessness' (1991) 21 Socialist Review 13.

Epstein, R., 'The Harm Principle and How It Grew' (1995) 45 U.T.L.J. 369.

Fudge, J. 'The Public/Private Distinction: The Possibilities and the Limits to the Use of *Charter* Litigation to Further Feminist Struggles' (1987) 25 Osgoode Hall L.J. 485.

Furedy, J., 'Academic Freedom, Opinions and Acts: The Voltaire–Mill Perspective Applied to Current Canadian Cases' (1995) 44 U.N.B.L.J. 131.

Gintis, H., 'The Political Economy of School Choice' (1995) 96 Teachers College Record 492.

Glasbeek, H.J., 'Some Strategies for an Unlikely Task: The Progressive Use of Law' (1989) 21 Ottawa Law Rev. 387.

Greschner, D., and E. Colvin, 'Expanding the Boundaries of Constitutional Obligation: Lessons from the Canadian Experience' (1985) 22 Comp. Jur. Rev. 1.

Grey, J., 'Freedom of Expression in a Canadian University Context' (1995) 44 U.N.B.L.J. 119.

Havel, V., 'The Power of the Powerless.' In A. Wilson, ed., *Open Letters* (London: Faber and Faber, 1991).

Hough, J., 'The Logic of Collective Action' (1990) Journal of Soviet Nationalities 61.

Hughes, P., 'Reconciling Valuable Interests; or Academic Freedom as Academic Responsibility' (1995) 44 U.N.B.L.J. 87.

Hughes, P., 'Workplace Speech and Conduct Models: Reconsidering the Legal Model' (1998) 77 Can. Bar Rev. 105.

Ionescu, G., 'Political Undercomprehension or the Overload of Political Cognition' (1989) 24 Government and Opposition 413.

Jervis, R., 'Realism, Game Theory and Cooperation' (1998) 40 World Politics 371.

Kausikan, B., 'Asia's Different Standard' (1993) 92 Foreign Policy 24.

Kramar, R., 'Obscenity: Return to Old Morality Play or New Approach?' (1992) 35 Crim. L.Q. 77.

Lamrock, K., 'Free Speech on Campus: The Principle beyond the Crucible' (1995) 44 U.N.B.L.J. 103.

Landes, R.G., 'Political Education and Political Socialization.' In Jon H. Pammett and Jean-Luc Pepin, eds, *Political Education in Canada* at 15–20 (Halifax: Institute for Research on Public Policy, 1988).

Lessig, L., 'Cyberspace's Architectural Constitution.' Draft dated 12 June 2000 of lecture given at Amsterdam, Netherlands. Available on the Web at *http://cyber.law.harvard.edu/works/lessig/www9.pdf.*

Loader, L., 'Trespass to Property: Shopping Centres' (1992) 8 J.L. and Soc. Pol. 254.

Macfarlane, J., 'Beyond a Right to Offend' (1997) 20 Dal. L.J. 78.

McIntyre, S., 'Backlash against Equality: The "Tyranny" of the Politically Correct' (1993) 38 McGill L.J. 1.

McKenna, I., 'Canada's Hate Propaganda Laws – A Critique' (1994) 26 Ottawa L. Rev. 159.

Mahoney, K., 'Obscenity, Morals and the Law: A Feminist Critique' (1985) 17 Ottawa L. Rev. 1.

Mahoney, K., 'Language as Violence v. Freedom of Expression: Canadian and American Perspectives on Group Defamation' (1988–9) 37 Buffalo Law Review 337.

Mahoney, K., '*R. v. Keegstra*: A Rationale for Regulating Pornography' (1992) 37 McGill L.J 242.

Mayton, T., 'Seditious Libel and the Lost Guarantee of Freedom of Expression' (1984) 84 Columbia L. Rev. 91.

Meiklejohn, A., 'The First Amendment Is an Absolute.' In P.B. Kurland, ed., *Free Speech and Association: The Supreme Court and the First Amendment* (Chicago: University of Chicago Press, 1975).

Minsky, M., 'Will Robots Inherit the Earth?' (October 1994) Scientific American 108.

Neier, A., 'Asia's Unacceptable Standard' (1993) 92 Foreign Policy 290.

Petter, A., 'The Politics of the *Charter*' (1986) Sup. Ct L. Rev. 473.

Phillips, S., 'Meaning and Structure in Social Movements: Mapping the Network of National Canadian Woman's Organizations' (1991) 24 Canadian Journal of Political Science 781.

Prutschi, M., 'Anti-Semitism on Trial: Zundel Convicted, Media Indicted' (1985) Bulletin 13.

Prutschi, M., 'Hate Groups and Bigotry's Fellow Travelers' (1990) 6 Currents 1.

Prutschi, M., 'A Jewish Perspective on Racism in Canada' (Summer 1990) Canadian Jewish Congress: Joint Community Relations Committee. 'Anti Semitism, Anti-Semites, the Community, the Media and the Law.'

Prutschi, M., 'Organized Anti-Semitism in Canada' (1985) 25(1) Orah 8.

Putnam, R., 'Bowling Alone: America's Declining Social Capital' (1995) 61 Journal of Democracy.

Putnam, R., 'Diplomacy and Domestic Politics: The Logic of Two-Level Games' (1988) 42 International Organization 427.

Putnam, R., 'Tuning In, Tuning Out: The Strange Disappearance of Social Capital in America' (1995) 28 Political Science and Politics 664.

Rogin, M., 'The Countersubversive Tradition in American Politics' (1986) 31 Berkeley Journal of Sociology 1.

Schabas, W., 'Free Speech on Campus: Lessons from International and Comparative Law' (1995) 44 U.N.B.L.J. 11.

Schrank, B., 'Academic Freedom and University Speech' (1995) 44 U.N.B.L.J. 75.

Sinn, H., 'Social Insurance, Incentives, and Risk Taking,' *Working paper Series, No. 5335*, National Bureau of Economic Research (Cambridge, Mass.: Nov. 1995).

Skilling G., and S. Precan, eds, 'Parallel Politics: Essays from Czechoslovakia from Czech and Slovak Samizdat' (1981) 3 International Journal of Politics 3.

Skilling, H., 'Charter 77 and the Musical Underground' (1990) 22 Can. Slav. Papers 20.

Students' Federation of the University of Ottawa, 'News Release' (7 July 1982).

Tarrow, S., 'Struggle, Politics and Reform: Collective Action, Social Movements and Cycles of Protest,' Centre for International Relations, Cornell University, Western Societies Program, Occasional Paper No. 21 (Ithaca, N.Y.: 1989).

Taylor, E., 'Hanging up on Hate: Contempt of Court as a Tool to Shut down Hatelines' (1995) 5 N.J. Con. L. 163.

Ternowetsky, G., 'Hunger in Regina: Where Do We Go from Here?' (1994) 34 Canadian Review of Social Policy 100.

Turpel, E., 'Aboriginal Peoples and the *Canadian Charter of Rights and Freedoms*' (1989) 10 Canadian Woman Studies 102.

Walsh, B., 'Canadian Dissident' (1993) 59 Quill and Quire 9.

Walzer, M., 'Philosophy and Democracy' (1981) 9 Political Theory 379.

Weiler, P., 'The Supreme Court and the Law of Canadian Federalism' (1973) 23 U. of Toronto L.J. 307.

Woodcock, G., 'Voter's Block: What If They Called an Election and Nobody Came?' (1986) 65 The Canadian Forum 1.

Index